# WORLD CHRISTIANITY

## Central America and the Caribbean

# WORLD CHRISTIANITY

## VOLUME 4

# Central America and the Caribbean

Clifton L. Holland, Editor

**MARC**

919 West Huntington Drive, Monrovia, California 91016
A Ministry of World Vision International

World Christianity is an ongoing project in conjunction with the Strategy Working Group of the Lausanne Committee for World Evangelization. The present status of Christianity among various people groups in different countries is explained in order to motivate the Church throughout the entire world to respond to the visible and hidden task of WORLD EVANGELIZATION.

PREVIOUS VOLUMES

1.  WORLD CHRISTIANITY: MIDDLE EAST
    Covering 16 countries of vital importance where
    Islam, Judaism and Christianity converge.

| | |
|---|---|
| Bahrain | People's Democratic |
| Cyprus | Republic of Yemen |
| Iran | Qatar |
| Iraq | Saudi Arabia |
| Israel | Syria |
| Jordan | Turkey |
| Kuwait | United Arab Emirates |
| Lebanon | Yemen Arab Republic |

2.  WORLD CHRISTIANITY: EASTERN ASIA
    Covering 18 countries which contain 37% of the
    world's population. Extreme contrasts are
    evident in this area of diversity and
    opportunity.

| | |
|---|---|
| Brunei | Laos |
| Burma | Macao |
| Cambodia | Malaysia |
| China (People's Republic) | Mongolia |
| Hong Kong | Philippines |
| Indonesia | Singapore |
| Japan | Taiwan |
| Korea (North) | Thailand |
| Korea (South) | Vietnam |

3.  WORLD CHRISTIANITY: SOUTH ASIA
    Highlights a region in which Hindus, Muslims,
    Animists, Buddhists, Christians, Communists,
    Marxists and Secularists live close to one
    another physically but "worlds apart"
    culturally, socially and philosophically.

| | |
|---|---|
| Afghanistan | India |
| Bangladesh | Overview |
| Bhutan | 22 State Profiles |
| Nepal | Selected Union |
| Pakistan | Territories |
| Sri Lanka | |

Library of Congress Number 79-89819

Copyright © 1981 by
MISSIONS ADVANCED RESEARCH AND
COMMUNICATION CENTER
A Ministry of World Vision International

# CONTENTS

Reprinted with permission*

*From MAPS ON FILE, a registered trademark.
© Martin Greenwald Associates, Inc., 1981
© Facts On FIle, Inc., 1981

# I
# INTRODUCTION

This program is jointly carried out by the Strategy Working Group of the Lausanne Committee for World Evangelization and MARC, a ministry of World Vision International. For further information on the program, please write: MARC, 919 West Huntington Drive, Monrovia, CA 91016 U.S.A.

# FOREWORD

This is the fourth volume in the World Christianity series published by MARC.

The Missions Advanced Research and Communication Center (MARC) was launched in 1966 at the Congress on World Evangelism held in Berlin, Germany. The phrase "That Everyone May Hear" became the theme for everything that MARC attempted in subsequent years. MARC was founded in response to the growing recognition that there were major segments of the world's people who were receiving no opportunity to hear the Good News that Jesus is Lord of all and Savior of all.

The early 1960s marked a turning point in world missions. Once again we came to realize that not only could people not hear without a preacher, but that the preacher could never reach them if they had not been identified. There was much lost time to be made up in rediscovering both the immensity and complexity of the task of world evangelism, even as we discovered new ways to go about it. In direct response to this need MARC began producing country profiles in 1971 on the status of Christianity, completing fifty-three Status of Christianity Profiles in preparation for the International Congress on World Evangelization held in Lausanne, Switzerland in 1974. Since that time a number of other countries have been added, and older profiles have been revised. Meanwhile, a parallel effort was under way to describe the world in terms of unreached people groups. Caste, tribe and ethnic group were supplemented as delimiters by the identification of specific groups found within the boundaries of occupation, income, geography, religion and age. Descriptions of unreached peoples, compiled in the annual directories Unreached Peoples '79, Unreached Peoples '80, Unreached Peoples '81 and Unreached Peoples '82, are now part of the country profiles as well.

However, the production of such profiles on a one-by-one basis presented a problem both for the compilers and the users. Consequently, in the autumn of 1978, we began to issue country profiles in a format that would cover one particular area of the world at a time. World Christianity: Central America and the Caribbean is the fourth in this series of volumes.

This work has been carried out in close cooperation with the Strategy Working Group of the Lausanne Committee for World Evangelization. The information contained in this and previous volumes is part of the LCWE attempt to display the task of world evangelization in a way that will help the church identify and evangelize the unreached in the many different countries of the world.

Of necessity, some material in such a compilation is fresher than the rest. Any report like this must be considered "work in progress." Therefore, we welcome comments, corrections or additions that Christians throughout the world may supply.

We wish to express our thanks to Clifton L. Holland who has been responsible for the overall editing of this issue. Mr. Holland serves as director of PROCADES (Central America Socio-Religious Studies Project) in conjunction with INDEPTH, (Institute of In-Depth Evangelization). His years of experience as a field missionary and coordinator of research projects have combined to make this issue what it is.

I also wish to express my thanks not only to the men and women from Central America and the Caribbean who have contributed information for World Christianity but to those on MARC's staff who have so painstakingly and carefully attempted to compile and analyze what has been handed to them.


Samuel Wilson, Director
Missions Advanced Research and
Communication Center (MARC)

## CENTRAL AMERICA AND

## THE CARIBBEAN OVERVIEW

The Central American and Caribbean regions, often described as the "backyard" of the United States, are much in the news today. There is great concern about recent social upheavals in several countries, due to right-wing military dictatorships on the one hand and Marxist-led revolution on the other. Countries with moderate or centrist governments are characterized as struggling "democracies" with shaky economies. The island nations of the Caribbean and the coffee and banana republics of Central America have experienced many armed struggles since 1945 as political factions attempt to move their countries farther to the right or to the left. The left justifies their movement as a struggle to bring about social justice, while right-wing groups seek to maintain their position of power and control in the name of stability.

Some observers tend to blame the social turmoil in the Caribbean and Central America on Marxist-led revolutionary movements inspired or aided by Cuba, but others point to complex social problems as the basic source of conflict. One hotspot in the area is El Salvador. The Roman Catholic Church in that small, overpopulated nation accuses the Salvadoran government and its military forces of repression, violation of human rights, persecution against the Catholic Church and of betraying the Salvadoran people for a "few pieces of silver" in order to keep the ruling oligarchy in power. Thousands of Christians, Catholics and Protestants alike, have marched in the streets of Washington, San Francisco and other major cities where they have protested U.S. military aid to the government of El Salvador and have supported social reforms and human rights policies.

After generations of human abuse and political misrule by the Salvadoran government, many observers feel that the root of the present struggle in El Salvador is deeply imbedded in institutionalized social injustice and not in a Marxist-led revolutionary movement. The latter may be a response to social injustice rather than the cause of unrest.

While the struggle continues in El Salvador, there is growing apprehension over Nicaragua and the course that the new revolutionary government may take in the future. Will social justice, human rights, political pluralism and a mixed-economy be maintained by the Sandinista Government, or will Nicaragua follow in the footsteps of Cuba, or experience an attempt at counter-revolution?

The desperate cries for social justice by oppressed and marginalized peoples rise from the dust of many Central American and Caribbean streets, while the political forces battle for advantage and power in the small, struggling nations. The majority of the population are poverty-level peasants and industrial workers who have seldom, if ever, experienced the freedom of living in a truly democratic society, of equal opportunity, of guaranteed human rights and of honest elections. Communist Cuba has recently produced interference in the political spectrum from the left. History records a much longer period of instability from the despotic right in terms of dangers to democratic societies in the Caribbean and Central America. Authoritarian rule from the left or right produces oppression and creates the conditions for revolutionary struggle to achieve social justice and respect for human rights. Either ideology may produce anti-Christian conditions.

Geographically, the Caribbean and Central America represent two distinct regions, with some similarities but with more contrasts. The two regions contain racial and cultural diversity: Amerindian (native American Indians), Spanish, English, French, Dutch and African origins predominantly, but in different proportions within each country. After centuries of intermarriage and cultural blending, several ethnic groups have emerged as dominant: Hispanized mestizos (Spanish-speaking), West Indian Creoles (English-speaking), other Afro-American peoples (Black Haitians, Black Hispanics, Black Caribs, etc.) and Amerindian peoples along with small immigrant groups (Chinese, East Indians, Arabs, Jews, North Americans, Europeans, Japanese, etc.). In most countries of the area, the Hispanized population, regardless of racial mixture (Indian, Spanish or Black), is considered "latino" culturally and "mestizo" racially. However, a subtle racial prejudice against Blacks and Indians often exists on the part of those who are of more direct white European descent.

Religion also shows great diversity. The animism of Amerindian peoples was the base for the Spanish and French Roman Catholic overlay; the British, Germans and North Americans added Protestantism; the slave trade brought African animism; and other religious systems accompanied smaller ethnic groups to the Caribbean and Central America. Although Roman Catholicism is the dominant religion of most of Central America and the Caribbean, there are several exceptions: Jamaica, the Bahamas, the Leeward Islands (except Guadalupe), Barbados and St. Vincent in the Windward Islands, and Belize are predominantly Protestant. In a few other countries the Protestant population is a sizeable minority: Guatemala (20%), Haiti (15%), Panama (12%) and Nicaragua (10%). In some countries, non-Christian religions are a significant minority: Cuba (49% secular), Trinidad and Tobago (25% Hindu, 6% Muslim) and Jamaica (16% other).

The growth of religious groups is distinctly different between the Caribbean and Central American regions. In the Caribbean, only a few countries have experienced notable changes in religious affiliation in recent years: Cuba, where both Catholics and Protestants have declined in numbers and secularists have increased to 49% of the total population; and Puerto Rico, where Protestants are now 8% of the total population in what was predominantly a Roman Catholic country. By contrast, in Central America the total Protestant membership has grown at an average annual growth rate (AAGR) of 10.5% since 1967. Belize (6.6% AAGR) and Panama (7.8% AAGR) grew slower than the rest of Central America while Honduras (13.7% AAGR), Nicaragua (12.5% AAGR) and Guatemala (12.1% AAGR) had the highest rates of Protestant growth between 1967 and 1978.

Although Caribbean and Central American countries are both included in this volume, there is a notable difference in the quality and quantity of data available on Protestant church growth in the two regions. The information on Central America is much more complete and reliable than that of the Caribbean since a major church growth study of Central America was recently completed based on extensive fieldwork.

The Central America Socio-religious Studies Project (PROCADES), a ministry of the Institute of In-depth Evangelization (INDEPTH), with headquarters in San Jose, Costa Rica, conducted scores of interviews with major Protestant denominations in each country of Central America during 1978-1980. This research has produced a more accurate historical and statistical overview of Protestant growth in Central America. Therefore, the profiles on Central America produced in this volume represent a condensation of the church data obtained from the Central American

Church. PROCADES collected the data with the intention of publishing in Spanish for the Church in Central America. No such study has been done recently for the Caribbean countries. For the latter region, the MARC staff has relied on older and secondary materials for this volume. The two regions are included here for the sake of completeness in dealing with the geographical areas of the western hemisphere, and because of the historical continuity in the expansion of Christianity in the two regions.

As General Editor of World Christianity: Central America and the Caribbean, I would like to thank Burt Singleton, Jr. of the MARC staff for coordinating this publishing project, and John Pentecost and Steve Crosby for assisting me with the writing and editorial work, especially for the "Nation and its People" sections. Steve and John were responsible for the research and writing of the Caribbean countries, while the Central America portion was my major responsibility. We trust that our combined efforts will generate new interest in the continuing expansion of evangelical Christianity in Central America and the Caribbean, especially in the urgent task of evangelizing and planting new churches among the unreached people groups of these two regions, as well as aiding in the emergence of a truly indigenous church within each people group.

Our motivation has been to aid in the fulfillment of the Great Commission in this generation, and our inspiration has been to be faithful to the command of the risen Lord as Head of the Church. We have been encouraged and challenged by the spirit of the Lausanne Covenant to the end that "the whole earth (every people group) may hear the sound of His voice," and have the opportunity to believe and obey Jesus Christ as Lord and Savior. Hallelujah!

Clifton L. Holland, Editor
Director, PROCADES
San Jose, Costa Rica

# II
# STATUS OF CHRISTIANITY
# COUNTRY PROFILES
# CENTRAL AMERICA

*This program is jointly carried out by the Strategy Working Group of the Lausanne Committee for World Evangelization and MARC, a ministry of World Vision International. For further information on the program, please write: MARC, 919 West Huntington Drive, Monrovia, CA 91016 U.S.A.*

# STATUS OF CHRISTIANITY COUNTRY PROFILE

# BELIZE

## SUMMARY

AREA - 22,973 sq. km. (8,867 sq. miles)
POPULATION - 126,000 (1979 estimate)
RELIGION - 54.4% Protestant, 43% Roman
    Catholic, 2.6% Other

Located on the east coast of Central America, Belize has more historical ties to the Caribbean than to the rest of Central America. It was settled by British buccaneers who used its sheltered cays and coves as hideouts from which they could prey upon Spanish shipping. British influence continued to grow while the Spanish neglected the area. British colonists and their African slaves came from the other British Caribbean lands. Hence, the Belizeans have developed a Caribbean culture and Belize is often called a Caribbean country.

Because of its British influence, Belize is the only country in Central America where English is the primary language and Protestantism is the dominant religion. However, due to large scale immigration of Latin and Indian people groups from Guatemala and Mexico, Spanish and Catholicism are becoming increasingly important. Now, Latin and Indian influences are dominant in the interior of

the country while the coastal sections are still Caribbean-oriented.

## UNREACHED PEOPLES

Amerindians: 22,400 or 19% (1970 Census)

The majority of the Indian peoples in Belize are descendants of the ancient Mayan civilization, and are nominally Catholic. In the south, Mopan Maya speakers migrate between the Peten Province of Guatemala and the Toledo District of Belize. This group numbers about 5,500 but the Mopan evangelical community in Guatemala totals only about 120 people in three small churches. Both the Nazarenes and the Mennonites are known to have a few believers among the Mopans in Belize, but the largest denomination among them is an independent Pentecostal group entitled; the "Kekchi and Mayan Churches of Belize." This group reported 15 congregations and about 750 Kekchi and Mayan believers in the Toledo District in 1978. The New Testament has been translated into Mopan by Wycliffe. Sixteen New Testament stories and several

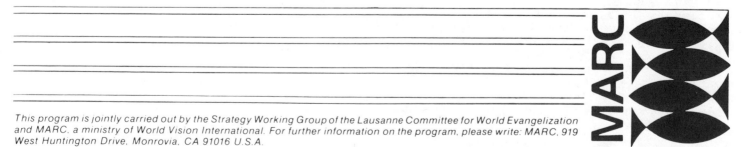

*This program is jointly carried out by the Strategy Working Group of the Lausanne Committee for World Evangelization and MARC, a ministry of World Vision International. For further information on the program, please write: MARC, 919 West Huntington Drive, Monrovia, CA 91016 U.S.A.*

tracts are also available in Mopan, in addition to a hymnal.

The Kekchi live mainly north of Coban in the Guatemalan Department of Alta Verapaz, but they are expanding into Izabal, Baja Verapaz and Peten Departments, and also into Belize. In Guatemala a Kekchi people movement has occurred, where the evangelical population now numbers about 18,000 out of nearly 300,000 Kekchi. The exact size of the Kekchi population in Belize is unknown, but their receptivity to the gospel in Guatemala has apparently extended into Belize, where the Nazarenes also reported a people movement among the Kekchi and Mopans in the southern lowlands. Numerous Kekchi churches have been planted and some form part of the newly organized "Kekchi and Mayan Churches of Belize." The entire New Testament is available in Kekchi, along with a hymnal, several Old Testament books, and a dozen gospel tracts.

The Yucatec Maya, numbering about 540,000, live in the Mexican states of Yucatan, Campeche and Quintana Roo, and in the districts of Orange Walk and Corozal in Belize. Whereas an estimated 45,000 Yucatec speakers are associated with evangelical churches in Mexico, there are only about 120 believers in Belize. Four small congregations have been established since 1958 in the Corozal District by the National Presbyterian Church of Mexico, no doubt following up on some of their members who migrated into Belize. Rapid acculturation has taken place among the Yucatec Maya and many are now fluent in Spanish. However, the older adults still prefer their native language. Parts of the New Testament were translated into Yucatec as early as 1844, but the entire New Testament was not available until 1961 and was revised in 1977.

## Mestizos: 25% (1978 estimate)

The mixed Indian and Spanish population lives mainly in the northern lowlands and in the western regions of Belize, near the Mexican and Guatemalan borders. Although traditionally nominal Catholics, growing numbers of mestizos have responded to the message of the gospel and have become members of Protestant churches during the past two decades. The Nazarenes, Gospel Missionary Union, Adventists and newer Pentecostal groups have grown considerably in the Orange Walk and Cayo Districts since the 1950s. However, the Spanish-speaking mestizo population continues to practice a syncretic "Cristo-paganism" with little understanding of the risen Christ or of the Scriptures.

## Black Caribs: 10,600 or 8% (1974 estimate)

Racially, the Black Caribs are descendants of runaway African slaves who intermarried with the Red Carib Indians in the West Indies during the 18th century. The British deported about 5,000 Black Caribs from the islands of Dominica and St. Vincent in 1797, and relocated them in the Bay Islands of Honduras. From there the Black Caribs gradually dispersed and established settlements along the northern coast of Honduras, south to Pearl Lagoon in Nicaragua, and north to the Livingston area of eastern Guatemala, and into Belize in 1823. Most Caribs in Belize make their living from fishing and subsistence farming, near Punta Gorda and Stann Creek on the south coast. A few Caribs have become teachers, businessmen, doctors and lawyers. An estimated 2,000 Caribs live in eastern Guatemala and 6,000-8,000 live in the southern lowlands of Belize.

The Black Caribs (also known as "Garifuna") have maintained their separate identity in spite of the fact that, physically, they differ little from the Creoles. While retaining their own languages, many Caribs also speak English. A growing number are learning some Spanish due to trading contacts with the Kekchi and Mopan Maya who live nearby. Generally, Caribs do not marry outside their own group. Most Caribs are Animists and few are practicing Christians. Although many are considered to be at least nominally Catholic or Protestant, their religious life is dominated by spirit worship, black magic and ceremonial dances of mixed African and Indian origin. Few Caribs actively attend Protestant churches even though the Anglicans, Baptists and Methodists have had schools and mission stations in their settlements since the 1830s. Other Protestant groups have worked among the Caribs more recently, notably the Nazarenes since the 1960s. Portions of the Bible were first translated into Caribe and Waike by a Baptist missionary, Alexander Henderson, in the 1840s. More recent translations have been done by Wycliffe in Guatemala.

## East Indians: 2,700 or 2.2% (1970 Census)

During the 1870s, East Indian workers were brought to Belize by large landowners, who hoped that the importation of these agricultural laborers would be as successful as in Trinidad and British Guiana. But only a small number of East Indians actually arrived in Belize, where they worked on the large sugar estates of the Toledo Colony. Their descendants still grow rice in the Toledo District or other crops in the Corozal area. Most are small farmers, while others have become merchants. Although their beliefs have apparently persisted over the years, a few attend Catholic or Protestant churches (largely Methodist).

## Chinese: 200 (1970 Census)

In the 1860s a group of Chinese were imported to the Colony as indentured servants, but the venture was not very successful, with some dying from disease and others fleeing to live among the Indians of Yucatan. Descendants of these early immigrants continue to live in Belize, but most of the present Chinese population have arrived since the 1930s. Few have become Christians. The majority continue to worship their ancestors, while pursuing age-old customs and operating stores and restaurants.

## Syrians: 170 (1970 Census)

Some of the most successful businessmen in Belize are Syrians or Lebanese, who have lived there for two or three generations. Although few in number, the Syrians have fulfilled an important economic role in the community, along with the Chinese merchants. Family ties are strong, but little is known about their religious beliefs.

**CURRENT STATUS OF CHRISTIANITY**

The country of Belize, known as British Honduras until 1973, is predominantly a Christian nation (97.4%). In 1970, about 65% of the population was Catholic, 33% was Protestant and 2.6% were members of other religions, mainly Animists, Hindus and Chinese religions. The Catholic population has increased in recent years due to the immigration of Mayan Indians and mestizos from Guatemala and Mexico. However, by 1978, the Protestant Community of Belize totalled 68,600 or about 54.4% of the total population. Resurgence of beliefs rooted in African Traditional religions has been reported among Belizeans of West Indian descent who have traditionally preserved a Protestant heritage. Few West Indian Belizians actually attend church or in any way express an active commitment to Christianity. Black Caribs, are largely Animists and constitute the largest non-Christian element within Belizean society. Nominal Christianity characterizes most people of Belize.

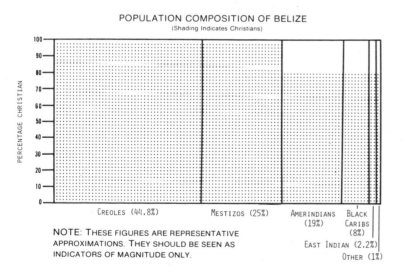

POPULATION COMPOSITION OF BELIZE
(Shading Indicates Christians)

NOTE: THESE FIGURES ARE REPRESENTATIVE APPROXIMATIONS. THEY SHOULD BE SEEN AS INDICATORS OF MAGNITUDE ONLY.

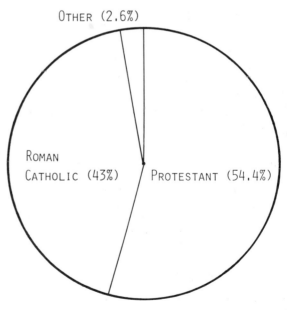

RELIGIOUS COMPOSITION OF BELIZE

# NATIONAL CHURCHES

## PROTESTANT CHURCHES

Historically, the majority of Protestants in Belize have been Anglicans and Methodists. Anglicans accounted for 46.5% of all communicant members in 1978, excluding those who are inactive or nominal adherents. Evangelical Non-Pentecostal Churches totaled 35%, the Adventist Family 24.3%, the Pentecostal Family 16.2% and miscellaneous 0.2%.

Nevertheless, the most notable increases in the Protestant community since 1960 have been among the Pentecostals, increasing from about 550 in 1960 to 9,800 in 1978. Most of the increase since 1970 was among a multitude of small Pentecostal groups. The Adventist community more than doubled between 1960 and 1970, from 1,056 to 2,519, but jumped to almost 12,000 by 1978. Of this number, 3,897 were communicant members. Among the Evangelical Non-Pentecostal groups, both the Methodist Church and the Belize Baptist Mission showed a decline since 1960, while other groups reported slight to moderate gains, mainly among the Nazarenes, Gospel Missionary Union, Christian Brethren, the Churches of Christ, and several independent Baptist groups. The Mennonites have shown a large gain since 1960, but nearly all of this increase was due to the migration of Mennonites to Belize from Mexico, the United States and Canada. The chief exception to this pattern is the Belize Evangelical Mennonite Church, related to the Eastern Mennonite Board of Missions and Charities, that entered Belize in 1960, specifically to do mission work among the Spanish-speaking population. However, their present total membership is only about 150 in five small congregations. By 1978, total Protestant membership in Belize was estimated to be 16,446 distributed among 254 organized local congregations. The total Protestant community was 68,000 or 54.4% of the Belizean population. Most Protestants in Belize are nominal Christians. Many of the older Protestant churches are almost empty now during services.

## CATHOLIC CHURCHES

Although the Catholic Church was not officially present in British Honduras until 1851 when the first Catholic missionaries arrived, by 1860 the Catholic community in Belize City accounted for 15% of the total population. However, the growth of the Catholic Church in Belize prior to 1900 occurred chiefly among the Indian and mestizo peoples in rural areas, and not among the Creoles in Belize City. Even as the early Protestant Churches in Belize grew mainly from the influx of West Indian migrants, so also the Catholic Church increased principally due to the arrival of Indian refugees from Yucatan who settled in the northern lowlands of Belize during the late 1840s, as well as from the migration of other Indian and mestizo peoples from Guatemala after 1850.

The missionary zeal of the English Jesuits prior to the 1890s, and to that of the American Jesuits from Missouri since that date, has strengthened the position of the Catholic Church in Belize. The Vicariate of Belize was created in 1893, but it was not until 1956 that a Bishopric was organized. The Jesuits, aided by other religious orders, established schools and social ministries, in addition to parish churches, throughout the country among the larger ethnic groups.

Today, Catholics predominate in every administrative district with the exception of the District of Belize where 55% of the population are Protestants, most of whom are Creole.

As the mestizo and Indian segments of the population increase during coming years, along with a corresponding decrease in the proportion that is Creole, the size of the Catholic community will tend to expand as well.

## COOPERATIVE AGENCIES

Although the Protestant Council has existed for many years, it includes only a few of the major denominations and is very limited in its activities. However, the Christian Social Council encompasses a wider range of Christian groups and maintains cooperative relationships with the Caribbean Council of Churches and with the World Council of Churches through the Division of Inter.-Church Aid, Refugee and World Service. Members of the Council include the Anglicans, Methodists, Church of the Nazarene, Church of God in Christ, Scottish Presbyterians, Seventh-day Adventists, Salvation Army and the Roman Catholic Church. This organization grew out of a common desire for greater unity among Christian churches and for programs that express the life and mission of the Church. Present ministries include an adult education program for the educationally and economically disadvantaged, a tutorial program for children and youth to help them complete primary and secondary educational requirements, a children's home, several pre-schools and a social welfare program for poor families and disaster victims.

# FOREIGN MISSIONS

## PROTESTANT MISSIONS

During the first century of Protestant influence in the British Colony of Belize, the Anglican Church was dominant. In all probability, the Church of England was present in the colony in the days when British buccaneers used the mouth of the Belize River as a base for plundering Spanish ships in the Caribbean. The more honorable buccaneers frequently carried Anglican chaplains aboard their ships, and even their lawless successors, the pirates of the Caribbean, occasionally kidnapped parsons to invoke blessings upon their exploits and to comfort the dying. The Church of England was present and it is likely that Anglican chaplains, sponsored by the British colonists, existed among the scattered logwood settlements that dotted the coast of Belize during the late 1700s. But it was not until 1815 that the first permanent Anglican place of worship was constructed, making St. John's Cathedral the oldest Protestant church in Central America. From 1776, when the first Anglican chaplain was sent to Belize by the Society for the Propagation of the Gospel in Foreign Parts, until the 1860s, the Anglican Church was the established Church of the colony.

Throughout Central America, historically, the Anglican Church has ministered largely to the West Indian immigrant population and to an expatriate community of British and Americans, who reside mainly in the capital cities and in the Caribbean coastal towns. In Belize, the majority of Anglicans are English-speaking West Indians of African descent, known locally as Creoles. Included in this social group are not only Negroes from Jamaica and other Caribbean islands, but also native Belizeans who are descendants of British buccaneers and the womanfolk of various races and nationalities that accompanied them. There are few Anglicans among the Mayan and mestizo peoples of Belize, although some Black Caribs have been influenced locally by Anglican tradition through the efforts of priests and catechists in south coast villages. However, the center of Anglican church life remains Belize City.

In many remote Belizean settlements in the southern lowlands and in Belize District, the Anglican church and school is the center of village community life. Many Anglican missions in these areas have been served by English laymen testing their missionary vocation, or by local catechists trained for the work and officiating in school and church under the direction of the Bishop and the educational authorities.

The size of the Anglican community has gradually increased over the years, mainly due to population growth. From about 12,000 adherents in 1936, the number of Anglicans increased to 17,783 according to the 1970 Census. This Census also revealed that 90% of all Anglicans resided in the Districts of Belize and Stann Creek (67% of all Anglicans resided in Belize City, alone). In 1978, about 4,000 communicants and 20,000 adherents were scattered among 26 organized churches and missions. The Anglican Church also operated 23 primary schools and two secondary schools.

During the early 1800s, groups of nonconformists or dissenters (meaning non-Anglicans) began arriving in British Honduras, which led to a decline in Anglican influence. English Baptist and Methodist missionaries were sent to the colony in 1822 and 1825, respectively, and Scottish Presbyterians began work in Belize City during the 1820s. By 1856 the Protestant Community of Belize City, where most of the inhabitants of the colony resided, included 2,500 Anglicans, 500 Baptists, 500 Methodists and 200 Presbyterians, in addition to 1,000 Catholics and 2,260 "others," out of a total population of 7,000 people. In 1901 the Baptist Mission reported 353 baptized members and 1,324 adherents among nine organized congregations. In 1978 Baptist work in Belize consisted of six organized churches and 330 baptized members. During the 1970s, other Baptist groups have initiated ministries in Belize, including the Southern Baptist Convention in Belize City in 1978, and two independent Southern Baptist missionaries in the interior. Most Baptists in Belize are Creoles.

The active membership of the Methodist Church in Belize declined between 1960 and 1978. In 1960, 1,800 members were reported, but by 1978 there were only 1,695 members among 15 organized congregations. In the same period, the total Methodist community decreased from 14,500 to 10,700, mainly due to emigration. Most Methodists in Belize are Creoles and have been since Methodist missions started in the colony. In 1970 the Methodist population was concentrated in two districts: Belize District with 71.4% of all Methodists, and Stann Creek District with 13.7%.

It was not until the early 1900s that other Protestant groups began working in British Honduras. The Adventists, arriving in the Bay Islands of Honduras in the 1890s, sent out workers along the entire Caribbean coast of Central America from their base on Roatan. Occasional visits were made to Belize by Adventist missionaries prior to the 1920s, but it was not until 1922 that the Belize Adventist Mission was formally organized. By 1960 the Adventist community numbered about 1,050, then grew to 2,500 by 1970, and increased to about 12,000 in 1978. According to the 1970 Census, Adventists were mainly concentrated in the Districts of Belize (37.5% of all Adventists) and Corozal (34.5%).

The Church of the Nazarene entered Belize from Guatemala in 1934 and began planting churches among the Spanish-speaking inhabitants of Benque Viejo in the Cayo District, near the Guatemalan border. Nazarene work grew slowly, from 300 members in 1946 to 456 members in 1966. However, the number of churches grew from seven to 27 in the same period. Furthermore, a Bible school to train national workers was built in 1950. The Nazarenes have been working among several ethnic groups since the 1960s, resulting in several new congregations. Reports in 1978 indicate that a people movement was in progress among the Maya and Kekchi peoples. Although the Bible School was shut down in 1965, the Church of the Nazarene in Belize has been striving for indigenity. Theological Education by Extension (TEE) has been developed, along with three extension centers established to train pastors and Christian workers in their native tongues. In 1978 there were 18 organized churches and missions operated by the Nazarenes with a membership of 632 people and a community of 2,500. Nazarenes are mainly located in the Districts of Cayo, Stann Creek and Toledo. Unconfirmed reports indicated that the newly-formed "Mayan and Kekchi Churches of Belize" grew out of the Nazarene work in southern Belize due to the influence of the Pentecostal movement in this region.

Few new Protestant denominations entered Belize until the 1950s, undoubtedly due to the dismal prospects for church planting among the small, economically depressed population. The population of British Honduras numbered only 59,220 people in 1946. The first Pentecostal denomination to enter the area was the Church of God - Cleveland in 1944. Five additional Pentecostal groups started work there during the 1950s, including the Assemblies of God (1951), the Church of God in Christ from Memphis, Tennessee (1953), the Pentecostal Church of God of America (1956) and the Church of the Lord Jesus Christ of the Apostolic Faith (1957). Most of these newer denominations formed

churches among the Creole population, mainly in Belize District, while only a few reached out to the Indian and mestizo peoples. Although these five Pentecostal denominations had only 200 members among them in 1960, by 1978 they had grown to 67 organized congregations with 2,656 members and representing 16% of the total Protestant membership. The largest Pentecostal body, with 15 churches and 750 members is the indigenous "Mayan and Kekchi Churches of Belize." Today, only three Pentecostal denominations are known to have mission work in Belize: The Church of God - Cleveland, Tennessee, the Assemblies of God, and the Church of God in Christ. Most of the Pentecostal growth is among small independent churches.

Notable among the non-Pentecostal groups that arrived in Belize during the 1950s were the Gospel Missionary Union in 1955 and several groups of Mennonite colonists from Mexico in 1958, who were followed by numerous other Mennonite groups during the 1960s, mainly from the United States and Canada. In 1956 the Gospel Missionary Union bought a tract of land where they opened a camping and conference center and a Bible school, known as Carol Farm. Ministry was initiated among the Yucatec Mayans in Orange Walk District in 1960, and a Christian bookstore was begun in Belize City a few years later. By 1978 there were seven organized churches and five mission stations with 326 baptized believers.

The Mennonites received special permission by the Belizean government to settle and establish agricultural colonies which have subsequently made a vital contribution to the Belizean economy and diet. Mennonite agencies have also assisted with disaster relief and development. Some of the Mennonite groups have arrived solely for the purpose of establishing agricultural colonies while others have come for the purpose of planting churches. An example of the latter is the Eastern Mennonite Board of Missions and Charities that sent their missionaries in 1964. By 1978 they had established five congregations with 122 communicant members, which were a part of the Belize Evangelical Mennonite Church. This Church body is ministering to the Creoles in English, to the mestizos and Mayans in Spanish and to the Black Caribs in their own language in the Stann Creek area.

During the 1960s, ten new mission agencies or groups entered Belize. Of these, three were Pentecostal, most were Mennonite. At least 15 new Protestant groups or agencies arrived during the 1970s, ten of which were Pentecostal. Most of them were from the United States, but four were

Spanish-speaking groups from Guatemala or Mexico and two were Mennonite. The Southern Baptists were among the new groups that arrived late in the decade.

## ROMAN CATHOLIC MISSIONS

The majority of new arrivals in the northern lowlands of Belize during the late 1840s were Mayan refugees from the Yucatan Peninsula of Mexico who were nominal adherents to the Roman Catholic Church. In 1848, the Mayas revolted against both the Mexican government and the large landowners who had oppressed them since the Spanish conquest, causing heavy losses of life and property for several years. The resulting race war in Yucatan between the Mayas and the mestizos forced many Indians to flee across the border into British Honduras to escape persecution and death, a migration that led to the subsequent growth of the Catholic Church in northern Belize.

The first two Jesuit priests arrived in the colony in 1851, sent by the Vicar Apostolic of Jamaica "to preach the faith and convert the heathen." By 1856 the Catholic population was already second in size to the Anglicans in Belize City. However, the increasing strength of the Catholic Church in Belize was not only due to the missionary zeal of the Jesuits, but also their readiness to leave the comforts of city to work in the remote and backward villages of the interior, where they found greater responsivness among the Indians and mestizos, rather than the Creoles in the coastal settlements.

The growth of the Catholic Church in the colony during the late 1800s led Pope Leo XIII to create the Vicariate of Belize in 1893. Although the English Jesuits, always few in number, were responsible for the early advances of the Catholic Church, after 1893 the Vicariate was administered by the American Society of Jesus from Missouri. It was not until 1956, however, that a Bishopric was created in Belize, but the Missouri Jesuits maintained their control of the Church. Aiding the Jesuits were several other religious orders, notably the Pallitine Sisters, the Holy Family and the Sisters of Mercy. These priests and nuns extended the Catholic faith into the most inaccessible parts of the country and to every ethnic group, where they established churches, schools and social ministries. The fruit of their labors is evident in the present position of dominance enjoyed by the Catholic Church in Belize, which has increased from 59% of the population in 1935 to 65% in 1970. Catholics comprised at least 70% of the population in every district of the country in 1970, except for Belize

District where Catholics totaled only 44.4%. By 1980, however, the total Catholic population had decreased to about 58.5% largely due to recent growth among Protestant denominations among the Indians and mestizos.

**MAJOR CHRISTIAN ACTIVITIES**

## EVANGELISM

The impact of the 1858-1859 revival in the United States and Great Britain was felt immediately in the British West Indies among the emancipated slaves and their children. The revival in Jamaica was particularly strong, following the September 1860 awakening that began at Moravian chapel in Cornwall County. Although the movement's greatest intensity lasted only a couple of years, its impact was felt for a whole generation. In the Colony of British Honduras, news of the Jamaican Revival led to spiritual awakening during 1861-1862, particularly among the Methodists and Baptists.

The effects of a worldwide awakening between 1900-1910, particularly the Welsh Revival of 1904-1905, soon reached Jamaica where thousands of conversions were reported during 1906. The impact of these events were also felt in other West Indian islands, and also in British Honduras where the Baptists and Methodists were again touched by revival power. Robert Cleghorn, pastor of the Queen Street Baptist Church in Belize City, reported that the years 1905-1914 were "years of ingathering," with 166 new additions to his congregation alone, mostly among young people. Beginning in 1910, daily Bible classes were held by the Baptists in Belize City, attended by large numbers of young men. High attendance was reported at camp meetings in Crooked Tree Village in May, 1910. Soon, church buildings were too small to hold the crowds of people attending services in Belize City, and plans were made for constructing larger churches. However, the outbreak of World War I brought an end to religious revival in Belize, as well as the beginning of a period of economic decline that continued for over 30 years.

Not until the 1950s were there signs of new spiritual life among the churches of Belize. In 1951, the Rev. Efraim Alphonse arrived in Belize City from Panama to hold a city-wide evangelistic campaign, sponsored by the Latin America Mission of Costa Rica. Alphonse, a noted Panamanian Methodist pastor and evangelist who had been a pioneer missionary among the Guaymi Indians in northwestern Panama, preached in a series of evangelistic meetings along the Caribbean coast from Belize City in the north to Panama City in the south. Although this was a good beginning among the English-speaking population of Central America, Belize was by-passed during the decade of Evangelism-in-Depth campaigns of the 1960s, even though special meetings were held in Puerto Cabezas and Bluefields in Nicaragua, Port Limon in Costa Rica, and in several Panamanian cities among English-speaking West Indians.

Most evangelistic efforts in Belize have been denominationally oriented, with the exception of the Alphonse Crusade in 1951, when temporary interdenominational cooperation made united meetings possible. However, the fruits of mass evangelistic efforts have been notably limited in Belize, even along denominational lines, especially among the West Indian population that largely resides in Belize City. More recently, greater success has been reported by churches working among the Spanish-speaking and Indian population rather than among the Creoles. Nazarenes, the Gospel Missionary Union and various Pentecostal groups have spearheaded new evangelistic efforts among non-Creoles, aimed at planting new churches.

During the late 1970s, chapters of the Full Gospel Businessmen and Women's Aglow were established in Belize City, where the Charismatic movement has kindled fires of love and unity among both Protestants and Catholics, mainly of the upper classes.

## BROADCASTING

There are no Christian radio stations in Belize, but several denominations sponsor programs on Radio Belize, operated by the government. Although most of these programs are aired in English, some Spanish broadcasting is also permitted under the sponsorship of the Church of the Nazarene and the Belize Evangelical Mennonite Church. Presently, no evangelical television programs are broadcast in Belize.

## LITERATURE

Christian literature is available in all the denominational schools, which are operated by many churches in Belize. Since English is the national language, literature is most abundant in that language, although Spanish materials are also obtainable. Four Christian bookstores exist in Belize City, operated by the Adventists (Belize Adventist Book Center), the Anglicans (The Belize Bookshop), the Gospel Missionary Union

(The Christian Literature Center) and the Mennonites (a book deposit is located at the Mennonite Center). Bibles are also distributed by local representatives of the Bible Society and the Gideons. Films are available from the Christian Brethren, the Mennonite Center, the Outreach Ranch (operated by Outreach for Belize) and King's College (run by the Gospel Missionary Union). Correspondence courses for evangelism and Christian growth are offered to the public by at least six Protestant denominations.

## BIBLE TRANSLATION AND DISTRIBUTION

Although the British and Foreign Bible Society arrived in Belize as early as 1818, its work has been intermittent and its volume low. In spite of the high literacy rate in Belize, the distribution of the scriptures, mainly in English, has not been noteworthy. However, an office of the Bible Society apparently existed in Belize City in the 1840s, because Fredrick Crowe, a converted English seaman, is reported to have served as a colporteur of the Society in Belize at that time, and as a missionary in Guatemala from 1843 to 1846, under the sponsorship both of the Bible Society and of the Belize Baptist Mission. More recently, the Honduran Bible Society has supplied Belize with Christian literature from their San Pedro Sula office, with increasing demands for Spanish materials. A local committee related to the Bible Society exists in Belize City and a representative of the Gideons is also present.

Few efforts at Bible translation were made in Belize, mainly due to the large number of English-speaking people in the colony since logging days. However, Alexander Henderson, an English Baptist missionary, is reported to have made translations of the Bible into the Carib and Waike languages as early as 1850, and attempts were also made to translate the Scriptures into Mayan tongues. Little is known about these early translations, either as to the extent or quality of the work, but several books of the Bible were apparently printed in Carib. More recent translations into Carib have been done by Wycliffe Bible Translators in Guatemala. The entire New Testament has also been translated into the Mayan languages of Mopan and Yucatec and into Kekchi by Wycliffe and other translators working in Guatemala and Mexico. Hymnals, tracts and Scripture portions and selections are also available in some of these languages.

## EDUCATION

Theological. There are relatively few theological schools in Belize for the training of laymen or ministers. The Anglicans, Methodists and Baptists traditionally have sent ministerial candidates to Jamaica or Great Britain for advanced theological training, but since World War II a number of theological institutions have come into existence in Belize. Although no theological seminary exists here, four denominations operate Bible institute programs in residence, and Theological Education by Extension (TEE) programs are sponsored by the Nazarenes, the Conservative Baptists and the Southern Baptists.

The Nazarenes founded the Fitkin Memorial Bible College at Benque Viejo in 1950 to train pastors for Belize, but this college was closed in 1965 due to low student enrollment. Now prospective ministerial students are encouraged to attend the Central American Nazarene Seminary in Costa Rica. However, the Nazarenes also developed a TEE program to meet the multi-language and multi-racial needs for leadership training in Belize at various levels: (1) continuing education for trained pastors, (2) special training for prospective theological students and (3) in-service education for pastors with little or no formal Bible training. Instead of a central campus, courses are offered to part-time students at three regional centers. Other students are encouraged to take correspondence courses. Through this flexible program, theological training is offered at various levels and in several languages, according to the special needs of each student.

Christian. The lack of public education in Belize during the early 1800s stimulated the early missionaries to set up schools for the inhabitants of the colony. Although the first "free school" was established by the Public Meeting in 1807, the Baptists and Methodists started their own educational programs soon after their arrival during the 1820s and 1830s. Although most of the early schools were located in Belize City, the Methodists were particularly successful in starting schools on their mission stations in rural areas, notably in the Stann Creek area among the Black Caribs. It was not until after the emancipation of the slaves that the government of the colony began to assume greater responsibility for public education. In 1850 legislation was passed to provide for more schools and to make new regulations for education, including the formation of a Board of Education. But primary and secondary education in Belize has historically been provided for along denominational lines, aided by government grants.

The present educational system is administered by the Ministry of Education through school managers who may be religious or secular authorities. Managers are responsible for the appointment and supervision of teachers under their direction, including transfers, suspensions or dismissals, and for all other matters relating to the establishment, organization and maintenance of their respective schools. Education at the primary level is free and compulsory for children between the ages of six and fourteen years. In 1976 there were 166 denominational and 11 government primary schools with 32,200 pupils enrolled. At the secondary level there were 18 denominational and four government schools with a total enrollment of 5,210 pupils. The state paid the full salaries of primary school teachers and met up to 50% of the cost of buildings, maintenance, furniture, textbooks and equipment of the denominational schools, whereas each approved denominational secondary school received an annual basic grant in addition to other subsidies depending on the size of the institution. In 1978 there were 112 primary and eight secondary schools operated by Protestant denominations in Belize, with the Anglicans, Methodists, Mennonites and Adventists reporting the largest number of schools. The remainder of the denominational schools were operated by the Catholic Church, particularly the Jesuits who regarded education as a basic means of propagating the gospel. As a consequence, most Catholics send their children to Catholic schools.

The denominational character of the educational system, however, has led to some fragmentation of vital resources and to a duplication of efforts among religious groups. During the early history of Belize, all education was in the hands of the churches. Of course, the churches were by no means reluctant to assume major responsibility for public education, since they regarded this as an essential part of their religious duties. However, in rural areas, Protestant and Catholic schools were often established side by side in small villages. More recently the government has exercised greater control over denominational schools and has made greater efforts to improve educational standards.

## SOCIAL CONCERN

A number of medical and social service programs are administered by Protestant agencies in Belize. In terms of medical work, Amigos Internacionales conducts a medical caravan ministry in Punta Gorda, the Mennonites maintain clinics in the Blue Creek and Spanish Lookout Colonies, the Nazarenes operate the Holland Memorial Clinic in Benque Viejo del Carmen, and the Adventists sponsor the Mundall Clinic in Santa Elena. Social service programs are operated by the Adventists (Ask Program), the Baptist Association of Belize (Self-Help Program), the Christian Social Council (various social welfare, educational and childcare programs), the Salvation Army (Farm's House, Grant's Home for Men, and Over Sixty Clubs) and the Mennonites (numerous internal social service programs in the colonies). Several Mennonite agencies sponsor agricultural and rural development ministries, mainly among the Mennonite colonies, although some help is offered to non-Mennonites. Since 1977, an independent Southern Baptist missionary has led a new ministry called "Outreach for Belize," where assistance is given to local farmers in the Cayo District at Outreach Ranch.

Specialized ministries for children and youth also exist in Belize, in addition to numerous denominationally operated primary and secondary schools. The Christian Social Council operates a Children's Home in Belmopan, and several nursery and pre-schools for children of working mothers in Belize City. The Christian Brethren sponsor a number of "Four F Clubs" (Faith, Fun, Fitness and Fellowship) for 11-13 year olds.

## NATION AND ITS PEOPLE

POPULATION

The population of Belize, the smallest country of Central America, totaled about 126,000 in 1979. Most of the country is sparsely populated. Almost half of the population is under age 15, about 36% are between the ages of 15-44, and only 15% are over 45 years of age. The rate of population increase is offset by the number of people who emigrate, mainly to the United States. Whereas, before World War II the trickle of Belizean emigrants were mostly mestizos, the late 1970s witnessed an exodus of Creoles and Caribs. This caused a decline in the total population, from 130,000 in 1975 to 126,000 in 1979. At the same time, the number of immigrants to Belize mainly includes mestizos and Indians who cross the borders from Mexico and Guatemala, both legally and illegally. As a result,

the population of Belize is experiencing a gradual Latinization, now estimated to be 25% of the total population.

Most Belizeans live in towns (54%) and nearly one-third of the nation's people live in Belize City (45,000) in 1975). The development of Belmopan as the administrative capital will probably lower the concentration of people living in Belize City. However, Belmopan's population today is still small.

Since the earliest days, people have tended to settle on the fertile lowlands where communication for trade was possible by either road or water. This is readily observed by the number of settlements on the coast, and by a chain of smaller villages along the Hondo and Belize Rivers. Major population centers in 1975 in addition to Belize City were: Dangriga Town (8,053), Orange Walk (6,613), Corozal (5,482), San Ignacio (5,013), Punta Gorda (2,418) and Benque Viejo del Carmen (2,230).

There are still large areas of the country with very few inhabitants, notably the Cayo District dominated by the Mayan Highlands, which contained only 13.3% of the total population in 1975. The Northern Lowlands (composed of the districts of Belize, Corozal and Orange Walk) had 68.4% of the population, compared to only 18.3% in the Southern Lowlands (formed by the districts of Stann Creek and Toledo). The Toledo District registered the lowest population density with only 4.3 inhabitants per square mile. About one-third of the country is yet to be developed, which offers Belize a great potential asset for agricultural development.

COMPOSITION

The pattern of settlement in Belize has produced a great variety of racial types within a relatively small population. While the Creole language and culture have historically dominated Belizean life, the growth of the mestizo (mixed Spanish and Indian) population during the 1960s and 1970s has been significant. By 1980 mestizos comprised about 25% of the total population. Although Creoles still form a majority of the population of Belize City, they have declined as a percentage of the country's total population. Other large ethnic groups include: Amerindians (19%), Black Caribs or Garifuna (8%), Caucasians (4%) and East Indians (2.2%). There are also small numbers of Chinese and Lebanese immigrants.

Creole is the name given to all those of Negro origin who have English as their first or second language. The same name is also used, although rather imprecisely, for mixtures of Negro people with any other groups; but terms like mulatto, or colored are rarely used. The Creoles, first brought to Belize as slaves from Africa and later as laborers from the West Indies, still dominate the coastal settlements. Belize City, for example, is largely Creole (63% in 1970).

The mestizos are Spanish-speaking and concentrated in the northern and western areas of the country, not far from the Mexican border from where most of them came. Their Roman Catholic religion, their customs and their language set this ethnic group apart from the larger Creole population. Most mestizos engage in subsistence agriculture.

The Mayas are descendants of the first inhabitants of Belize and of subsequent immigrant Indian groups from Mexico and Guatemala. While constituting about 19% of the total population, they are proportionally larger in certain districts, notably Orange Walk (29%), Corozal (41%) and Toledo (51%). The Mayas tend to remain inland where, in several parts of the country, they form distinct population units, notably in the Southern and Northern Lowlands. The mestizos, by intermarriage, have helped draw the Mayas from these isolated areas. Mayan people generally speak their own languages, as well as some Spanish.

The Black Caribs or Garifuna, originally deported by the British from the West Indies to the Bay Islands of Honduras in the 1790s and later migrating to the coastal areas of Honduras, Guatemala and British Honduras, tend to retain their own language and culture. They do not generally marry outside their own cultural group. Black Caribs greatly outnumber all other ethnic groups in the towns of Stann Creek and Punta Gorda, and have formed separate villages along the coast in the Southern Lowlands. Although most Black Caribs are small boat fishermen or small farmers, some have achieved upward social mobility through education.

Other ethnic groups include a small Caucasian population of Europeans, mainly British, some of whom are descendants of the early buccaneers that roamed the coast and established logging settlements during the 1600s and 1700s. The "white" population is mainly found in Belize City and principally engaged in commerce. This group includes other European immigrants, notably German Mennonite colonists who began arriving in the late 1950s from Mexico, Canada and the United States, as well as North American businessmen. East Indian laborers were brought to Belize during the 1870s to work in the emerging sugar industry in the Toledo District, and their descendants (about 3,000) are principally small farmers or merchants in the Toledo or Corozal areas.

LANGUAGE AND LITERACY

More than 90% of the population of Belize is considered literate, with wide variations in functional literacy between urban and rural areas. The high literacy rate is due to the strong emphasis traditionally put on primary education in this former British Colony. English is the official language and is taught in all public schools.

However, the phenomena of diverse cultures that coexist in this small country is reflected in the languages spoken here. The Belizean lingua franca is Creole, a conglomerate language that is spoken mainly by Afro-Belizeans. Belizean Creole is an English-based pidgin Creole similar to Jamaican Creole, but these languages are often mutually unintelligible with Standard English. Of the nearly 25,000 Mayas, less than half continue to use Mopan, Kekchi or Yucatec as their primary language. The majority have gained some measure of fluency in Spanish, but few speak English. The mestizos and Mayas account for most of the Spanish-speaking population of the country. While increasing numbers of Black Caribs are adopting Belizean Creole as their principal language, many continue to speak Carib, and some use Spanish as a trade language with the Mayas. Finally, many of the recent Mennonite immigrants are of German heritage and use Low German in their daily conversation within their segregated agricultural colonies, while using English or Spanish to communicate with outsiders.

RELIGION

Belize holds the distinction of being the only Protestant nation in Central America, owing to its historical development as a Colony of Great Britain. Although the 1970 Census of Population reported that 65% were Catholic, more recent estimates give the size of the Protestant Community at 54%, or approximately 68,600. The largest active memberships were reported by the Anglican Church (24% of all active Protestant church members), Seventh-day Adventist Church (24%), all Pentecostals (16%), all Mennonites (11.6%) and the Methodist Church of the Caribbean and the Americas (10%). However, the Anglicans and Methodists also reported large numbers of inactive members - those who were baptized as infants but who seldom or never attend church services. In fact, nominal Christianity, among both Protestants and Catholics, characterizes most Belizeans.

The Catholic population greatly increased in size during the 1850s, due to the influx of refugees from the Yucatan Peninsula. Most Catholics are Mayan Indians or mestizos from Guatemala or Mexico. Although the Black Caribs of southern Belize are reported to be nominal Catholics, most observers indicate that this unique people have retained strong elements of their native African and Indian beliefs and practices. Only a few Black Caribs are known to be Protestants. According to the 1970 Census, only 2.6% of the population was non-Christian, mainly Animists, Hindus or adherents of Chinese religions.

## GEOGRAPHY AND CLIMATE

Belize is located on the east coast of the Central American mainland, adjacent to the Yucatan Peninsula. It is bordered by Mexico on the north and northwest, and by the Republic of Guatemala on the west and south. Belize is separated from the Republic of Honduras by about fifty miles of Guatemalan territory and is bounded on the east by the Caribbean Sea.

With a total land area of only 23,000 square kilometers (8,866 square miles), including square kilometers (266 square miles) of coastal islands, Belize is the smallest country in Central America. There are several natural regions within the country.

The Northern Lowlands occupy most of the northern half of the country and consist of gently sloping limestone hills and level plains. Much of the valuable timber of this region has been cut. But where there is good drainage for the many rivers that flow through the plains, the soils are fertile. Land use in this case is intensive with widespread fields of sugar cane, rice, some forestry and many small farms.

The Coastal Plains, although often the least accessible and least useful districts, are the most densely settled areas. Many of the suitable settlement sites are only just above sea level, with the danger of seasonal flooding from the sea. The Coastal Plains are badly drained and numerous swamps stretch along the coastline.

Karst is the name given to areas of limestone in which caves, hollows, conical hills and steep cliffs dominate. Vegetation in the karst areas is very thick and the hollows tend to be badly drained. Since the relief is difficult to cross and the soils on the hill slopes are thin, there has been little development in these regions.

The Maya Mountains, which include the highest peaks in Belize, dominate the West and South. While in the lower areas porous soils favor the development of an open pine forest cut by clear, sparkling streams, the Southern Maya mountains are practically inaccessible, making development very difficult.

The Southern Lowlands consist of many low, rounded hills and the wetter climate of this area produces a dense vegetation comparative to the true rainforest. The coastal zone of mangrove and the presence of badly drained swamps keep this area isolated from the rest of Belize. Though bananas and forestry products are produced in some of the larger settlements, land use is limited to small plots along the coast and permanent cultivation by the Indians in the interior.

The Cays form the surface of a great barrier reef that extends some 640 kilometers (400 miles) down the length of the Yucatan Peninsula to the Bay of Honduras. While some cays are covered by mangrove, others are bare coral reefs or have sandy lagoons and palm trees. Approach to the coast is through the cays and thus is difficult and dangerous.

Belize enjoys tropical to sub-tropical climatic conditions, with the northern sector classifiable as wet/dry tropical and the southern sector as wet/tropical or rainforest. In the southwest the Maya Mountains produce a marked lowering of temperature. On the coast, temperatures range from a minimum of 15 degrees C. (50 degrees F.) to a maximum of 27 degrees C. (81 degrees F.). Readings of over 38 degrees C. (100 degrees F.) are not uncommon in the interior during April, while in the uplands some December nights are cooler than 5 degrees C. (40 degrees F.). The mean annual temperature in the mountains is around 22 degrees C. (72 degrees F.).

Relative humidity is distinctly noticeable in the coastal areas. However, the heat and humidity are usually mitigated by easterly trade winds and diurnal sea breezes.

Annual rainfall ranges from less than centimeters (60 inches) in the north to over centimeters (160 inches) in the south. The dry season usually extends from January to April. The rainy season normally begins in May and continues until December. The country lies within the hurricane belt and has experienced many damaging storms in the past, like the one in 1978 that caused considerable damage throughout the country.

## HISTORY

The first known inhabitants of Belize were Mayans, whose civilization reached a peak between the 4th and 9th centuries. While the Spanish conquest had little effect on Belize, around the middle of the 17th century an assorted group of British pirates was successful in founding a settlement on the Bay of Honduras. Under their control, a flourishing log-wood trade, reinforced with slave labor, was established. The log-wood trade was gradually surpassed in importance by mahogany, and more slaves were brought in and soon outnumbered the Europeans

The government of the settlement was originally in the hands of a Public Meeting, which passed and executed laws and annually elected magistrates. When, in 1862, British Honduras was declared a Crown Colony, the population had become more varied due to the immigration of Caribs, mestizos and people of African origin from the Caribbean. Her population, which then stood at 25,600, mainly produced goods for overseas markets.

More recently, new economic patterns have developed, and these, as well as the political movement towards independence, have brought together groups of people previously isolated from each other. After a period that witnessed the rise of coherent party politics (1954-1960), the growth of trade unions and the obtention of universal suffrage, Belize became internally self-governing in 1963. Belize became totally independent in September, 1981. However, Guatemala still claims Belize as part of her territory. Many Belizeans are apprehensive about their country's future in response to the Guatemalan threat. Great Britain still maintains a military presence in order to at to the new nation's security.

## GOVERNMENT AND POLITICAL CONDITIONS

In 1963, a constitution was adopted that provided complete internal self-government to Belize for the first time in its history. That constitution was intended as a transition stage toward full

independence and several powers still remained in the hands of a Governor appointed by the British Government.

The Belizean system of government is based generally on the British Parliamentary system. There is the usual division between legislative, executive and judicial functions. The Constitution provides for a bi-cameral legislature: the National Assembly, comprising a House of Representatives and a Senate. The House consists of eighteen elected members and is the body that introduces laws. The Senate is made up of eight members nominated by the Governor. Its main function is to consider and ratify laws passed to it by the House.

Executive functions reside in the Premier, appointed by the Governor as that member of the House of Representatives who is best able to command the support of the majority of members of the House. The Premier chooses a Cabinet of Ministers. The Cabinet is the chief policy-making body in the government machinery, and is colletively responsible to the National Assembly.

Political parties may be freely formed in Belize and may present candidates for all national and local elections. The party presently in government is the People's United Party, which was founded in 1950, and has since 1956 been led by George C. Price, now Premier. The opposition party represented in the National Assembly is the United Democratic Party which was formed in 1974 as a coalition of various opposition groups, and is led by Dean Lindo.

## ECONOMY

After 300 years of dependence on forestry, by 1978 the Belizean economy was no longer dominated by the exportation of timber. Agriculture is now the predominant activity, with sugar as the number one crop. Other major exports are citrus, fish products, clothing, lumber and bananas. Belize is self-sufficient in the production of beans and is approaching this goal for the staple grains of corn and rice. The Mennonite colonies are the country's largest single producers of domestic crops.

Land for farming is plentiful and there are large areas awaiting development. Even today, only 15% of the land suitable for agriculture is being used. Most of Belize's potential 2.2 million acres of agricultural land is in private ownership, and absentee landlords have control over the most fertile lands. The Belizean legislature is attempting to make more of these lands available to farming through a progressive program of land distribution. The total area of Belize, classified according to land usage, is as follows: cultivable area, 38%; useful forest, 46%; unproductive hills and swamps, 16%.

Belize's small industrial base consists primarily of a number of light industries geared exclusively for the domestic market (clothing, flour, fertilizers, furniture, cigarettes, etc.). The major industrial activity for the domestic market is building construction. Export-oriented industries include the processing of citrus products, a honey-producing industry, an animal feed plant, a clothing factory, a small furniture and boat-building industry.

Belize's economy is quite weak with Belizeans having to pay high prices for fuel, food and manufactured goods. A major plan for economic development is being implemented in order to ensure greater self-reliance. In 1975, the GNP was 130 million ($B). That same year total imports were valued at $102 million (US) and exports at $73.1 million (US).

Belize dollar: 1.65 = $1 (US)

## CHURCH STATISTICS FOR BELIZE

NOTE: Statistics are from the 1978 PROCADES survey of Protestant Churches and are based on official denominational reports or estimates. Although definitions of membership vary slightly among churches, the data is highly comparable and reliable. All known churches are included in this list.

| Church or Mission Name | Number of Congregations | Membership | % of Total |
|---|---|---|---|
| PROTESTANT | | | |
| Liturgical | 26 | 4,000 | 24.3 |
| Anglican | 26 | 4,000 | |
| Evangelical Non-Pentecostal | 118 | 5,757 | 35.0 |
| Association of Evangelical Church of Belize (Gospel Missionary Union) | 12 | 326 | |
| Belize Baptist Mission | 6 | 333 | |
| Christian Brethren | 5 | 233 | |
| Church of the Nazarene | 18 | 632 | |
| Churches of Christ | 1 | 191 | |
| Mennonites | 37 | 1,909 | |
| Methodist Church | 22 | 1,695 | |
| Presbyterian Church (Mexico) | 4 | 120 | |
| Presbyterian Church (Scotland) | 1 | 75 | |
| Others | 12 | 243 | |
| Pentecostal | 67 | 2,656 | 16.2 |
| Assemblies of God | 6 | 96 | |
| Church of God - Cleveland, TN | 8 | 101 | |
| Church of God in Christ | 7 | 540 | |
| Kekchi and Mayan Churches | 15 | 746 | |
| Others | 31 | 1,173 | |
| Adventist | 40 | 3,997 | 24.3 |
| Seventh-day Adventist | 39 | 3,897 | |
| Independent Adventist Church | 1 | 100 | |
| Miscelaneous | 3 | 36 | 0.2 |
| TOTALS | 254 | 16,446 | 100.0 |
| Estimated Community (1978) | | 68,586 | |

## SELECTED BIBLIOGRAPHY AND INFORMATION SOURCES

The sources listed below are to help the reader find additional information on this country and Christian ministries there.  This list does not try to be comprehensive or complete.

DOCUMENTS

General

Ashcroft, Norman, Colonialism and Underdevelopment: Processes of Political Economic Change in British Honduras, New York:Teachers College Press, 1973.

Belize Institute of Social Research and Action (BISRA), Belizean Studies, (A journal of Social Research and Thought), St. John's College, Belize City.

Bruckdown, The Magazine of Belize, Belize City: Bruckdown Publications.

Government of Belize, Belize: A New Nation in Central America, Belmopan: The Government of Belize, 1976.

Grant, Cedric, The Making of Modern Belize: Politics, Society and British Colonialism in Central America, Cambridge, England: Cambridge University Press, 1976.

Dobson, Narda, A History of Belize, Trinidad and Jamaica: Longman Caribbean Ltd., 1973.

Waddell, David A.G., British Honduras:A Historical and Contemporary Survey, London: Oxford University Press, 1961.

Christian

Caiger, Stephen L., Honduras Ahoy!, London: The Society for the Propagation of the Gospel in Foreign Parts, 1949.

Cleghorn, Robert, A Short History of Baptist Missionary Work in British Honduras: 1822-1939, London: The Kingsgate Press, 1939.

## ACKNOWLEDGMENTS

The information in this profile was taken from many sources which were the best available to the editors at the time of preparation.  However, the accuracy of the information cannot be guaranteed.  Views expressed or implied in this publication are not necessarily those of World Vision.  The editors have tried to present the ministries of various organizations in an objective manner, without undue bias or emphasis.  Where we have failed, we apologize for erroneous impressions that may result and request that comments and corrections be sent to MARC, 919 West Huntington Drive, Monrovia, California, 91016, USA.  We appreciate and acknowledge the comments and contributions of various organizations and individuals in the preparation of this publication.

# STATUS OF CHRISTIANITY COUNTRY PROFILE

# COSTA RICA

### SUMMARY

AREA – 51,000 square kilometers
    (19,647 square miles)
POPULATION – 2,285,700 (1980)
RELIGION – 98.5% Christian (89.7% Roman
    Catholic, 7.9% Protestant and 0.9%
    other), 1.5% non-Christian religions

Costa Rica, known as the "Switzerland of Central America", has a long tradition as a peaceful, democratic and highly literate country, with more school teachers than soldiers. Its capital, San Jose, is now home of the Inter-American Court of Human Rights of the Organization of American States. In recent history, Costa Rica has been a model of civil and religious liberty. Although small in size and population, Costa Rica exerts a stabilizing influence over the Central American region.

The homogeneity of the population, which is 97% white-mestizo, plus its relative isolation and self-sufficiency has created a strong sense of nationhood. The heritage from the colonial era when everyone was poor but independent, with equal opportunities for most of the population, has created an atmosphere that permits social progress for the majority.

The dominant political party since the Civil War of 1948 is the National Liberation Party (PLN) led by Jose Figueres. It is liberal and reformist of Social Democrat tradition. The Unity Party, a split off of the PLN led by Rodrigo Carazo, is now in power.

Because of the increasing cost of living and the growing instability of the economy, Costa Ricans have become angrily impatient with government policies and have taken their protests to the streets to demand higher wages and lower prices. When Costa Rica's international monetary reserves dropped $200 million by mid-1979, leading economists began to warn of the country's growing economic crises and to demand major policy changes for 1980. Disastrous economic conditions throughout the early 1980's thrust the government into virtual bankruptcy. The national currency was radically devalued and foreign credit curtailed while high inflation persisted. National elections can invoke significant changes in leadership, but even if new policies are implemented immediately, it will take years for the economy to be rebuilt.

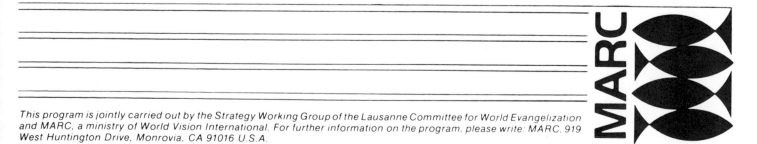

*This program is jointly carried out by the Strategy Working Group of the Lausanne Committee for World Evangelization and MARC, a ministry of World Vision International. For further information on the program, please write: MARC. 919 West Huntington Drive, Monrovia, CA 91016 U.S.A.*

## UNREACHED PEOPLES

### Amerindians: 15,000, 0.15%

Although few in number, American Indians constitute significant groups of unreached peoples in Costa Rica. The major Indian groups are the Bribris, Cabecares, Borucas, Guaymi and Terrabas who live in settlements near the southern border, and the Guatusos who live in the north. Costa Rica's Indians belong to six language groups, but most adults speak some Spanish; some speak only Spanish. Only about 20% are literate in any language.

Some Indians are nominally Catholic, a few are Protestants, but the great majority are Animists. Taboos and superstitions continue to permeate everyday life. Increased efforts will be needed to reach this neglected segment. The only known work among the various Indian groups is being done by the Central America Mission, the Evangelical Mennonites, the Assemblies of God and the Foursquare Church. Bible portions are available in Cabecar, Bribri and Guaymi.

### Chinese: 4,500, 0.2%

This ethnic minority includes Cantonese-speaking Chinese from Hong Kong as well as Mandarin-speaking and Hakka-speaking Chinese from Taiwan. The earliest arrivals were contract laborers who worked on the coffee plantations during the mid-1800s, and in construction of the railroads beginning in the late 1880s.

Many Chinese who live in Costa Rica operate restaurants and hotels, others own stores or act as middle-men in the selling of agricultural products. They are less visible in cosmopolitan San Jose than in outlying areas. In 1950, 39% of the Chinese resided in Limon Province, 22% in Guanacaste, 23% in Puntarenas and 14% in San Jose. The total Chinese population at that time was about 1,000. Since 1950 many Chinese have arrived from Hong Kong and Taiwan and are now living in the San Jose area.

The older generation of Chinese tends to be conservative and resists assimilation, adhering to traditional Chinese religions in many cases. The newer generation is assimilating to Spanish culture, becoming Roman Catholics, and intermarriage is common. Only a few Chinese are Protestants.

### Jews: 2,000, 0.1%

The Jewish colony is primarily located in the capital city. The first Jews came from Spain in the 17th and 18th centuries and were largely assimilated into Costa Rican society. However, in the period 1929-1939, several hundred Jewish people immigrated to Costa Rica from Poland, Austria and Germany. After World War II, 60-70 Jewish families came to Costa Rica from Eastern Europe and Russia, mainly young Jews who had escaped the Holocaust.

Today, the sons and daughters of these poor immigrants are businessmen or professionals. Although many do not observe strict orthodox rules, intermarriage is uncommon, with ethnic homogeneity being fostered by the synagogue and the Jewish school. However, some of the descendents of those who intermarried have become Protestants or Catholics.

## OTHER PEOPLE GROUPS

### Popular Catholicism

Although an estimated 80-85% of the Catholic population does not attend mass regularly, many Costa Ricans consider themselves to be religious. The majority practice a "pick and choose" kind of religion that is becoming the concern of the Catholic Church. Invocation of the aid of saints, fatalism and superstition are characteristic of the majority, while sheer indifference among the educated upper and middle classes is commonplace, especially among the males. For many Catholics, the extent of their religious devotion is represented by the annual Holy Week processions, or special celebrations in honor of a favorite saint and the Virgin of the Angels at the Basilica in Cartago. Most Cathoics attend church only for baptisms, weddings or funerals, but rarely for confession and mass. However, it is still quite common to see people make the sign of the cross and kiss their thumbs when passing a Catholic church.

The practices of witchcraft, fortune-telling and herb-healing ("curanderismo"), though not widespread, are significant indications of the lack of faith and general distrust common among the majority of Costa Ricans. Many devout Catholics, from illiterate campesinos to educated inhabitants of the capital, consult the local "bruja" (witch) in order to bring about cures, attain success and avoid misfortune. During the 1970s, an increasing number of cases of demon possession and oppression have been reported by evangelical pastors, who have participated in exorcisms.

## Upper Class Costa Ricans: about 6% of the population

Composed mostly of nominal Catholics, the upper class are the least penetrated by Protestant churches. This population segment includes successful businessmen, wealthy professionals and owners of large land holdings. Growing receptivity among the upper classes is evidenced by the success of such diverse groups as the Full Gospel Businessmen's Fellowship, Women's Aglow, International Students, Ministry to the Student World (MINAMUNDO), Christian Ministry to the English-Speaking, the Center for Christian Development (publishers of the magazine New Wine in Spanish), and numerous small Bible study groups that meet in upper class homes throughout the San Jose area.

## Negroes: 45,700 (2%)

Though African Negroes were brought into Costa Rica at the time of colonization, most Negroes in the country today are descendants of West Indian migrant workers, mainly from Jamaica. Beginning in the mid-1880s, the West Indians immigrated to Costa Rica to participate in the construction of the railroad from Port Limon on the Caribbean coast to San Jose in the central highlands. Later, most of these workers remained in the lowlands near Limon to work on the banana plantations being developed at that time by the United Fruit Company. There they were isolated from the highlands both by choice and by legal restrictions which prohibited them from living in the Central Valley. The Negroes were allowed to preserve their British West Indian life-style, as well as their English-speaking Protestant heritage, while living in a Spanish-speaking Catholic country.

The Census of 1927 shows 19,136 Jamaican Negroes in Costa Rica, (4.1% of the total population) of which 94% resided in the Province of Limon. In the 1930s, due to the spread of a banana disease, the plantations were abandoned, and the entire Atlantic coast suffered severe economic problems. Most Negroes were forced into subsistence farming, others found jobs as stevedores or as workers on the cacao plantations, while others simply left Costa Rica.

In 1949 travel prohibitions were removed and Negroes became full citizens of Costa Rica. Although a majority of Negroes continue to live in the Province of Limon, where they comprise about 30% of the population, a period of assimilation to the highland culture has occurred in recent years. English is still taught in the schools of Limon, but Costa Rica's Negroes are rapidly adopting Spanish as their primary language. Although some Negroes have become professionals and many hold white-collar positions, the majority are numbered among Costa Rica's poor. Former pride in their distinctiveness has given way to a more ambivalent attitude. Frustration mounts as increased expectations are met with government indifference, especially in the Limon area.

Though most Costa Rican Negroes consider themselves Protestants, church membership statistics, showing only about 9,600 West Indian communicants, indicate that this ethnic group includes a large number of non-practicing Christians. The percentage of Negroes that have converted to Catholicism remains very low. They are primarily Anglicans who resisted liturgical changes introduced when the Church shifted from British to American jurisdiction in 1947. Much lingering superstition and African Animism (Pocomia and Obeah) can be found in this group.

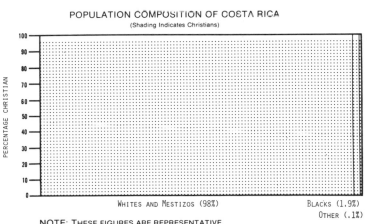

POPULATION COMPOSITION OF COSTA RICA
(Shading Indicates Christians)

PERCENTAGE CHRISTIAN

WHITES AND MESTIZOS (98%)   BLACKS (1.9%)
OTHER (.1%)

NOTE: THESE FIGURES ARE REPRESENTATIVE APPROXIMATIONS. THEY SHOULD BE SEEN AS INDICATORS OF MAGNITUDE ONLY.

Christianity in Costa Rica is represented primarily by the Roman Catholic Church. About 90% of the total population are baptized Catholics. However, the number of practicing Catholics (those who attend mass at least once a week) is estimated at only 15-20%.

The Protestant Community numbers 180,000, about 8% of the population. There are sixty-five denominations and independent groups. Since 1967, Protestant membership has grown at a 216% Decadal Growth Rate (DGR) or 11% Average Annual Growth Rate (AAGR). The average Sunday School attendance is double the membership, which means that about 67% of the Protestant Community is considered active.

Pseudo-Christian groups such as the Church of Jesus Christ of Latter Day Saints and the Jehovah's Witnesses constitute about 0.9% of the population. Non-Christian religions include Animism, Baha'i, Chinese religions, Judaism and Psychic movements. Approximately 31,500 people (1.5% of the population) belong to these groups.

An estimated 430,500 people attend Catholic and Protestant churches each week. Of these, 72% are Catholic (310,700) and 28% are Protestant (119,800), which is about 15% of all Catholics and 67% of all Protestants. This means that only 19% of the total population are active Catholic or Protestant, leaving at least 81% yet to be reached.

## RELIGIOUS COMPOSITION OF COSTA RICA

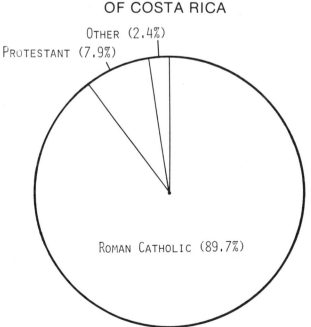

OTHER (2.4%)
PROTESTANT (7.9%)
ROMAN CATHOLIC (89.7%)

## CATHOLIC CHURCH

In spite of its official status, the Catholic Church in Costa Rica is relatively poor. Less than 0.01% of the national budget is allotted to the Church. Nevertheless, after the State, the Catholic Church is the nation's strongest institution. Catholic doctrine is taught in all public schools and Catholicism influences most national traditions.

In the late 1930s the Costa Rican Church began to emerge from a characteristically limited role that had kept it in the background of the country's social and political life. It entered the fields of social welfare and politics but never to the extent of favoring one political party over another. Church participation in these activities has been widely accepted and supported by the population. Relations between Church and State are amicable.

Besides being poor, the Catholic Church as an organization is small. The country is divided administratively into one archdiocese and four dioceses. There are about 400 priests to take care of 1,100 churches, which is one priest for every 5,700 people. About 70% are diocesan priests and the rest are members of 18 religious orders. The majority of the diocesan priests are Costa Ricans, while those belonging to religious orders are mostly foreign missionaries. About 970 nuns support the work of the Catholic Church by their involvement in social, correctional, educational and medical institutions. They are organized in 26 religious orders and 60% are Costa Ricans.

Since 1958 the Christian Family Movement and, more recently, the Charismatic Movement have made their impact on the Costa Rican Catholic Church. Since its beginning in 1971, the Charismatic Movement has experienced growing popularity, especially in the San Jose area. About 40,000 people attended a recent Catholic Charismatic rally held in the National Stadium, although only about 3,000 are considered to be committed Charismatics.

At present, the Catholic Church in Costa Rica is being directed by a conservative archbishop, who is anti-charismatic and anti-ecumenical. The Council of Costa Rican Bishops, in a recently published document, has stressed the importance of re-evangelizing non-practicing Catholics, as well as ministering to the youth and to the poorer classes. Though this document reflects recent conclusions of the Latin American Bishop's Conference held in Puebla, Mexico, its stress on re-evangelization acknowledges the laxness and superficiality of religious faith and observance among many Costa Ricans. An estimated 80-85% of the Catholic population do not attend mass.

PROTESTANT CHURCHES

Until the late 19th century, Protestant worship was found almost exclusively among immigrant groups. The Protestant Church of San Jose, composed mainly of Europeans, was founded in 1848. Work among the West Indians by Baptists (1887), Methodists (1894) and Anglicans (1896) was concentrated in the Caribbean coastal province of Limon. Most of the Spanish-speaking national churches originated from efforts by North American foreign missionary societies. The first to arrive was the Central American Mission in 1891, followed by the Methodist Episcopal Church in 1917 and by the Latin American Evangelization Campaign in 1921.

In 1900 English-speaking West Indian Negroes constituted about 68% of the total Protestant membership, and they remained the majority ethnic group within the Protestant Community until the late 1930s. After 1914 adverse economic conditions along the Caribbean coast seriously affected the West Indian churches. They declined rapidly after 1935, and by 1940 only about 900 communicant members remained, which represented only 39% of the total Protestant membership. Since 1940 the proportion of Protestants who are native Spanish-speaking Costa Ricans has steadily increased, so that by 1980 they constituted 83% of the total membership of nearly 60,000.

The largest Protestant group in Costa Rica today is the Seventh-day Adventist Church. Arriving in 1900, the Adventists soon had work both among West Indians in Limon and among Latins in San Jose. They grew from 148 members in 1928 to 1,500 in 1960. Since 1965, Adventists have been the largest Protestant Church in the country, with 2,412 members in 1967 and 5,700 in 1978. Between 1967 and 1978 they had an average annual growth rate of 7.7%.

From 1930 to 1960, the Anglican Church was the largest Protestant church in Costa Rica. The vast majority of Anglicans were West Indians in the Atlantic zone. Bishop Ormsby, of the Diocese of British Honduras, visited Costa Rica in 1896 and instituted Anglican worship among Anglo-Americans in San Jose and among West Indians in Limon. By 1935 four churches

and several missions had been established with a total of 500 members. In 1947 the work in Costa Rica was transferred from British to American jurisdiction. Although membership increased notably between 1947 and 1960 (from 947 to 1,500 members), only 1,015 were reported in 1967. From 1960 to 1978, the Episcopal Church had an annual growth rate of 4.9%. The latest report shows 4,200 baptized members, though only 2,049 were communicants.

Seven small Lutheran churches exist in the San Jose area with about 375 members. They represent three denominations: the Evangelical Lutheran Church of Germany (1956); the Lutheran Synod of Costa Rica and Panama (1978), a break-off from the Missouri Synod's work that began in 1964; and the Evangelical Lutheran Synod of Mankato, Minnesota (1978).

Since 1960, the Pentecostal family of churches has grown rapidly: 14.7% (AAGR) between 1960 and 1978. At present, twenty-four Pentecostal groups have a total membership of about 21,000. Pentecostals clearly comprise the largest portion of the Protestant Community, increasing from 20% in 1960 to 45% in 1978. The largest denominations are the Assemblies of God, the Church of God - Cleveland, Tennessee and the International Church of the Foursquare Gospel.

Some of the Evangelical Non-Pentecostal groups have also grown considerably since 1960, but the majority still have less than 1,000 members. Of the larger denominations, only the Association of Bible Churches (related to the Latin America Mission/CLAME), the Baptist Convention (Southern) and the Baptist Bible Fellowship Churches have increased more than 5% per year. For example, between 1967 and 1978, the Association of Bible Churches grew 9.7% (AAGR) and the Baptist Convention 6.7%. However, the Bible Baptists, who only had 287 members in 1974, increased at the amazing rate of 79% per year between 1974 and 1978, recording 2,950 members in 1978.

Looking at total Protestant growth in Costa Rica since 1900, slow growth was the norm prior to 1940. However, total membership more than doubled between 1940 and 1950 and then doubled again by 1960, with about 10,000 members reported for that year. Between 1960 and 1970, a somewhat slower growth pattern was evident, with membership increasing to 16,580 in 1970. Then Protestant membership more than tripled in the last decade, increasing to almost 60,000 by January, 1980. That was a jump of 261% since 1970, compared to 66% in the period between 1960 and 1970. If the present trend continues, we can expect the total Protestant membership to reach 100,000 by 1985, 155,000 by 1990, and 400,000 by the year 2000.

Several important factors have contributed to this upward spiral of numerical church growth in Costa Rica, especially among the larger denominations: improved leadership training programs (there are 20 Bible institutes and seminaries in Costa Rica) and a strong evangelistic orientation together with a heavy emphasis on church planting (some 260 new congregations were established between 1974 and 1978).

Externally there has been a growing openness and responsiveness among the general population. This receptivity seems to be linked to several key elements: (1) The good public image of evangelicals (since the 1920s), created by the leaven of the evangelical movement in Costa Rican society - the positive testimony of evangelicals as individuals and of the evangelical institutions that serve the general public. (2) The special role of evangelical radio station TIFC (since 1948) in creating a positive image through both religious and cultural programs, in communicating the gospel and in stimulating Christian growth, especially among new believers. (3) The emphasis on Bible reading among Catholics (since the 1950s), when low-priced Bibles and New Testaments became available through the Bible Society and religious and secular bookstores, promoted by evangelicals and by a new generation of priests and nuns. (4) The effects of the Second Vatican Council and Medellin (late 1960s) on religious concepts and attitudes, which produced a growing crisis of faith, that led some to search for a more personal and vital religious faith, and led others to become more secular, with greater religious indifference or loss of faith. (5) The emergence of the Catholic Charismatic Movement (early 1970s), which provided new alternatives from within the Catholic Church, but with an evangelical spirit of renewal and Christian growth.

All of these factors emerged in the context of a liberal, progressive, Social Democratic political and social milieu, with no threats to internal tranquillity since 1948 other than the increasing cost of living, resulting mainly from external economic pressures and government inefficiency.

In 1978 the total Protestant Community numbered about 141,000. There were over 600 ordained and lay ministers serving 580 churches, 150 missions and more than 600 preaching points. To a great extent the Protestant Churches of Costa Rica have become indigenous in leadership and operation, and the majority of the members are from the majority society. In addition, five English-speaking churches serve the Anglo-American Community in San Jose, and one Lutheran congregation has ministered to the German colony since 1956. Several Beechy-Amish Mennonite groups from Belize and Mexico have formed agricultural colonies since the early 1960s, and one Quaker colony is located at Monteverde.

## FOREIGN MISSIONS

### ROMAN CATHOLIC MISSIONS

The first foreign missionaries in Costa Rica were Roman Catholic priests who accompanied Gil Gonzalez Davila on his explorations of the Nicoya Peninsula in the early 1500s. Since one of the goals of the Spanish conquest was the conversion of the Indians to Christianity, each succeeding expedition included priests. The Costa Rican tribes, however, neither submitted to Spanish domination nor embraced the Catholic religion. As a result, the Catholic Faith in Costa Rica remained relatively free of the process of syncretism so prevalent in countries with large Indian populations.

In the colonial era, the Church, like the country as a whole, was desperately poor. A small number of priests, the majority of whom worked on isolated Indian mission stations, serviced the few churches that were constructed. Visiting bishops were appalled at the poverty and ignorance prevalent in the country.

Church influence and power began developing in the late 17th century. Schools and brotherhoods flourished as did missionary work among the Indians. In the late 18th century, an Episcopal order forced colonists to settle around existing churches. This helped reinstate the traditional Spanish family pattern and respect for religion.

With the advent of independence in 1825, Roman Catholicism was established as the state religion. A series of mild anti-clerical laws was passed in 1826, a trend that continued in succeeding years. After the creation of the independent bishopric of Costa Rica, a concordat with the Vatican was signed. It granted jurisdiction over church property to civil authorities.

Harmonious relations between Church and State prevailed except for two notable periods: during the presidencies of Juan Mora (1858) and of Prospero Fernandez (1883). The latter abrogated the concordat with the Vatican, secularized the cemeteries, forbade the establishment of monastic orders and barred all religious orders from entering the country.

After the death of Fernandez, tenuous relations with the government were restored, though succeeding bishops continued to adhere to a limited role, keeping the Church in the background of public life. This role was encouraged and approved by the government, controlled by liberals during the first 40 years of this century.

The late 1930s marked a change in this relationship, with the Church's entrance into the field of social welfare. Under the direction of archbishop Victor Sanabria, an intellectual and a social visionary, the Church began to exert its influence in political matters, helping bring about advanced social reform. Since then Church participation in social welfare activities and non-partisan politics has been accepted and supported by the population.

One out of every three priests in Costa Rica belongs to a religious order. There are eighteen such orders for priests, including the Jesuits. Almost all priests belonging to orders are foreigners, mainly from the U.S., Spain, Germany and Italy. At present, nine high schools, including prestigious technical and vocational schools, are serviced by religious orders.

Today, there are 26 congregations or religious orders for women with 970 nuns, which is a notable decline from 1,503 nuns in 1970. That same year, 60% of the nuns were Costa Ricans, 37% were from other Latin American countries and 3% were non-Latins.

Generally, nuns do social work among the poor, administer the prison for women, provide institutional child care, teach in primary and secondary schools and work in hospitals. In a country that has 13,277 inhabitants per parish, and where rural priests may have to serve up to 15 churches, nuns play an important role in the life of the Church. In some outlying villages, where a priest comes only occasionally, the nuns baptize, teach catechism, visit homes, teach in the schools and administer communion.

## PROTESTANT MISSIONS

Missions Among West Indians

The first Protestant missionary work in Costa Rica was undertaken by the Jamaican Baptist Missionary Society in 1887. It sent the Rev. Joshua Heath Sobey to minister among English-speaking Jamaicans who had migrated to Costa Rica to work in railroad construction and banana industries in the Province of Limon. The following year, the First Baptist Church was organized in Limon, under the newly formed Jamaican and Central American Baptist Mission. During the 20th century, Baptist work among West Indians grew very little. In 1967 the Conservative Baptist Home Mission Society was invited to take over the work in Limon Province, but not much progress has been made. Membership in 1978 totaled only 200 among four churches.

Formal Wesleyan Methodist worship was initiated among the West Indians around Limon in 1894. It was not until 1896 that the shepherdless Methodists had their own permanent pastor. Edward Pitt, a Jamaican layman, was sent from Panama as an agent of the Missionary Committee of the Methodist Conference. Pitt was ordained in 1901 and became supervisor of the work when the Costa Rican Methodist Circuit was created in 1905. When he retired in 1927, the West Indian Methodist work had 600 members, twice as many adherents, and was entirely self-supporting. The latest report in 1978 showed four churches and about 260 members.

The Anglican Church has been present in Central America since the eighteenth century, when the Society for the Propagation of the Gospel sent its first representatives to British Honduras, now Belize. By 1906, there were twelve well-organized missions between Limon and San Jose. In 1947 the Anglican Diocese of British Honduras was transferred to the American Protestant Episcopal Church, under the missionary district of the Panama Canal Zone. With the formation of a new Diocese in 1956, the Episcopalians began to do missionary work among the Spanish-speaking population and to cooperate more closely with other missionary organizations. In Costa Rica, this resulted in a notable membership increase from 956 in 1947 to 1,950 in 1960. However, outside the San Jose area, the majority of Episcopalians are still West Indians.

The Seventh-day Adventists arrived in Limon about 1900 to begin work among West Indians, and by 1906 they were also working among Latins in the San Jose area.

Since 1965, Adventists have reported the largest Protestant membership in the country. Prior to 1955, about two-thirds of their members were West Indians, but since then the Spanish-speaking membership has increased to about 50%.

The Salvation Army, following the tide of West Indian migration to Panama, established work on the Isthmus in 1905. Two officers were sent to Costa Rica in 1907. By 1960, churches and schools were operating in Limon, Matina and Zent and about 500 adherents were reported. In the mid-1970s the Salvation Army entered the San Jose area to work among the Spanish-speaking population, where they now have several congregations and social ministries.

Missions Among Latins

The first Protestant missionary work among Spanish-speaking Costa Ricans was begun by the Rev. and Mrs. William McConnel of the Central American Mission (CAM) in 1891. From the outset, the CAM emphasis was on widespread evangelism, but was weak on church planting. Mission workers preached and distributed Bibles throughout the Central Valley and along the Atlantic coast. Meetings were held in private homes until 1902 when the first chapel was built. During the early years, CAM work was often met by persecution. From 1912-1920 CAM workers were divided and frustrated over hyper-dispensationalism. These factors help explain why the CAM experienced slow growth during the early period. From 190 baptized believers in 1900, the CAM work grew to 721 members in 1919, with eight organized congregations in five provinces. However by 1921 few CAM missionaries remained in Costa Rica and the work, in general, had deteriorated. Only five congregations remained and all but two national workers had abandoned the mission. Another twenty years passed with very little growth; only 300 members were reported in 1937. It was not until the 1940s and 1950s that a new group of missionaries, together with national pastors and workers, brought about an extension and consolidation of CAM work in Costa Rica. Churches founded by the CAM were organized as the Association of Central American Evangelical Churches, becoming autonomous in 1948 and almost entirely self-supporting by 1956. Not until the 1940s were national workers ordained as pastors and sufficient emphasis given to formal training for Christian work. Church membership increased from 650 in 1955 to 1,064 in 1960. Since 1960 the number of churches and members has remained about the same. In 1978, the CAM reported 30 churches and 1,122 members.

The Methodist Episcopal Board of Foreign Missions began work in Costa Rica in 1917. By the mid-1930s, churches were planted in several communities of the Central Valley, in the rich agricultural region of San Carlos and in the southwestern coastal plain. Methodists have always stressed the social implications of the gospel. Since 1921 the Methodist School in San Jose has provided quality primary and secondary education for middle and upper class students, thereby removing prejudice and creating a good public image for the growing evangelical community. In 1953, an agricultural project was initiated in San Carlos, known as the Methodist Rural Center. From the first Conference report in 1920, when 49 communicant members were reported, the Methodists grew to 262 in 1937, 633 in 1955, and by 1960 numbered 865. A total membership of 1,135 was reported in 1978. Between 1967 and 1978, the Methodists had an annual growth rate of 1.8% which was less than the population increase.

The interdenominational Latin America Evangelization Campaign, later known as the Latin America Mission (LAM), entered Costa Rica in 1921 under the leadership of the Rev. and Mrs. Harry Strachan. The mission began as a promoter of evangelistic campaigns throughout Latin America, and soon came to have a major role in the evangelical movement in Costa Rica. This was accomplished by means of local evangelistic campaigns and cooperative institutional efforts. The new mission was established in San Jose for the express purpose of engaging in: (1) Systematic evangelistic campaigns in the larger cities and towns of Latin America; (2) Itinerant evangelization; (3) Training of native workers. Some of Latin America's best evangelists were recruited as preachers for campaigns between 1921-1934 in Latin America, the Caribbean, Spain and Morocco.

Campaigns were held in Costa Rica with Juan Varetto in 1922, and with Angel Archilla Cabrera in 1927. During the first campaign, there was no organized opposition and people from all social classes filled the largest theatre in San Jose. But the second campaign in 1927 provoked a great religious controversy, with public defamation of Protestants by Catholic priests. However, this seemed to encourage people to attend the meetings. Sympathy had been created for the evangelical cause and hundreds were converted. New converts were so numerous that the existing churches could not care for them, which motivated the Strachans to build a large tabernacle-like structure in 1929, seating 1,000. This was the origin of the Bible Temple in San Jose, which served as an "evangelistic center" for the extension of the work in the capital and to outlying areas.

One of the Strachan's concerns was theological education for national workers. They established a Women's Bible Training School in their home, beginning in 1923 with eight students. In 1924, when a two-story structure was built for the Training School, eight young men were brought down from Nicaragua and the school became a "Bible Institute." By 1925 the Institute was functioning with 19 students and a faculty composed of missionaries from various denominations. This interdenominational Institute met a long-felt need and was well received in evangelical circles, resulting in the decision of many missions to send students to the school. The name was changed to the "Latin America Biblical Seminary" in 1941 when its academic standards were raised to meet the growing needs of the evangelical movement.

The Bible Clinic grew out of a small nursing school that was established by the mission in 1928. Loving care was given to the sick and helpless in an evangelical hospital. This resulted, both directly and indirectly, in winning many to the Lord and improving the public image of the evangelical movement in Costa Rica. New hospital facilities were constructed in 1975 which doubled overall capacity to 60 beds.

In 1941, the Latin America Evangelization Campaign changed its name to the "Latin America Mission" (LAM) to reflect the expanding interests and ministries of the mission. The 1940s also brought the organization of the Association of Bible Churches (AIBC), which grew out of the mission's evangelistic work. Expansion occurred naturally, as a result of evangelistic work by students and faculty of the Bible Institute and from evangelistic campaigns. In 1945 the AIBC was formed with 14 congregations and 406 baptized members. In 1960 the AIBC had increased to 13 churches, 18 missions and 37 preaching points, with a total membership of 1,055. By 1967 the membership had grown to 1,574, and by 1978 had reached 3,984 with 44 churches, 18 missions and 34 preaching points. The annual membership increase between 1967 and 1978 was 9.7% (AAGR).

Several other ministries emerged in Costa Rica under LAM sponsorship including the Children's Bible Home (now Roblealto Child Care Association), established in 1931, Camp Roblealto in 1947 (one of the earliest camping ministries in Latin America), and Latin America Mission

Publications in 1949 (Editorial Caribe, now located in Miami, and one of the largest publishers and distributors of evangelical literature in Latin America).

Under Kenneth Strachan's leadership, the LAM sponsored mass evangelistic campaigns through Latin America and the Caribbean during the 1950s, aided Billy Graham's Caribbean Crusade in 1958, and launched a decade of Evangelism-in-Depth campaigns throughout the continent during the 1960s. After the first nationwide Evangelism-in-Depth program in Nicaragua in 1959, a team of workers arrived in Costa Rica for a similar effort during 1960-1961. The cooperation of evangelical groups was nearly 100% and it had a great unifying effect on the evangelical community. Church leaders remember the year of Evangelism-in-Depth as a turning point in the history of the evangelical movement in Costa Rica. Evangelicals no longer viewed themselves as a persecuted minority but rather as a growing army of God's people who were no longer afraid to give public testimony of the faith in Christ.

In 1971 the LAM was restructured under national leadership to provide a new organizational framework for the expanding ministries of the former departments of the mission. The Community of Latin American Evangelical Ministries (CLAME) was formed as an international federation of Christian organizations serving the evangelical community and aiding her to penetrate "all groups, classes and levels" with the gospel.

The first Pentecostal missionaries came to Costa Rica in 1918, under the auspices of the Pentecostal Holiness Association, but they stayed only a few months. In 1926 they returned but again stayed only a short time. They were followed by other Pentecostal missionaries who also remained for brief periods. In 1933, however, the Rev. Amos Bradley took over this pioneer work, and later established a number of small groups around San Jose. These groups were turned over to the Pentecostal Holiness Church in 1955. By 1960 seven churches with 180 members were reported. In 1974 the membership had increased to 672 and by 1978 it numbered 1,104. The annual growth rate was 13.2% between 1974 and 1978.

The Church of God - Cleveland, Tennessee began work in Limon in 1937 when a small English-speaking independent congregation was taken under its care. The first Spanish-speaking church was organized in San Jose in 1951, and by 1955 four churches were reported with 281 members. Some early Pentecostal preachers did not enjoy the respect of older evangelical groups because of their "scandalous behavior." However, under the Rev. Jaime Aldama's leadership, the Church of God became more identified with the evangelical movement in Costa Rica, especially after their participation in the Evangelism-in-Depth campaign. The work expanded to 14 congregations with 835 members in 1960, with over 2,000 reportedly attending Sunday school. In 1974 the membership totaled 1,235 and by 1978 it had increased to 2,100, distributed among 48 organized churches and 17 missions. Between 1967 and 1978, the total membership grew 9.7% per year.

The largest Pentecostal church in Costa Rica, the Assemblies of God, was established by the Rev. and Mrs. Lawrence Perrault in 1942. The Assemblies of God workers also experienced some difficulties during those early years. However, this initial period of noncordial relationships was soon overcome when Perrault left and Arthur Bauer took his place. When the Evangelical Alliance was formed in 1950, the Assemblies of God was a charter member.

In 1945, the Assemblies expanded their work to the town of San Isidro de El General, an important market center located on the Pan-American Highway to the south of San Jose. This led to the development of the work in the large southwestern sector of Costa Rica. Here, the Assemblies found a large field for evangelism and church planting. By 1956 eleven churches had been formed in this region. The Bible Institute which had been established in San Jose during 1953 trained national leaders to fulfill pastoral responsibilities.

Since 1953, the Assemblies of God have grown to become the largest Pentecostal denomination in Costa Rica, and the second largest Protestant body, after the Adventists. From 189 baptized believers in 1953, the work grew to 556 members in 1960, and by 1967 a total membership of 846 was reported. Between 1967 and 1978, membership grew 19.2% per year, which was the highest rate of growth among the larger denominations. Membership more than doubled between 1974 and 1978, from 2,128 to 4,492, with 120 congregations in existence by 1978.

Much of this growth has been due to concentrated evangelistic efforts since 1970 in the San Jose area and throughout the Central Valley, which have met with considerable success. Several large new churches have been planted, like those in in Desamparados and Moravia, after a series of year-long evangelistic campaigns

with wide publicity from radio, T.V. and newspaper advertisements. Thousands were drawn to the meetings by a strong emphasis on divine healing, and hundreds stayed to become founding members of newly formed congregations. Special training sessions were held for new converts before the evening evangelistic services, and new leaders were prepared to teach Sunday school classes and to shepherd new congregations. The Desamparados Church is now one of San Jose's largest churches, reporting 500 members and an attendance of 800. Many new churches and missions have been started as result of these extended evangelistic campaigns by the Assemblies of God throughout Costa Rica. Energetic young pastors from the Bible Institute in Moravia have become leaders in the new churches.

The International Church of the Foursquare Gospel initiated work in Costa Rica in 1953 as an extension of its strong work in Panama, where it is the largest evangelical group. Due to the immigration of Panamanian banana workers into the southwestern region of Costa Rica, many new Foursquare congregations were formed there. In 1978, 19 out of a total of 31 Foursquare churches were located in this region. From 56 members in 1956, the Foursquare work increased to 250 members in 1960. The total membership tripled between 1960 and 1967, with 758 members recorded in 1967. The annual growth rate between 1967 and 1978 was 14.4% (AAGR). Of the larger Protestant denominations in Costa Rica, the Foursquare Church had the second highest rate of growth for this period.

The Southern Baptist Convention is one of the largest of the ten different Baptist groups in Costa Rica. Their first church was a group that broke away from the Central American Mission in 1943. Many early Baptists in Costa Rica had been members of other evangelical groups. However, dissention soon arose within the new Baptist movement, leading to the formation of a splinter group known as the National Baptist Church. The expansion of the Baptist work began in 1944 when missions were begun in Cinco Esquinas, Moravia, Puriscal and Nicoya, and the following year in Limon, Naranjo and Alajuela. The first Annual convention was held in 1946 with representatives from six churches and missions. By 1949, when the Convention was transferred from the Home Mission Board to the Foreign Mission Board, there were three organized churches and six missions, with about 220 members.

The period between 1950 and 1960 witnessed the organization of six new churches, the construction of new church buildings and the initiation of a theological seminary. After the founding of the Baptist Theological Seminary in 1951, new fields were opened by graduates with economic support from the Mission. In 1955 a breakaway movement became affiliated with the World Baptist Fellowship. Baptist bookstores were started in San Jose (1958) and San Ramon (1960). Beginning in 1957 there was a turnover in missionary personnel, with nine new missionary couples arriving in 1970. Among them were seminary professors, literature workers, general missionaries, urban church developers and pioneer workers. Three new fields were opened for evangelistic missionaries in Turrialba, San Ramon and San Isidro. By 1960 total membership had increased to 613 and Sunday school attendance to 1,278.

Beginning in 1960, the Southern Baptist Convention began a ten-year program aimed at self-support. By 1973 most of the churches were self-supporting, although many of the pastors were working part-time outside the church. Lay participation increased and the churches continued to grow both in number and membership. Between 1967 and 1978, the Baptist Convention had a 6.7% annual growth rate, increasing from 1,107 members in 1967 to 1,626 in 1974 and with 2,260 reported for 1978. In that year there were 27 organized churches and 13 missions.

There are several church associations in Costa Rica that are related to the Baptist Bible Fellowship movement in the United States. The largest of these was established in San Jose about 1958. By 1974 the work had increased to 287 members, and several new missionary couples had arrived in Costa Rica. Filled with youthful enthusiasm, the new missionaries embarked on an aggressive evangelistic ministry in several new, middle class neighborhoods in San Jose, where they successfully established new churches. Their approach was to set up a tent ministry in a vacant lot which they purchased, conducting evangelistic meetings in the evenings and training new leaders in the mornings. This was similar to Strachan's approach during the 1920s. Later, after the congregation had become fairly large, permanent buildings were constructed with the aid of stateside churches.

By 1978 the Bible Baptists had established four churches and three missions with a total membership of 2,950. This is an average congregational size of 421 members, which is the highest for any group in Costa Rica. The Bible Baptists' annual growth rate between 1974 and 1978 was a remarkable 79%.

In historical perspective, eleven church planting organizations initiated work in Costa Rica prior to 1940, eleven more in the period of 1940-1960, and 20 between 1960-1980. By 1981 there were 280 protestant missionaries active in ministries of 55 different mission agencies. Most individuals, 210 to be precise, were supported by churches and organizations in the Unites States. Other countries with a large representation were Puerto Rico (16), Nicaragua (6) and Canada (6). Forty agencies are involved in church planting, with 140 missionaries assigned to church work. The rest of the missionaries (140) were serving with agencies not engaged in church planting, but in church-related institutions or in specialized ministries. The agencies with the largest missionary staffs were the Latin America Mission/CLAME (98), followed by the Adventists (16) and the Southern Baptists (15).

## MAJOR CHRISTIAN ACTIVITIES

### EVANGELISM

Most mission agencies and denominations have continuing evangelistic thrusts. These efforts range from personal evangelism to church planting and large city-wide campaigns. Church bodies specializing in evangelization include the Assemblies of God, the Foursquare Church, Pentecostal Holiness, Baptist Convention, Bible Baptists, Bible Church Association, and other groups. The Assemblies of God sponsor extended crusades for the purpose of planting new churches. The others include evangelism as an active part of their ongoing ministries.

A number of evangelistic outreach projects have been sponsored by international organizations. Billy Graham held a well-attended campaign in San Jose in 1958 and the Latin America Mission conducted "Evangelism-in-Depth", a nation-wide evangelistic program, during 1960-61. Both the Graham campaign and Evangelism-in-Depth resulted in large membership increases in San Jose churches and unity within the greater evangelical community.

41

EVANGELISM continued...

In 1968, Pablo Finkenbinder (Hermano Pablo) held a city-wide crusade in San Jose, followed by Luis Palau in 1972. More recently, crusades were held by Domingo Pilarte of the Pentecostal Holiness Church (February 1978), by the PTL Club (January 1979) with Dr. Cho of Korea, and by Yiye Avila (June 1979), a Puerto Rican evangelist.

Groups and agencies specializing in evangelism in Costa Rica include: the Institute of In-Depth Evangelization (INDEPTH), Child Evangelism Fellowship, Ministry to the Student World (MINAMUNDO), Campus Crusade for Christ (known as "Alfa y Omega"), International Students, Full Gospel Businessmen's Fellowship and the Latin American Evangelical Center for Pastoral Studies (CELEP). These same groups provide for leadership training.

BROADCASTING

The Latin America Mission founded radio station TIFC, "The Lighthouse of the Caribbean", in 1948. This was the second missionary station in Latin America. TIFC maintains studios and transmitters in San Jose and operates on AM, FM, and three short-wave frequencies, with 17 hours of broadcasting daily. TIFC has had a major role in exposing Costa Ricans to the evangelical movement and in creating an openness to the gospel.

In 1951, representatives from most of the evangelical radio stations in Latin America drew up plans for a "Panamerican Christian Network". This organization subsequently extended itself beyond broadcasting stations. It became an international service agency called DIA (Difusiones Interamericanas) in 1952, with headquarters in San Jose. DIA duplicates and distributes radio programs to secular and Protestant radio stations in Latin America, and serves as a center for cooperative efforts in providing many broadcasting services.

In addition, a number of Christian agencies and churches place radio programs on commercial stations. Television programs also being transmitted include, the 700 Club, PTL Club and a new program produced by the Assemblies of God.

The Catholic Church broadcasts over its own station (Radio FIDES) as well as over commercial radio and television stations.

LITERATURE

Because most of the population is literate (89%), Christian literature distribution is an important ministry in Costa Rica. Presently, nine Protestant book distributors offer books in Spanish and English from the major publishing houses. Editorial Caribe, founded in San Jose in 1948 by the LAM, now operates from Miami, Florida, but maintains an editorial office in San Jose. It continues to be one of the most important producers and distributors of evangelical literature in Latin America.

There are six Protestant bookstores, five of which are located in the San Jose Metropolitan Area. APROLIC, a book distributor affiliated with CLAME, is trying to overcome this handicap through a bookmobile service to population centers removed from the Central Valley. This ministry now has 225 distribution points in stores and churches throughout the country. There are two Baptist bookstores in San Jose, and the Baptist Convention also has a bookmobile ministry.

The commercial bookstores of San Jose sell books from many Catholic publishing houses, as well as some Protestant literature. Charismatic books are now in popular demand.

BIBLE TRANSLATION AND DISTRIBUTION

Because of high literacy rates, Spanish Bibles can be read by most people. The majority of indigenous peoples are bilingual or speak only Spanish, rather than speaking their native language. Three groups, the Cabecares, Bribris, and Guaymis have some Bible portions available to them in their language. Other ethnic groups (North Americans, Europeans, and Chinese) have Bibles available to them in their primary language. The increased interest in Bible reading among the Catholics is revealed in Bible Society statistics for 1978 and 1979. (These reports do not include the figures of commercial publishers and distributors.)

| | |
|---|---|
| Bibles | 20,236 |
| New Testaments | 29,745 |
| Portions | 142,722 |
| Portions for new readers | 9,028 |
| Selections | 2,531,806 |
| Selections for new readers | 2,356,677 |
| Total 1979 | 5,090,214 |
| Total 1978 | 2,816,034 |

## EDUCATION

### Christian

Two large Protestant schools and a new, smaller one are operated in Costa Rica, all offering kindergarten, primary and secondary education. Methodist School, founded in 1921 by the Methodist Church, and Monterey School, established in 1955 by the LAM, have full government recognition. The International Baptists have recently opened a new school in English, called the International Christian School. Government concern for education accounts for the relatively small emphasis on this type of ministry.

### Theological

Three major seminaries in Costa Rica are the interdenominational Latin American Biblical Seminary, founded by the LAM in 1923 as a Bible Institute, the Adventist Vocational College (1927) and the Nazarene Seminary (1970). Besides these seminaries, 17 Bible Institutes, largely missionary operated and nearly all denominational in character, also offer theological education. Of these, six belong to Pentecostal and 11 to non-Pentecostal denominations. Among these theological institutions, eleven offer theological education by extension (TEE) programs with about 1,070 students enrolled, with some living outside of Costa Rica. The large number of leadership training institutions in Costa Rica has greatly improved the quality of pastoral preparation, as well as stimulating evangelism and church planting.

## SOCIAL CONCERN

### Agriculture and Rural Development

Several missions and national churches carry out agricultural programs. These are usually centered in a specific agricultural community, radiating their influence to the surrounding region. Currently, there are five agricultural and rural development programs, and three relief and community development programs. Examples are the Rural Center maintained by the Methodist Church in Ciudad Quesada and the centers operated by Goodwill Caravans, the Bible Church Association, the Evangelical Mennonites and Adventists. Agricultural and development projects include experiments with seeds and crop production, extension services and technical assistance, development of cooperatives and drilling of wells.

## Medicine and Public Health

The two major Protestant medical services, both related to CLAME, are those operated by Goodwill Caravans and the Bible Clinic.

Since 1960 Goodwill Caravans has been serving rural communities of Costa Rica in public health, dental care, agricultural assistance, literacy, family counselling, and religious education. Volunteer doctors, dentists, nurses and agricultural experts, in a joint effort coordinated by the staff of Goodwill Caravans, travel throughout the country to isolated communities about 30 times a year. For many years, Caravans has operated a permanent rural clinic in Rio Naranjo in the northern province of Guanacaste. Official government support has been given to Caravans since 1970, when it was declared a public service organization.

The Bible Clinic, established in San Jose in 1929 by the Latin America Evangelization Campaign, offers out-patient and complete hospital services. Dr. Marie Cameron, a Canadian, served as medical director of the hospital from 1930 to 1968. In that year, the Clinic became independent of LAM, under the leadership of a national board of directors. The Association of Costa Rican Medical Services, the new legal entity, added a new five-story building to the hospital in 1975, increasing its capacity to 65 beds.

### Other Social Ministries

The Roblealto Child Care Association (CLAME) has two day-care centers in San Jose and a foster home program. It also maintains a home for children who need care over an extended period. The Episcopal Church also operates two day-care centers for children of working mothers. In addition, Goodwill Caravans has a special department for helping disadvantaged children. Interest in youth, the majority segment of the population, is reflected in the relatively high number of camps and camping programs (15) run by Protestant churches and agencies in Costa Rica.

Various specialized ministries for adults have come into existence because of special needs. The Good Samaritan Home, founded in 1955, is a cooperative evangelical effort to care for the elderly. Goodwill Caravans operates the Christian Women's Center as a part of its Department of Urban Development. Since 1973, the Salvation Army has established alcoholic rehabilitation centers in San Jose and Tres Rios.

43

## ECUMENICAL RELATIONSHIPS

Some 25 churches, agencies and organizations constitute the Evangelical Alliance of Costa Rica, a unifying force in the life of the evangelical community, founded in 1950. In its thirty years of existence, the Alliance has sponsored seminars, retreats, public worship services and short courses. It has been effective in protecting the rights of the evangelical minority. As a channel for cooperative service, the Alliance has been most effective in assisting those affected by national emergencies, such as floods and earthquakes. The work carried out by its Rural Work Committee paved the way for the creation of Goodwill Caravans in 1960. However, some of the larger denominations (such as the Episcopal Church, Adventists, Baptist Convention, and Central American Mission-related churches) are not affiliated with the Alliance.

## GENERAL SERVICE AGENCIES

There are a number of Costa Rica-based agencies whose services extend to most of Latin America.

ALFALIT, founded in 1961 by Methodist missionary, Justo Gonzalez, is primarily aimed at "enabling everyone in Latin America to read the Bible". The name is formed from two Spanish words: alfabetizar (to make literate) and literatura (literature). The program of ALFALIT is to produce materials for literacy and guidance for new readers. However, the organization has branched out into community development, agricultural promotion, various aspects of functional literacy, adult education and leadership training, in addition to literacy evangelism.

The international offices of ALFALIT are located in Alajuela, and autonomous national organizations of ALFALIT now exist in twelve countries of Latin America. Over 50 titles are now offered and nearly two million copies of ALFALIT books have helped over 300,000 people to read and write.

The Community of Latin American Evangelical Ministries (CLAME), is a federation of autonomous organizations that grew out of the various departments of the LAM. It was formed in 1971 in response to creative pressures within the Latin America Mission. All of the new entities are under national leadership, but are assisted by missionary personnel on loan from the LAM or other missionary or service organizations.

CLAME, by nature international and interdenominational, exists to aid the evangelical movement in Latin America by providing various support ministries. The basic purposes of CLAME are: (1) to participate in the evangelization of Latin America; (2) to contribute to the unity, mobilization, growth and edification of the Church; (3) to aid the strategic penetration of the Gospel into all groups, classes and levels of society through relevant Christian testimony and action; (4) to stimulate a missionary vision among Latin churches and help mobilize their resources for the local, national and international extension of the Gospel; and (5) to develop Christian leaders at all levels in service for Christ both in the Church and in the community.

The office of the General Secretary is located in San Jose, with special services provided to members in Costa Rica: Association for Christian Literature (APROLIC), Association of Bible Churches (AIBC), Bible Clinic, Christian Ministry to the English-speaking, Cultural Association, "Lighthouse of the Caribbean" (Radio station TIFC), Disfusiones Interamericanas (DIA), Editorial Caribe, Goodwill Caravans, Institute of In-Depth Evangelization (INDEPTH), Latin American Biblical Seminary (SBL), Latin American Evangelical Center for Pastoral Studies (CELEP), Ministry to the Student World (MINAMUNDO), Monterrey School and Poblealto Childcare Association.

Difusiones Interamericanas (DIA), founded in San Jose in 1952, is an international and interdenominational service agency and center for cooperative broadcasting services. DIA produces, duplicates and distributes evangelical radio programs to over 600 secular and Protestant radio stations in Latin America. Additional services include: listener follow-up by telephone and personal correspondence; technical assistance; conferences and workshops on program production, station management and communications in general; and rental service of films and other audio-visual aids and equipment.

The Institute of In-Depth Evangelization (INDEPTH) is an interdenominational and international team of evangelical leaders who are dedicated to the task of stimulating and developing holistic Church growth, primarily in the Central America region. With the restructuring of the Latin America Mission in 1971, INDEPTH emerged out of the former Department of Evangelism-in-Depth. Help is offered to pastors and churches through the following ministries of INDEPTH advisors: (1) Consultation services; working with church

44

leaders to develop strategies and programs of discipleship and evangelization for churches at various levels - locally, regionally or nationally; (2) Leadership seminars: on discipleship, evangelization and holistic church growth; (3) Church growth research: to find out why churches are or are not growing, in order to help them increase their fruitbearing; planning and participation: in evangelistic crusades, pastoral retreats and conferences, training seminars and workshops, etc. (5) Publications and audio-visual aids: producing materials on discipleship, evangelization and church growth.

The Latin American Evangelical Center for Pastoral Studies (CELEP) promotes the pastoral ministry of the Protestant Churches in Latin America and the Caribbean. CELEP engages in research; has a publications program; sponsors workshops, seminars and consultations; and undertakes special projects. Examples of the latter are the Women's Pastoral Project and the Program for Facing National Emergencies. More recently it has accepted responsibility for the Coordination of the Education for Communication Program (EDCOM), which aims at helping church leaders understand the complexities of religious communication. These activities revolve around the desire of CELEP "to motivate and train leaders to serve as catalysts for the mobilization of the Church for a comprehensive witness in the world." This leadership training program focuses on: (1) The meaning of pastoral ministry in the Latin American context; (2) the pastoral problems that arise within both the Church and secular communities; and (3) the pastoral practice and models of pastoral action in contemporary Latin America. CELEP's international headquarters are located in San Jose.

Ministry to the Student World (MINAMUNDO) is a fellowship of Christian student workers, who are dedicated to the task of bringing the gospel to the student population of Latin America. The MINAMUNDO team is composed of about 15 couples who minister at various levels: among high school and university students, among professionals, and through Christian camping programs.

MINAMUNDO owes its existence in part to a concern expressed within the Evangelism-in-Depth Movement that a much greater emphasis should be given to a ministry among the students of Latin America. Out of this concern the Ministry to the Student World of Latin America Mission was born in 1968. At that time three major activities were brought

together: Camp Roblealto, founded in 1947, the university work, started in 1960, and the high school work begun in 1967. With the advent of the Community of Latin American Evangelical Ministries in 1971, the organization took on legal status as an association under the laws of Costa Rica and became known as MINAMUNDO International. At present MINAMUNDO serves in Mexico, Costa Rica, Panama, Colombia and Ecuador.

The Spanish Language Institute is a center for the language and cultural preparation of missionaries to Latin America. Established in Colombia in 1942 and transferred to San Jose in 1950, the Institute has served the majority of mission boards and agencies of the United States, Canada and Europe, now with an average of 350 students each year from 80 denominations.

## NATION AND ITS PEOPLE

## POPULATION

Costa Rica's population of 2.3 million makes it one of the least populated nations of Central America. Only Panama has fewer people. Between 1950 and 1970, Costa Rica experienced a "population explosion" when it doubled in size. Since 1970, it became the only country in Latin America to reduce its birth rate drastically within a short period of time, from 3.3% to 2.5%. Today 39% of Costa Rica's population is under 14 years of age, 57% are between 15-64 years, and 4% are over 65 years of age. The population density is only 45 people per square kilometer (116 per square mile). Two out of three Costa Ricans lived in rural areas in 1980. In this general breakdown, two extremes are noted; one third live in scattered rural communities of less than 500 people, while one fourth live in the San Jose Metropolitan Area that measures only 4% of the national territory. The Central Valley is the principal area of attraction: its population grew 50% between 1963 and 1973. Internal migration patterns reveal existing regional inequalities. Between 1968 and 1973, 43% of all migrants over 5 years of age moved to the Central Valley in search of greater opportunities for social mobility. The Atlantic and South Pacific regions each received about 20% of the migrants, mainly attracted by jobs on banana plantations. The country's capital, San Jose, is located in the Central Valley and its population of 508,000 in 1980 made it the largest city. Nearby cities of Cartago

(40,900), Alajuela (40,700) and Heredia (31,100) grew significantly during the 1970s. Other important cities are Limon (36,900) and Puntarenas (30,300), the major Caribbean and Pacific ports, respectively.

## COMPOSITION

Costa Rica has one of the most homogeneous populations in Central America. The majority are of Spanish descent or of Spanish-Indian (mestizo) origin. There is no cultural or racial distinction between whites and mestizos. The latest census to use racial categories (1950) revealed that 98% of the population were white or mestizo, while 1.9% were black and the remainder Indian or Chinese. The most important ethnic minorities today are the West Indian Negroes (2%), who live mainly in the Caribbean province of Limon, and several small Indian tribes scattered around the country, numbering about 15,000. Other ethnic minorities include the Chinese (4,500) and the Jews (2,500). According to the 1973 Census, only 2.5% of the total population were foreign born, of which 66% were Central Americans, 10% North Americans, 9% South Americans, 7% Europeans, 2% Mexicans and 2% Asians.

## LANGUAGE AND LITERACY

Costa Rica is a nation which has more teachers than soldiers. Education is both free and compulsory. The largest percentage of the national budget is spent on education. As a result, the country has the highest literacy rate of Central America, almost 90%. However, the functional literacy rate is much lower, with wide variation between urban and rural areas. Both elementary and secondary education are free, with the former being compulsory. Spanish is the dominant language of the country and it is a purer form of the language than that found in the rest of Central America. This is largely due to the relative isolation of individuals living in the Central Valleys. The Spanish spoken by those living near the borders of Panama and Nicaragua, more closely resembles that of the neighboring countries. English is spoken primarily by Negroes of West Indian descent who predominate in Limon Province. However, English as a second language is becoming a valuable asset in industry and business where bilingualism is highly desirable. English is now being taught in most of the country's private high schools. Although six different Indian languages exist in Costa Rica, Spanish is generally spoken by most Indian adults.

Not only are Costa Ricans highly literate, they are also well informed on national and international events. According to a recent study on mass media, 87% of the population listen to the radio daily, 60% watch television, and 43% read the newspapers. Naturally, these figures are higher for urban areas and for the Central Valley than for outlying areas.

## RELIGION

Christianity is the dominant religion of Costa Rica. About 90% of the people are baptized Roman Catholics. However, only 15-20% of these attend Mass regularly. Because of recent rapid growth among Protestant churches, the Protestant Community now totals 7.9% of the total population. Since 1967, the average annual growth rate (AAGR) has been 11% among Protestants. The lack of strong religious convictions among nominal Catholics may explain recent growth patterns among religious groups, both Christian and non-Christian. The Church of Jesus Christ of Latter-Day Saints (The Mormon Church) and the Jehovah's Witnesses report 5,400 and 13,250 adherents, respectively. However, the Christadelphians, Christian Science and Children of God only claim a small number of adherents, about 150.

Psychic movements have found growing response, especially among the more highly educated. The Great Universal Fraternity and the Universal Gnostic Movement claim adherents totaling 5,000. The Theosophical Society, Spiritists and Rosicrucians have about 1,650 adherents. Many newspapers and popular magazines carry astrological charts and advertise psychical groups.

At the same time, inroads are being made by other non-Christian groups who are finding Costa Ricans to be very open to new religious experiences. Totaling about 3,000 adherents, Baha'i, Hari Krishna, the Unification Church, Yoga, Transcendental Meditation, Silva Mind Control and Islamic groups are all present in the capital city of San Jose. The effects of the popular philosophies of Marxism, secularism and materialism are being felt at all levels of society.

## GEOGRAPHY AND CLIMATE

Costa Rica is the second smallest Central American country. A volcanic mountain system composed of three ranges extends the length of the country, making it considerably mountainous. The highest elevations are found in the southern Talamanca range with mountains of over 3,962 meters (13,000 feet) in height.

46

Many streams and rivers drain the mountain regions. About two-thirds of the total land area is forested. The Caribbean coast, 130 miles long, is flat, hot and humid. The Pacific coast, 630 miles long, has hilly or mountainous peninsulas, coastal lowlands and deep gulfs and bays. Six distinct ecological regions can be distinguished: the Central Valley, the North Pacific, South Pacific, Central Pacific, North and Atlantic.

The climate is tropical with two seasons: the wet season (May through November) and the dry season (December through April). The Caribbean plain, however, receives rainfall year round. Temperature varies with elevation. The lowland plains have maximum temperatures averaging 30 degrees C. (90 degrees F.) while the highland regions average between 20-25 degrees C. (70-80 degrees F.).

## HISTORY

Costa Rica was discovered and probably named by Christopher Columbus on his last voyage to America. In the colonial era that followed, Costa Rica was one of the poorest of Spain's colonies, isolated geographically and culturally from the rest of Central America. Cacao, and not precious metals, formed the base of her exports as a colony. The Indians, enslaved and ill-used, died off rapidly, forcing the early settlers to cultivate their own land. This condition gave rise to a pattern of small land-ownership which was to prevail during the centuries. Costa Rica had little contact with the outside world, including the two neighboring territories of Panama and Nicaragua. As a result, the colony developed an independent and individualistic society. But from 1823-1838, Costa Rica formed part of the United Provinces of Central America, becoming an independent republic in 1836. The 19th century witnessed the beginning of the economic transformation of Costa Rica with the cultivation of coffee for export. The free public school system, established in 1890, contributed to the formation of a literate and politically active people. During the first three decades of this present century, the exportation of bananas by Standard Fruit and United Brands greatly added to the country's economic stability.

Compared with other Central American governments, Costa Rica's is remarkably stable. The elections of 1889 are considered to be the beginning of the modern political era of Costa Rica. Except for two interruptions of constitutional government (one in 1917 and the other in the aftermath of the revolution of 1948), Costa Rica has a strong tradition of democratic government. The decade of the 1940s witnessed a transition for the small nation from a liberal to a social democracy. Beginning with advanced social and labor legislation proposed by President Calderon Guardia (1940-1944), successive presidents implemented sweeping changes through social reform. This process was not detained by the revolution of 1948, which was principally caused by electoral dishonesty. The victor was revolutionary hero Jose Figueres who governed 18 months, a time in which 834 laws were emitted. Most notable of these were nationalization of the banks, the abolition of the army and the right of women to vote. Constitutional government was restored in 1949, initiating a time of rapid modernization of the country.

## GOVERNMENT AND POLITICAL CONDITIONS

Costa Rica is one of the leading democratic countries in Latin America. Formally, the country is governed by three political institutions provided for by the Constitution of 1949: the executive, legislative and judicial branches. The president and two vice presidents are elected for one four-year term. Likewise, the unicameral legislature is elected at the same time for a four-year term. Legislators cannot be reelected for successive terms. Judicial authority is vested in the Supreme Court of Justice and by lesser courts. The 17 Magistrates of the Supreme Court are elected by the Legislative Assembly for eight-year terms. Informally, however, numerous interest groups and an elaborate bureaucratic apparatus play an equally important role in formulating and conducting government policies. This political system, is partially responsible for the non-extremist changes that have taken place in the country, earning itself an image of a liberal democracy.

It has been characteristic of Costa Rican governments to stress education, implement labor reforms and provide for social welfare. The National Liberation Party (PLN) is the country's major ideological party when in power. It has implemented programs in accord with its concept that the state is the institution charged with promoting the general welfare of society as a whole. Since its origin in 1952, the National Liberation Party has been largely responsible for the government's involvement in the economic system as a producer, consumer and provider of jobs. Its founder, Jose Figueres, continues to be an important leader in the political mainstream.

Chief among other political groups in Costa Rica is the Unity Party, a loose coalition of opposition groups led by ex-Liberationist lawyer, Rodrigo Carazo. The Unity Party gained sufficient strength on a "clean government" campaign to win national elections in 1978, ousting PLN leader, Daniel Oduber, from the Presidency. Carazo won 51% of the vote, a notable landslide victory. Serious campaigning has already begun for the 1982 elections, with growing predictions of a PLN victory. Other moderates are divided and split into a number of smaller parties. Although leftist parties are legal, their activities are concentrated in labor unions and not in winning national elections; however, the United People's Party did win a few seats in the present Legislative Assembly. Suprisingly, this strongly democratic and pro-U.S. nation also maintains diplomatic relations with the USSR, Romania and Cuba.

Undoubtedly, Costa Rica will play a key role in the future of the Central America region. After the fall of the Somoza dynasty in Nicaragua, and due to continuing political and social unrest in El Salvador and Guatemala, a democratic alignment is taking place between Nicaragua, Costa Rica and Panama to counter-balance the power of rightist military governments in the northern part of the region. Costa Rica has strongly supported human rights and social justice issues in Latin America, so much so that the Organization of American States (OAS) made San Jose its headquarters for the newly established Court of Human Rights, and the United Nations has recently approved a project to create in Costa Rica an international University for World Peace.

PUBLIC ORDER AND INTERNAL SECURITY

Costa Rica is one of the few nations of the world that has renounced the maintenance of a military establishment. Although the Constitution states that military forces may be organized for specific needs, such as territorial defense, the country has generally placed its reliance on the Organization of American States.

The maintenance of public order is assigned to the Civil and Rural Guard, more of a police force than an army. Though Costa Ricans are fundamentally an orderly and law-abiding people with a tradition of respect for authority, there is growing alarm over increasing delinquency and organized crime in the recent years, along with an increasing number of illegal strikes and other public manifestations of unrest. There is also concern about the increasing militarization of the Civil Guard and the number and sophistication of munitions. More professional methods of military management have been implemented in response to tension produced by the recent civil war in Nicaragua. The Minister of Public Security recently resigned amidst charges that he was trafficking in arms, and this has led to a Watergate-type of investigation by the National Assembly.

HEALTH, EDUCATION AND WELFARE

The mortality rate of 4.6 for 1,000 inhabitants is the lowest in Central America and compares favorably with that of other progressive countries of the Western Hemisphere. Life expectancy is 68 years for men and 72 for women.

Though infant mortality rates have decreased sharply (now calculated at 29 per 1,000), it must be noted that malnutrition is present, in some degree, in over half of the children under five years of age. Malnutrition, compounded by diarrhea and infectious diseases, constitutes a major cause of infant mortality.

Health care, in general, has undergone rapid modernization. Preventive medicine is mainly the concern of the Ministry of Health; all other health services are handled, for most of the population, by the country's Social Security System. This system, financed by workers, employers and the State, offers complete health care services. Complaints against this system have to do with the quality and availability of the services rendered, especially in rural areas.

In 1978, almost one third of the national budget was destined for education by Costa Ricans. Primary and secondary education are free, with primary school being compulsory. There are 226 high schools. Higher education is provided by four universities, one of them private and one a university-level extension program. These universities had a total enrollment of 44,000 in 1979.

Though registration is high at all educational levels, the drop-out rate is a great concern. Whereas about 90% of all 10 year olds were in school in 1973, only about 35% of all 15 year olds were enrolled. In 1978, only 1.1% of the total population had completed five or more years of university, 3.3% had some university studies, 19.1% had some secondary education, 63.3% had some primary education and 12.1% had no formal instruction.

Added to the high value placed on formal education and the increasing levels of health, the increasing availablity of public services (roads, bridges, water, electricity, telephone) is an important factor in general welfare of Costa Ricans. The National Institute of Electricity is responsible for electrical power and communications systems, which are among the best in Central America. Two hydroelectric projects, located in Cachi and Arenal, provide the country with electrical power and water for consumption and irrigation.

The Ministry of Public Works and Transportation has spent millions of dollars on roadbuilding and improvements during the past decade. Costa Rica now claims the best road system in Central America. Good all-weather roads now link San Jose with both Caribbean and Pacific ports. The Pan-American Highway crosses Costa Rica from the borders of Nicaragua in the north to Panama in the south. Most Costa Ricans depend on buses for transportation, both in urban and rural areas. The majority of private automobiles are concentrated in the Central Valley.

ECONOMY

Costa Rica enjoyed the highest per capita GNP ($1,540) within Central America in 1978. Although the economy is essentially dependent on agriculture, the proportion of the labor force in agriculture declined from 55% in 1950 to 37% in 1973. Coffee, bananas, cacao, sugar and meat constitute the major export products. However, by devoting a large portion of agricultural production to cash crops for export, the intense cultivation of staple foodstuffs needed to supply a rapidly growing population is often neglected. Though the contribution of the industrial sector to the gross national product (from 12% in 1950 to 24% in 1978) has been growing, this increase is not reflected in the number of jobs available. The proportion of the labor force in industry only increased slightly from 11% to 15% between 1950 and 1978. Commerce and public services account for the majority of the remaining active labor force, which totals 33% of the population.

The economy has experienced significant growth since 1960, due mainly to the exportation of agricultural products to Europe and North America. Since the mid-1970s, however, Costa Rica has encountered growing economic problems. The trade deficit with other Central American countries reached $36.5 million in 1979, which may indicate that Costa Rica´s participation in the Central American Common Market has been detrimental to her economy. The total foreign debt was estimated at $1.6 billion in 1979 and over 3.7 billion in 1980. Inflation rose more than 13% during 1979, with gasoline prices surpassing $3.25 per gallon (U.S.) The value of the colon dropped from 8.6 per $1 U.S. to 40 per $1 U.S. in 1981 and the nation itself was on the verge of bankruptcy. Negotiations with the World Bank may provide much needed relief through special financing of foreign debt.

Unbalanced trade relationships, increased foreign indebtedness, deficit spending and rapid inflation have had a negative impact on the national economy. The importation of high cost energy resources creates further dependence and weakens the economy. Facing food shortages and with their buying power sharply reduced, Costa Ricans are becoming increasingly impatient with the way in which the government tackles major problems. Comprehensive policy changes are being demanded by leading politicians, by business and labor leaders and by the masses.

Exchange rate: 40 Colon = $1

49

# CHURCH STATISTICS FOR COSTA RICA

NOTE: Statistics are from the 1978 PROCADES survey of Protestant Churches and are based on official denominational reports or estimates. Although definitions of "membership" vary slightly among churches, the data is highly comparable and reliable. All known Protestant Churches are included in the list.

| Church or Mission Name | Number of Congregations | Membership | % of Total |
|---|---|---|---|
| PROTESTANT | | | |
| Adventist | 47 | 5,700 | 12.1% |
|   Seventh-day Adventist | 47 | 5,700 | |
| Evangelical Non-Pentecostal | 284 | 15,653 | 34.9% |
|   American Baptist Association | 13 | 540 | |
|   Association of Bible Churches | 62 | 3,984 | |
|   Baptist Convention (Southern) | 39 | 2,260 | |
|   Bible Baptist Churches | 7 | 2,950 | |
|   Central American Churches | 60 | 1,117 | |
|   Holiness (four groups) | 28 | 875 | |
|   Mennonites (two groups) | 11 | 400 | |
|   Methodists (two groups) | 24 | 1,395 | |
|   Other Baptists (11 groups) | 40 | 2,132 | |
| Liturgical | 24 | 2,424 | 5.4% |
|   Episcopal Church | 17 | 2,049 | |
|   Lutherans (three groups) | 7 | 375 | |
| Pentecostal | 370 | 21,052 | 47% |
|   Assemblies of God | 120 | 4,900 | |
|   Association of Christian Churches | 10 | 965 | |
|   Church of God - Cleveland | 66 | 2,100 | |
|   Crusade of Faith | 1 | 720 | |
|   Evangelical Pentecostal of Cartago | 9 | 1,200 | |
|   Foursquare Church | 31 | 2,900 | |
|   Independent Christian Churches | 4 | 660 | |
|   National Evangelical Church | 8 | 1,280 | |
|   Pentecostal Church of God | 14 | 1,200 | |
|   Pentecostal Holiness Church | 26 | 1,100 | |
|   Other Pentecostal Holiness groups | 20 | 665 | |
|   Pentecostal "Jesus Only" (two groups) | 29 | 846 | |
|   Rose of Sharon | 3 | 500 | |
|   Misc. Pentecostal | 29 | 2,016 | |
| TOTAL (1978) | 725 | 44,829 | 100.0% |
| ESTIMATED TOTAL FOR 1978 | | 141,000 | |

The sources listed below are to help the reader find additional information on this country and Christian ministries there. This list does not try to be comprehensive or complete.

## DOCUMENTS

### General

Blutstein, Howard I., et al. Area Handbook for Costa Rica, Foreign Area Studies, The American University, Washington, D.C.: U.S. Government Printing Office, 1970.

Biesanz, Mavis, et al. Los Costarricenses (The Costa Ricans), San Jose, Costa Rica: Editorial Universidad Estatal A Distancia, 1979.

Denton, Charles F., Patterns of Costa Rican Politics, Boston: Allyn and Bacon, Inc., 1971.

Duncan, Quince and Melendez, Carlos, El Negro en Costa Rica (The Negro in Costa Rica), San Jose, Costa Rica: Editorial Costa Rica, 1974.

Fernandez, Mario E., et al. La Poblacion de Costa Rica (The Population of Costa Rica), San Jose, Costa Rica: Editorial Universidad de Costa Rica, 1976.

### Christian

Nelson, Wilton M., A History of Protestantism in Costa Rica, Lucknow, U.P., India: Lucknow Publishing House, 1963.

PROCADES/INDEPTH, Directorio de Iglesias, Organizaciones y Ministerios del Movimiento Protestante: Costa Rica (Directory of Churches, Organizations and Ministries of the Protestant Movement: Costa Rica), San Jose, Costa Rica: PROCADES/INDEPTH, 1978.

PROCADES/INDEPTH, Evaluacion Panoramica del Crecimiento Numerico de los Grupos Protestantes entre 1967 y 1978 (Panoramic Evaluation of the Numerical Growth of Protestant Groups between 1967 and 1978), Costa Rica Report 4, San Jose, Costa Rica: PROCADES/INDEPTH, 1979.

## ORGANIZATIONS

Bible Society of Costa Rica, Apartado 5672, San Jose
Community of Latin American Evangelical Ministries (CLAME), Apartado 1307, San Jose
Evangelical Alliance of Costa Rica, Apartado 10250, San Jose
Institute of In-Depth Evangelization (INDEPTH), Apartado 1307, San Jose
Institute of Social Studies in Population (IDESPO), Universidad National de Heredia

## ACKNOWLEDGMENTS

The information in this profile was taken from many sources which were the best available to the editors at the time of preparation. However, the accuracy of the information cannot be guaranteed. Views expressed or implied in this publication are not necessarily those of World Vision. The editors have tried to present the ministries of various organizations in an objective manner, without undue bias or emphasis. Where we have failed, we apologize for erroneous impressions that may result and request that comments and corrections be sent to MARC, 919 West Huntington Drive, Monrovia, California, USA, 91016. We appreciate and acknowledge the comments and contributions of various organizations and individuals in the preparation of this publication.

# STATUS OF CHRISTIANITY
# COUNTRY PROFILE

# EL SALVADOR

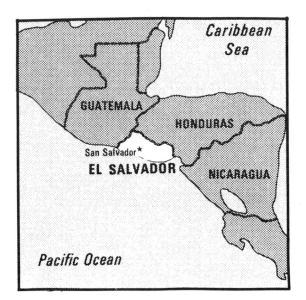

## SUMMARY

AREA - 21,156 square kilometers (8,260 square miles)

POPULATION - 4.9 million

RELIGION - 92% Catholic, 7% Protestant, 1% Other

After brewing beneath the surface for years, civil unrest boiled over in El Salvador following the Sandinista victory in Nicaragua in 1979. Tens of thousands of people have been killed in the fighting between the army, guerrilla bands and right-wing para-military forces. Several Catholic priests, nuns and Protestant ministers have been killed, intimidated or forced to flee from the escalating conflict. The endless cycle of poverty for landless peasants, the unequal distribution of land, the terrorist acts of leftist groups, the stern counter-revolutionary measures by the government and the support of both sides by outside powers have all contributed to this seemingly unresolvable conflict. Thus, Christians in El Salvador are forced into difficult decisions. In spite of the social unrest, the Protestant Church has grown at an average annual growth rate of 11.3% during the 1970s.

## PEOPLE GROUPS

### Latinos (94%)

As in other countries of Central America, most of the population is Latino and largely mestizo (92%), along with some of white Spanish ancestry (2%). Although the majority are nominal Catholics, few attend Mass or take an active part in religious activities other than annual festivals. Only a few Latinos have church weddings and common-law marriages are the rule. Among the lesser acculturated Latinos, the older Indian belief system has only a thin veneer of Catholicism, with traditional religious life finding its most important public expression in the annual fiesta honoring the patron saint of the parish, town or city.

Most Protestant growth has occurred among the Latino population, but no more than 6.5% could be considered Protestant adherents. If active Catholics total 15-20% of all Latinos, then there still remains approximately 75-80% who are yet to be reached with the gospel.

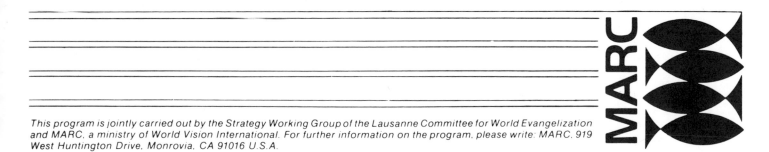

This program is jointly carried out by the Strategy Working Group of the Lausanne Committee for World Evangelization and MARC, a ministry of World Vision International. For further information on the program, please write: MARC, 919 West Huntington Drive, Monrovia, CA 91016 U.S.A.

## Amerindians (6%)

Since the Indian groups in El Salvador are predominantly Spanish-speaking, no Christian churches, either Catholic or Protestant, use an Indian dialect. Consequently, there is little obvious distinction between Latino and Indian ethnic groups in terms of general religious practices, and it is difficult to determine the extent of Protestant penetration among the Pipil and Lenca. However, in the early 1900s, several Protestant missions began work among the Pipil in southwestern Salvador using Spanish, and it is assumed that there are still congregations composed largely of Indian believers.

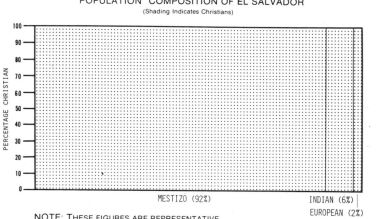

POPULATION COMPOSITION OF EL SALVADOR
(Shading Indicates Christians)

NOTE: THESE FIGURES ARE REPRESENTATIVE APPROXIMATIONS. THEY SHOULD BE SEEN AS INDICATORS OF MAGNITUDE ONLY.

## Other People Groups

Until 1979, the majority of social groups were difficult to reach for Christ. However, due to the political conflict and the violence that has affected the country, a sound revival has been experienced in all the social sectors and especially among university students, urban middle class, urban working class, the elite upper class, (prosperous merchants and highly paid professionals) and military people.

A people group that merits to be mentioned is the one made up of migratory flows resulting from the present crisis. These groups are of two types: 1) displaced groups (130,000-180,000) who are people that fled within the Salvadoran territory escaping from confrontations between guerrillas and the national army;

and 2) Refugees who have fled to many countries, with large concentrations in Honduras (30,000 to 40,000, mainly in camps along the border), Costa Rica, Mexico and the United States, especially in the Los Angeles area. Estimates of the number of orphans in El Salvador range from 5,000 to 10,000. Refugees and orphans are being cared for by Catholic and Protestant relief organizations, the International Red Cross and local Red Cross agencies, the UN High Commissioner for Refugees and World Vision International.

### CURRENT STATUS OF CHRISTIANITY

Although 92% of the Salvadoran population are baptized Catholics, serious internal tensions and external conflicts face the Catholic Church during the 1980s. After decades of conservatism the Salvadoran Church, led by Archbishop Oscar Romero, has officially taken its stand with the poor and oppressed in Salvadoran society, following the pastoral guidelines enunciated by the Latin American bishops at Medellin and Puebla. On the other hand, conservative bishops within the Salvadoran hierarchy have supported the government in its war against insurrection. However, a growing number of Catholic organizations and institutions in El Salvador are now openly supporting the revolt against the oligarchy and military establishment that has ruled the country since the 1930s.

The Salvadoran Church's stand for human rights and social justice has resulted in severe persecution against socially active priests and nuns, including foreign missionaries, by right-wing terrorist organizations and government military forces. Since 1977, twelve priests, including Archbishop Romero, and four Catholic women missionaries from the United States, have been murdered in the escalating violence between the government and the insurrectionists. Jesuits and Maryknolls have been special targets of persecution by forces supporting the Romero and Duarte governments. Over 30 Salvadoran priests are now in exile for alleged political activities.

Most Protestants in El Salvador, politically conservative like most Catholics prior to the mid-1970s, are now taking a more critical look at their past record on human rights and social justice issues. Many are becoming politically and socially active. A growing number of these socially active pastors and laymen have been harrassed, tortured, murdered or exiled by government supporters, while others have experienced the same treatment from left-wing terrorists because they were voices of moderation or of support for the government.

In 1978, the estimated Protestant population of El Salvador was about 295,000 or 7% of all Salvadorans, predominantly Hispanicized mestizos and Indians (Latinos). The Protestant movement is characterized by a large proportion of Pentecostals within the total membership (about 68%), compared to slightly more than 50% for the entire Central American region. Whereas the total Protestant membership in El Salvador increased by an Average Annual Growth Rate (AAGR) of 11.3% during the 1970s, the Pentecostal rate of increase was 12.6% (AAGR). The largest Protestant denominations are the Assemblies of God - 22,500 members, Seventh-day Adventists - 12,000, Church of God, Cleveland - 9,850, the Evangelical Church of El Salvador, related to the Central American Mission - 6,000 and the Prince of Peace Church - 5,000.

## RELIGIOUS COMPOSITION OF EL SALVADOR

Other 1%

Protestant 7%

Roman Catholic 92%

**NATIONAL CHURCHES**

## PROTESTANT CHURCHES

The history of the Protestant movement in El Salvador is distinct from other Central American republics, in that pioneer

foreign mission efforts here were directed towards the Spanish-speaking population from the very beginning. Since the English-speaking Creole and West Indian immigrants were largely absent from El Salvador, Protestant missionary activity was initiated among Hispanics or Latinos, and among small American Indian groups - the Pipil and Lenca. The earliest Protestant groups to enter El Salvador were the Central American Mission (1896), the California Friends Mission (1902), independent Pentecostals (1904), American Baptists (1911) and the Adventists (1915).

The Protestant movement can be subdivided into families of denominations to allow us to see growth trends more clearly. The Evangelical Non-Pentecostal Family of Churches (ENPs) composed 63% of the total Protestant membership in 1936, while the Pentecostal Family was 30.3% and the Adventist, 6.8%. However, the Pentecostals and Adventists have progressively become a larger proportion of the total Protestant membership, while the ENPs have declined. By 1950, Pentecostals were 55.8%, Evangelical Non-Pentecostals, 34.9% and Adventists, 5.8%. Between 1960 and 1970, Pentecostals decreased slightly in proportional size, from 68.5% to 64.6%, but rose again by 1978 to 67.7%. Adventists progressively increased, while ENPs declined proportionally during the same period; in 1978, Adventists were 13.9% and ENPs, 15.3%. The Liturgical Family of Churches arrived in El Salvador during the 1960s, and by 1970 represented 2% of the total Protestant membership. In 1978 the remaining 1.2% of the total membership was not yet classified by family types.

The period of greatest Protestant church growth in El Salvador was during the 1970s (11.3% AAGR), compared to 6.9% during the 1960s, 7.1% for the period 1945-1960 and 9.2% between 1930 and 1945. Whereas the ENPs experienced a slump during the 1950s (slowing to 2.9% AAGR) and the Pentecostals during the 1960s (6.3% AAGR), the Adventists are the only group that has declined in growth since 1970 - from 13.8% (AAGR) in the 1960s to 8.5% (AAGR) since 1970. The Liturgical Family of Churches, mainly Lutherans, have an annual growth rate of 11.4% for the 1970s. Overall, the Protestant communicant membership increased from 41,800 in 1970 to about 111,400 in 1980, when the Protestant population totaled about 334,000, or 6.9% of all Salvadorans.

An examination of the geographic distribution of Protestant congregations reveals that the Pentecostal Family predominates in all three regions :- western (77.6%), central (64%) and eastern

55

(69%). The ENPs are better represented in the central region, where San Salvador is located, whereas the Adventists are strongest in the eastern region, near San Miguel. Proportionally, 51% of all ENP congregations are located in the central region, 45% of Liturgical work is in the eastern region, along with 38.5% of all Adventist congregations, whereas 40% of Pentecostal work is located in the western region dominated by Santa Ana, El Salvador's second largest city.

## CATHOLIC CHURCHES

About 91% of the population are baptized Roman Catholics. El Salvador is an ecclesiastical province composed of an archdiocese and four dioceses. The first diocese was established in San Salvador in 1842, while the dioceses of Santa Ana and San Miguel were formed in 1913. Santiago de Maria was added in 1958. The diocese of San Salvador was raised to the level of an archdiocese in 1929.

There has always been a shortage of priests and other religious workers in El Salvador. In 1944, there were 106 parishes with 203 priests and 357 nuns, which increased to 175 parishes, 373 priests and 803 nuns in 1968. Today, among 229 parishes, there are 373 priests (173 diocesan and 200 religious), 70 lay brothers and 735 nuns. In 1970, about 62% of the priests and 19% of the nuns were native Salvadorans, which is a high percentage of national priests and a low proportion of indigenous nuns compared to other countries of Latin America. The proportion of priests per inhabitant in El Salvador went from 1 per 7,692 in 1970 to 1 per 12,860 in 1980.

Relations between the Catholic Church and the State became strained after the rise to power of General Carlos Humberto Romero in January, 1977. At about the same time Oscar Romero was appointed archbishop of San Salvador, apparently the more conservative of the two candidates for that position. However, in a country dominated by terror and injustice, Archbishop Romero soon became a voice for Christian compassion and reason, denouncing the military's repression of the people and pleading for redistribution of land and unification of the country. Romero and other priests began to speak out against the alleged injustice and repression by the government and its military forces. Their solidarity with the poor and oppressed and their denunciations brought them into serious conflict with the ruling aristocracy, often called the "fourteen families," who have ruled El Salvador with the support of the military since the early 1930's. Many

priests and other religious workers were soon accused of being communists because of their support of the poor and their denunciation of the growing repression by General Romero's security forces.

The distinguishing feature of the Salvadoran Catholic Church today is its strong stand on human rights and social justice, based on the pastoral "option for the poor" enunciated by the Latin American bishops at Medellin in 1968 and reiterated at Puebla in 1979. Since 1977, many priests in El Salvador have been harrassed by government military forces and right-wing terrorist groups that support the government in its war against alleged communist insurrection. An assassin's bullet struck Archbishop Romero in the heart in March 1980, while he was saying Mass in San Salvador. In these ways, the Catholic Church has experienced persecution by the Romero and Duarte governments, both of which have been condemned by Latin American and North American Catholic bishops in pastoral letters and official declarations.

## FOREIGN MISSIONS

## PROTESTANT MISSIONS

The Pentecostal movement had its origin in El Salvador about 1904, with the arrival of an independent Canadian missionary, Frederick F. Mebius. Mebius apparently arrived in El Salvador about 1904, staying until about 1906, then he made a missionary journey to Bolivia, where he encountered much opposition. He returned to El Salvador in 1907 or 1908. The first Pentecostal believers in San Salvador were former members of churches established by the Central American Mission, and those in Santa Ana were from Baptist churches. A notable Pentecostal revival occurred in Colonia Montserrat in San Salvador, before Mebius left the capital to extend the movement to the western region of the country. Eventually, Mebius established a strong church at Las Lomas de San Marcelino in Izalco. This church became the center for the Apostolic movement in El Salvador which later spread to Honduras, in 1931.

Mebius, together with several lay evangelists, inspired by the Apostolic faith, traveled throughout the countryside in an itinerant preaching ministry that eventually produced 25 organized congregations, with about 750 members and perhaps 1,500 adherents, by 1930. The Apostolic movement became an entirely indigenous movement, without any outside funds from foreign mission agencies.

The work founded by Mebius came to be known as "Free Apostolic Churches." After the arrival of the Assemblies of God in El Salvador in 1929, efforts to organize this independent movement were partially successful. Twelve existing congregations became the founding churches of the Assemblies of Cod in El Salvador in 1930. The Assemblies of God had entered the country at the request of Francisco Ramirez Arbizu, one of the leading pastors in the Apostolic movement.

However, over half of the Apostolic congregations and pastors did not want to submit themselves to the authority of the Assemblies of God. Therefore, they continued as an independent movement, using the name "Free Apostolics." Each group was an independent congregation with only fraternal ties with other congregations and pastors in the movement. Part of the tension was over the form of ecclesiastical organization, since the Assemblies of God practiced a modified episcopal system of church government which was contrary to the congregational polity that the Free Apostolics had adopted.

None of the early Apostolic leaders had any formal training for the ministry, and few had any education beyond basic literacy, if that. As with many early Pentecostals, the Free Apostolics represented an anti-intellectual movement with strong separatist tendencies. But about 1935, some of the churches in the movement began to organize themselves in order to be recognized by the government. Involvement of lay personnel in the life of the local churches was limited by dependence on "apostles" and "prophets" for guidance and authority.

Several ecclesiastical bodies emerged out of the Free Apostolic Movement. The Apostolic Church of the Apostles and Prophets, formed in 1935, had 80 congregations and about 3,800 members in 1980. Apostolic Church of the Upper Focm, established in the 1930s, had 26 congregations and about 1,245 members in 1980. The Apostolic Church of God in Christ, established in 1950, reported six congregations and about 230 members in 1980. The Apostolic Church of the New Jerusalem split from the Apostles and Prophets in 1977. They reported two churches and 172 members. The Free Apostolics represent about 50 independent congregations and 3,200 members. Totals for the other church associations growing out of this movement were 114 churches and 5,500 members in 1978.

In 1940, the Rev. H.S. Syverson, general overseer of Central America for the Church of God - Cleveland, visited Mebius in El Salvador. The two agreed that they should work together under the auspices of the Church of Cod. Therefore, in February, 1940, the work of the Church of God began in El Salvador.

During the first four years of ministry in El Salvador, until Mebius' death in 1944, the Church of God grew slowly. After four years of labor, the Church of God field began to show signs of revitalization and expansion. In 1944, Syverson initiated the first short-term Bible school for training pastors and lay workers.

Although short-term missionaries aided in the development of the Bible Institute and in the general advancement of the Church of God in El Salvador, most of the evangelization efforts were done by Syverson and the national leaders. Not until 1953 were additional missionaries assigned to the work in El Salvador.

Growth over the next twenty years shows a consistent pattern of expansion and development in the Church of God. By 1970, total membership had increased to 4,300 among 117 organized churches and 78 missions; in 1972, membership climbed to 4,956 and by 1974 it reached 6,708. Continued development of the work gave the Church of God 170 churches and 50 missions in 1978, with 9,850 members, which was an annual rate of increase of 10.9% (AAGF) for the period 1970-1978, compared to 4.6% (AAGF) between 1958 and 1970.

Meanwhile, the Assemblics of God began to build on its base of 12 small churches that were inherited from the Apostolic movement in 1930. Under the supervision of Ralph Williams, existing churches were strengthened, advances were made toward self-support for pastors, and new congregations and preaching points were formed. By 1936, the Assemblies of God reported 21 churches and 14 missions, with 655 members and 965 adherents. The work had almost doubled in six years.

However, these advances were only the beginning of a phenomenal period of growth among the Assemblies of God. It has made this field a showcase for their mission work in Latin America. This solid growth is attributed to the employment of indigenous church principles.

The statistical record of the Assemblies of God in El Salvador is marked by plateaus and spurts of growth. Starting with about 500 believers in 1930, the membership had only increased to 684 in 1935, but jumped to 2,560 in 1945; the rate of growth between 1930 and 1945 was 11.5% (AAGR). Growth accelerated and church membership increased from 1,798 in 1951 to 3,065 in 1954. By 1955, the membership almost doubled to 5,982 and remained at this level until 1959, when 6,220 members were reported. The AAGR between 1945 and 1959 was 6.5%. By 1970, the total membership had increased to 9,600, or 4.0% (AAGR) for the period 1959-1970. But the growth picture is not complete without a look at the decade of the 1970s: the Assemblies of God reached 22,477 members in 1978, with 531 churches and 1,267 missions and preaching points. Membership growth for the period 1970-1978 was 11.2% (AAGR).

Training institutions and programs have greatly aided in these advances by the Assemblies of God. A short-term training program for leaders was established at Las Lomas in Santa Ana in 1930, which eventually developed into the Bethel Bible Institute in Santa Ana in 1936-1937. Until about 1960, this institute served the leadership training needs for western El Salvador, where the work of the Assemblies was mainly concentrated. However, after work in the capital and its surrounding areas experienced remarkable growth in the 1950s, the Assemblies relocated their central offices and the Bible Institute to San Salvador in 1964-1967.

In retrospect, the Assemblies of God have not been immune to schismatic movements, with several occurring during the 1960s. At least five church associations have been formed by leaders who left the Assemblies of God and started their own organizations: the Pentecostal Evangelical Union (1954), the Evangelical Mission of the Holy Spirit (1960), the Garden of Eden Evangelical Church (1962), the Evangelical Mission of the Voice of God (1969), the largest of these groups, with 28 churches and 1,340 members, and the Evangelical Church of El Salvador (1974). These five groups have about 62 churches and 2,830 members.

Two newer Pentecostal groups in El Salvador that have historical ties with the Assemblies of God are the Pentecostal Church of God of New York and the Pentecostal Church of God of Puerto Rico. Doctrinally and administratively, there are few differences between the three ecclesiastical bodies, but all three are organizations with a missionary thrust and have sent workers to El Salvador. The Puerto Rican group arrived in 1966 and now has seven churches in the region of San Miguel, while the New York group, also founded in 1966, has 21 churches, 10 missions and 1,172 members, but is concentrated in San Salvador.

The Prince of Peace Evangelical Church was founded in El Salvador in the 1950s as part of the Prince of Peace Movement that began in Guatemala in 1956 under Jose Maria Munoz. Many people in El Salvador were converted while listening to Munoz by radio, others were healed, and soon a number of congregations had grown up in El Salvador that used the name "Prince of Peace." Other independent Pentecostal churches became related to this movement, which was organized under the Rev. Salomon Portillo in the early 1960s, although only fraternal ties exist with the Prince of Peace Association in Guatemala. During the mid-1960s, a Bible institute was formed in San Salvador to provide pastors and lay workers with more formal training. Between 1967 and 1978, the total membership grew from about 2,000 to 5,050 - 8.8% (AAGR), and in 1978 there were 171 churches and 121 missions and preaching points.

Another Pentecostal church which started in Guatemala and spread to El Salvador is the Elim Church, begun in 1961 by the Rios family in their home in Guatemala City. In 1964, their son, Dr. Otoniel Rios Paredes, a medical doctor, became the central force in the development of Elim Church following his introduction into the Charismatic movement. Like Munoz, Dr. Rios extended the Elim Church movement by means of a popular radio broadcast from Guatemala City. By 1978, a large central church had been constructed and 52 congregations had been formed along with a Bible institute program. One of the students in the Bible institute was a young Salvadoran, Sergio Solorzano, who was converted through Dr. Rios´ ministry. Sergio returned to San Salvador shortly thereafter and became pastor of a growing house church. Strong leaders were trained by Sergio through his teaching ministry. Elim Church leased a large warehouse in a new industrial park a few miles ouside the capital. The congregation began to fill the large new auditorium with 500 to 1,000 people on Sundays, and over 300-500 for a mid-week Bible studies. This large, growing congregation, consisting mostly of middle and upper class Salvadorans, is an important part of the growing Charismatic movement in El Salvador.

The Church of God of Prophecy began its ministry in El Salvador in the early 1950s, but has encountered numerous difficulties over the years due to schismatic movements among its leaders and among the groups that have broken away from the mother church (due largely to leadership conflicts). The parent body is called the Universal Church of God of

Prophecy (related to the Church of God of Prophecy in Cleveland, Tennessee), which reported 38 churches and four missions with 1,726 members in 1978. The first division occurred about 1952, leading to the formation of the Church of God of Prophecy "Holy Zion," now with 64 churches and 5,430 members. Then, in 1969, another schism produced the Evangelical Church of Prophecy "Fountain of Life," which grew to 12 churches and 645 members by 1978. Other similar groups were formed during the 1970s: the Fundamental Church of God of Prophecy (1972), the Church of God of Prophecy "The Holy Zion" (1974) and the Church of God of Prophecy "The City of Zion (1974). The total membership of all these groups in 1978 was 9,871 among 175 organized churches.

The Apostolic Movement of the Name of Jesus ("Jesus Only") is represented in El Salvador by three denominations. The first to arrive was the Apostolic Church of Faith in Jesus Christ in 1948, now with 33 churches, 25 missions, but only 600 baptized members. The membership was much larger prior to the arrival of the United Pentecostal Church in 1975. They apparently attracted the majority of the members of the older group. In 1978, the United Pentecostal Church reported 47 churches and missions, 372 preaching points and 2,400 members. Also during the 1970s, the "Light of the World Movement" (Luz de Mundo) began work in El Salvador, now with 25 churches and 1,200 members. Both the former and latter groups have their international headquarters in Mexico, while the United Pentecostal Church is from the United States.

The Evangelical Non-Pentecostal Family of Churches has a long history of work in El Salvador. After six years of work in Costa Rica, the Central American Mission (CAM) made plans to enter El Salvador in 1894, but the two missionaries they sent died en route. The Rev. and Mrs. Samuel Purdie became the first CAM missionaries actually to serve in the country, arriving in July, 1896. The first CAM church was started in Ilapango, a few miles from San Salvador, in 1889. The work then spread to the capital and neighboring areas, so that by 1910 there were 25 churches with over 600 members. The CAM, by 1937, had organized churches in eight of the 14 Departments of El Salvador, and reported 21 churches and 83 outstations, with 1,890 members and 3,200 adherents. In 1935, the CAM-related churches were organized under a national council and became known as the Evangelical Church of El Salvador.

However, a series of reversals caused the CAM work to decline between 1935 and 1940, although it had regained this loss by

1945, when 2,084 members were reported. Then the CAM churches entered a period of slow growth that lasted until 1967, when the AAGR was only 1%. The growth rate picked up slightly during the 1960s (3.2%, AAGR), and then almost doubled during the 1970s (6.2%, AAGR). Periodic losses between 1910 and 1945 can be attributed to many causes; the growth of the Pentecostal movement, the political and social turmoil during the 1930s, competition with the Baptist Convention for members among non-Pentecostals and tensions between missionaries and nationals over CAM policies.

It appears that perhaps some new solutions to old problems are being attempted by the CAM and the Iglesia Evangelica de El Salvador. The growth rate improved during the 1970s as a result of a new optimistic spirit, and effective evangelistic and discipling ministries. From 60 churches and 36 "congregations" (missions) in 1970, the work grew to 83 churches, 32 "congregations" and over 180 preaching points. The membership almost doubled from 3,300 in 1970 to over 6,000 in 1978.

The American Baptist Home Mission Society entered El Salvador in 1911, where it soon developed strong educational and church work, especially in San Salvador and Santa Ana. By 1937, a chain of 19 churches and nearly 50 outstations had been established. Many of the organized congregations were completely under national leadership, and work had begun among the Pipils in the western coastal region. The Baptist Association of El Salvador was organized in 1934, but the development of trained national leaders was a slow process. By 1937, a Baptist training college had been founded for ministerial preparation with an enrollment of eight students.

The American Baptist work in El Salvador has not been characterized by rapid expansion, but by slow and steady increases over the years. The rate of growth between 1925-1945 was 3.4% (AAGR), and almost identical growth was recorded from 1945-1967 when there was 3.3% (AAGR). Growth between 1967 and 1978 was 4.0%. From 19 organized churches in 1937, the work expanded to 41 churches in 1978, with 3,665 communicant members. All American Baptist and Southern Baptist missionaries have now left El Salvador because of the recent civil war.

Other Baptist groups are now working in El Salvador, most of whom have entered the country during the 1970s. Of the six groups that are known to exist, only two have more than 1,000 members: the Good Samaritan Baptist Churches, with 15 congregations and the Miramonte Baptist Church (Independent) with 16 congregations. These six groups have a total of 62 congregations and about 5,500 members. A related group in the Baptist Family of Churches is the Church of Christ, which began work in El Salvador in 1963 and now has 53 congregations and about 2,000 members.

Several other Evangelical Non-Pentecostal agencies working in El Salvador are: the United World Mission, with only 10 churches and 480 members, the Church of the Nazarene (1964), now with 15 churches and missions and about 500 members and the California Yearly Meeting of Friends (1902), with only six churchs and 205 members.

The Liturgical Family of Churches is represented here by the Episcopal Church (six churches and 135 members), and by several Lutheran groups: the Lutheran Church, Missouri Synod (1953) reported six churches, eight missions and 1,700 members, and two small Lutheran groups with only two congregations and about 80 members.

The Seventh-day Adventist Church sent a couple to El Salvador in 1915 to begin work in San Salvador, where their first church was organized in 1916 with 19 members. By 1937, the Adventists reported five churches with 325 members and about 550 adherents. Apparently during this early period the Adventists suffered a curtailment of their work due to competition with the growing Pentecostal movement.

However, Adventist growth has continuously increased at a steady rate until the present. Between 1925 and 1945, Adventist membership grew at the annual rate of 13.8% (AAGR), compared to 7.5% in the period 1945-1960. During the 1960s, growth averaged 9.2% (AAGR) and it was 8.5% during the 1970s. By 1978, 61 churches and 59 missions ("groups") reported a total membership of 12,067.

Two additional Adventist groups have established themselves in El Salvador. Both are independent movements within the Adventist Family of Churches. The Seventh-day Adventist Reform Movement began work in 1956 and had ten churches and 420 members by 1980, whereas the Church of God, Seventh Day (known as the God of Israel Movement, in El Salvador) reported 25 churches and 1,200 members.

## ROMAN CATHOLIC MISSIONS

The evangelization of Central America by Catholic missionaries followed the Spanish conquest and occupation of the region in the 1520s. Although the Pipil (Toltec origin) and Lenca (Mayan origin) Indians in El Salvador had a highly developed religion based on the worship of forces of nature, there were a number of parallels between their religious practices and Catholicism, which made Spanish missionary efforts somewhat easier.

Following the defeat of the Indian armies by Pedro de Alvarado in 1525, the old Indian gods seemed powerless before the Spanish conquerors and their new religion. The missionary friars, after driving out the Indian priests and destroying the images of their gods, offered a new religious system to the Indians that was generally accepted by them, or at least superimposed on their old belief system. Thousands of Indians were converted to Catholicism during the Spanish colonial period.

However, due to the chronic shortage of Catholic priests and other religious workers, the people of the smaller towns and villages learned to conduct their religious life with only occasional assistance from the Catholic clergy. To fill this need, the "cofradia," a voluntary religious association, developed among the people for planning, organizing and paying for local religious celebrations during the year.

The status of the Catholic Church changed in the post-colonial era, depending on who was ruling the country, the Conservatives or the Liberals. The first anticlerical laws were established by a Liberal government in 1824. In 1871, the Liberal revolution proclaimed freedom of thought and religion, removed cemeteries from clerical control, legalized civil marriage, made education nonclerical and abolished monastic orders. These policies have remained in force until the present, except for the prohibition of religious orders. The government does not contribute in any way to the support of religion, but since 1962, the Church has been allowed to acquire real estate for other than religious purposes. There is no concordat between El Salvador and the Vatican, but diplomatic representatives are exchanged. The Constitution of 1962 reiterated the separation of Church and State and guaranteed religious freedom for all faiths, but precludes the clergy from belonging to political parties and holding public office.

In 1980, 200 Catholic priests belonged to religious orders. The most numerous were the Salesians and the Jesuits. About 50% of the religious clergy were dedicated to parishes, 20% to teaching, 10% to training other priests and the rest to work in the archdiocese. The religious priests assigned to parishes were mainly foreign missionaries, largely from Italy and Spain. The Catholic Church also sponsors 161 schools with more than 35,000 students. Catholic personnel from the United States included 15 men (6 diocesan, 5 Franciscans and 4 Maryknoll) and 13 women (11 nuns and 2 lay workers).

The Salvadoran government is increasingly distrustful of Catholic priests and nuns, especially foreign missionaries, because of the Catholic Church's growing commitment to human rights and social justice issues. While some Catholic missionaries have been deported for alleged political activity, 12 priests have been assassinated by right-wing terrorist organizations who strongly support the present government. Although most of the murdered priests were Jesuits, three Maryknoll sisters and one female lay workers from the United States were murdered by some government troops in December, 1980. Over 30 Salvadoran priests are in exile because of suspected political activity. Therefore, most of the foreign missionaries are now engaging in pastoral work due to the increasing shortage of parish priests.

### MAJOR CHRISTIAN ACTIVITIES

EVANGELISM

Prior to the 1950s, interdenominational evagelistic campaigns were apparently unknown in El Salvador. During the 1950s, a new dimension was added to Salvadoran church life with the introduction of mass evangelistic campaigns, led by international evangelists and held in public meeting places. Many denominations worked together in city-wide crusades. The first interdenominational campaign was conducted by T.L. Osborn at Santa Ana, during January, 1953. Large crowds attended these meetings with over 500 inquirers registering decisions. Three years later, Richard Jeffery held a "Great Campaign of Divine Healing and Evangelism" in San Salvador, sponsored by the Assemblies of God, but with many denominations taking part and reaping the results of a notable spiritual awakening. Six months later, during a mass ceremony at Lake Ilopango, 1,500 new converts were

baptized. Between 1954 and 1956, the membership of the Assemblies of God doubled to 6,000 as a result of these crusades.

After this promising beginning in mass evangelism, El Salvador was bypassed by two large-scale evangelistic efforts during the 1950s and 1960s: Billy Graham's Caribbean Crusade in 1958 and Evangelism-in-Depth (EID) sponsored by the Latin America Mission during the 1960s.

Argentine evangelist Luis Palau conducted a series of campaigns in Central America during the 1970s, beginning in San Salvador in 1970. During the ten day crusade, Palau produced a dozen one-hour television programs, based on an informal format that included gospel singing, a fifteen minute talk by Palau and then Palau responded to questions called in by viewers. The program was an instantaneous success and generated a flood of letters, which inspired Palau to include similar TV programs in later campaigns in other countries. The San Salvador crusade resulted in 1,500 professions of faith and many new church members were added among participating churches.

Since the mid-1970s, Campus Crusade for Christ has been working with local churches in a series of city-wide crusades patterned after their "I Found It!" campaigns in the United States. Staff workers assist local churches in the training of Christians to follow up on contacts made during the campaign, discipling new converts and guiding them into local churches where they can become responsible members and continue to follow Christ. During 1980, more than 169,000 people were contacted and 60,000 made professions of faith in the "Yo lo encontre!" programs in several cities. Campus Crusade maintains a national office in San Salvador but works in cities across the country using committed Salvadoran staff workers.

In November, 1980, Jorge Raschke, an Assemblies of God evangelist from Puerto Rico, attracted a crowd of more than 80,000 people in San Salvador, where a crusade was held in the national stadium. Then in April, 1981, a similar crusade was conducted in Santa Ana with more than 70,000 in attendance, where the evangelist not only invited those present to "believe on the Lord Jesus Christ and be saved!" but also to believe God for physical healing. A great number of conversions were reported, along with miracles of healing, which had a great impact on the city.

## BROADCASTING

During the 1960s, the Assemblies of God and three other denominations joined forces to establish an evangelical radio station in San Salvador, located on the grounds of the Assemblies of God Bible Institute. This 10,000 watt station, known as Radio Imperial (YSHQ), is used by many evangelical groups to spread the gospel throughout El Salvador and into neighboring countries. In the mid-1970s, another evangelical station, Radio VEA, was established near San Salvador, under the leadership of Pentecostals. In addition to these two evangelical stations, many evangelical programs are also broadcast on commercial stations throughout El Salvador.

One of the early pioneers in radio and television broadcasting in San Salvador was the Rev. Paul Finkenbinder, now one of Latin America's leading evangelists and radio personalities, popularly known as "Hermano Pablo." Finkenbinder, son of Assemblies of God missionaries in Puerto Rico, is exceptionally fluent in Spanish and is often considered a Latino, although he is a North American. After 21 years of ministry in El Salvador with the Assemblies of God (1944-1965), Finkenbinder returned to the U.S. and established Hermano Pablo Ministries.

More recently, several evangelical TV programs have been aired in El Salvador, produced by the PTL Club and the 700 Club. A special TV program was produced by Luis Palau in 1970 during his ten day crusade in San Salvador. Christian films are distributed by the Assemblies of God and other denominations, including films produced by Hermano Pablo during the 1960s.

## LITERATURE

Although the Salvadoran government made serious efforts to reduce illiteracy during the 1960s, the literacy rate was only 63% in 1970. The Roman Catholic Church began literacy education via radio in 1962. In 1978, at least a dozen Protestant denominations had begun literacy programs, often using materials published and distributed by ALFALIT International of Alajuela, Costa Rica.

Other Christian literature ministries include Bible correspondence courses, which are offered by at least six denominations, specifically for inquirers and new converts. Several local bulletins and evangelical newspapers are produced by Protestant denominations, largely for communication among their members.

Ten Protestant bookstores provide Sunday school materials, cassette tapes, phonograph records and books to the general public in four different cities. The CAM operates a bookmobile for residents of rural areas in El Salvador.

## BIBLE TRANSLATION AND DISTRIBUTION

An area office of the American Bible Society was established in 1969 at Tegucigalpa to handle distribution in Honduras, El Salvador and Nicaragua. In 1975, an ABS national office was organized in El Salvador, and in 1979 the Bible Society in El Salvador became an associate member of the United Bible Societies, with the following statistics reported for 1980:

| | |
|---|---|
| Bibles | 42,424 |
| New Testaments | 18,446 |
| Portions | 327,779 |
| New Reader Portions | 28,024 |
| Selections | 1,729,813 |
| New Reader Selections | 49,250 |
| TOTAL 1980 | 2,195,736 |

The translation of the scriptures into Pipil or Lenca has not been necessary because only a few Indians still speak their native languages. Other smaller Indian groups are entirely Spanish-speaking.

## EDUCATION

Christian. Protestant groups in El Salvador did not place much emphasis on education prior to the 1960s. Only the American Baptists and the Seventh-day Adventists were operating schools in 1960. However, during the 1960s, the Assemblies of God and other groups began to develop programs of Christian education. The Liceo Cristiano was founded in 1962 under the leadership of the Rev. John Bueno, pastor of the Centro Evangelistico in San Salvador. Today, this school offers primary and secondary education at six locations, depending on the student's grade level. The Adventists have six combined primary and secondary schools in El Salvador. The American Baptists continue to operate schools in San Salvador and Santa Ana that serve many denominations and offer excellent education at the primary and secondary levels. Other denominations have also started schools: the Evangelical Mennonites, Lutherans, the Central American Mission and the Church of the Nazarene. There are at least 15 primary and secondary schools operated by Protestant denominations.

Theological Education. For many years, the American Baptists and the Assemblies of God were the only Protestant groups to offer programs of theological education. Both of these programs were apparently established during the 1930s: the Baptists in Santa Ana and the Assemblies of God at Quezaltepeque. About 1935, the Assemblies of God established a Bible institute in Santa Ana which was later moved to San Salvador in 1964, known as the Bethel Bible Institute.

Today, there are a dozen programs of Theological Education by Extension (TEE), 15 Bible institutes and three theological seminaries in El Salvador. The seminaries are all operated by Baptist groups - the American Baptists, the Bible Baptists and the Baptist International Mission. However, some seminary programs in Latin America operate at the university level, rather than at the graduate level. Bible institutes often function at the high school level, requiring only a primary graduation certificate for admission to the program.

## SOCIAL CONCERN

Community and rural development. The only programs known to exist are those sponsored by the Episcopal Church and the Evangelical Mennonites, although CESAD (the Evangelical Salvadoran Committee for Relief and Development) had plans to begin projects of rural and community development.

Medicine and Public Health. About a dozen clinics are operated by Protestant denominations, but no hospital has yet been established. Clinics are provided by the Episcopal Church (2), Baptist Association (3), Lutherans (3), Mennonites (1), Assemblies of God (1) and the Universal Church of God (1). During the current political crisis, CESAD and other groups work with the Red Cross and other agencies to provide emergency medical attention to refugees and other victims of the civil unrest.

Other Social Ministries. Cooperative credit unions, providing savings and loan services, are operated by the Episcopal Church and the Baptist Association.

Special student ministries at the high school and university level are provided by the Lutherans, Miramonte Baptist Church (independent) and Campus Crusade for Christ.

Vocational training is offered by the Lutherans, the Evangelical Mennonites and the Baptists.

A home for the elderly is sponsored by the Central American Mission.

Several ministries are being provided for orphans and abandoned children, or for children in needy families, by World Vision International, the Evangelical Mennonites, the Baptist International Mission and the Central American Mission.

Work among refugees is provided by CESAD, World Vision International and many other organizations which provide food, clothing, shelter, medical treatment and counseling.

## ECUMENICAL RELATIONSHIPS

Relationships among Protestant groups have always been rather weak and often quite tense. Few interdenominational efforts have enjoyed a broad base of support, although some denominational programs or institutions have served the general Christian public. This is especially true of Protestant schools. Radio YSHQ is an example of cooperation among four evangelical mission agencies or national church bodies. The efforts of the national offices of the American Bible Society and ALFALIT International have also generated a spirit of cooperation among many evangelicals. During the last two years, several Protestant groups have participated in an ecumenical committee on human rights in San Salvador, in which the Catholic Church has also been represented. However, no evangelical alliance or national council of churches has ever existed in El Salvador.

## GENERAL SERVICE AGENCIES

In November, 1979, the Evangelical Salvadoran Committee for Relief and Development (CESAD), patterned after similar agencies in Central America, was organized under the leadership of individual evangelicals from many churches and organizations within the evangelical community, although few denominations are officially represented. CESAD's leadership and support has basically come from the following groups: Church of the Apostles and Prophets, Assemblies of God, Baptist Cultural Association, Bible Society of El Salvador, Central American Mission, Christian Reformed Church, Church of God, Church of God of Prophecy "Holy Zion," Evangelistic Center of the Assemblies of God, Prince of Peace Church, Radio Imperial (YSHQ) and Radio VEA.

In the period following the ouster of General Romero in 1979, evangelical leaders began to see the need for a cooperative relief and development organization among evangelicals that would provide spiritual and social assistance to needy Salvadorans. The supporters of CESAD are united in a common commitment to serve where needed, without bias (ideological or religious), in programs throughout the country, working together with international organizations like World Vision International, Christian Reformed World Relief, Church World Service and the Red Cross. Administrative and technical assistance has been provided by CEDEN (Evangelical Committee for Development and National Emergency) from Honduras, at the request of CESAD.

Emergency committees of individual Christians working on a volunteer basis, supervised by CESAD, have now been formed in 12 of the 14 departments of El Salvador. These committees are composed of evangelicals of different denominations, who provide food, clothing, shelter, medical care and counseling to those in need. The committees organized under CESAD at the local or regional level also form part of a national emergency plan under the direction of the Salvadoran Red Cross. Although community and agricultural development projects were envisioned as part of CESAD's overall program, the present political crisis has forced CESAD to concentrate its efforts in refugee work. Its policy is to help anyone who does not bear arms. Under the present difficult conditions that exist, evangelicals are beginning to work together to provide for both the spiritual and physical needs of their suffering "neighbors." CESAD's slogan is "Do good to everyone in the name of Jesus Christ."

Although new to El Salvador, World Vision has developed its programs through more than 70 projects such as: child assistance, community development, evangelism and relief programs to assist people affected by the political crisis. As a result of the ordinary work programs, about 120,000 Salvadorans have been helped both in El Salvador and in neighboring countries. Some 500 tons of food and other items have been distributed among these people. World Vision sponsors some 8,000 children in El Salvador.

## NATION AND ITS PEOPLE

### POPULATION

El Salvador is the most densely populated nation in the western hemisphere. Of the 4.8 million people, 61% live in rural areas. Three-quarters of the population live in the central highland plateau and the adjoining river valleys where there are heavy concentrations of both rural and urban dwellers. The population is distributed fairly evenly throughout the rest of the country. The most sparsely settled sector is the arid mountainous terrain near the Honduran border.

In the past 30 years many landless farmers have left the central highlands and moved east of the Lempa River to work as laborers on the cotton plantations. Smaller migrations have occurred from the mountain regions of Sonsonate Department to the western coastal plain and there has been a significant move away from the overcrowded rural areas into the cities, especially into San Salvador, which had a population of 857,800 in 1980. A great many people have fled the growing violence by emigrating to other Central American countries, mainly Honduras.

### COMPOSITION

El Salvador has one of the most homogeneous populations in Central America, with only a few ethnic minorities. Racially, the population is composed of 92% mestizo, 6% Indian and 2% white. The term Latino transcends racial distinctions to denote all Hispanized inhabitants.

Only a few ethnic minorities can be found in the country, mainly Indian groups who have been able to remain in remote areas of the country and have retained indigenoues cultural patterns. Various estimates have been given for the Indian population, ranging from 100,000 to 400,000 people (4 to 16% of the total population), but the majority of Indians are now classified as racially mestizo and culturally Latino.

The two major Indian groups are the Pipil and the Lenca. The Pipil, with only a few native speakers remaining, are descendents of the Toltec civilization in Mexico. The Lenca are believed to have a Mayan origin.

The foreign-born population in El Salvador has always been small, with most non-Salvadorans coming from the Central American countries. Although the foreign business community is not large, it is diverse and includes Germans, Swiss, Turks, Lebanese, Syrians, Chinese and North Americans.

### LANGUAGE AND LITERACY

Spanish is the official language and is spoken by virtually all the inhabitants. Most of the Indians, especially those most acculturated, speak only Spanish. Some of the Indians in the southwest towns of

Panchmalco, Izalco and Nahuizalco speak Pipil as well, but the number is steadily decreasing. Many Pipil words have become part of the current vernacular where no acceptable Spanish equivalent existed to describe such things as indigenous animals, plants and food.

The literacy rate of El Salvador is 40%. The rate in the rural areas is even lower, about 25%.

## RELIGION

Though only a small percentage of Salvadorans attend Mass, some 92% of the population consider themselves Roman Catholic. Nominality is a problem recognized by Catholic bishops and priests. However, due to the current civil strife and an already short supply of priests and religious workers, little change can be expected.

The Protestant Church in El Salvador grew at a healthy 11.3% average annual growth rate during the 1970s. Over two-thirds of the Protestants in El Salvador are affiliated with the Pentecostal Family of Churches.

## GEOGRAPHY AND CLIMATE

El Salvador is the smallest mainland nation of the Western Hemisphere, with a total area of 21,156 square kilometers (8,260 square miles). Its terrain is varied with about half considered lowlands and half highlands. The country has the largest number of volcanoes in Central America, with four of them still active. Mountain ranges run east and west across the country and roughly divide it into three distinct physical zones, characterized by their general climatic conditions.

The southern coastal plain, called the "torrid" land, consists of a narrow, relatively flat coastal belt extending the length of the country. It is an area of extensive agriculture with some developing industry and fishing.

The northern latitudinal zone is known as the "cold" land. It consists of the northern lowlands of the wide valley of the Lempa River and the northern east-west range, the Sierra Madre, which extends to the Honduran border. Although called the "cold" land this area is actually quite warm along the river valley and has a pleasant, temperate climate on the upper mountain slopes. It is an arid and semi-barren region which is sparsely populated and has little farming or other development.

The third zone is known as the "temperate" land, lying between the other two regions. It is composed of the central highlands and includes most of the national territory. It is a large plateau that runs the length of the country between the two mountain ranges to the north and south. It is characterized by lush valleys of rich volcanic soil interspersed with mountains and volcanoes.

Temperatures vary with the altitude. The coastal lowlands have the maximum heat and humidity, the central plateau has a temperate climate bordering on semitropical and the northern mountains experience the coolest temperatures in the country.

The entire country experiences two distinct seasons. The dry season, and the rainy season (which lasts from May to October but sometimes extends into early December). Precipitation during the wet season averages about 25 centimeters (10 inches) monthly. The average annual rainfall for the country is about 180 centimeters (72 inches) and is heaviest along the coast where it averages 213 centimeters (85 inches).

## HISTORY

Pedro de Alvarado, one of Cortez's principal lieutenants in the conquest of Mexico, invaded El Salvador in 1524 with a small army. The Pipil were one of the few Central American Indian tribes who were able to defeat the Spanish. However, in 1525, Alvarado returned and defeated the Pipil. El Salvador was made a province of New Spain (Mexico) and was placed under the control of the Captaincy General of Guatemala, where it remained until its independence in 1821.

El Salvador was the first Central American country to challenge the Spanish rule. Abortive uprisings were led by Father Jose Matias Delgado in 1811 and Manuel Jose Arce in 1814. They sparked the successful Central American drive for independence. On September 15, 1821, the Captaincy General of Guatemala declared its independence from Spain. In 1823, the United Provinces of Central America were established at a constitutional assembly of the five Central American states in Guatemala City. In 1838, El Salvador declared its independence from the United Provinces.

Although there were a number of violent overthrows of government in the period following independence until 1899, the situation was a bit more stable than the other Central American countries during this era. From 1899 to 1931 El Salvador had a period of political stability, with only one violent upset in 1913. However, in 1931 the president was overthrown and the military has maintained control since that time. Although elections were regularly conducted, the military controlled the selection of candidates for office and the election results.

In the summer of 1969, El Salvador and Honduras were involved in a brief war caused primarily by the migration of landless Salvadoran farmworkers to Honduras. After two weeks of fighting, the Organization of American States helped establish a ceasefire and the withdrawal of occupied Honduran land.

Since 1977, El Salvador has experienced increased outbreaks of violence. In that year, General Carlos Humberto Romero was declared President through what was generally recognized as election fraud. In the face of demonstrations against this fraud a state of siege was declared and the government began persecuting anyone who criticized it. Different leftist groups developed guerrilla armies and the amount of violence steadily increased. General Romero was overthrown in 1979 by a group of younger and more progressive officers. They set their objective to conduct an equitable distribution of land and invited all the political parties to join in establishing a government. Unfortunately, the leftists and rightists have thwarted most attempts at land reform. In its attempts to gain control, the government has often taken harsh measures, for which it has been criticized by religious groups and other governments.

## GOVERNMENT AND POLITICAL CONDITIONS

El Salvador has had 14 constitutions as an independent nation, the current one coming into existence in 1962. The constitution provides for three branches of government. The presidential term is set at five years, and any attempt by a chief executive to succeed himself is recognized as a cause for insurrection.

In 1977, a law of defense and guarantee of public order was passed, suspending some constitutional rights and giving extraordinary power of search and seizure to the army and government. The security forces were given the right to arrest anyone suspected of subversion and all meetings and publications were banned. The law was not repealed until March, 1979.

In response to these types of actions, the leftists increased their violence. More than a dozen businessmen were kidnapped during this period, embassies were taken, assassinations and military campaigns conducted and a number of strikes initiated. The rightists counteracted by forming their own guerrilla movement made up of 50,000-100,000 farmers, called Orden.

After Romero was ousted, the new ruling Junta promised far-reaching land reforms. The new government nationalized the banks and exterior commerce and tried to begin agrarian reforms. Violent tactics utilized by various groups on opposite ends of the political spectrum made it impossible to carry out these reforms in six of the 14 departments. The leftists wanted nothing less than complete revolution. Opposition also came from landowners who had their own guerrilla forces.

The Junta, headed by Jose Napolean Duarte, directed the Army to suppress leftist guerrillas. Violence escalated and deaths were multiplied. A "final offensive" by guerrilla forces, supported by arms from Cuba, was put down by government forces in January, 1981. However, the unrest continues.

## ECONOMY

The economy relies heavily on agriculture, which provides roughly one-fourth of the gross national product (GNP), employs 60% of the labor force and generates 90% of the nation's foreign exchange. Coffee accounts for about 50% of all exports. El Salvador is the number three world exporter of coffee, after Brazil and Colombia. Yields are the highest in the world, averaging about 770 pounds per acre, compared with 300 to 400 pounds per acre in the other producing countries. Coffee is grown in every department of El Salvador. Cotton production has expanded dramatically since the 1950s. Nearly all cotton is grown along the Pacific coast. Sugar cane is another major export crop, having grown greatly in importance in the 1960s. Corn and beans are the basic food crops in the Salvadoran diet. Rice is another important domestic crop. However, because of the unstable social conditions, export crop production is down greatly and there is a lack of the basic food grains.

Industrial production doubled in the 1960s, outpacing the rest of the economy. By 1969, this sector produced about 20% of the GNP. The percentage of the economically active population involved in industry rose from 3.6% in 1950 to 11% in 1971. El Salvador's industry has been hard hit by the violence and economic instability.

## CHURCH STATISTICS FOR EL SALVADOR

NOTE: Statistics are from the 1978 PROCADES survey of Protestant Churches and are based on official denominational reports or estimates. Although definitions of membership vary slightly among churches, the data is highly comparable and reliable. All known churches are included in this list.

| Church or Mission Name | Number of Congregations | Membership | % of Total |
|---|---|---|---|
| PROTESTANT | | | |
| Liturgical | 22 | 1,913 | 2.0% |
|   Episcopal Church | 6 | 135 | |
|   Lutherans (3 groups) | 16 | 1,778 | |
| Evangelical Non-Pentecostal | 298 | 15,036 | 18.0% |
|   Baptist Association | 46 | 3,664 | |
|   Baptist Inter. Mission | 9 | 844 | |
|   Church of Christ | 55 | 2,000 | |
|   Evangelical Church of El Salvador (CAM) | 115 | 6,022 | |
|   Miramonte Baptist Church | 16 | 2,600 | |
|   Other Smaller Groups (14) | 73 | 2,506 | |
| Pentecostal | 1,565 | 66,407 | 66.0% |
|   Assemblies of God | 531 | 22,477 | |
|   Church of Apostles and Prophets | 80 | 3,800 | |
|   Church of God - Cleveland | 220 | 9,850 | |
|   City of Zion Church of God of Prophecy | 23 | 1,254 | |
|   Free Apostolics | 50 | 2,400 | |
|   Holy Zion Church of God of Prophecy | 64 | 5,430 | |
|   Light of the World Church | 25 | 1,200 | |
|   Pent. Church of God (NY) | 31 | 1,172 | |
|   Prince of Peace Church | 171 | 5,050 | |
|   United Pentecostal Church | 47 | 2,400 | |
|   Universal Church of God of Prophecy | 42 | 1,726 | |
|   The Upper Room Apostolic Church | 26 | 1,248 | |
|   Voice of God Mission | 28 | 1,000 | |
|   Other smaller Pent. groups | 227 | 7,400 | |
| Adventist | 155 | 13,687 | 14.0% |
|   Adventist Reform Movement | 10 | 420 | |
|   Church of God, Seventh Day | 25 | 1,200 | |
|   Seventh-day Adventist | 120 | 12,067 | |
| Misc./Unclassified Groups | 19 | 1,181 | |
| TOTALS (1978) | 2,059 | 98,224 | 100.0% |
| TOTAL PROTESTANT COMMUNITY (1980) | | 334,000 | |

## SELECTED BIBLIOGRAPHY AND INFORMATION SOURCES

The sources listed below are to help the reader find additional information on this country and Christian ministries there. This list does not try to be comprehensive or complete.

DOCUMENTS

General

Blutstein, Howard I., et al. Area Handbook for El Salvador, Washington D.C.: U.S. Government Printing Office, 1971.

Cozean, Jon D., Latin America 1980, Washington, D.C.: Stryker-Post Publications, Inc., 1980.

Herring, Hubert, A History of Latin America, New York: Alfred A. Knopf, 1968.

Woodward, Ralph Lee, Jr., Central America: A Divided Nation, New York: Oxford University Press, 1976.

Christian

"Directorio Geografico de las Iglesias y Misiones Evangelicas de El Salvador," San Jose, Costa Rica: INDEPTH Publications, 1980.

Dominguez, Roberto, Pioneros de Pentecostes: En el Mundo de Habla Hispana, Vol. 2, "Mexico y Centroamerica," Hialeah, FL: Literature Evangelica, 1975.

Grimes, Barbara F., ed., Ethnologue, Huntington Beach, CA: Wycliffe Bible Translators, 1978.

Grubb, Kenneth G., Religion in Central America, London: World Dominion Press, 1937.

Orr, J. Edwin, Evangelical Awakenings in Latin America, Minneapolis, MN: Bethany Fellowship, 1978.

Ramirez, Cristobal, Las Asambleas de Dios en El Salvador, San Salvador: Tipografia Comercial Santa Ana, n.d.

Read, William P., Victor M. Monterros, Harmon A. Johnson, Latin American Church Growth, Grand Rapids: Eerdmans, 1970.

Taylor, Clyde W. and Wade T. Coggins, eds., Protestant Missions in Latin America: A Statistical Survey, Washington, D.C.: EFMA, 1961.

## ACKNOWLEDGMENTS

The information in this profile was taken from many sources which were the best available to the editors at the time of preparation. However, the accuracy of the information cannot be guaranteed. Views expressed or implied in this publication are not necessarily those of World Vision International. The editors have tried to present the ministries of various organizations in an objective manner, without undue bias or emphasis. Where we have failed, we apologize for erroneous impressions that may result and request that comments and corrections be sent to MARC, 919 West Huntington Drive, Monrovia, California, 91016, USA. We appreciate and acknowledge the comments and contributions of various organizations and individuals in the preparation of this publication.

# STATUS OF CHRISTIANITY COUNTRY PROFILE

# GUATEMALA

### SUMMARY

AREA - 108,880 square kilometers (42,031
    square miles)
POPULATION - 7,262,400 (1980 est.)
RELIGION - 78% Roman Catholic, 21%
    Protestant, 1% Other

Guatemalans are caught in the middle of many social conflicts, including political power struggles. The government sees itself forced to employ emergency crackdown measures in order to maintain order. Polarization of opinion results. Right-wing leaders think all such measures are necessary for the preservation of society. Left-wing leaders think they stifle not only dissidents and terrorists, but all expression of contrary opinions. There seems to be too little sensitivity to the impact of policies upon the lives of thousands of individuals who own very little land.

Conservatives may resist public discussion of social justice, human rights or equal opportunity programs. Guerrilla groups have some disruptive effect on the economy of the country. Discrimination, persecution and assassination may be employed against those suspected of socialist activism. Kidnappings and killings are common, and have included pastors, priests, journalists and university professors.

Christianity remains a strong and vital force in Guatemalan society, despite the current unrest. Protestant churches in Guatemala are experiencing phenomenal growth. Protestants represented only 2.8% of the population in 1950, but after three decades of explosive growth, one out of five Guatemalans is now a Protestant. Most of this growth has occurred among the Ladino population, but several people movements are reported among a few Amerindian groups.

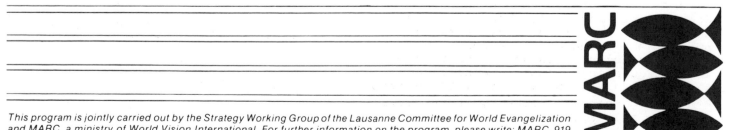

*This program is jointly carried out by the Strategy Working Group of the Lausanne Committee for World Evangelization and MARC, a ministry of World Vision International. For further information on the program, please write: MARC, 919 West Huntington Drive, Monrovia, CA 91016 U.S.A.*

## PEOPLE GROUPS

Three major classifications, based on ethnic differentiation, are commonly cited in Guatemala: Indian, mestizo and white. Significant overlap is indicated by varying sources and the statistics given are only estimates. Each classification should be studied carefully in order to identify the unique sociological groups contained within each major "ethnic" classification.

### AMERINDIAN (44%)

The actual number of Amerindian people has never been ascertained. Various sources report that they comprise anywhere from 36% to 55% of the total population. Official government estimates reported in the 1973 Census indicated that 44% of the total population were part of indigenous groups. Practically all of the Amerindians in Guatemala are descendants of the Mayans. Approximately 40 Mayan dialects are still spoken in Guatemala. The Quiche form the largest group with nearly 27.5% of all descendants of the Maya. Seven different dialects are prevalent among the Quiche who are scattered widely throughout the mountains and plains.

The Mam comprise about 14.6% of the Mayan descendants. Significantly fewer Christians live among the Mam than among the Quiche or the Cakchiquel, which comprise the third largest group. They constitute 12% of the Mayan population. Language differences present a major challenge since seven local dialects are spoken by the Mam alone. The only other sizeable group, with more than 12% of the Maya population, is the Kekchi. The Kanjobal, Pocoman, Chorti, Tzutujil, Ixil, Pocomchi, Achi and Chuj each comprise between 1% and 4% of the peoples of Mayan descent. Several other groups comprise less than 1%.

A recent study of Indigenous groups in Guatemala (Coke, 1978) reveals notable differences in the size of the Protestant population among various groups. Some smaller tribal groups have responded very favorably to the gospel while others have shown little interest. People movements are evident among a few specific groups of Mam who speak particular dialects, and are not evident among other groups of Mam. Christian communities have also been identified among groups of Kekchi, Chuj, Aguacatec and Kanjobal. Early Protestant ministries were initiated by individuals who knew only Spanish. More recent endeavors, however, have been conducted in the indigenous languages. Wycliffe Bible Translators have been particularly successful in developing ministries which incorporate cultural patterns and language forms unique to each group. Slightly more than 6% of all Mayans were considered to be Protestants in 1977 as compared to 17.6% of all Guatemalans.

### LADINO (55%)

In Guatemala, the term "Ladino" is used instead of the standard term "Latino" to refer to individuals who reflect Hispanic culture and language patterns. Most Ladinos are mestizo (mixed white and Indian) although approximately 2% of the total population are of direct European descent are also classified as Ladino. "Ladinos" comprise between 42% and 56% of the total population, depending on the source of information. The 1970 census states that 55% of the population of Guatemala are Ladino.

### OTHER PEOPLE GROUPS

The Afro-American population in Guatemala is quite small. About 5,500 Black Caribs, a few thousand Creoles (Negroes of West Indies heritage who speak English), and a few hundred other blacks who speak French or Spanish, reside in Guatemala.

Several thousand Salvadoran refugees settled in Guatemala during 1980 and 1981 in order to escape the turmoil of civil war in El Salvador.

Small numbers of East Indians, Chinese, Lebanese, Syrian, British, German and North American individuals live in Guatemala.

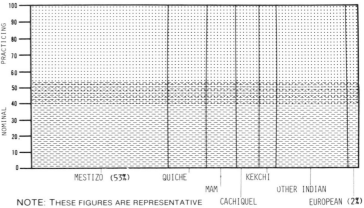

POPULATION COMPOSITION OF GUATEMALA
(Shading Indicates Christians)

NOTE: THESE FIGURES ARE REPRESENTATIVE APPROXIMATIONS. THEY SHOULD BE SEEN AS INDICATORS OF MAGNITUDE ONLY.

Guatemala has more "Cristo-pagans" than any other country in Central America. Many of the indigenous peoples of Mayan descent practice syncretism. Animistic beliefs are strongest among the least acculturated Indians who live in the mountains of the central highlands or the rain forests of the lowlands in the Peten region of northern Guatemala. A small group of Black Caribs live on the Caribbean coast, near Livingston, and are also predominantly Cristo-pagan.

Catholic sources report that 88% of the total population are baptized Catholics. A recent survey of Protestants in Guatemala has revealed that there are over 200 denominations with 286,000 baptized Protestant church members. The total Protestant population of Guatemala in 1978 was estimated to be 17.6%, up from the official census figures of 8.2% in 1964 and 2.8% in 1950. According to a survey compiled in 1973, about 36% of all Protestants in Guatemala were of Mayan descent while 64% were listed as Ladino. Recent people movements among the Quiche and other indigenous groups have significantly altered these statistics, but no definite data is available. The Protestant population growth rate was 12.1% (AAGR) between 1967 and 1978. If this growth has continued, then 21% of Guatemalans were Protestant in 1981.

## RELIGIOUS COMPOSITION OF GUATEMALA

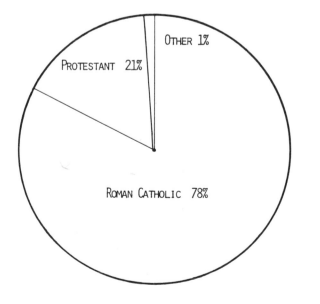

OTHER 1%

PROTESTANT 21%

ROMAN CATHOLIC 78%

## PROTESTANT CHURCHES

The growth of the Protestant church has not come easily. Efforts of many Evangelicals have not been received favorably, but in spite of great hostility, the evangelical church as a whole has grown immensely.

The highest rates of increase occurred from 1960 to 1964 and from 1973 to 1978 when average annual growth was 18.3% and 20.1%, respectively. Whereas evangelical growth rates slumped in many Central American countries during the early 1960s, in Guatemala they rapidly increased and the number of Protestants doubled in four years. Church membership slowed to 6% annually between 1964 and 1973 and then increased to 20% annually between 1974 and 1978. Most Protestant growth was reported among the Ladinos, although a few notable people movements were apparent among the Yucatec Maya, Mam, Tzutujil, Chuj and Aguatec.

Seven large denominations constitute 64% of the total Protestant population. The Prince of Peace Church reported 33,670 members; the Association of Central American Evangelical Churches - 32,353; the Assemblies of God - 31,506; the Church of God (Cleveland) - 30,000; Seventh-day Adventists - 17,200; National Presbyterian - 16,262; and the Church of the Nazarene - 8,400. Twenty-three of the largest denominations account for 89.4% of all Protestant members while 175 denominations comprise the remaining 10.6% of the membership.

In 1935, approximately 97% of all communicant members were related to non-Pentecostal churches. Church growth among Pentecostals was more rapid than among other groups and by 1950 they comprised 13% of the Protestant population. The increase continued. In 1960 they comprised 19.6%, in 1970 31.4% and in 1978, 52.1%. Only six of the fifteen largest Protestant denominations are Pentecostal. The three largest Pentecostal groups account for 35% of the Protestant population in Guatemala. Of the 6,216 organized congregations in 1978, approximately 3,430 were Pentecostal. Eighty-eight associations of Pentecostal churches have been identified within Guatemala, compared to 59 among non-Pentecostal Evangelicals, four among liturgical denominations and three among Adventists.

## CATHOLIC CHURCHES

The Roman Catholic Church is undergoing a minor revolution within its ranks. Propagation of "Liberation Theology" has polarized reformists from conservatives.

Historically, the Roman Catholic Church sought to be a major influential entity among the Ladinos and Europeans. In 1872 an official census of clergy provided information regarding 119 expatriate priests. An official government sanction imposed thereafter established measures to suppress the strength and influence of the Church and affiliated religious orders. Though the national population doubled in the 75 years following the census, the number of priests remained constant. This shortage of priests limited the extent of ministries among individuals who lived in remote villages. Many indigenous people groups accepted only certain aspects of Catholic doctrine and appended them to existing beliefs. Thus, Cristo-Paganism flourished.

The majority of the clergy have always been expatriates, primarily from Spain, Italy and North America. Indigenous leaders were seldom trained. Native languages, values and music were usually ignored and sometimes repudiated. Reform within the Catholic Church structure has been slow, and many nominal Catholics have chosen to participate in revival movements of indigenous religions. Others have chosen to ignore formal religion and others are involved in reform movements within the Church.

A new emphasis on individual study of the Bible, coupled with availability of Scriptures in native languages, has provided impetus for revitalization of Catholicism. The Charismatic Movement within Catholic spheres gained tremendous popularity until official restrictions were implemented. As a result, many Catholics have chosen to leave the church.

In 1976, official Catholic publications stated that 88% of the total population of Guatemala were at least nominally Catholic. The hierarchical structure consisted of one archdiocese with eight dioceses. One archbishop, 15 bishops, 641 priests and 1,104 nuns served in 341 parishes.

## PROTESTANT MISSIONS

In 1824, the English Baptists became the first Protestant group to enter Guatemala. Their initial ministry was to a small British colony located near Lake Izabal, but the work soon expanded to Ladinos and Indians. Frederick Crowe, a missionary with the Belize Baptist Mission who also represented the Auxiliary Bible Society of Belize, entered Guatemala in 1841. He spent two years in Abbotsville as missionary and school teacher, and then moved to Salama and Guatemala City. His activities as colporteur, school teacher and missionary were not well received and community leaders had him deported in 1846.

Religious freedom was finally established by law in 1873 by direction of President Justo Rufino Barrios, who wanted to modernize the country and regulate the control of the Catholic Church. Barrios sent a personal letter to the Presbyterian Board of Missions in New York inviting them to conduct ministries in Guatemala.

The Presbyterians responded by sending personnel who formed an American school and held church services in English. In order to avoid antagonizing the local Catholic leaders, no religious instruction was offered at the school. A small congregation was formed which later became the Union Church of Guatemala. Edward Haymaker established the Central Presbyterian Church of Guatemala City in 1888, one year after he arrived. It was the first Spanish-speaking Protestant church in Guatemala. A hospital and nursing school were founded by the Presbyterians in Guatemala City in 1912. Presbyterian workers established a bookstore in 1915, a girl's school in 1918 and an industrial training center in 1919.

A separate presbytery was formed for ministries among the Mayan Indians. The Mam Center was opened in 1922 to provide training in industrial arts, health, education and literacy. The Mam New Testament was published in 1939 after 17 years of work by a number of missionaries who represented different agencies. The Quiche Bible Institute became a joint project of several groups including the Primitive Methodists. It was recognized that displacing indigenous leaders for higher education was detrimental to the welfare of the community fellowship. Thus a program of Theological Education By Extension (TEE) was developed by the Presbyterians during the 1960's. The concept developed at that time has been widely accepted in every continent of the world.

The Presbyterian Church of Guatemala was the first in Central America to become an autonomous national body of its own accord. Full integration of the Presbyterian Mission and the National Presbyteries was accomplished in 1961. All expatriates have served under the ecclesiastical jurisdiction of the National Presbyterian Church since that time. In the process of nationalization, some Presbyterian property was sold so that most ministries would be self-supporting. Close cooperation has been maintained with the Program Agency of the United Presbyterian Church in the U.S.A. In 1935 the Presbyterians reported 22 organized churches and 198 preaching points with 2,805 communicant members. Membership totaled 4,700 in 1951, 8,000 in 1960 and 11,500 in 1967. The National Presbyterian Church reported 106 congregations, 118 missions and 16,163 members in 1978. A church was formed in 1962 which reported 150 members in four congregations.

Several churches seceded from the National Presbytery. The Horeb Conservative Presbyterian Church was formed in 1962. Six congregations, with 180 members, aligned themselves with the Horeb Church. The Fundamental Bible Presbyterian Church in Guatemala City also seceded in 1962. More than 3,100 members were attending 18 churches by 1979. The Bethany Presbyterian Church of Quezaltenango became a Pentecostal church and broke away from the National Presbytery in 1972. Bethany Church reported 23 congregations and 10 missions with 1,435 members during 1978.

Ministries of the Central American Mission were established in Guatemala in 1899. During the 1920s and 1930s, definite steps were taken to develop ministries among Ladinos and among Mayan peoples, particularly in the Central Highlands. Evangelization of the Indians began in earnest in 1919. Indigenous language dialects were utilized, and training of pastors and teachers was initiated when the Robinson Bible Institute was established. The total number of CAM missionaries who have worked among Indians in Guatemala is second only to Wycliffe Bible Translators. The first New Testament for an indigenous group was translated and published in 1931 by William C. Townsend, a CAM missionary. CAM related churches have the largest number of Indian members of any Protestant group. Theological education was a major concern of many CAM missionaries. Four

Bible Institutes and a seminary provide training in church leadership and theology. National churches established by CAM personnel have been fully autonomous since 1927. In 1935, 63 churches and 185 preaching points with 13,700 adherents and 6,500 members were affiliated with CAM ministries. The Evangelism-in-Depth program initiated in 1962 inspired growth and vitality among many CAM groups. Church growth among CAM churches increased to 7.3% (AAGR) during the 1960's and to 9.5% (AAGR) between 1967 and 1978. Total membership increased from nearly 12,000 in 1967 to 13,000 in 1970 and 32,353 in 1978 among 509 congregations. In 1973, approximately 43% of CAM church members were Ladinos and 57% Mayans.

Ministries of the Church of the Nazarene in Guatemala began in 1901 when a missionary couple from the Pentecostal Mission of Nashville, Tennessee, arrived. They were joined by other workers in 1904 and ministries were extended to the Coban. The original mission station was transferred to the Friends. Nazarene ministries were conducted in Spanish but many Indians responded to the claims of the gospel. Ministries among Kekchi expanded rapidly when the Kekchi New Testament became available. The Church of the Nazarene has become the seventh largest denomination in Guatemala. Beginning with 417 members in 1920, the Nazarene Church grew to 700 in 1935, 893 in 1950, 2,123 in 1960, 2,700 in 1970 and 8,400 among 75 congregations in 1978. Of the 3,000 members reported in 1973, 61.8% were Indian and 38.2% Ladino.

The California Yearly Meeting of Friends began work in Central America in 1902 when pioneer missionaries with a ton of Bibles settled in southeastern Guatemala. The first two men died within two years but they prepared the field for the Friends Mission in three countries. Intensive evangelism, training of national leaders and development of an indigenous Friends Meeting were established shortly after the arrival of personnel in 1904. By 1925 there were over 2,000 adherents. In 1935, 4,325 were reported. Between 1940 and 1955 the number of Friends adherents grew from 4,340 to 7,494 and by 1971 approximately 10,000 individuals were affiliated with the Friends movement. In 1978, 3,413 members were part of 264 organized congregations. Many members of Friends Meetings were Salvadorans who were displaced by the hostilities which erupted in the "Soccer War" of 1969.

Seventh-day Adventists began ministries in Guatemala City in 1908. An English language school was purchased as a missionary enterprise. The Guatemala Mission was organized in 1913 with ministries in Quezaltenango and Guatemala City. Work among Quiche was begun in 1940 and the Indian Cultural Center was formed in 1948. In 1964 there were six churches, 16 organized groups and numerous sabbath schools among the indigenous peoples. Medical ministries began in 1962. Total membership in 1934 was nearly 300 in six churches and 18 preaching points. By 1960 there were 21 churches, 48 preaching points, 2,950 members among a community of 5,624. Membership increased rapidly to 4,597 in 1964 and to 17,207 in 1978 among 68 churches and 148 preaching points.

Ministries of the Church of God - Cleveland were initiated when Charles Furman and Thomas Pullin planted a number of churches among Quiche Christians whom they had evangelized. Although Furman and Pullin had originally been Primitive Methodists, they encouraged all the churches which they had founded to join the Church of God - Cleveland. Ministries in the capital began in 1940 because of a revival in churches of the National Evangelical Mission which had been formed in 1923 by a group of 20 families who led the Cinco Calles Church. Two Ladino leaders convinced most members to join the Church of God - Cleveland. These same leaders later started a sister denomination, the Church of God of Prophecy, which became affiliated with the North American headquarters, also in Cleveland, TN. A few years later another group of believers followed one of the leaders in joining ministries of the Missionary Church of God of Houston, TX. The Missionary Church of God reported 4,500 members in 100 churches in 1978. The Church of God -Cleveland- which had only 1,100 members in 1950, has become one of the largest denominations in Guatemala.

Approximately 6,150 members were active in 110 churches in 1960, 10,250 members in 287 churches and 296 missions in 1970 and 30,032 members in 599 churches and 284 missions in 1978.

Primitive Methodists have worked primarily among Quiche and Ixil Indians of the western mountains since 1922. Several missionaries cooperated with Presbyterians in production of the Quiche New Testament in 1946. Most activities were conducted in Spanish and most pastors were Ladinos. In 1980 the Primitive Methodists were responsible for 5 clinics, a hospital, a primary school, a secondary school, two literacy centers and five weekly radio programs. Total membership numbered 6,533 among 43 churches in 1978.

In 1917, the Pilgrim Holiness Church began work in El Progreso, but in 1945 their missionaries united with the Emmanuel Missionary Church. The latter group had entered Guatemala in 1941 and established a mission station near Guatemala City. The same missionaries began a new work in Jalapa. There are now several Emmanuel Church groups in Guatemala. The Emmanuel National Evangelical Church, which was founded in 1967, is the largest one. It relates to the Evangelistic Faith Mission of Bedford, Indiana. In 1978, this group reported 17 churches and 20 missions with 1,078 members.

Ministries of the Plymouth Brethren were started in 1924 by Carlos Kramer, a Guatemalan of German ancestry. Fourteen churches and 20 preaching points were reported in 1934 with 425 members. By 1965 there were 102 assemblies with 2,500 members and by 1975 - 160 assemblies with 4,500 members among a community of 9,000. Among the Cakchiquel, Mam and Quiche there were 63 churches, 1,770 members and a community of 3,540 adherents in 1974. By 1980, there were 12,500 active participants in 250 "congregations" of the Brethren Assemblies.

Baptists in Guatemala trace their origins to the founding of the Independent Evangelical Mission in 1928. This group adopted Baptist policies and practices as well as maintaining contacts with the other Baptist Churches in Central America. In 1946, six congregations from this mission became founding members of the Guatemala Baptist Convention, which was organized with 10 churches and 369 members. They later became affiliated with the Southern Baptist Convention. In 1960, the Baptist Convention reported 19 churches and 28 preaching points with 3,091 communicants including 1,513 members. By 1965 there were 26 churches and 40 preaching points with 4,000 members and by 1978, 62 churches and 69 preaching points with 6,924 members.

The first permanent worker from the Assemblies of God arrived in Guatemala in 1937. The Central Bible School was established in 1943 and by 1980 there were Assemblies of God fellowships in nearly every department of the country. The John Franklin Bible Institute was formed in Panajachel to train leaders to minister among indigenous people groups, specifically the Cakchiquel, Tzutujil and Quiche. In 1975, Indian individuals comprised 14% of the total population of the churches. From the three churches and four preaching points with 100 members in 1930, the Assemblies of God ministries grew to 95 churches, 112 preaching points and 3,300 members in 1960; 315 churches,

460 preaching points and 11,000 baptized members in 1970; and 633 churches, 51 preaching points and 31,500 members in 1978.

The Interdenominational Evangelical Mission (IEM) was established by a former CAM missionary who established the Garden of Roses School. Ministries included a day care center, orphanage and Bible Institute. One church formed when individuals working with the school requested assistance from the Chrstian and Missionary Alliance. The CMA assumed responsibility for many of the Evangelical Mission churches in 1963. In 1970, the CMA reported 20 churches with 2,019 members; in 1976 they reported 31 churches with 2,413 members and in 1979, 35 churches and three preaching points with 2,992 members. The Philadelphia Church, the largest and strongest individual church, decided to become independent along with several related sister churches. A small group of churches chose to preserve their existing affiliation and formed the Evangelical Interdenominational Churches of Guatemala. In 1979, they reported six churches with 610 members. The remainder of the churches joined World Missions which reported 23 churches with 1,315 members in 1979.

The Association of the Spanish American Churches of Guatemala began as a result of ministries initiated in 1947 by the Spanish American Indian Mission. The Mission was originally of Baptist tradition, but in 1963 a revival occurred at a Pastor's conference and it spread throughout the churches. The revival included an outpouring of charismatic gifts, including tongues and a rather spectacular deliverance from demon possession. The members formed the Calvary Church Association (El Calvario), which reported 30 churches, 35 preaching points and 3,500 members in 1965. By 1974, there were 100 churches with 4,500 members, and in 1978 nearly 6,500 members in 118 churches and 32 preaching points.

Lutheran immigrants from Germany began arriving in Guatemala during the 1870's. Attempts were made as early as 1907 to establish a Lutheran congregation in Guatemala City, but it wasn't until 1929 that "La Epifania" was organized. Since this church depended upon pastors from Germany, the small congregation ceased meeting because of World War II. The Lutheran Church (Missouri Synod) responded to requests of English, German and Spanish speaking groups in 1947. A church was established in Guatemala City and outreach ministries were directed to Zucapa and Puerto Barrios. By 1960 there were four churches and nine preaching points with 813 members. In 1977, 1,040 members were reported among six churches and 15 preaching points, and in 1979, 962 members among 10 churches and seven preaching points.

Ministries of the Church of God (Anderson) were established in 1954 by a Guatemalan who returned from the U.S. No North American missionaries have been associated with the work, which has grown to include 60 churches and 120 preaching points among 5,000 members. In 1974 37 churches with 2,600 members were among indigenous peoples.

Foursquare Gospel activities began in Guatemala in 1955. In 1967 there were 2,000 members; in 1974, 2,500 members in 40 churches. But in 1978, there were only 1,250 members in 25 churches. Divisions within the denomination have significantly affected ministries.

The Prince of Peace Evangelical Association was formed in 1956 by Jose Maria Munoz and a group of believers who had been a part of the Central Assembly of God. Many of the original members of the Prince of Peace movement had transferred from various Assemblies of God congregations. As the new churches were formed and began to evangelize, the movement spread quickly. One of the main reasons for its rapid growth was a daily thirty minute radio message directed to pastors, teachers and lay leaders in remote areas where limited resources were available. By 1974 there were 14 radio programs in Guatemala, Mexico, Honduras, El Salvador and Nicaragua. From 100 individuals in 1956, membership increased to 4,500 in 1967. In 1975 there were 270 churches with 8,606 members and by 1979, 518 churches with 33,670 members.

The Elim Christian Mission is one of the fastest growing denominations in Central America. It began as a small house church in Guatemala City during 1961. One of the first members of this group, Dr. Otoniel Rios, a well known medical doctor, significantly influenced the direction taken by the movement following a personal charismatic experience. He was responsible for the development of a large central church in Guatemala City and began a radio ministry in 1970 which became very popular and attracted many individuals to the church. In 1973, Dr. Rios terminated his medical practice to devote himself to full-time pastoral ministries. By 1978, the Elim Christian Mission had increased to 52 chuches with over 3,000 members in Guatemala alone. In 1981 the total membership exceeded 15,000 and the Elim Christian Mission continued to grow as fast as any denomination in Central

America. Equally significant is the fact that the Central Elim Church now has the largest membership of any single congregation in Central America. The average Sunday attendance at "Elim Auditorium" in Barrio Rosario grew from 2,500 in 1978 to 8,500 in 1981. Approximately 7,000 baptized members are active in ministries of the church. Two worship services are held each Sunday in the new auditorium which seats 6,500. Between 150 and 200 new members have been baptized each month including many individuals from the middle and upper classes who were formerly nominal Catholics.

Other large denominations in Guatemala include: The Apostolic Church of Faith in Jesus Christ with 41 churches and 2,422 members; the Assemblies of Christian Churches with 22 churches and 1,132 members; the Churches of Christ with 150 churches and 6,840 members; and the Church of God "New Testament" with 84 churches and 4,591 members.

## CATHOLIC MISSIONS

One of the stated goals of the Spanish colonists and explorers was the conversion of Indians to Christianity. Armies were always accompanied by members of religious orders. The Franciscans, Augustinians, Dominicans and Mercedarians accompanied Pedro Alvarado when he invaded Guatemala. By 1545 these four orders had a program of conversion in which Indians were forcibly gathered into towns and around monasteries. Priests visited a few outlying areas at different times but the geography prevented extensive contact with remote groups. In early years of colonization, the clergy protected indigenous peoples who lived near missions. Laws were passed in 1542 at the instigation of priests. They attempted to eliminate some of the harsher practices of exploitation which had been imposed on Indians living in remote areas. By 1750, more than 424 churches and 23 missions had been constructed. In 1871 a liberal government instituted a series of anticlerical laws. All monastic orders were forbidden and foreign clergy deported. Church property was confiscated and civil marriage required of all citizens. The government which had imposed such restrictions was overthrown and the Catholic Church was granted access to property and rights of entry. Expatriate clergy were permitted to teach in public schools and priests were granted rights to officiate in weddings. During the 1970s the Catholic orders began an intensive missionary effort in isolated areas where the indigenous groups practiced Cristo-paganism. A school was established

to train expatriate missionaries in the cultural practices of the indigenous groups, and in language acquisition, politics and social concerns. In 1979, there were 95 priests and nuns from the U.S. working in Guatemala, in addition to 38 priests and nuns from Canada. These missionaries represented approximately 35 different religious orders in North America. Even in 1970, less than 15% of all Catholic religious workers in Guatemala were nationals.

**MAJOR CHRISTIAN ACTIVITIES**

## EVANGELISM

Early evangelistic efforts in Guatemala were largely denominational in character, but there were a few interdenominational crusades prior to the 1950s. In 1921, Harry Strachan and Juan Varetto of the Latin America Evangelization Campaign conducted an evangelistic crusade in Guatemala City under the sponsorship of the larger denominations. In 1932, evangelist Joaquin Vela engaged in three months of campaigns. A large united campaign was held in Guatemala City during 1950 in conjunction with the Central American Sports Games.

During the 1950's, interdenominational mass evangelistic crusades began to play an important role in the growth of the Protestant movement in Guatemala. The month long crusade was led by Ramon Cabrera and Israel Garcia. They preached to thousands of individuals who filled a large tent erected near the Olympic Stadium especially for the occasion. Other mass evangelistic campaigns followed in succeeding years with Evangelists Hyman Appleman, T. L. Osborn, Merv Rossel and David Garcia. In 1953, evangelist T. L. Osborn from Tulsa, Oklahoma, held a notable evangelistic and healing campaign that stimulated the growth of many Pentecostal churches in the capital. It simultaneously caused consternation and alarm among non-Pentecostal groups. The Presbyterians and churches affiliated with Central American Mission lost many members at that particular time. Osborn conducted a series of 48 open air meetings which attracted crowds of 8,000 to 25,000 every night. Reports of healings and other miracles were widely circulated and revival touched many denominations throughout cities and villages of Guatemala. As a result of the Osborn campaign, the Assemblies of God baptized 2,300 new believers and added 1,000 new members to the 11 churches.

In 1956 David Garcia, a Puerto Rican evangelist, conducted a crusade among 10,000 individuals who attended the meetings at the Olympic Stadium.

Two other significant evangelistic crusades during the 1950's brought national recognition to the growth of evangelical churches in Guatemala. In 1957, in conjunction with the celebration of the 75th anniversary of Presbyterian work in Guatemala, a nationwide series of evangelistic campaigns was held with participation by representives of most evangelical denominations in the country. The festive celebration culminated in a parade by evangelicals through the streets of Guatemala City with about 20,000 to 25,000 participants. The local newspapers reported twice this number and there was clear recognition of the growing evangelical presence and strength in Guatemala, and especially in the capital.

As part of the Billy Graham Caribbean Crusade coordinated by the Latin America Mission, campaigns were held in many of the larger cities of Guatemala. They were led by evangelists Estuardo Bundy, Ramon Cabrera, Mariano Gonzalez and Jorge Sanchez. Cabrera conducted a four day crusade in Guatemala City prior to the arrival of Billy Graham. He preached to a crowd of 40,000 to 42,000 individuals attending one of the two final meetings.

These noteworthy earlier efforts were followed by two national movements of evangelism during the 1960s that solidified gains obtained during the 1950s. At the invitation of the Evangelical Alliance of Guatemala, the Latin America Mission brought its Evangelism-in-Depth team into the country in 1962. Over 15,000 professions of faith resulted from this united effort which mobilized 30,000 lay workers in a variety of evangelistic activities all across the country.

Guatemala was the first country in which the Evangelism-in-Depth program was repeated. The churches of Guatemala coordinated their efforts and sponsored "La Campana de los Cien Mil" in 1968. More than 30,000 decisions were reported as a direct result of the program.

Luis Palau conducted a campaign in Guatemala City in 1971 which received extensive radio and television coverage. Later campaigns in November 1972 attracted over 115,000 people in five western cities. In 1978, Manuel Bonilla, a Mexican evangelist and popular gospel singer, filled the National Stadium in Guatemala City during a brief crusade. Puerto Rican evangelist Yiye Avila conducted a campaign during 1979 in the national stadium with an aggregate attendance of 60,000.

The Charismatic Movement began in Guatemala in 1970 with small group meetings among both Catholics and Protestants, led by Tim Rovenstine of World MAP. The Charismatic Movement among Catholics grew remarkably in the mid 1970's after Father Francis McNutt and Ruth Stapleton from the USA held a retreat in Guatemala and 35 Catholic leaders were baptized in the Holy Spirit. By September 1979, the Charismatic Movement had grown strong enough to fill the National Stadium during a rally led by Father McNutt. There are now chapters of the Full Gospel Businessmen's Fellowship and Women's Aglow Fellowship in Guatemala City, along with several Charismatic churches such as Bethel Community, the Christian Fraternity and Iglesia Cristiana Verbo.

BROADCASTING

Guatemala is the only country of Central America to have five Protestant radio stations. The first was Radio Cultural TGN established by the Central American Mission. In 1963, a group of Pentecostal leaders founded Radio VEA (Voz Evangelica de America). Later, a commercial station in Morales, Izabal Department, became "Radio Izabal" under evangelical leadership. Two addional stations have been added recently: Radio Maya (TGBA) in Varillas, Huehuetenango, operated by the CAM, which transmits all of its programs in Indian dialects; and Radio Union (TGMU), founded by the Seventh-day Adventists in 1980.

Scores of evangelical programs are also broadcast on commercial radio stations in Guatemala. There were at least 50 such programs in 1969. One of the most popular evangelical programs is called "Amaneciendo con Cristo," produced by the Rev. Jose Maria Munoz of the Prince of Peace Association, now the largest denomination in Guatemala. A principal reason for the growth of this movement is reported to be Munoz' daily radio program which attracted listeners from all over Guatemala and parts of El Salvador, Honduras and Mexico. This program, originally heard over Radio Sonora, then over Radio Nuevo Mundo, is now heard on Radio VEA and is produced by Josue Munoz, son of the founder who died in late 1979.

Dr. Otoniel Rios, founding pastor of the Elim Christian Mission, has also developed a popular program on Radio VEA that has contributed significantly to the growth of the Elim movement, which had 52 churches and 3,000 members in 1978. The central

Elim Church is the largest congregation in Guatemala City with a Sunday attendance of 8,000 to 8,500.

Most of the evangelical television programs aired in Guatemala are produced in the United States: PTL Club, 700 Club and Elmer Bueno Presents. Evangelist Luis Palau, during his 1972 campaign, produced a popular program for local television by responding to questions phoned in by viewers. The Rev. Jorge Lopez produces a daily, one-minute T.V. program on Channel 5. He is pastor of the Iglesia Fraternidad Cristiana which meets in a banquet room at the Hotel Fiesta in Guatemala City. There each Sunday 300-400 middle and upper-class worshippers enjoy services with a distinct Charismatic flavor. The high cost of producing and airing programs has kept most evangelical groups from utilizing this medium.

## LITERATURE

The production and distribution of Christian literature is more complicated in Guatemala than in the rest of Central America, since over 40 Indian dialects are spoken. Most of the nonliterates are found in rural areas among the Indian communities. Alfalit and other literacy materials are being used by many denominations and service agencies to teach basic literacy skills. For those who can read, Christian books and materials are available in about 20 Protestant bookstores in Guatemala City, and in another 20 or so bookstores scattered throughout the country, including four in Quetzaltenango. However, most of the literature in Christian bookstores is available only in Spanish. The Christian Literature Crusade works with local churches and service agencies towards the goal of distributing Gospel tracts to every home in Guatemala. Christian films and other audio-visual materials are available from a number of organizations.

## BIBLE TRANSLATION AND DISTRIBUTION

Building on earlier Bible distribution efforts by agents of the British and Foreign Bible Society (BFBS) between 1824 and 1846, the American Bible Society established a Central America regional office at Guatemala City in 1892 (later moved to Panama about 1905). Until the 1960s, Bible distribution was handled mainly by foreign mission agencies aided by visiting colporteurs from the Bible House in the Panama Canal Zone. However, in 1961, a new regional office of the American Bible Society was opened in Guatemala City to coordinate distribution efforts in Guatemala, El Salvador and Honduras. In 1969, the Guatemalan Bible Society was officially established under a full-time national director.

Prior to the 1890s, the only Bibles available were in Spanish or English. But in 1898 the Gospel of Mark was published in Quiche by the BFBS in Guatemala City. This was followed by the Gospel of Mark in 1898 and the Gospel of John in 1901, published in Carib by the BFBS. In 1902, the BFBS published the Gospel of Mark in Cakchiquel. Beginning about 1920, the Central American Mission began serious translation work through the ministry of William Cameron Townsend, who later co-founded the Wycliffe Bible Translators. In 1931, the American Bible Society published the entire New Testament in Cakchequel. Wycliffe entered Guatemala in 1952 and has worked on about 30 of the 41 Amerindian language groups in the country. Of the 27 New Testaments that have been published to date, 14 were translated by Wycliffe workers and seven were translated by workers who have been trained by Wycliffe. Many denominations have done translation work. By 1978, eleven different missions had translated and published at least one book of the Bible in a Mayan language.

| Bibles | 40,951 |
|---|---|
| New Testaments | 28,645 |
| Portions | 385,676 |
| For New Readers | 23,799 |
| Selections | 4,851,943 |
| New Reader Selections | 212,611 |
| | -------- |
| Total (1979) | 5,543,625 |
| Total (1978) | 3,489,864 |

## EDUCATION

Christian. The first Protestant misssionaries in Guatemala founded Christian schools as a point of contact with the upper classes, using English as a means of sharing the Gospel. Forty Protestant schools were reported in Guatemala in 1969. The largest Christian school is the Latin American Evangelical Institute (IEAL) in Guatemala City. Established in 1954, IEAL now offers primary, secondary and junior college education in both day and night school programs, as well as adult education in an extension program. In addition to the main campus in the capital, IEAL operates a day school, development and nutrition center and a handcraft training school in Chimaltenango, as well as a day school and adult development center in Palencia. The total enrollment in all of these programs in 1980 was 5,285 students. IEAL is reported to be the largest evangelical school in Latin America.

Guatemala has the only Protestant university in Central America, Universidad Mariano Galvez, founded in Guatemala City in 1966 by a group of evangelical professionals from a number of denominations. The University offers bachelor's, master's and doctoral-level programs in various departments: business, economics, law, engineering, humanities and theology.

Theological. The training of pastors and lay workers in formal programs of theological education has grown signiificantly over the years, from five Bible institutes in 1935, to 23 Bible institutes and six seminaries in 1978. Eleven of the Bible institutes and three of the seminaries are located in Guatemala City.

The influential Central American Theological Seminary (SETECA), founded in 1929 by the CAM as a Bible institute, has provided theological education for pastors and workers of many conservative and non-Pentecostal denominations in Guatemala and neighboring countries. The CAM also operates four Bible institutes in Guatemala.

Other seminaries include the Southern Baptist Theological Institute, the Fundamentalist Bible Presbyterian Seminary, the Latin American Theological Seminary (Church of God - Cleveland) and the Department of Theology of the Mariano Galvez University. There are at least six programs of theological education by extension (TEE), with the Presbyterian Seminary in San Felipe providing an early TEE model that has stimulated similar programs around the world.

SOCIAL CONCERN

Prior to 1976, there were few Protestant missions or agencies involved in relief and development activities. Following the major earthquake in February, 1976, dozens of Protestant relief and development organizations and denominational agencies, along with Catholic agencies, were soon aiding victims and assisting in the rebuilding of whole towns, villages and urban neighborhoods.

In addition to denominational programs of social concern, the following international Protestant service agencies have assisted in relief and development projects in Guatemala since the earthquake: AMG International, Baptist World Relief, Christian Children's Fund, Christian Nationals Evangelism Commission, Church World Service, Food for the Hungry, Heifer Project International, Lutheran World Relief, MAP International, Mennonite

Central Committee, Mennonite Economic Development Association, Norwegian Church Aid, Wycliffe Bible Translators/Summer Institute of Linguistics, World Relief Commission of the National Association of Evangelicals and World Vision International.

These and other Protestant agencies have participated either directly or indirectly in a variety of programs in the areas of community development, economic assistance, education, equipment and material aid, literacy, medicine and public health, nutrition, reconstruction, rural and agricultural development, industrial development, aid to businesses, family planning, social welfare and vocational training.

Prior to the earthquake in 1976, several members of Calvary Church Association received a vision of a future major earthquake, and reported this to leaders of the central church in Guatemala City. In response to this warning from the Lord, church leaders and members began to stock-pile emergency items. Therefore, when the earthquake hit, leaders of Calvary Church were prepared and met that same day to formally organize the Emergency Committee of Calvary Evangelical Church (CEMEC), and immediately sent out representatives all over the country to determine the extent of the disaster. Special service brigades were organized and sent out to distribute food, clothing, medicine and other emergency items. After obtaining building supplies and organizing work crews, CEMEC began the task of reconstruction, in coordination with the National Emergency Committee of the Guatemalan government.

During 1976, CEMEC worked in 22 different projects, including the building of 1,750 houses. As work progressed, CEMEC began to develop more long range projects that included programs of community development, health, education, small industries, agriculture, cooperatives, construction, reforestation and similar projects. But at the same time, CEMEC and Calvary Evangelical Church ministered to the spiritual and psychological needs of the people. In 1980, after four years of valuable experience, CEMEC was reorganized as the Christian Foundation for Education and Development (FUNDACED).

ECUMENICAL RELATIONS

The first interdenominational Protestant council was formed in 1935, originally among the leaders of the Presbyterian Mission and the Central American Mission, and later joined by the Nazarenes, Friends and Primitive Methodists in 1937. The name was changed to the "Federation of Evangelical Churches" and the organization became more representative of the national churches rather than foreign missions. The Federation sponsored a series of activities in 1958 related to Billy Graham's Caribbean Crusade.

In 1960, the Evangelical Alliance was formed with a broad base of support among leading denominations, building on the spirit of fraternal unity that existed previously in the Federation of Evangelical Churches. The Evangelical Alliance (or Alianza) officially sponsored the Evangelism-in-Depth program in 1962 and a National Campaign for Evangelism in 1968. However, several original members have withdrawn from the Alianza.

The Evangelical Alliance created a special emergency committee in 1972 to aid those suffering from the effects of the Managua earthquake. This committee was reactivated in 1974 and named the Permanent Evangelical Committee for Relief (CEPA). In 1979, CEPA was restructured to meet the needs and opportunities of the post earthquake period, and was renamed the Evangelical Committee for Integral Development (CEDI).

During the 1970s, several new ministerial associations were formed that represent the majority of the evangelical ministers in Guatemala, with membership composed of individual pastors rather than denominations, whereas the Evangelical Alliance is composed of church associations and service agencies. The new ministerial associations give evidence of a growing spirit of unity among evangelical pastors in Guatemala. The Association of Evangelical Ministers of Guatemala (AMEG) represents pastors in Guatemala City and its environs, although its scope is national; whereas the Association of Evangelical Ministers of Quezaltenango (AMEQ) is composed of pastors in the nation's second largest city. In actuality, AMEG and AMEQ are more broadly representative of Protestant groups in Guatemala than is the Evangelical Alliance, since some of the major denominations are not presently members of the Alliance, such as the CAM, Assemblies of God, Church of God - Cleveland, Church of the Nazarene, Friends, Primitive Methodists and Southern Baptists.

More recently (December, 1979), a new evangelical organization was formed among Amerindian pastors and workers, called Asociacion Indigenista de Evangelizacion (ASIDE). This organization has sponsored two congresses on indigenous work in Guatemala, with participation of representatives from most language groups and denominations in the country. Their purpose was to promote the integral growth of Amerindian evangelical churches. Although most of the members of ASIDE are Amerindians, the membership includes some foreign missionaries and Ladinos who work among the Indian communities.

## General Service Organizations

A number of international Protestant service organizations have national offices and programs in Guatemala. Campus Crusade for Christ, Child Evangelism Fellowship, Church World Service, Institute of In-Depth Evangelization (INDEPTH), The Latin American Evangelical Center for Pastoral Studies (CELEP), Missionary Aviation Fellowship and O. C. Ministries (SEPAL) all have significant ministries in Guatemala.

## NATION AND ITS PEOPLE

## POPULATION

The population of Guatemala was 5,730,092 at the time of the last census in 1973. The 1980 population was estimated to be 7,262,400. The capital and largest city, Guatemala City, has a population of 860,000. Over 60% of the people live in rural areas. In general, the Indian population lives in dispersed settlements in the western highlands; some have migrated to the plantations near the Pacific coast, to the lowlands of southern El Peten and to Guatemala City. Most of the Ladino population is found in the lower eastern highlands and the urbanized areas of the western highlands. The lowlands are sparsely populated, but are predominantly Ladino.

## COMPOSITION

The population of Guatemala is composed primarily of two major ethnic groups, the Ladinos and the Indians. Virtually every other group has been absorbed into these two main groups. The Ladinos speak Spanish while the Indians speak various Mayan dialects. The distinction between Ladino and Indian is based more on cultural and social lines than racial differences. Ladino is usually applied to any person who speaks Spanish and generally accepts Hispanic customs and values.

The percentage of Indians was decreasing until recent years because of an official government policy aimed at acculturating the Indians. In 1973, the Amerindian population was estimated to be 44% of the total population.

Present divisions among the Indians date from colonial times when the Spaniards divided them into municipios or townships, either arbitrarily or on the basis of tribal groupings. The Indians rebuilt their society, integrating many European elements, while retaining most of their traditional customs. Each township developed its own dialect and customs. Nevertheless, a general Indian culture serves to unite all of the communities.

The largest Mayan Indian groups are the Quiche, who compose 27.5% of the Indian population and 12% of the Guatemalan population, the Mam (14.6% and 8.9%, respectively), the Cakchiquel (12% and 7.3%) and Kekchi (12.0% and 7.3%). Other groups include the Pocoman, Kanjobal, Chorti, Tzutujil, Ixil, Pocomchi, Achi, Chuj, Uspantec, Jacaltec, Aguacatec and Maya Mopan.

About 5,500 Black Caribs live along the Caribbean coast of Guatemala. They live in small villages, speak their own language and depend on agriculture or wage labor for their livelihood. It is common for the men to leave home for intervals of two or three years in order to work for higher wages.

## LANGUAGE AND LITERACY

The literacy rate is between 30% and 40%, although it is close to 65% in urban areas. The average education level is second grade of primary school.

Spanish is the official language and is spoken by a majority of the people. It is the language of government, schools, newspapers and media. The trade language of all people is Spanish. Almost all Indian males speak Spanish while most Indian women do not. There are over 42 major language groupings. The Kekchi, Quiche, Cakchiquel and Mam are the four major Indian linguistic groups. The Carib language is somewhat unique because the men spoke Carib and the women, Arawake. Most distinctions have now disappeared, although separate vocabularies are still maintained.

## RELIGION

Roman Catholicism is the dominant religion but most of its adherents are nominal in practice. Several elements of indigenous religions have crept into Guatemalan Catholicism, particularly among the Indian population. Roman Catholics total about 78% of the population, while Protestants comprise approximately 21%. Protestant churches are growing at an annual rate of 12.1%.

## GEOGRAPHY AND CLIMATE

The area of Guatemala is 108,880 square kilometers (42,031 square miles). The country can be divided into four natural regions: the Pacific Coast, the Highlands, the Caribbean Coast and El Peten.

The Pacific Coast is straight and open, with no natural harbors and relatively shallow offshore waters. The soil is fertile and well drained, becoming more forested as the altitude increases.

The Central Highlands are covered by the remnants of an extensive pine and oak forest which was cleared for agriculture. Most of Guatemala's people live in this area. Some 30 volcanoes are scattered about this area, some of which are active. There are 18 principal rivers flowing from the mountains into the Pacific, some of which provide hydroclectric power.

The Caribbean Coast is flat and exposed to Caribbean storms. The country's major port, Puerto Barrios, is located in the Bay of Amatique. Much of the coastal area is covered by tropical rainforest. Three valley corridors extend inland from the Caribbean coast. These serve to link various parts of the interior, particularly the highlands, with the coast.

The vast area of El Peten, which comprises about one-third of the national territory, extends as a distinct appendage into the Yucatan Penninsula. It is a rolling limestone plateau covered with dense tropical rainforest interspersed with wide savannas. The soils are relatively poor for agriculture. The entire region is sparsely populated and served by few good roads.

The entire country lies within the tropics, but the climate is varied because of the differing altitudes and the proximity of the regions to the coast. The difference between the average temperatures of the coldest and warmest months in any given place is usually not more than 9 degrees C. (15 degrees F.). The hot country, which extends from sea level to approximately 750 meters (2,500 feet) has average temperatures of 30 to 32 degrees C. (85 to 90 degrees F.). The highland areas have a temperate climate with temperatures between 24 and 27 degrees C. (75 and 80 degrees F.)

81

## HISTORY

Guatemala was conquered by Spanish forces from Mexico in 1523 and it became the seat of Spanish government in the Central American region. Because there were few valuable natural resources, the Spanish government rapidly lost interest in the region. The Spanish settlers intermarried with the Indians, and Catholic missionaries sought to Christianize the Mayan-Quiche people. The mountain valleys were developed into large agricultural estates and worked by the virtually enslaved Indians. The majority of the Indians withdrew from the Spanish-speaking community and maintained their traditional ways of life. The Indians retained their religion, simply adding Christian elements to it.

Independence from Spain was achieved in 1821. However, Augustin de Iturbide, Emperor of Mexico, annexed the Central American states to Mexico in 1822. With Iturbide's death in 1823, they declared themselves independent and formed the United Provinces of Central America. This confederation collapsed in 1838.

From the time of the confederation's dissolution until 1944, Guatemala was ruled by dictators. Elections were held in 1945 and 1950 and were won by liberal reformers. After a miltary coup in 1954, the military has had a strong influence in Guatemalan politics. The last three Presidents have been military.

Issues of social justice and human rights are elements in the civil strife which is evident in Guatemala. Leftist guerrillas regularly clash with the military and para-military forces of the right-wing government. Much of the support for the guerrilla forces comes from the rural population. During the early 1970s, the government was able to keep the insurrectionists under control. But following the major earthquake in 1976, four separate guerrilla fronts sprang up. It is estimated that over 20,000 people have been killed in fighting since then.

## GOVERNMENT AND POLITICAL CONDITIONS

The Constitution of 1965 established a republican, democratic and representative form of government. There are three branches of government: the executive, legislative and judicial, of which the executive is the most powerful. The current president is General Romeo Lucas Garcia, who came to office in 1978. The government attempted to make the election an honest one by inviting international observers. However, only military candidates ran for the office and a majority of eligible voters stayed away from the polls. As it was, no candidate received a majority and the outcome had to be determined by the National Congress.

The guerrilla movements, active since the early 1960s, have forced the government to take emergency measures in order to stay in power. A number of people involved in political and social opposition movements have been killed.

## ECONOMY

Guatemala's economy is based almost exclusively on agriculture. The major crops include coffee, bananas, beef and cotton. Due to Guatemala's natural beauty and historical sites, tourism was also an important industry, but it has been affected by the current political conditions.

Most farmland is controlled by huge estates. For instance, 2.1% of the population owns 62.5% of the farmland. The large Indian population grows subsistence crops on small plots in the highlands. The average per capita income is about $400, but in rural areas it is about $80.

Although the 1976 earthquake disrupted the economy by destroying roads, bridges and some industry, the economy has rebounded at an annual growth rate of 8%. Oil deposits were discovered in the El Peten region in 1975. Guatemalan industry has experienced phenomenal growth since 1960, although industry still exerts relatively small influence on the overall economic picture. However, industry in Guatemala accounts for a higher percentage of the GNP than does industry in any other Central American country. The food-processing industry is the largest, followed by clothing, textiles, beverages, petroleum products, chemicals, furniture and wood and paper products.

## CHURCH STATISTICS FOR GUATEMALA

NOTE: Statistics are from the 1978 PROCADES survey of Protestant Churches and are based on official denominational reports or estimates.  Although definitions of membership vary slightly among churches, the data is highly comparable and reliable.  Not all known churches are included in this list.

| Church or Mission Name | Number of Congregations | Membership | % of Total |
|---|---|---|---|
| PROTESTANT | | | |
| Liturgical | 41 | 2,119 | 0.7% |
| Episcopal | 20 | 1,056 | |
| All Lutherans (3 groups) | 21 | 1,063 | |
| Evangelical Non-Pentecostal | 2,397 | 111,446 | 38.9% |
| Assoc. of C.A. Churches (CAM) | 823 | 32,353 | |
| California Friends | 264 | 3,413 | |
| Christian and Missionary Alliance | 41 | 2,992 | |
| Church of Christ | 150 | 6,840 | |
| Church of God - Anderson | 180 | 5,000 | |
| Church of the Nazarene | 75 | 8,409 | |
| Evangelical Faith Mission | 37 | 1,078 | |
| Fund. Bible Presbyterian | 18 | 3,115 | |
| Indep. Evangelical Mission | 16 | 1,000 | |
| All Mennonites (7 groups) | 73 | 1,723 | |
| National Presbyterian Church | 224 | 16,263 | |
| Plymouth Brethren | 200 | 9,000 | |
| Primitive Methodist | 43 | 6,533 | |
| Southern Baptist | 131 | 6,924 | |
| Others (38 groups) | 122 | 6,803 | |
| Pentecostal | 3,429 | 149,082 | 52.1% |
| Apostolic Church of Faith in Jesus Christ (Mexico) | 41 | 2,422 | |
| Assemblies of Christian Churches | 22 | 1,132 | |
| Assemblies of God | 684 | 31,505 | |
| Bethany Evangelical Church | 23 | 1,435 | |
| Calvary Church (Cont. Miss. Crusade) | 150 | 6,450 | |
| Church of God - Cleveland | 994 | 30,032 | |
| Church of God "New Jerusalem" | 84 | 4,591 | |
| Elim Church | 52 | 3,000 | |
| Evang. Assoc. "Springs of Life" | 25 | 1,200 | |
| Evang. Mission of Holy Spirit | 50 | 2,542 | |
| Foursquare Church | 25 | 1,250 | |
| Missionary Church of God | 100 | 4,500 | |
| Mt. Basan Evang. Church | 19 | 1,943 | |
| Palestine Pent. Mission | 25 | 1,150 | |
| Pent. Church of God of America | 184 | 3,215 | |
| Prince of Peace | 518 | 33,670 | |
| Universal Church of God of Prophecy | 89 | 3,532 | |
| Others (71 groups) | 344 | 15,513 | |
| Adventist | 231 | 17,897 | 6.3% |
| General Conf. of Seventh-day Adventists | 216 | 17,207 | |
| Church of God, Seventh-day | 10 | 460 | |
| Seventh-day Adventist Reform Movement | 5 | 230 | |
| Misc. or Unclassified | 118 | 5,585 | 2.0% |
| All groups (36) | 118 | 5,585 | |
| TOTAL (1978) | 6,216 | 286,129 | 100.0% |
| Estimated Protestant Community (1978) | | 1,161,600 | |

The sources listed below are to help the reader find additional information on this country and Christian ministries there. This list does not try to be comprehensive or complete.

DOCUMENTS

General

Cozean, Jon D., Latin America, 1980, Washington, D.C.: Styker-Post Publications, 1980.

Dombrowski, John, et al, Area Handbook for Guatemala, Washington, D.C.: U.S. Government Printing Office, 1970.

Herring, Hubert, A History of Latin America, New York: Alfred A. Knopf, 1968.

Christian

Cadwallader, Samuel, "Historical Background for an Understanding of the Guatemala Baptist Mission," Guatemala: Guatemala Baptist Mission, 1974.

Coke, Milton, An Ethnohistory of Bible Translation among the Maya, Pasadena; Unpublished dissertation, Fuller Theological Seminary, 1978.

Dominguez, Roberto, Pioneros de Pentecostes: En el Mundo de Habla Hispana, Vol. 2, Mexico y Centroamerica, Healeah, Florida: Literatura Evangelica, 1975.

Grimes, Barbara F., ed., Ethnologue, Huntington Beach, CA: Wycliffe Bible Translators, 1978.

Grubb, Kenneth G., Religion in Central America, London: World Dominion Press, 1937.

Lloret, Julian, "The Maya Church," Ph.D. dissertation, Texas: Dallas Theological Seminary, 1975.

Orr, J. Edwin, Evangelical Awakenings in Latin America, Minneapolis, MN: Bethany Fellowship, 1978.

PROCADES, "Directorio Geografico de las Iglesias y Misiones de Guatemala," San Jose, Costa Rica: PROCADES/INDEPTH, 1980.

Read, William R., et al, Latin American Church Growth, Grand Rapids, MI: Eerdmans, 1969.

Teague, Denzell, "A History of the Church of God in Guatemala," M.A. thesis, unpublished, Deerfield, IL: Trinity Evangelical Divinity School, 1974.

Weerstra, Hans, "Maya Peasant Evangelism," Ph.D. Dissertation, Pasadena, CA: Fuller Theological Seminary, 1972.

**ACKNOWLEDGMENTS**

The information in this profile was taken from many sources which were the best available to the editors at the time of preparation. However, the accuracy of the information cannot be guaranteed. Views expressed or implied in this publication are not necessarily those of World Vision. The editors have tried to present the ministries of various organizations in an objective manner, without undue bias or emphasis. Where we have failed, we apologize for erroneous impressions that may result and request that comments and corrections be sent to MARC, 919 West Huntington Drive, Monrovia, California, USA, 91016. We appreciate and acknowledge the comments and contributions of various organizations and individuals in the preparation of this publication.

# STATUS OF CHRISTIANITY COUNTRY PROFILE

# HONDURAS

## SUMMARY

AREA - 112,088 square kilometers (43,244 square miles)
POPULATION - 3.9 million (1981)
RELIGION - 92% Roman Catholic, 8% Protestant

Impoverishment has remained one of the few stable and consistent factors in the lives of citizens and refugees in Honduras. Political instability, economic disparity and class distinctions have rendered Honduras the most underdeveloped nation in the western world, after Haiti. Recent reports indicate that less than 1% of the population own nearly all of the arable land. Although peasants comprise 87% of the population, they own virtually no land and what they do own is hilly and subdivided for subsistence farming.

Over 25,000 Salvadoran refugees have settled in Honduras and in so doing have provoked both real and imagined fears and pressures. Right-wing military personnel contest the presence of guerrilla support units who provide manpower, food, ammunition and arms to insurgents in El Salvador. Thus many Salvadoran refugees have been forcibly removed from camps and farms along the border. They have been

dispersed in scattered villages throughout Honduras. Most refugees fled suppression and war in El Salvador but have been greeted with suspicion and apprehension. The "soccer war" of 1969, between Honduras and El Salvador, has not been forgotten and discrimination against Salvadorans is common. Many refugees do not plan to remain in Honduras, but for the present time there is no viable alternative. Honduran officials are afraid that the refugees will instigate revolutionary philosophies among the peasants.

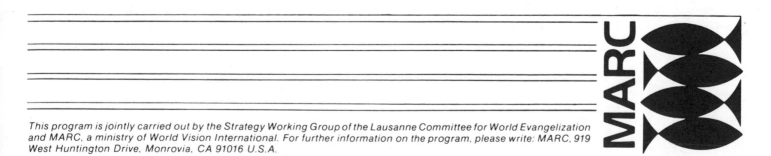

*This program is jointly carried out by the Strategy Working Group of the Lausanne Committee for World Evangelization and MARC, a ministry of World Vision International. For further information on the program, please write: MARC, 919 West Huntington Drive, Monrovia, CA 91016 U.S.A.*

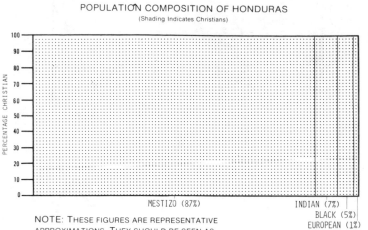

POPULATION COMPOSITION OF HONDURAS
(Shading Indicates Christians)

PERCENTAGE CHRISTIAN

MESTIZO (87%)          INDIAN (7%)
                       BLACK (5%)
                       EUROPEAN (1%)

NOTE: THESE FIGURES ARE REPRESENTATIVE
APPROXIMATIONS. THEY SHOULD BE SEEN AS
INDICATORS OF MAGNITUDE ONLY.

**PEOPLE GROUPS**

Black Caribs (2.5%)

Black Caribs comprise about 2.5% of the
total population. An estimated 77,000
Caribs live in scattered settlements along
the northern coast, between the Rio Sico
in the east and the Guatemalan border in
the west. The Black Caribs are often
considered to be a Roman Catholic,
Afro-American population. However, they
have retained strong elements of their
original Red Carib religion and culture.
They were deported from St. Vincent to the
Bay Islands by the British in 1797. From
the Bay Islands, the Black Caribs migrated
to the mainland where small settlements
were formed along the Caribbean coast from
Belize to Nicaragua. The largest
population of Black Caribs is found in
Honduras.

Many Black Caribs are afraid of spirits of
the dead. Cures for sickness often
involve all-night dances and spirit
possession. Polygyny is practiced to some
extent. Special community festivals are
held in honor of the village patron saint.
Few Black Caribs are Evangelicals,
although the Anglicans, Methodists,
Plymouth Brethren, Mennonites and other
Protestant groups attempted to establish
churches among them. No Protestant
missionaries were known to be working with
Black Caribs in Honduras on a regular
basis in 1980. The New Testament was
recently translated into Carib by the
Summer Institute of Linguistics (SIL) in
Guatemala. Scripture portions are
available in Carib, and many Black Caribs

are also literate in English or Spanish.

Afro-American (5.5%)

The Afro-American population of Honduras
(about 5.5%) has resulted from the
intermarriage of Negroes with other racial
groups, mainly whites and American
Indians. Most speak English or Creole as
their first language, and many are
becoming bilingual as the use of Spanish
increases. Many of the early
Afro-Americans in Honduras were residents
of the Bay Islands, which were under
British control until 1859. Most Bay
Islanders originally came from the British
Cayman Islands in the 1830s, but many
eventually migrated to the mainland in
search of employment, along with later
Afro-American immigrants from the West
Indies. Most West Indian Negroes were
nominal Protestants, having been baptized
in Anglican, Methodist or Baptist Churches
formed in the West Indies by British
missionaries during the 1700s. However,
after arriving on the mainland of
Honduras, most West Indian Protestants
found themselves isolated from churches,
and only a few congregations were
organized among them prior to 1900.

Most Afro-Americans in Honduras are
nominal Protestants in the same way that
most Latinos or mestizos are nominal
Catholics. Although there are Protestant
congregations among them — mainly
Adventist, Episcopal, Church of God -
Cleveland, Methodist and Baptist -- less
than 10% of the Afro-American population
are committed Protestants and few of them
have become Catholics.

Amerindian (7%)

There are several Amerindian tribal
peoples in Honduras, including the
Miskito, Sumo, Paya and Jicaque, who have
maintained their unique culture and
language. Other Indian groups have been
largely assimilated into the Latino
Spanish-speaking culture, although a few
older people are still bilingual in their
Indian dialect and Spanish. Official
statistics are not available on the size
of the Indian population in Honduras but
older estimates indicate that
approximately 7% of the total population
could be considered Amerindian. Since
only 1% have resisted Hispanization, this
leaves about 6% who are in the process of
being assimilated into the Latino culture
-- including the Lenca (Departments of
Intibuca, La Paz and Lempira), Chorti
(Copan), Pipil (Ocotepeque) and Jicaque
(Olancho, Yoro and Morazan). There is
still one isolated, unacculturated group
of Jicaque in Montana de la Flor in
central Honduras. In 1972, SIL workers

86

were living among the group in La Flor, where translation work was difficult and progress slow. They have a small group of believers and a building.

The largest group of unacculturated Amerindians is the Miskito population who inhabit the Mosquito Coast in northeastern Honduras.

The Miskito live in the Caribbean coastal lowlands in communities of 100 to 500 people. They use canoes and rafts on the rivers, and larger canoes or boats on the ocean. They make their livelihood from fishing, hunting, and slash-and-burn agriculture. The men usually clear the land, while the women do the planting, cultivating, and harvesting. Although culturally Indian, the Miskito manifest some Negro traits as well. This is due to their intermarriage with Afro-Americans during the early period when African slaves were imported to Central America by the Spanish and British, and in subsequent contacts with West Indian immigrants to the Mosquito Coast.

Although the Miskito have preserved their language and culture, significant changes have occurred in their religious beliefs. The Moravians have won many converts among them since 1930. Ministries of the Baptists among the Miskito have been particulary successfull since the 1960s. Early efforts by English Methodists had no lasting result, whereas Anglican missionary activities produced a number of congregations in the coastal settlements both among the Miskito and among the West Indian residents in the larger towns on the Mosquito Shore.

Today, most of the 26,900 inhabitants of the Department of Gracias a Dios are Miskito, although an unknown number are of West Indian descent. The Moravian Church claims about 6,200 baptized members and perhaps 12,000 adherents among the Miskito. The Baptist Association reports 1,300 members and about twice as many adherents. Therefore, about half the Miskito population is at least nominally Protestant. The Catholic Church also has a number of missions there. Although a viable Church exists among the Miskito, it is doubtful that 20% are committed Christians.

The smaller tribes have sought to maintain their separate language and culture and have been resistent to outside influences. The Sumo number only about 500 in Honduras, although a larger group of about 2,000 Sumo (who speak a different dialect) live across the Rio Coco in Nicaragua. Although no Bible translation has been carried out among them, many Sumos are bilingual, speaking Miskito as well as Sumo. Some are trilingual, speaking Miskito, Spanish and Sumo. The Moravians have formed Sumo congregations using the Miskito Scriptures and hymnal.

The Paya now live in the higher mountains of Olancho, where they inhabit the river towns of Dulce Nombre de Culmi, Santa Maria del Carbon and Malancones. The total Paya population is only about 300. They still use their own language, although many Paya men are bilingual. In 1972, SIL reported an independent Protestant congregation of about 100 believers in Malacones, where most of the 30 Paya families had been converted. They were holding their own worship services and were reading the Scriptures in Spanish. The World Gospel Mission had a preaching point in Culmi, but there was no gospel witness in El Carbon, located about two-days hike from Culmi.

Other small people groups in Honduras are the East Indians, Syrians, and Chinese that live along the Caribbean coast or in the Bay Islands. However, most of these peoples live in the port cities of La Ceiba and Puerto Cortes, or in San Pedro Sula. There are also a small number of Jews in Honduras, although the exact size of the community is not known.

Approximately 25,000 refugees from El Salvador live in six or more camps inside Honduras. Few males between the ages of 14 and 40 live in the camps because they are either involved in the current civil war in El Salvador or have been killed. Most of the refugees are women, children and older men. Between 75,000 and 80,000 refugees residing in El Salvador may cross the borders into Honduras if they are allowed to do so. It is estimated that 99% of the refugees are "Campesinos" (farm workers).

## Latino (85%)

The majority of the Latino population of Honduras (about 85%) can be described as Catholic, although "Popular Catholicism" or "Cristo-paganism" are terms that are often used to indicate the nominal character of their Roman Catholic faith. Although most Latinos are baptized Catholics, few take an active part in church activities other than religious festivals, pilgrimages to shrines, funerals, weddings and baptisms. Attendance at Mass, confirmation, and confession is usually infrequent. Civil marriages and free unions are the rule, while only the few practicing Catholics have church weddings. Animistic practices are stronger among the lesser acculturated Indians and mestizos and there is wide reliance upon "brujas" (witches) and "curandos" (herb specialists) to achieve good fortune or healing.

It is among the Spanish-speaking population that Protestant Churches have shown most of their growth since 1900. Yet less than 10% of all Latinos are Protestant adherents. Assuming that practicing Catholics total no more than 20% of the Latino population, there remains an estimated 70% who are Cristo-pagan, or about 2,082,500 individuals.

## RELIGIOUS COMPOSITION OF HONDURAS

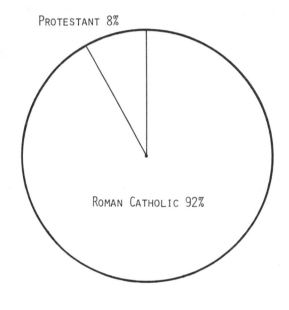

PROTESTANT 8%

ROMAN CATHOLIC 92%

### CURRENT STATUS OF CHRISTIANITY

The Roman Catholic Church is the predominant religious group in Honduras. Although 90% of the people are nominal Catholics, few regularly attend Mass. The Roman Catholic Church is poor financially, and weak administratively, with few religious workers (priests, nuns and lay-workers) to care for a widely scattered population. Normally conservative, the Church is now experiencing tensions due to two internal developments: social reform and the Charismatic Movement.

The Protestant community has grown from less than 1% of the total population in 1935, to 2.2% in 1965, and now represents 8% of all Hondurans. Between 1965 and 1980 the annual rate of increase in Protestant membership was 13.4% (AAGR) while the general population growth was only 3.5%. The largest Protestant denominations are the Seventh-day Adventists, the Moravian Church, the Plymouth Brethren, and the Assemblies of God.

Other religious groups can also be found in Honduras. In addition to Christian sects like the Church of Jesus Christ of Latter Day Saints (Mormons) and the Jehovah's Witnesses, spiritist groups appear to be growing among the Honduran population, especially in the San Pedro Sula area. African animistic practices can still be found among the Black Caribs, as well as among the Negroes of West Indian heritage. Obeah, Pocomania, Myalism and Vodun are a few of the popular forms of animism. Cristo-paganism is characteristic of many Hondurans of Indian descent, especially among those who are least acculturated to Latino culture and Catholic doctrines. Animism remains strong in some of the isolated Indian communities, especially among the Paya, Sumo, and Jicaque tribes. Both the Black Caribs and the Miskito show evidence of animistic beliefs and rituals of African and Indian origin.

### NATIONAL CHURCHES

#### PROTESTANT CHURCHES

Before 1900 the majority of Protestants in Honduras were English-speaking Negroes who inhabited the Bay Islands and adjacent coastline. They were principally Anglicans, Methodists and Baptists who migrated to this region from the British West Indies. Since 1900 growth has primarily occurred among the Spanish-speaking population.

Protestants are distributed among various denominations in Honduras. The Liturgical Churches (Episcopal and Lutheran) with 1,724 communicant members comprised 2.2% of the total Protestant membership in 1978. The Evangelical Non-Pentecostal Churches, with 35,218 members, comprised 45.7%; the Pentecostal Family of Churches, with 30,136 members, comprised 39%; and the Adventist Family of Churches with 9,976 members, 13%. The total Protestant communicant membership in 1980 was 77,000 and the Protestant community was nearly 300,000.

Total Protestant membership in Honduras increased at an annual rate of 1.6% between 1936-1950, 7.4% between 1950-1960 and 12.4% between 1965-1978. If the present rate of increase continues, it will reach 177,800 members by 1985 with a total Protestant community of 553,500 or 12.2% of the national population.

Between 1965 and 1980, Protestant membership in Honduras grew at an average annual rate of 13.4%. Since 1965 a number of larger denominations have increased more than 10% annually. They include: Plymouth Brethren (more than 20%), Assemblies of God (16%), Moravian Church (13%), Evangelical and Reformed Church (12%), Seventh-day Adventists (12%), and the Church of God - Cleveland (10%).

Although Pentecostal churches have grown significantly during the past 30 years, only a few denominations have more than 1,000 baptized members, specifically: Church of God - Cleveland with 4,550; the Prince of Peace Church (4,000): Free Pentecostal Church (3,500); Foursquare Church (1,870); Philadelphia Church (1,200); and the Church of God of Prophecy (1,065). Compared to other countries of Central America, with the exception of Belize, the Pentecostal churches in Honduras are proportionately the smallest (39%).

On the other hand, compared to the rest of Central America, Honduras has the largest proportion of the non-Pentecostal churches (46%). Other large denominations not previously mentioned are: the Central American Church of Honduras, related to CAM International (4,813); Association of Holiness Churches, related to the World Gospel Mission (2,300); and the Southern Baptist Convention (2,270). The remaining denominations each have less than 2,000 members.

The Pentecostal churches are not the only ones growing in Central America; Seventh-day Adventist churches in Honduras increased from 3,000 to more than 10,000 baptized members between 1965 and 1980, which makes them the largest Protestant denomination in Honduras.

Geographically, 55% of all Protestant congregations in Honduras are located in the Central Mountain Region, which had 57% of the population; 7% of the congregations are in the Pacific Coastal Region (10.4% of the population); and 38% are in the Caribbean Coastal Region (32.6% of the population). The Departments of Valle and Intifuca have proportionately fewer congregations than any other departments in the country.

## CATHOLIC CHURCHES

The power and influence of the Catholic clergy was significant in the Colonial era. During the Independence period, however, a series of liberal reforms sought to restrict the activities of the Church. Between 1880 and 1965, a series of constitutional changes alternately added or removed restrictions on the Catholic Church in Honduras. Under the 1965 Constitution, the Church remains independent of the State which has generally not interfered with the operations of the Church as long as the hierarchy and the priests have remained out of politics. The government does have a diplomatic representative at the Vatican, and the Holy See maintains a representative in Honduras. Church property and income are tax-free, but the Church is restricted by law from holding any income producing property.

The Catholic Church in Honduras derives its income from fees and contributions, and thus it is very poor. The government provides no funds for the church except subsidies for certain parochial school programs.

Organizational structure is not particularly strong. The heirarchy of the Catholic Church has been challenged to go beyond traditionally conservative stands, interact with the people and recognize the changing needs and desires of the majority of the population. Some of the younger priests have come into conflict with their superiors because of their active concern and involvement in matters of economic and social welfare. Despite the Catholic Church's limited abilities to respond to the pressing needs of the masses, the roots of the church are deep and permeate many aspects of life. Most Hondurans are nominally Catholic, but attendance at Mass is minimal.

The Catholic Church is administratively divided into one archdiocese, headed by the archbishop, and into three dioceses with two prelatures which are each headed by a bishop. In 1970, only 5% of the 233 priests and 18% of the nuns were Hondurans. Honduras had the highest proportion of expatriate priests of any Latin American nation. By 1975 there was one priest per 12,500 Hondurans.

### FOREIGN MISSIONS

## PROTESTANT MISSIONS

As early as 1739, Miskito chiefs requested that their children receive religious instruction in the Anglican faith. They sent several young men to Jamaica where they could receive formal education in British schools and training in Anglican doctrines.

89

The first missionary known to arrive on the mainland of Honduras was Christian Frederick Post (1768 - 1785), who represented the Society for the Propagation of the Gospel in Foreign Parts. Post arrived at the Black River (Rio Sico) settlement in 1768, where services were conducted in the Superintendent's Hall.

Other Anglican chaplains were sent to preach the gospel among the British settlers, Indians and Negroes that inhabited the Mosquito Coast during the mid-1700s. Many were unable to bear the heat and primitive conditions and they either left or died. Nevertheless, Anglican schools and chapels were established among the Indians and Negroes.

The Rev. M. Newport, a chaplain in Belize, became a pioneer missionary in the Bay Islands, where a small British settlement came into existence during the 1730s. The Island of Roatan, which achieved fame as a pirate refuge during the 1600 - 1700s, had been subsequently settled by migrant workers from the British Cayman Islands who arrived in 1835. Newport visited Roatan in 1839 where he established a school and organized the parish. It was not until 1847 that the first Anglican church was constructed.

In the early 1870s Anglican parishioners emigrated from the British Antilles, Belize and the Bay Islands to the northern coast of Honduras, where workers were needed to help build a railroad. The Anglican bishop in Belize extended his pastoral care to this region of Honduras. Large Anglican churches were established at Tela, Puerto Cortes and La Ceiba, and a number of missions along the rail and banana lines. In 1935 the Anglican Church in Honduras reported eight churches, 250 communicants and about 1,250 adherents.

Anglican work in the Republic of Honduras was transferred to American jurisdiction in 1947, and became a missionary district of the Protestant Episcopal Church. By 1978 the Episcopal Church in Honduras reported a total of six churches, eight missions and 1,615 communicants in the entire Republic, which included the Bay Islands.

Following initial efforts on the Mosquito Coast, the Methodists concentrated their efforts in Belize and the Bay Islands. A Methodist society of 36 members was formed in 1844 - 1845. By 1860 the Methodist church in Honduras numbered close to 1,000 members. Roatan became a separate station with its own resident missionary. Several British missionaries worked among the Islanders during the next 20 years.

Between 1887 and 1892, the Belize District of the Wesleyan Methodist Church formally entered the mainland of Spanish Honduras, where congregations were formed among Belizean and West Indian Methodist migrants. By 1913, only 41 Methodist members could be counted on the circuit. In 1930 the Wesleyan Methodist Missionary Society formally withdrew from the mainland of Spanish Honduras due to economic hardships that affected their work there. Only a few struggling Methodist congregations were able to survive this difficult period, notably the churches in La Ceiba and Puerto Cortes, which soon became affiliated with a Methodist group from the United States, the African Methodist Episcopal Zion Church.

In 1949, the United Brethren in Christ Mission went to Honduras to take over the work begun by the African Methodist Episcopal Zion Church in the 1930s. In 1952 work was begun among the Spanish-speaking people. However, by 1970 there were only 300 members in 13 congregations. In 1978, 25 churches and six missions were reported with a membership of 1,382.

Still another Methodist missionary society entered Honduras in 1957. The Wesleyan Church of Marion, Indiana, reported four churches and two mission stations in 1960, with 129 church members, three missionaries and one national worker. By 1978, six churches were reported with 260 members.

The Baptists in British Honduras responded to invitations from West Indian Baptists living in the Bay Islands and sent their first representative in 1846. Ministries of the Bay Islands Baptist Mission were greatly expanded in 1849. By 1850, the first Baptist church had been organized and native workers were being trained. Baptist work in Belize and the Bay Islands became independent in 1904 under the British Honduras Baptist Trust Association.

A spiritual renewal known as the "Great Awakening" occurred in Belize and the Bay Islands from 1905 to 1914. Hundreds of new converts were added to the churches. The days of renewal were followed almost immediately by turmoil in the First World War. Lack of employment opportunities and failing export markets motivated thousands of islanders to emigrate. Rampant destruction by a major hurricane caused further economic depression and hindered church growth during the 1930's.

Following the Second World War, a new wave of missionaries from North America journeyed to Central America. In 1960 there were five churches with 128 members among a community of 630 adherents on the Bay Islands. By 1978 the Bay Islands Baptist Association reported seven churches with 110 members. Ministries on the mainland grew substantially from 700 members in 1970 to 1,470 members among 66 churches in 1978.

In 1887 a Seventh-day Adventist minister from New Orleans made an exploratory visit to the Bay Islands, where he distributed tracts and books. That same year, the first resident minister arrived and established the Adventist Mission on Roatan Island. In 1893 the first Adventist church was formally organized with 25 members and a Sunday school of 60. An Adventist school was founded and by the end of 1893 there were three congregations and 100 members. By 1905 the combined membership, most of which was located in the Bay Islands, totaled 160 in five churches and five out-stations. By 1937, the Adventist Mission reported 15 churches with 624 members. Growth continued so that by 1970 Adventist membership increased to 3,700 among 26 churches and by 1978 to 9,933 members in 38 churches and 70 mission stations, making it the largest Protestant denomination in Honduras. Adventist work has grown equally among Spanish-speaking and English speaking people groups throughout Honduras. About half of all Adventists reside on the north coast and in the Bay Islands.

Personnel with the Central American Mission (CAM International) entered in 1896 with the express desire to evangelize Spanish-speaking groups in the interior, rather than English-speaking peoples on the Caribbean coast. Five CAM missionaries launched a pioneer work in the mountain villages. In 1936 there were 21 churches with 1,175 members. In 1975, there were 77 churches with 2,375 members. Church membership had doubled in 35 years. In 1979, 4,304 members were reported in 83 churches and 106 other congregations. In 1948, churches planted by CAM formed the autonomous Association of Central American Churches. Most CAM International missionaries are involved in support ministries related to ongoing operations of the American Academy and the Evangelical Hospital. Other expatriate personnel work in the primary and secondary schools, the Bible Institute, bookstores or campground facilities.

Ministries of the Plymouth Brethren were inititated by Alfred Hockins, a missionary who had a very distinguished career in Honduras. His initial stay was not for long since he was forced to return to England in 1902 due to illness. But he did return in 1911 as a missionary with the Christian Missions in Many Lands, and remained actively involved until his death in 1978. By 1936, twelve small congregations were established in the San Pedro Sula and Trujillo regions by Hockins and John Rudouck, another Brethren missionary, The Rudoucks had been in Guatemala from 1926-1931 and relocated to Honduras with a working knowledge of the language and culturally appropriate ministries. The Plymouth Brethren work was concentrated in the coastal regions until 1950 when four new missionary couples were able to establish inland ministries. In 1950, there were 25 small assemblies; by 1960, there were 45 congregations with a total membership of 900 and by 1970 there were 65 congregations with 1,950 members. The most notable growth occurred from 1970 to 1980 when the number of congregations reached 120 and membership totaled 7,200. Brethren leaders attributed this growth to several factors: (1) During the Hurricane Fifi crisis in 1974, many people became Christians and began attending Brethren Assemblies. (2) Many Christians were forced to migrate because of flood damage and as they did, they introduced many new people to the gospel. (3) A great deal of assistance was received from foreign countries following the Hurricane. (4) "Special Assemblies" lasting three to four days were held at that time for 1,000 individuals representing most of the Brethren Assemblies. Unity and spiritual growth among Brethren Christians became more pronounced. (5) Regional Bible studies provided training for numerous individuals who became involved in leadership of the growing number of newly formed Assemblies. (6) Brethren missionaries began visiting local Assemblies on a regular basis and provided training in spiritual growth and evangelistic outreach.

For 30 years the California Yearly Meeting of Friends supported two separate fields in Honduras. By 1935 there were two dozen churches and nearly 50 preaching points in the western region with 1,500 members and 2,280 adherents. By 1960 there was little change with 22 churches reporting 1,068 members and 3,000 adherents. The war with El Salvador in 1969 severely hindered ministries of the Friends because many of the church members were Salvadorans who resided in Honduras. Believers from that people group fled to El Salvador, Guatemala and the interior regions of Honduras. In 1979 there were 63 congregations scattered throughout the region with membership totaling 700.

Ministries in the south-central region were established in 1914. In 1944, the Friends Board of Missions turned over their Tegucigalpa field to the National Holiness Missionary Society (Now known as the World Gospel Mission). Accute shortages in finances and personnel brought about the transfer which affected five churches and about 500 individuals.

The Honduran Holiness Church became autonomous in 1956, but not much growth was recorded during those early years. In 1951 only five churches were reported, with 564 members. Although 16 churches existed in 1965, there were still fewer than 600 members. By 1968, however, 32 churches reported 1,781 members, including new believers who had not yet been baptized. The Holiness Church lost many members during the war with El Salvador in 1969, because Salvadorans were either sent home or detained by the government during this tense period. From a low of 700 members in 1969, membership grew to 2,324 in 1975. However, in 1979 there were only 2,309 members in 76 Holiness congregations. Several schools are operated in Tegucigalpa, and Bible Institutes at El Hatillo and Juticalpa.

By 1935 the Evangelical and Reformed Church (ERC) was a well established mission in northern Honduras. The Foreign Mission Board of the Evangelical Synod of North America began work in Honduras in 1921. Schools, clinics, house visitation and evangelistic ministries were established in San Pedro Sula. Similar activities were extended to the surrounding region, from Puerto Cortes on the north coast to Santa Barbara in the southern interior and east into Yoro Department.

In contrast to most work in northern Honduras, the Evangelical and Reformed Church concentrated on the Spanish-speaking population. The strategy of the Synod was to achieve "personal regeneration by means of the proclamation of the gospel and social regeneration through the formation of a middle class by means of education." In keeping with the latter goal, the Evangelical Theological Seminary was established in Pinalejo, Santa Barbara, in 1934. A short time later, a school was added for training lay evangelists. Medical work was begun in Concepcion in 1947. In 1962, the theological institute was transferred to San Pedro Sula. From three churches and five stations with only 75 communicants and 250 adherents in 1935, the work increased to 17 churches and 106 preaching points in 1960, with 718 communicants and 3,628 adherents. Also functioning were 25 Sunday schools, four primary schools, a secondary school, a bookstore, two clinics and the theological institute, assisted by 18 foreign workers, five ordained national pastors and 12 lay workers. By 1978, there were 23 churches with 3,500 members. Extensive ministries were conducted in education, medicine, agriculture, literature and communications in cooperation with the United Church Board for World Ministries, the mission arm of the United Church of Christ in the U.S.A. Prior to 1930, numerous Miskito congregations had been established along the banks of the Coco River, the border between Nicaragua and Honduras. By 1935, the Moravians had established three churches and three mission stations among the Miskito with 75 communicants and about 250 adherents in the sparsely populated coastal lowlands. Living in this remote region were tens of thousands of Miskito and a few hundred Paya and Sumo Indians, largely unevangelized since the first frustrated attempts by Anglican and Methodist missionariss during previous centuries.

However, the Moravians persisted in their efforts and were successful in winning many Miskito to faith in Jesus Christ. By 1960 the Moravian Church reported 989 communicants and 1,850 adherents, among 41 churches cared for by 12 foreign workers and a number of national pastors, in the Department of Gracias a Dios. Medical, educational and agricultural work was conducted, in addition to evangelistic and church planting activities. The Honduran Synod of the Moravian Church claimed 2,829 communicants in 37 organized congregations, with a Moravian Community of 6,300 adherents in 1978. The total Miskito population numbers about 28,000.

**Southern Baptists started their work in Honduras in the 1940s.** Beginning in 1946, Baptist churches were organized in Tegucigalpa from congregations that had been using Baptist literature. Separate Baptist conventions were formed in Honduras and Guatemala in 1959.

Soon after the first missionaries arrived in the 1950s, a bookstore was established in Tegucigalpa that continues to provide a vital source of Christian literature for all of Honduras. A theological training institute was soon established in the capital as well. Harold Hurst pioneered in television with the program, "La Iglesia en el Hogar" (The Church in the Home), which is well known through the country. In the field of medicine, a mobile unit operates out of El Porvenir, and a physician and family nurse practitioner were appointed for Honduras in 1972. Student work began in 1970. A Baptist campground has been established on the shores of Lake Uojoa in central Honduras.

By 1960 the Southern Baptists had established churches in the Departments of Francisco Morazan, Choluteca, Comayagua and Cortes with the center of the work in the capital. Six churches and 20 preaching points were reported in 1960, with 161 baptized members and 531 adherents. In 1970 eleven churches had been formed with about 700 members, but by 1979 there were 32 churches, 55 missions/preaching points, 2,374 members, and a total Sunday school enrollment of 3,140. Twenty-six students were attending the Baptist theological Seminary in Comayaguela, and a program of theological education by extension had begun with five students enrolled. In 1974, the Southern Baptists became known as the "National Convention of Baptist Churches of Honduras" (CONIBAH).

Another Baptist group began work in Honduras in 1967, known as Caribbean Baptist Outreach of Popular, Florida, under the leadership of an independent Southern Baptist missionary. Since that time, about 30 churches have been formed among the Miskito in addition to a Bible institute in Puerto Limpira for training Miskito pastors. Only one church is Spanish-speaking while the majority use Miskito. These churches have been formed into the Baptist Association of the Mosquitia. Nine of them are also members of CONIBAH and are included in their statistical reports. The 30 Baptist churches in the Mosquitia were estimated to have about 1,300 members in 1980.

Baptist Mid-Missions entered Honduras about 1955 and had formed four small churches in the San Pedro Sula area by 1970 under the supervision of six missionaries. In 1979 there were 19 organized churches with about 500 baptized members, known as the Independent Evangelical Baptist Churches of Honduras.

The first missionaries with the Eastern Mennonite Board of Missions and Charities arrived in Honduras in 1950. Evangelistic and medical work was established in Trujillo, Tocoa and Gualaco on the north coast. Church growth during the first decade was slow. In the face of local Catholic opposition, Mennonites advocated education and development, establishing a primary school and bringing in the Voluntary Service Program. Young Mennonites from the USA worked in organizing cooperatives, planting gardens, selling veterinary medicines and similar projects aimed at serving local community needs.

During the 1960s, the infant church began to organize itself, and the Honduras Evangelical Mennonite Church emerged. National leaders attended institutes for training in theological and pastoral concerns and a formal Bible Institute program was established in Trujillo.

During the 1970s, the Mennonites witnessed the growth of urban churches. Church members from the north coast and the Agua and Sula Valleys, where rural Mennonite churches had been established, began moving to La Ceiba, San Pedro Sula and Tegucigalpa-Comayaguela (the federal capital). During the 1950s and 1960s, the emphasis was on establishing rural churches, but during the 1970s urban church planting and development received priority. The clinics, schools and Voluntary Service Program were discontinued, and a new Extension Bible Institute was developed at La Ceiba. It includes vocational training for pastors and lay workers.

Spiritual and organizational renewal became an important part of Mennonite church life in Honduras during the 1970s. Some congregations became less dependent on one strong pastor and turned to the multiple personnel ministry model which makes use of pastoral teams. Group decision-making became the pattern. Although previous social ministries were discontinued on the north coast, Mennonites in Honduras consider social concern and action to be integral parts of the church's lifestyle. Youth teams began teaching health, sewing and literacy classes, in addition to leading small group Bible studies and building discipleship into the lives of new converts as well as older believers.

Edward King and his team of workers in Tegucigalpa have demonstrated how Charismatic renewal can be combined with social concern and action in a rehabilitation program for delinquent youth, known as the Living Love Program (Grupos de Amo Viviente). Over a dozen of these Charismatic discipleship groups have been established in the capital, where they are having far-reaching effects among Honduran young people and their families. A special lay program of Bible instruction and discipleship has been developed to train young people in an informal Bible institute setting.

Looking at the overall growth picture, the Mennonites grew between 1962-1967, then consolidated the work between 1968-1972, followed by 20% AAGR in the period 1973-1976. From a base of 25 churches and 300 members in 1970, the Mennonites increased to 35 churches and 805 members in 1978.

The first known Pentecostal missionaries in Honduras were probably those who visited the Bay Islands in the 1890s. However, in 1931, an independent Pentecostal missionary from Canada, Frederick Mebius, crossed the border from El Salvador and helped establish a number of churches in western Honduras. The first Pentecostal believers were apparently former members of the Friends Church.

The Assemblies of God were requested to send a pastor to care for the growing flock of Pentecostal believers in western Honduras. Two men responded and established several congregations. In 1936 a Pentecostal church was formed following an earthquake, when a group of villagers were filled with the Holy Spirit and began to boldly testify about the Pentecostal experience.

In 1940, the first Assemblies of God missionaries arrived in Honduras from the United States. The Honduran Bible Institute was opened in 1946. Since 1965 it has operated in San Pedro Sula. From the very beginning, the work in Honduras has been indigenous and self-supporting, although the Assemblies of God Board of Missions has aided the work by sending missionaries and funds for special projects. However, the construction of church buildings, operating expenses, and pastoral salaries have uniformly come from the Honduran believers themselves with little outside assistance.

In 1960 there were 30 churches and 44 preaching points with 680 baptized members, aided by six foreign workers and served by 34 national pastors. By 1965 the total membership had increased to about 1,200 among 40 churches and numerous preaching points, and by 1978 to 5,900 members in 196 churches and 243 preaching points. The resulting AAGR of 15.6% means that the Assemblies of God was the second fastest growing denomination in Honduras between 1965 and 1978.

The Evangelical Association of the Prince of Peace churches is an indigenous movement which spread to Honduras from Guatemala in 1960. Pastoral training is accomplished through an extension Bible institute program, brief seminars conducted in each geographical area where the movement exists, and a permanent Bible Institute in Guatemala City that gives basic pastoral courses lasting five months.

By 1974 about 50 Prince of Peace Churches had been established in Honduras, mainly in the western and central regions of the country. In 1978 there were 125 churches and over 60 preaching points in Honduras, with an estimated 4,000 members.

The Church of God - Cleveland arrived in the Bay Islands in 1944. On the Island of Roatan, special services were held at French Harbor, Jonesville and Coxen Hole. But the greatest success occurred on the Island of Utila, where revival meetings lasted for three months and led to over 500 reported conversions, or approximately one-third of the island population. In April of 1945, the first Church of God was established on Utila with 40 members. The building purchased for the new church had been the island's only movie theatre and gambling hall, which shows that the revival had considerable impact on the Islanders. However, it wasn't until 1950 that the first believers received the promised "baptism of the Holy Spirit" in the Bay Islands. The Church of God opened an elementary school in 1948 which met an important need for education on the island.

The Church of God movement spread to the mainland when an English-speaking congregation was organized at La Ceiba in 1951-1953. During the next few years several new churches were established in the Bay Islands and on the northern coast of Honduras. By 1960 there were five churches and four missions in the Bay Islands with 169 baptized members and 408 adherents, while on the mainland two churches and two missions had been established with 63 members.

The Church of God - Cleveland was also established in the interior of Honduras by Josue Rubio beginning in 1950. Rubio, a native of northwestern Mexico, arrived in Tegucigalpa and began door-to-door visitation. In 1951 a small congregation was formed in his home. It soon became the first Church of God in the capital, with 53 members. By 1960 there were 24 churches and 10 missions under the supervision of the Church of God in the Central Mountain Region of Honduras, with 1,054 members and about 2,150 adherents.

The most significant growth had occurred in the Departments of Copan and Barbara, located in the rugged mountain country along the border with Guatemala. Repeated visits to this region after 1952 resulted in the formation of many new congregations, with the revival spreading into Guatemala during the period 1956-1958. Because of this growth, a new district of the Church of God was formed along the border in 1958. In 1960, 15 churches had been organized in Copan Department with 734 members and 1,505 adherents, while in the neighboring Department of Santa Barbara, four churches reported 156 members and about 300 adherents.

Throughout Honduras in 1960, the Church of God - Cleveland reported 32 churches and 10 missions, which had increased to 59 churches and 29 missions by 1970. During the same period, membership increased from 1,279 to 2,100 under the leadership of lay pastors who had little formal pastoral or theological training. In 1978 there were 144 churches and 74 missions with a combined membership of 4,548. Between 1965 and 1978, the Church of God grew at an annual rate of 9.9% (AAGR).

Another Pentecostal denomination, the International Church of the Foursquare Gospel, arrived in Honduras in 1951 and began an evangelistic ministry in the capital. By 1960 the work had spread to the Departments of Cortes, La Paz, Santa Barbara and Valle in addition to Francisco Morazan where Tegucigalpa is located. At this time, seven churches and 18 preaching points had been established, with 310 baptized members and about 1,000 adherents. By 1970 the total membership had increased to 1,109 and by 1977 it was 1,870. Part of this growth can be attributed to a strong Central Church in Comayaguela, where a Bible institute program has provided training for lay pastors.

Other large Pentecostal denominations include; the Church of God of Prophecy with 41 churches and 1,063 members; the Philadelphia Church, founded by Pentecostal missionaries from Sweden, with 14 churches and 1,200 members; the Pentecostal Church of God from Puerto Rico, with 42 churches and 1,800 members; and the Free Pentecostal Church of God, which is reported to have 80 churches and about 3,500 members.

During the 1970s, when the Catholic Charismatic Movement began to grow among the upper classes in Tegucigalpa, several new "ecumenical" groups were formed (fellowship groups of Catholics and Protestants). These groups have experienced significant growth, especially among young people and members of the business community, including the following: the Christian Love Brigade Association, led by Mario Fumero with four churches, four missions, and about 500 members; the Christian Center of Charismatic Renewal, pastored by Dr. Fernando Nieto, with two centers and about 500 members; Grupos de Amor Viviente (Living Love Groups), led by Edward King

who is related to the Eastern Mennonite Board for Missions and Charities. Approximately 700 people have been attending 15 Bible study and fellowship groups. Mennonite groups in San Pedro Sula and La Ceira also have a Charismatic emphasis.

## ROMAN CATHOLIC MISSIONS

Catholicism was introduced in Honduras when two Franciscan priests accompanied the first colonists in 1521 and began converting the Indians. The territory of Honduras, originally included in the Bishopric of Mexico, became independent in 1527. The systematic conversion of the Indians began in 1548 with the arrival of the Mercyite Missionary Order. The Franciscans who came to Honduras in 1574 are credited with firmly implanting Catholicism during the next two centuries.

The power and influence achieved by the Church during the Colonial era was restricted by the liberal reforms of the Independence period (1821- 1838). Severe restrictions were placed on the monastic orders, leaving only the parish priests to care for the spiritual needs of the people. Although the anti-clerical movement was strong throughout Central America at this time, its effects were less extreme in Honduras. The exodus of clergy and the emptying of the seminaries left the masses with few clergy to instruct them in the Catholic Faith. However, after 1838, most of the anti-clerical laws were revoked or ignored and Roman Catholicism became the religion of the State, to the exclusion of all others.

In 1880 Honduras again came under the control of liberal anti-clerical elements, and the constitution of that year granted complete religious freedom. Subsequent constitutions extended the scope of the attack on the privileges of the Church, culminating in the 1936 Constitution which provided for the separation of Church and State, and free exercise of all religions while prohibiting monastic orders, government subsidies to religious orders, and religious instruction in public schools. The 1957 Constitution removed the prohibitions, but it retained complete religious freedom, and the separation of Church and State, while prohibiting political activity on the part of the clergy.

Catholic personnel from the United States totaled 76 in 1979, including 19 Jesuit Fathers, 10 Franciscans and Capuchins, 11 other men and 35 sisters. Canadian Catholic personnel totaled 96 for a combined total of 172 from North America.

## MAJOR CHRISTIAN ACTIVITIES

### EVANGELISM

As elsewhere in Central America, mass evangelism in Honduras got off to a slow start in terms of large broad-based interdenominational efforts. No known campaigns of this kind took place in Honduras prior to the 1950's, perhaps due to the strong anti-Protestant climate among the nation's Roman Catholic clergy. But in 1952, many evangelical churches in Tegucigalpa supported evangelist Ernesto Leon of Laredo, Texas in a crusade sponsored by the Latin America Mission.

However, the most notable campaign in Honduran history took place in 1963-1964 during the Evangelism-in-Depth program sponsored by Latin America Mission. Fourteen denominations and a total of 296 local congregations participated in this united evangelistic effort. The results of this year-long school of evangelism spoke for themselves. Nearly 15,000 Honduran believers met regularly in 2,500 prayer cells, asking God to bring revival to His Church and salvation to the unconverted. During month-long institutes, over 6,000 laymen were trained to equip and mobilize the Honduran Church as witnesses of the power of God to transform lives through the simple preaching of the gospel. Over 75,000 homes were visited during several weeks of door-to-door visitation by trained workers. Over 5,000 individuals made professions of faith as a result of personal visits, evangelistic crusades in outlying areas or the large crusades in Tegucigalpa and San Pedro Sula. Evangelist Fernando Vangioni of Argentina preached to audiences of 1,000 or more during two-weeks of final campaigns. Churches in San Pedro Sula reported that their membership had doubled as a result of the crusades, while later reports indicated that at least 100 new congregations were formed during the Evangelism-in-Depth program in Honduras.

In the early 1970s, several large crusades were held by the Luis Palau Team. Radio and television programs aired during the crusades provided favorable public exposure to the growing evangelical movement. The image of evangelicals was greatly enhanced during that time.

Luis Palau held a crusade in San Pedro Sula in 1970, followed by another one in Tegucigalpa in 1971. Some critics have stated that the Palau meetings did not have broad backing among evangelicals, particularly the Pentecostals. Palau's local sponsor was the Central American Mission (CAM International) which was commemorating their 75th anniversay of ministry in Honduras. Total attendance at these crusades was 80,000. About this time another crusade was held with Hermano Pablo (Paul Finkenbinder) under the sponsorship of the Assemblies of God, although other Pentecostal denominations also participated.

In March 1980 the Full Gospel Businessmen held a banquet for business and professional people in Tegucigalpa, with Astronaut Charles Duke as the guest speaker. This and similar meetings in Tegucigalpa and San Pedro Sula have resulted in the conversion of many upper class Hondurans. Consequently, dozens of small Bible study groups have been formed. They are continuing to grow in size and number as others are attracted to the Charismatic movement. Some individuals have remained members of the Roman Catholic Church, while others have joined Evangelical churches. But many attend neither Catholic nor Protestant churches, preferring rather to participate in home Bible studies led by Charismatic leaders. Few of the new converts feel comfortable or welcome in many conservative evangelical churches, especially those of non-Pentecostal backgrounds. However, the Charismatic Movement in Honduras is apparently not as strong as similar movements in Guatemala and Costa Rica.

### BROADCASTING

In 1960 the Conservative Baptists established the first and only Evangelical radio station in Honduras: HRVC, the "Voice of Honduras." Broadcasting began on shortwave, but mediumwave was added in 1965. Many different denominations use the station to broadcast their own programs, which can be heard in many parts of the country.

Evangelicals also broadcast programs on at least a dozen commercial stations all over Honduras. There are also several evangelical T.V. programs on stations in Tegucigalpa which are produced locally (Christian Love Brigades and the Center for Charismatic Renewal), while other programs are produced in the USA in Spanish: 700 Club, PTL Club and Elmer Bueno Presents.

### LITERATURE

Since the literacy rate in Honduras is less than 50%, distribution of Christian literature is limited. Christians are therefore aware of the need to begin with literacy materials which encourage people to learn to read and write. This is being done by at least 10 different evangelical organizations in Honduras. Literacy classes are also being aired on radio HRVC. Alfalit of Honduras specializes in literacy and provides excellent materials and training for other organizations.

There are at least 13 Christian bookstores in Honduras including at least five in the capital, four in La Ceiba, two in San Pedro Sula, and one each in San Marcos (Ocotepegul), Siguatepeque and Brus Laguna (Gracias a Dios).

Christian films are available from at least four evangelical groups.

## BIBLE TRANSLATION AND DISTRIBUTION

Over the years, the distribution of the Scriptures has increased and particularly since the formation of the Area Office by the American Bible Society in 1969. This office is under the management of the Rev. Saul Gomez Diaz, a promotor of the Bible Society since 1958. The office has been responsible for distribution in Honduras, El Salvador and Nicaragua. In 1974, the Honduran Bible Society became a legal corporation, and became an associate member of the United Bible Societies in 1979.

Bibles, New Testaments, portions and selections are available in Spanish and English; and the New Testament, in Miskito. Portions are also available in Miskito and Carib. However, no translations have yet been completed in Jicaque, Paya and Sumo for the smaller tribes of Honduras. The larger tribes, except for the Miskito, have been acculturated to the extent that Spanish is their first language. The following statistics give an overview of recent distribution:

| | | |
|---|---|---|
| Bibles | | 24,987 |
| New Testaments | | 13,261 |
| Portions | | 100,229 |
| Selections | | 761,131 |
| New Reader | | |
| Selections | | 646,595 |
| | | --------- |
| Totals | 1980 | 1,546,203 |
| | 1975 | 1,523,161 |

This distribution is partly due to special denominational efforts, and also to the popularity of new versions among both Protestants and Catholics. The Good News Bible in Spanish has the official seal of approval from the Roman Catholic Church. Free distribution programs were carried out among students, prisoners, and refugees from neighboring countries (Salvadorans and Nicaraguans). The Gideons International have annually distributed a total of 30,000 New Testaments in jails, hospitals, hotels, educational centers and among army personnel. Bible Society promoters visited local churches, annual assemblies, conventions, retreats, etc., to tell about the work of the Society and to stimulate the distribution of the Scriptures. Special Penzotti training courses were offered in 1980, with the participation of 450 people from 15 denominations, to teach them how to develop an effective program. The Women's Auxiliary, called "Women in Action," actively supports the work of the Bible Society, helping with fund raising as well as distribution of materials. Interest in Scripture distribution is obviously growing among churches and their leaders.

## EDUCATION

Christian. The organization of primary and secondary schools by missionaries in Honduras was no doubt stimulated by the widespread illiteracy of the general population, especially in rural areas. Even today, at least half the people cannot read or write. By 1935, at least four denominations had primary schools, and the Evangelical and Reformed Church (ERC) operated the only evangelical secondary school at San Pedro Sula. Soon, other denominations launched educational projects, including the Friends in Ocotepeque and the Central American Mission (CAM International) in Siguatepeque.

By 1960 Protestants had organized at least 12 primary and two secondary schools in Honduras, with CAM International and the ERC being the dominant groups in education. Today, there are at least 12 kindergartens, 27 primary schools, nine secondary schools and three vocational schools operated by many denominations.

Theological. Formal theological education apparently got off to a slow start in Honduras. In 1935 only two groups -- the Friends in Tegucigalpa and the ERC in Santa Barbara -- had training programs for ministerial candidates at the Bible Institute level. By 1960, Bible Institutes had been established by CAM International, the ERC, the Assemblies of God, the Foursquare Church, the World Gospel Mission and the Southern Baptist Convention. In 1978 there were eight programs of theological education-by-extension, 15 Bible institutes and at least one seminary-level program operated by the Southern Baptists.

## SOCIAL CONCERNS

Community and Rural Development. At least a dozen denominations and service agencies are currently operating programs of this nature. While some denominations have developed their own programs, others work with CEDEN (the Evangelical Committee for Relief and Development), to promote development projects among their fellow Hondurans.

Medicine and Public Health. The evangelical hospital at Siguatepeque, operated by CAM International, is well known in Honduras. It was the only hospital run by Protestants in 1935, although at least six clinics had been established by several denominations. Today, there are a dozen clinics, three public health programs and two hospitals (CAM International and Adventist) sponsored by evangelical groups in Honduras.

Other Social Ministries. Christian camping has developed rapidly in recent years. Fifteen or more campgrounds or camping programs have been established by Evangelicals, especially for children and youth. In addition to providing needed recreational programs and facilities, Christian camping provides many opportunities for personal and social development.

Several specialized youth ministries are working with the high school and university students. In Tegucigalpa, the Christian Love Brigades and the Living Love Groups have special programs for the rehabilitation of young people with drug problems. Campus Crusade for Christ (Alfa y Omega), Inter-Varsity, MINAMUNDO, and the Southern Baptist Convention have a special interest in university students. MINAMUNDO workers are assisting local churches in northern Honduras by providing a variety of youth programs.

Some evangelical denominations operate nutrition programs, childcare centers and orphanages to help meet the special needs of children in Honduras. However, few centers for the elderly have been established by Evangelicals in Honduras.

ECUMENICAL RELATIONSHIPS

The Evangelical Alliance of Honduras, formed in 1959, was strong in the early 1960s during the years of the Evangelism-in-Depth program. However, the Alliance has tended to be a fairly weak organization, mainly dedicated to representing the evangelical community before the Honduran government in matters relating to religious education, taxes, customs duties, etc.

Prior to 1959 an inter-mission committee served a similar function, as well as establishing comity agreements and encouraging united witness. The general effectiveness of the Alliance has declined in recent years, due to the withdrawal of several member organizations and to the inherent difficulties of coordinating united efforts among diverse groups. There were 17 member organizations active in the Alliance in 1980. A recent activity of the Alliance has been to sponsor interdenominational pastors' conferences for mutual inspiration and training.

A new organization called CEDEN was formed in 1974, following the disastrous Hurricane Fifi. Many denominations and service organizations prefer to work with and through CEDEN to accomplish the same or similar goals that formerly were handled by the Alliance. CEDEN has about 30 member organizations.

GENERAL SERVICE ORGANIZATIONS

The Evangelcal Committee for Relief and Development (CEDEN) is a broad-based organization that draws support from at least 30 denominations and evangelical agencies in Honduras. Temporary relief committees had been formed by evangelicals to aid refugees during the war with El Salvador in 1969, to assist in earthquake relief in Managua in 1972 and to care for survivors of Hurricane Fifi on the northern coast of Honduras in 1974. In response to these emergencies, as well as to growing social concerns among evangelicals, CEDEN was organized on a permanent basis. Its present programs include: agricultural and community development, well-digging, public health, leadership training, communications and audio-visuals. The organization of regional committees and branch offices have given CEDEN a strong grass-roots support among Evangelicals throughout the country. Branch offices are located in San Pedro Sula, La Ceiba, Choluteca and Ocotepeque in addition to the main office in Tegucigalpa.

Missionary Aviation Fellowship (MAF) entered Honduras in 1949 to provide air service and support to existing evangelical organizations. MAF operates out of bases in Siguatepeque, Ahuas and Tegucigalpa. Service is provided to about 70 airfields in remote areas of Honduras, where low fares assist Evangelicals in the work of the ministry. However, about half of the total flying time is devoted to ambulance service. Presently, MAF operates four small planes and a helicopter in Honduras.

World Vision International is new to Honduras (1978-1979) but is now sponsoring about 25 projects throughout the country. The childcare programs benefited about

3,000 children during 1979-1980. The number of relief and development projects is growing. Cooperative efforts have been established with CEDEN, ALFALIT, the Evangelical Alliance and other service organizations in Honduras. Special attention is now being given to the growing problem of Salvadoran refugees who are fleeing across the border into Honduras to escape the violence and destruction of the civil war in El Salvador. During early 1981, in a coordinated effort by World Vision, the U.N. High Commission on Refugees and the Red Cross, refugee camps were established close to the border to provide food, clothing, shelter and spiritual care for about 25,000 refugees.

## NATION AND ITS PEOPLE

### POPULATION

The total population of Honduras, estimated at 3.9 million in 1981, is in a state of constant change due to migration of refugees. Urban areas are growing at approximately 5.2% per year while the entire nation grows at 2.8% per year. Even so, most of the residents live in rural areas. The valleys and plateaus between the major mountain ranges support the largest number of people. The coastal areas which have previously had sparse populations, are growing more rapidly than ever before.

### COMPOSITION

"Latinos" is a term used to refer to individuals of any racial mixture who have assumed many aspects of the dominant Hispanic-American culture. In Honduras, Latinos are descendants of Spaniards, Indians and Negroes who intermarried. They comprise 90% of the population.

Indigenous Indian groups in Honduras comprise 7% of the total population. The Lencas are the largest group with approximately 70% of all Indians. Most of them inhabit the mountainous regions of the southwest. Though they reflect cultural patterns similar to the Mayas, they speak Spanish, practice a syncretistic form of Catholicism and have become acculturated to the lifestyles of Latinos.

Several thousand Chorti Indians inhabit the forest-covered hills of western Honduras. They are part of a large people group which traverses national boundaries. Chorti reside in Guatemala as well as Honduras.

A small group of Pipil Indians of Mexican origin live near the border of El Salvador. Other smaller groups include: 3,000 Jicaque, 28,000 Miskito and several thousand Sumo along the rivers and coastal areas, and 300 Paya. The latter three groups believe in a remote deity who has little control over the events on earth, and in numerous spirits which indwell objects. Historically, they have practiced polygamy.

Black Caribs are descendants of African slaves who intermarried with Red Carib Indians of St. Vincent Island. The British government deported a large number of them to the island of Roatan in 1797 from which some migrated to the mainland. They were exposed to Catholicism but retained many elements of African traditional religions and continued to practice polygamy. Approximately 70,000 Black Caribs reside along the northern coastal regions.

English speaking blacks and a few white expatriates populate the Bay Islands. Many are becoming bilingual and adapting themselves to Latino cultural patterns or formulating new ones.

A small group of Turks, Syrians and other emigrants of Middle Eastern nations have played a significant role in commerce and small business. Cultural traditions have been modified as generations have passed.

### LANGUAGE AND LITERACY

The literacy rate is less than 50% despite free and compulsory education. Anyone who lives more than 3 kilometers (2 miles) from school is excused from attending. Thus thousands of families who live in remote farm areas do not send their children to school.

Spanish is the official national language of Honduras. Many individuals are bilingual since they retain an Indian dialect or English.

### RELIGION

Nominal Roman Catholics comprise 92% of the total Honduran population. Though Catholicism is intertwined with cultural traditions, attendance and involvement in church activities is minimal. Financial limitations and lack of committed personnel have restricted the efforts of Catholic churches. Significant changes have occurred within the church structure. The Charismatic movement within the Catholic Church, which began in the 1970's, has provided hope and vitality for members who do not want to leave the established church.

Protestants comprised 8% of the national population in 1980. The largest denominations were the Seventh-day Adventist, Plymouth Brethren, Moravian and Assemblies of God.

Remnants of traditional Indian spirit worship exist among indigeneous groups. African religions are evident, particularly among the Black Caribs.

## GEOGRAPHY AND CLIMATE

Honduras is the second largest republic in Central America with an area of 112,088 square kilometers (43,244 square miles). Over 80% of the land surface is mountainous. There are two distinct series of mountain ranges. The northern ranges are extensions of the Central American Cordillera, a mountain chain that stretches from Mexico to Nicaragua. One extension of these, offshore on the north coast, forms the Bay Islands. The southern area is elevated with a series of mountain ranges called the Volcanic Highlands. Valleys, savannas and plateaus between the mountains provide the only arable land except for the northern coastal region.

The north coast and Pacific Coastal Plains are classified as tropical. Between 175 and 250 centimeters (70 and 100 inches) of rain falls annually in the northern coastal areas and 150 to 200 centimeters (60 to 80 inches) in the Pacific Coastal Plains. Average humidity hovers around 84%. Mean annual temperatures range from 26 to 28 degrees C (79 to 82 degrees F) in the coastal areas and 19 to 23 degrees C (67 to 74 degrees F) in the mountains.

## HISTORY

The Mayans were the first inhabitants of Honduras to leave any records. Spaniards arrived in the early 16th century to explore the area. Gold and silver were discovered in the central mountain region and extensive mining with forced Indian labor provided wealth for rulers and explorers. Honduras gained independence from Spain in 1821 but remained a part of Mexico and then the United Provinces of Central America until 1839.

In 1839 a national assembly adopted the Republic's first constitution and a president was elected in 1840. Instability has marked the Republic's history with 12 different constitutions and more than 90 changes in leadership since the time of independence. Great Britain was involved in many national affairs during the 1800's and particularly in the Bay Islands. United States corporations played a major role in the development of banana industries.

## GOVERNMENT AND POLITICAL CONDITIONS

The government is highly centralized with most authority concentrated in the hands of the president. On December 4, 1972, the military took over the presidency of Honduras. On April 22, 1975, as the result of a decision by the Army Forces High Command, another military government assumed the responsibilities of governing Honduras. On May 31, 1978, Decree 633 was published, calling for the election of the National Constituent Assembly and on August 7, 1978, the Army Forces High Command named a ruling Junta consisting of three military officers which took responsibilities of ruling the country. On April 20, 1980, elections were held in order to form the National Assembly which was duly sworn into office on July 20, 1980. On the 25th of the same month the National Assembly named as Constitutional Provisional President of Honduras, General Policarpo Paz Garcia, the Commanding General of the Armed Forces.

The National Assembly established a new Constitution for Honduras in 1981. It contains the laws that govern Presidential and National Assembly elections.

## ECONOMY

Approximately 50% of the total land area is forested. Between 31% and 38% is suitable for pasture or cultivation. Land tenancy is characterized by many small holdings and a few very large holdings, the latter primarily along the Caribbean lowlands. The government owns 30% of the land.

Most agricultural production is accomplished without mechanization. Bananas, grown along the north coast, are Honduras' main export. Coffee is the second most important crop. Nearly 75% of all exports are agricultural products, and of these, 75% are bananas.

Industrial development has increased since 1940 as interaction and involvement of the Central American Common Market increased. Limited fossil fuels and few energy resources have hampered industrial growth. Only 15% of the homes had electricity in 1979.

All persons over 10 years old are considered to be part of the labor force. By this definition 40% are economically active with 60% in agriculture, 12% in services, 8% in manufacturing, 4.5% in commerce and the rest in mining, construction, communications, public utitilies and transportation.

The autonomous Central Bank of Honduras has extensive power and control of the monetary and credit system. It issues currency, sets interest rates and establishes foreign exchange rates which in 1979 equaled two lempira (peso) per $1 U.S.

## CHURCH STATISTICS FOR HONDURAS

NOTE: Statistics are from the 1978 PROCADES survey of Protestant Churches and are based on official denominational reports or estimates. Although definitions of membership vary slightly among churches, the data is highly comparable and reliable. All known churches are included in this list.

| Church or Mission Name | Number of Congregations | Membership | % of Total |
|---|---|---|---|
| PROTESTANT | | | |
| Liturgical | 17 | 1,724 | 2.2% |
| Episcopal Church | 12 | 1,615 | |
| Evangelical Lutheran | 5 | 109 | |
| Evangelical Non-Pentecostal | 831 | 35,218 | 45.7% |
| Baptist Assoc. of Mosquitia | 30 | 1,290 | |
| Brethren Assemblies | 120 | 7,200 | |
| Central American Churches | 132 | 3,320 | |
| Conservative Baptist Assoc. | 97 | 1,420 | |
| Evang. Holiness Church | 90 | 4,221 | |
| Evangelical and Reformed | 24 | 3,500 | |
| Moravian | 37 | 6,229 | |
| National Baptist Convention | 90 | 2,172 | |
| United Brethren in Christ | 32 | 1,382 | |
| Pentecostal | 907 | 29,922 | 38.9% |
| Assemblies of God | 196 | 5,909 | |
| Church of God - Cleveland | 218 | 4,548 | |
| Church of God of Prophecy | 41 | 1,063 | |
| Foursquare Church | 31 | 1,870 | |
| Pentecostal Church of God | 44 | 1,802 | |
| Pentecostal Free Church of God | 80 | 3,500 | |
| Philadelphia Church (Swedish) | 14 | 1,200 | |
| Prince of Peace Association | 125 | 4,000 | |
| Others | 159 | 6,030 | |
| Adventist | 114 | 10,190 | 13.2% |
| Seventh-day Adventist | 108 | 9,933 | |
| Others | 6 | 257 | |
| TOTALS (1978) | 1,869 | 77,054 | |

The sources listed below are to help the reader find additional information on this country and Christian ministries there.  This list does not try to be comprehensive or complete.

DOCUMENTS

General

Blutstein, Howard I.  et al, Area Handbook for Honduras.  Washington, D.C:
    U.S. Government Printing Office, 1971.

Conzemius, Eduard, Ethnographical Survey of the Miskito and Sumo Indians of Honduras
    and Nicaragua, Washington, D.C: U.S. Government Printing Office, 1932.

Helms, Mary and Loveland, Franklin O.  editors, Frontier Adaptations in Lower Central
    America, "Black Carib (Garifuna) Habitats in Central America," by William
    Davidson, Philadelphia: Institute for the Study of Human Issues, 1976.

Solien, Nancie L.  (Gonzales), Black Carib Household Structure: A Study of Migration
    and Modernization, Seattle: University of Washington Press, 1969.

Von Hage, Wolfgang, The Jicaque Indians of Honduras, New York: Heye Foundation,1943.

Christian

Bushong, Thelma, "The History of WGM in Honduras." Tegucigalpa, Honduras: Typewritten
    manuscript, World Gospel Mission, 1959.

Caceres, Oscar, "Ensayo Historico Parcial del Movimiento Protestante de Honduras." San
    Jose, Costa Rica; Unpublished thesis, Latin American Biblical Seminary, 1966.

Enyart, Paul, Friends in Central America, So. Pasadena, CA: William Carey Library,
    1970.

Mathews, Edward, "Planting the Church in Honduras: The Development of a Culturally
    Relevant Witness." Unpublished Thesis, Pasadena, CA: School of World Mission,
    Fuller Theological Seminary, 1970.

Mulholland, Kenneth B., Adventures in Training the Ministry: A Honduran Case Study in
    Theological Education by Extension, Presbyterian Reformed Publishing Company,
    1976.

"Directorio de Iglesias, Organizaciones y Ministerios del Movimiento
    Protestante: Honduras." San Jose, Costa Rica: Unpublished manuscript, PROCADES,
    1980.

ORGANIZATIONS

    CEDEN (Evangelical Committee for Relief and Development), Apartado 1478,
        Tegucigalpa

    Evangelical Alliance of Honduras, Apartado 1478, Tegucigalpa

    Honduran Bible Society, Apartado 747, Tegucigalpa

    Missionary Aviation Fellowship, Apartado T-227, Zona Toncontin, Tegucigalpa

    World Vision Office for Honduras, P.O.  Box, 97-C, Tegucigalpa

## ACKNOWLEDGMENTS

The information in this profile was taken from many sources which were the best available to the editors at the time of preparation.  However, the accuracy of the information cannot be guaranteed.  Views expressed or implied in this publication are not necessarily those of World Vision.  The editors have tried to present the ministries of various organizations in an objective manner, without undue bias or emphasis.  Where we have failed, we apologize for erroneous impressions that may result and request that comments and corrections be directed to MARC, 919 West Huntington Drive, Monrovia, CA. 91016, U.S.A.  We appreciate and acknowledge the comments and contributions of various organizations and individuals in the preparation of this publication.

# STATUS OF CHRISTIANITY COUNTRY PROFILE

# NICARAGUA

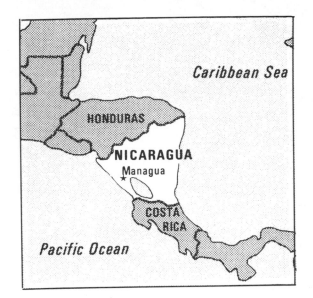

## SUMMARY

AREA - 147,900 square kilometers (49,163 square miles)

POPULATION - 2.5 million (1980)

RELIGION - 86% Roman Catholic, 12% Protestant, 2% Other

In July 1979, Nicaragua entered a new period of her history when the Sandinista Front of National Liberation (FSLN) succeeded in ousting the government of General Anastasio Somoza. Many Nicaraguan Christians, both Catholic and Protestant, not only actively supported the popular insurrection that deposed the Somoza regime, but have taken an active role in the new government at various levels. Several Catholic priests are Cabinet members in the National Reconstruction Government. One other Cabinet minister recently requested Bibles to be given to those who finished literacy training. Many Christians have served in worker's organizations and reconstruction projects, including the recent mass literacy campaign.

However, some Christians voice concern about the government's leftist leanings and its close relationships with the Cubans and the Soviets. Nevertheless, the government continues to allow religious liberty for all Nicaraguans. Consequently, the Protestant Church is still growing at an impressive rate of 12.5% annually.

## PEOPLE GROUPS

### AMERINDIANS (3.5% or 81,000)

Nicaragua's Hispanicized Indians (approximately 35,000) have largely adopted Roman Catholicism. The Matagalpas (18,000-20,000) form the largest group and are found in the Central Highlands, within the Departments of Matagalpa and Jinotega. The Matagalpas are sedentary subsistence farmers who occasionally work for wages on coffee plantations in the region. Most Matagalpas are nominal Catholics, but, unlike the "Latinos," it is the men who are more active in religious activities than the women. Local Catholic associations for aiding work in the parish are usually composed almost entirely of men. It is not known what type of Protestant activity, if any, occurs among the Matagalpas.

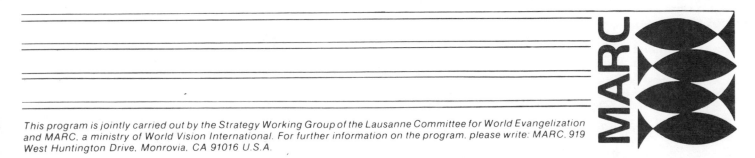

This program is jointly carried out by the Strategy Working Group of the Lausanne Committee for World Evangelization and MARC, a ministry of World Vision International. For further information on the program, please write: MARC, 919 West Huntington Drive, Monrovia, CA 91016 U.S.A.

The Subtiaba (5,000) and Monimbo (10,000) have retained few traits of their former pre-conquest Indian culture. Although most members of these two Indian groups are nominal Catholics, special importance is given to some Catholic rites, such as baptism. The Assemblies of God reported many believers among the Subtiaba, but only a few among the Monimbo. The United Brethren in Christ also have baptized a few among the Monimbo, and the Baptist International Mission has an ordained Monimbo pastor.

The Miskitos (40,000) and the Sumos (3,000) are largely reached. About half of these groups are reported to be Protestant adherents, especially among the Moravians. Many Protestant denominations now have churches and service ministries among the Miskito and Sumo, who now have strong indigenous churches with good evangelical leadership. Some Miskito and Sumo evangelists are also reaching out to the growing mestizo population that has steadily increased over the years, especially in the highlands of Zelaya Department.

The Rama and the Black Caribs, also living in the Department of Zelaya, are two small Amerindian groups that have maintained a high degree of cultural autonomy, and who are largely unreached. Although considered nominal Catholics, Animistic beliefs and practices appear to dominate their religious beliefs. The Rama Indians (600-1,000) now live in a few small villages on Rama Cay, near Bluefields, in the Coastal Lowlands where they subsist as hunters, small farmers and fishermen. They speak mostly Creole, with only a few older people speaking their native language. Only the Moravians have work among them.

The Black Caribs (2,000) live in several small villages along the shores of Pearl Lagoon, where they engage in subsistence agriculture and fishing. They are descendants of the Red Carib people who intermarried with escaped Negro slaves on the island of St. Vincent in the West Indies, and who were deported by the British to the Bay Islands of Honduras in the 1790s. Most have retained their traditional culture and language, although some speak Creole or English. The Moravians, Episcopalians and Catholics have churches among them, but most Black Caribs practice a mixture of African and Indian animism, overlaid with Catholic religious practices. Although some are nominal Christians, either Catholics or Protestants, most can be considered animists.

## Negroes and mulattoes (9%)

Afro-Americans in Nicaragua are ethnically diverse, but they are predominantly Protestant. The English-speaking Negroes and mulattoes, called Creoles, trace their origins to the British colonies in the West Indies. Large-scale migration of West Indians to Central America began about 1850 for railroad construction in Panama, then in Costa Rica and Honduras during the 1880s. After completing these construction projects, many West Indian laborers migrated along the Caribbean coast where they became workers on banana plantations, farmed coconuts and cocao, or became fishermen or dock workers. There are a few French-speaking Negroes in Nicaragua, in addition to the Spanish-speaking descendants of slaves who were brought to Nicaragua during the Spanish colonial period.

The latter two ethnic groups within the Negro population are basically Roman Catholics, whereas the majority of the English-speaking Negroes are nominal Protestants. However, remnants of African spiritism still exist among some Afro-Americans – Obeah, Poccmania, Myalism and Vodun – mixed with elements of Christianity. Although many Creoles are nominal Protestants, their Christian faith is similar to that of many mestizos who are nominal Catholics.

## Latinos (86%)

The mestizo and white racial groups amount to about 86% of the total population. Culturally, they are Latinos, bearers of Hispanic heritage. They are nominally Roman Catholic, but only about 15-20% practice their faith by attending Mass and participating in the sacraments. Few males attend church services, since religion is considered more appropriate for women. Men cannot be expected to conform to all the moral standards taught by the Church, it is argued; since these standards conflict with the popular male image of "machismo" (masculinity). Greater religious indifference is found among Latinos of the upper and middle classes in urban areas in the Pacific Coastal Region, although more participation is noted in the Central Highlands.

Latinos now account for about 70% of all Protestant church members, up from 39% in 1960. Spanish-speaking Protestants now number about 196,000 adherents, which is approximately 9% of all Latinos. Most recent Protestant growth has been among the Latino component of the population. At the present growth rate, about 26% of the total population will be Protestant by

## Other Religious Groups (2%)

The Church of Jesus Christ of Latter-Day Saints (Mormons) includes 13 "branches" with 3,091 adherents, while the Jehovah's Witnesses reported 68 congregations and 12,080 adherents, of whom 3,338 had attained the rank of "publishers." Bahai missionaries were active along the Caribbean coast during the 1960s, but few Bahai groups remain. Small groups of Lebanese and Arabs have existed along the Atlantic coast for many years, but most of them have left Nicaragua since the Sandinista Revolution. There is a small Jewish community of 200-300 people, the majority of whom live in Managua.

It is difficult to measure the extent of Marxist influence since the 1979 civil war, but it is assumed that more people are now open to Marxist-Leninist doctrine than ever before and that significant numbers of nominal Catholics, especially young Nicaraguans, will be influenced by it through the public schools. However, there has been some negative reaction against atheistic teaching by Cubans during the literacy campaign in 1979, notably among rural Nicaraguans. Although the National Reconstruction Government guarantees the freedom of religion, the teaching of atheism and evolution are also guaranteed freedom of expression by the constituition. This may become a source of further tension during the next decade as reconstruction efforts continue.

Roman Catholicism has been the dominant religion in western Nicaragua since the Spanish colonial period. The majority of the population in the Central Highlands and the Pacific Coastal Region are mestizos and are "nominal" Catholics; however, only 15-20% of all Catholics actually practice their faith. Women are more actively involved in Catholic activities than men.

Although Catholic sources in Nicaragua claim 93% of the total population as baptized Roman Catholics, a recent religious survey indicates that only about 86% can be considered Catholic adherents. The size of the Protestant community increased from 4% in 1950 to more than 12% in 1980. About 2% of the population are neither Catholics nor Protestants. The number of Protestant adherents totaled about 281,000 in 1980, with 93,700 communicant members: an increase of 12.5% annually since 1966. Protestant communicants among the larger denominations were represented as follows: Moravians (16.5%), Assemblies of God (10.8%), Adventists (7.7%), Church of God - Cleveland (6.7%) and the Baptist Convention (5.9%). This indicates that 47.6% of all Protestant church members in Nicaragua belong to five groups.

Prior to 1900, most inhabitants of eastern Nicaragua were Amerindians who practiced Animism, or Creoles who were nominally Protestant. By 1936, however, at least 31% of the population of the department of Zelaya was Protestant. Many individuals belonged to Moravian congregations and a few to Anglican, Baptist or Adventist groups. More than 50% of the population of some sections of Zelaya were Protestant by 1960.

## RELIGIOUS COMPOSITION OF NICARAGUA

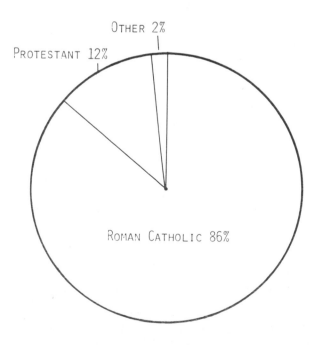

OTHER 2%

PROTESTANT 12%

ROMAN CATHOLIC 86%

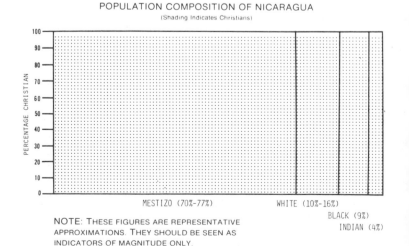

POPULATION COMPOSITION OF NICARAGUA
(Shading Indicates Christians)

PERCENTAGE CHRISTIAN

MESTIZO (70%-77%)   WHITE (10%-16%)
BLACK (9%)
INDIAN (4%)

NOTE: THESE FIGURES ARE REPRESENTATIVE APPROXIMATIONS. THEY SHOULD BE SEEN AS INDICATORS OF MAGNITUDE ONLY.

## NATIONAL CHURCHES

### PROTESTANT CHURCHES

Protestant growth was slow in Nicaragua prior to the mid-1960s. In 1937, only seven Protestant missions had begun labors on either coast. But by 1965, twenty-six Protestant groups were active in Nicaragua, and by 1978, forty-six new groups had been added. Today, there are at least 72 denominations and smaller independent groups working in the Republic. In 1978, over 1,500 Protestant congregations and missions were being served by at least 301 ordained national pastors, 760 unordained pastors and 83 Protestant missionaries (up from 41 missionaries in 1973).

The composition and growth rate of Protestant membership has shown notable changes over the years. Total membership in all Protestant congregations, missions and preaching points increased slowly between 1936 and 1950, from 6,242 to 10,521 (3.8% AAGR). The rate of membership growth increased to 4.1% AAGR in the period 1960-1966 (21,500 members in 1966). By 1978, the total Protestant membership reached 78,387 with a 12.5% AAGR between 1966 and 1978. The composition of the membership had changed from 75% "Costeno" (Indians and Creoles) and 25% "Latinos" (whites and mestizos) in 1936, to 62% Costeno and 38% Latino in 1966. Now, the total Protestant membership is 70% Latino and only 30% Costeno, which represents a drastic shift in the strength of Protestantism in Nicaragua during the past decade.

An overview of Protestant membership by families of denominations since 1950 reveals a notable shift in the type of church growth taking place among Protestants. Whereas the Pentecostal Family of Churches represented only 10% of all Protestants in 1950, this family had grown to 45% by 1978. The Evangelical Non-Pentecostal Family of Churches showed a proportional decline: from 83.1% in 1950 to 44.2% in 1978. The Adventist Family increased from 3.7% in 1950 to 7.8% in 1978, although Adventists represented 8.5% of all Protestant membership in 1966. The Liturgical Family of Churches, on the other hand, has shown little proportional change since 1950, when the Episcopal Church accounted for 3.3% of all communicants. By 1978, Episcopals and Lutherans totaled only 2.4% of all Protestant communicant members in Nicaragua.

An examination of annual rates of membership growth among Protestant families of denominations testifies to the vitality of Pentecostal expansion since 1950. Between 1950 and 1978, Pentecostals increased at 13.4% annually, compared to 5.1% for Evangelical Non-Pentecostals, 10.4% for Adventists and 6.1% for the Liturgical Family. The Pentecostals and Adventist Families have consistently shown more dynamic growth in Nicaragua since 1950 than other Protestant Families of Churches.

Under the Somoza regime, Protestant denominations benefitted from the principal of separation of Church and State, with the constitution guaranteeing religious freedom to all Nicaraguan citizens and to foreign residents. Consequently, most Protestant groups grew without hindrance, engaging in evangelistic activities and planting churches at will, supported by constitutional law and the power of civil authorities. The Nicaraguan police were occasionally called to protect Protestant missionaries or national believers from religious persecution by Catholic mobs, led by both Catholic laymen and clergy, who attempted to stop mass evangelistic activities. Protestants, in general, felt that the civil authorities were "ordained by God" for the common good and could be counted on for protection in time of crisis.

As a rule, Protestants abstained from assuming a critical stance toward the Somoza government, even though the National Guard increasingly used repression to try to stop political dissent. For many evangelicals, the revolutionary movement created a climate of fear, confusion and uncertainty, both for the present and the future. Nevertheless, some Protestants, especially young people, openly embraced the Sandinista cause; others adopted a more cautious "wait-and-see" attitude in an attempt to remain politically neutral; some even supported the Somoza government in passive obedience to the "powers that be."

During the months of insurrection and combat, the Evangelical Committee for Relief and Development (CEPAD), an interdenominational service organization that enjoys wide support among the evangelical community, played an important role in channeling aid to thousands of victims of the civil war during 1978 and 1979. After the National Reconstruction Government assumed power in July, 1979, CEPAD sponsored a national pastors' conference, with the participation of over 500 pastors and lay leaders. They drew up

a statement favorable to the programs of
the reconstruction government, but without
compromising their primary allegiance to
the Lord Jesus Christ. However there is
still a climate of uncertainty about the
direction in which the FSLN is heading.
This causes many evangelicals to proceed
with caution in the political arena,
hoping for a clear demonstration of the
promises made to the Nicaraguan public by
Sandinista leaders. But the evangelical
movement is making its presence felt in
revolutionary Nicaragua by actively
supporting many programs of the new
government.

## CATHOLIC CHURCHES

Catholicism was introduced to indigenous
Nicaraguans when Columbus arrived in 1502,
and it was established during the Spanish
Conquest of the 1520s. The first
Franciscan church was founded at Granada
in 1524. The Jesuits were leaders in
missionary work in Nicaragua during the
colonial period. Following the attainment
of independence by Nicaragua between
1821-1838, evangelization efforts by
Catholic missionaries greatly increased.
Except for a short period at the end of
the nineteenth century, Church-state
relations were generally good.

The Nicaraguan Catholic Church was
reorganized in 1913, with Managua as the
seat of the archbishopric. Nicaragua is
divided into four dioceses and one
apostolic vicariate in Bluefields, which
covers the missionary work of the
Franciscan Capuchins on the Atlantic
Coast. There are 190 parishes, about 390
Catholic churches, 304 priests (117
diocesan and 187 religious), 89 lay
brothers and 661 sisters. The Catholic
Church maintains about 275 schools and
over 90 charitable institutions.

Under the Somozas (1937-1979), the
Nicaraguan Catholic Church was not
constitutionally a state church. This did
not pose problems in its relationship to
the government. In fact, the Catholic
religion was recognized in practice and
received certain privileges. But in 1972
when 37 years of the church's acquiescence
toward the rule of the Somoza family
ended, Church-state relationships entered
a new phase.

In 1977, a pastoral letter by Nicaraguan
bishops condemned repressive activities of
the National Guard and particularly those
directed against peasants and political
dissidents. Archbishop Miguel Obando y
Bravo was an outspoken critic of the
abuses of the Somoza regime and a strong
supporter of democracy, human rights and
social justice.

However, the Church's strong human rights
stand made the government suspect it of
subversive activities. Somoza responded
by decreeing censorship on Church
broadcasts and publications. Though
religious liberty continued to be
respected formally, the National Guard
stepped up its harrassment of the clergy,
causing arbitrary detentions, expulsions
and even deaths.

In a pastoral letter after the FSLN came
to power in mid-1979, the archbishop urged
that all social structures in the new
Nicaragua be designed to promote human
dignity. Many Catholics, lay and clergy,
openly supported the revolutionary
struggle against the Somoza dictatorship.

Under the National Reconstruction
Government, a new phase of positive
relationships has begun between the Church
and State in Nicaragua. Three Catholic
priests are cabinet members in the
Sandinista government, specifically: the
Minister of Culture, Minister for Foreign
Relations and Minister of Social Welfare.
Officially, the Catholic Church has
supported new government programs aimed at
economic reconstruction and a massive
literacy program. Government spokesmen
have repeatedly assured the Nicaraguan
people that religious freedom will be
fully respected, and the new government
has ratified the International Declaration
of Human Rights. The new government's
image was greatly enhanced when Pope John
Paul II gave his approval of the
Sandinista Front's stated goals to build a
just society.

Nicaragua has a relatively small number of
priests compared to the size of the
population; only one per 7,483.
Consequently, the parish priests must not
only serve the larger Catholic population
of the main cities and towns but they must
also periodically visit a number of
smaller towns and rural villages to
celebrate the Mass and officiate at
special religious occasions. The diocesan
priests usually have little time to devote
to improving the quality of religious life
among the Catholic population. However,
the growth of Catholic lay organizations
has increased efforts aimed at more
serious study and meditation on the Bible.

**FOREIGN MISSIONS**

PROTESTANT MISSIONS

The earliest known Protestant missionary effort in Nicaragua was by an Anglican layman, Christian Frederick Post of Philadelphia, who received permission from the Miskito Indians to live among them during the mid-1700s. In 1767, Post was appointed catechist by the Society for the Propagation of the Gospel in Foreign Parts, and took up residence at Black River (Rio Sico) where a British settlement had existed since the 1730s. Several Anglican chaplains, sponsored by the Society, joined Post to labor on the Mosquito Coast. Several hundred Negroes, Miskitos and those of mixed races were baptized as Anglicans prior to 1785, when Post and other Europeans were forced to abandon the work because of hostilities with the Spanish.

Although there were few Anglican missionary efforts in Nicaragua between Post's departure and Britain's final withdrawal in 1860, it is significant that the Miskito king, George Augustus Frederick, was crowned by British authorities in 1825 at St. John's Cathedral in Belize City. The royal family, residing in Bluefields, requested the British to send chaplains and schoolmasters to instruct the Miskitos in the Christian faith. But despite earlier efforts, the first Anglican church was not built at Bluefields until 1896. Anglican work spread to other Creole communities along the Mosquito Coast and on the Corn Islands, as well as among Indian communities (Miskito, Sumo, Rama and Black Carib).

Since 1947, jurisdiction of Anglican work in Nicaragua was transferred to the American Protestant Episcopal Church, under the Missionary District of the Panama Canal Zone. Currently, the Episcopal Church has 16 churches, 1,800 communicants and a community of about 6,000, predominantly among Creoles.

The German Moravians sent their first missionaries to Nicaragua in 1849, invited by the Miskito king, Frederick. Early Anglican and weak Wesleyan Methodist efforts had been discontinued by this time, although a few Creole catechists carried on Anglican worship. By 1852, the first Moravian church in Nicaragua was constructed in Bluefields. At the official dedication of the church in 1855, the first Miskito convert was baptized. This led to intensified evangelistic efforts among the Indians north of

Bluefields in 1860. Work among the Miskitos grew noticeably after Moravian missionaries had acquired a basic knowledge of the Miskito dialect.

The period 1881-1900 was one of accelerated Moravian church growth due to the Great Revival of 1881 which resulted in thousands of conversions on the Mosquito Coast, not only among Creoles and Indians but also among the Hispanic population of the region. Moravian membership increased from 1,030 in 1881 to 3,294 in 1896.

Beginning in the 1920s, the American Moravians placed more emphasis on education in Nicaragua, believing that without it there could be little progress towards an indigenous national church. The missionaries and the Mission Board wisely saw that an indigenous church depended upon two principles: equipping believers to earn a better living in order to give more financial support to the national church, and building up national leadership so that foreign missionaries could be withdrawn from the field. The former task required the establishment of agricultural assistance programs and an industrial school, and the latter a more adequate program of Christian and theological education for training workers and ministers.

Administratively, Moravian work was operated as a mission province until the first District Church conference met in 1934. Originally, the field was served by German and British missionaries, but American Moravians were forced to take over the work during 1914-1918 due to World War I. Americans administered the Nicaraguan field until the 1960s. The Moravian Church is now under national leadership. In 1979, there were 12,950 communicants and a community of about 36,000 baptized Moravians among 120 congregations and numerous preaching points.

The earliest Baptist work was begun in the 1850s among the Creoles on the Corn Islands by the Jamaica Baptist Union. However, Baptist work was relatively isolated from the mainland of Nicaragua until Baptist churches were organized in Bluefields and Puerto Cabezas in 1922.

On the other hand, Baptists from the United States arrived on the Pacific coast prior to the 1920s. The First Baptist Church of Managua was organized in 1917. Baptist work soon spread throughout the Pacific Coastal Region during 1917-1920. By 1936, the Northern Baptists reported eight churches and 30 preaching points, with 960 members and 1,800 adherents. In this initial period of Baptist growth in the Pacific Region, there was a strong emphasis on evangelism and church planting among the Hispanic population. By 1937, when the Nicaraguan Baptist Convention was organized, 13 missionaries and eight national workers provided pastoral and lay leadership.

The relationship between missionaries and national leaders has been the source of many problems for the growing national churches. Several new churches have been formed following disagreements between missionaries and emerging national leaders.

The Baptist Convention, for instance, declined in strength between 1960 and 1967 because of the formation of the Association of Churches in Christ, which drew its leadership and members from the Baptists. The new group was an autonomous national church of Baptist convictions. This was basically a lay movement that grew out of the Baptist Convention as a reaction to missionary control and influence, as well as against the concept of professional ministers. With few exceptions, its pastors are not trained in seminaries or Bible institutes. They serve without salary and are appointed by their local congregations. By 1978 this Association had 46 churches, 15 missions and 1,877 baptized members.

Meanwhile, the Baptist Convention is now under indigenous national leadership and is self-supporting, although it still receives special assistance from the Board of International Ministries of the American Baptist Convention. In 1978, there were 46 churches and 128 missions and preaching points with 4,659 members. The annual membership growth rate has been 8.9% for the period of 1967-1978.

The Southern Baptist Convention has worked with the Nicaraguan Baptist Convention since 1968 by providing missionaries for literature and film distribution. A Baptist bookstore is also operated in Managua. However, the Southern Baptists are not engaged in church planting activities.

The National Evangelical Mission is an independent church body which split off from the Northern Baptists in 1930. Once more, tensions between missionaries and national leaders proved to be the primary cause of the split. The National Evangelical Mission adopted the policy of not receiving funds from outside Nicaragua, so that they would not be dependent on mission boards to determine policy or allot funds. In 1979, the National Evangelical Mission reported

eleven churches with a total membership of 570 people and an average attendance of 1,500.

The Baptist International Mission began its work in Nicaragua in 1959. By 1970 seven congregations had been formed in Managua, as well as a Bible institute. In 1980, under national leadership, the Baptist International Mission reported 14 congregations, 17 preaching points and a total membership of 3,040.

An offshoot of the Baptist International Mission was the formation of the Good Samaritan Baptist Churches, founded by a former missionary in 1972. By 1979, when the missionary left, the total membership was about 3,100. The Good Samaritan Bible Institute was established in La Trinidad in the mid-1970s to train pastors and workers.

The Central American Mission (CAM) initiated work in Managua in 1900. In spite of early opposition from the Catholic Church and resistance by the nominal Catholic population, by 1911 two mission stations had been established in and around Managua. By 1936, there were nine churches, 26 preaching points, 700 members and about 1,300 adherents. In 1948, the CAM work was organized under national leadership as the Federation of Central American Churches, but missionary-national tensions have plagued the Federation for many years.

In 1955, the Federation suffered a division that seriously affected their growth. In that year, ten of the 22 existing churches left the Federation to form the Convention of Central American Churches. However, this Convention has not had much growth, reporting only 13 churches and 647 members in 1978.

After this division, the CAM-related Federation was left with 12 churches and 386 members, but they continued to receive missionary and financial assistance from the CAM. However, in 1965, another split over missionary policies occurred. The new body was called the National Evangelical Missionary Association (AMEN). By 1978, AMEN had 17 churches, ten missions and about 2,000 members.

The Federation of Central American Churches also experienced growth after 1965, with 1,437 members, 36 churches and 30 missions in 1978.

The Church of the Nazarene entered in 1943 and founded its first church in Managua the following year. The Church of the Nazarene experienced slow growth prior to 1967, in spite of a heavy concentration of missionaries. There were only 915 members in 1967. In 1960, there were 21 Nazarene missionaries and 41 national workers; in 1970, the number of missionaries decreased to 17, while national workers doubled to 80. However, the Nazarenes experienced difficulties between nationals and missionaries during the early 1970s, which led some of the national pastors to form an independent body in 1976, called the National Church of the Nazarene. In 1978, this new group reported nine small churches and about 200 members. The Church of the Nazarene had 61 churches and 2,175 members, also under national leadership but still aided by the Nazarene Board of Missions.

The largest Pentecostal denomination in Nicaragua is the Assemblies of God, which entered the country during the 1930s as an extension of their work in El Salvador. They engaged in evangelistic activities and planted churches in the northwestern region, where few evangelical churches existed. By 1940, 12 churches had been formed. In 1937, the Nicaraguan Bible Institute in Matagalpa was established. (It was relocated to Managua in 1974). A revival in 1944-1946 added hundreds of new believers and the number of congregations increased to 32. In 1960 there were 23 churches and 32 missions with 796 members; and by 1966, the membership increased to 1,249. However, only four years later, they reported 2,200 members, an increase of 311% per decade or 15.2% per year. Growth continued during the 1970s, mainly due to new converts in the Central Highlands where scores of new churches were formed by lay pastors. Between 1970 and 1978, the AAGR was 18.4% as the total membership climbed to 8,500 among 150 churches and 30 missions.

In 1951, a group numbering 14 pastors and about 80 laymen withdrew from the Assemblies of God to form their own association, called "Obreros Unidos" (United Workers). The new association, later known as the United Pentecostal Evangelical Mission in Nicaragua, reported 45 churches and more than 100 preaching points in 1979, with approximately 3,000 members. The Obreros Unidos was a protest movement against missionary control and represented a desire for national leadership of the work. There were some doctrinal differences also: the main difference having to do with the role of dreams, visions and prophecy in the life of the churches.

In 1975, a group of 30 or more pastors and churches broke off from the Obreros Unidos and formed the Pentecostal Mission of Christian Churches. This group had about 30-40 churches and 1,800-2,000 members in 1979. Among themselves, the older group is called the "ancianos" (old men or elders), while the new group is referred to as the "jovenes" (young men). The jovenes group apparently led a reform movement back to Biblical authority and against an over-emphasis on dreams, visions and prophecy.

The Apostolic Movement of the Name of Jesus developed within Pentecostal Churches in the United States and spread around the world during the later 1910s. It had its beginning in Nicaragua about 1918-1919, when a Chinese Pentecostal missionary visited Leon and preached the doctrine of "Jesus Only." By 1940, there were about four organized congregations with about 200 members. In 1953, the Apostolic Church of Faith in Jesus Christ was provisionally organized under a missionary supervisor. By 1980, after considerable growth in membership and leadership, there were 60 congregations with 3,600 members. The national church achieved autonomy in 1970 under Nicaraguan leaders.

The Free Apostolic Church is a denomination that broke away 1953 from the Apostolic Church of Faith in Jesus Christ. This group did not accept the authority of the new organization. They do not accept civil marriage, do not practice tithing and have a strong emphasis on dreams, visions and prophecy. In 1979, this movement had 43 churches and about 3,000 members.

The Church of God - Cleveland initiated work in Nicaragua in 1951 when a Salvadoran missionary crossed the border and began to evangelize along the Pacific Coast. It is notable that the Church of God work in Nicaragua has been spearheaded and led by missionaries from other Latin countries. Considerable growth was experienced by the Church of God between 1960 and 1966. In 1960, there were only eight churches, eleven missions, 476 members and 1,150 adherents, assisted by 19 national workers and two missionaries. By 1967, the Church of God had increased to 1,288 members and 2,273 adherents among 30 churches and 14 missions. In 1966, the Church of God was officially recognized by the government. By 1978, the Church of God increased to 76 churches and 40 missions, with 5,250 members.

The Assemblies of Christian Churches (ACC) of New York sent two missionaries to Nicaragua in 1968 and organized two churches in Managua. During the early 1970s, the efforts of the Assemblies of Christian Churches increased in northwestern Nicaragua. In 1978, the work became an autonomous national church while retaining the same name. By 1978, the membership had increased to 1,027 and the average attendance to over 2,000 among 38 churches and five missions. However, by early 1980, the membership had almost doubled to 2,038 in addition to 800 new converts who were being prepared for baptism.

The Seventh-day Adventists got off to a slow start in Nicaragua in spite of an initial ministry that began in 1904 among the Creoles on the Atlantic coast. In 1936, the Adventists had only one church with 177 members and 275 adherents under the supervision of a missionary couple. Between 1960 and 1978, the number of congregations grew from 14 to 27. There were also 56 "groups" or preaching points in 1978. By 1978, Adventist membership had climbed to about 6,000, an annual increase of 10.4% between 1966 and 1978.

## ROMAN CATHOLIC MISSIONS

The first Catholic missionary orders to be established in Nicaragua were the Franciscans and the Jesuits, who trace their founding back to the colonial period. After independence, the number of religious orders rose sharply. Among the new orders were the Spanish and Italian Franciscans, Salesians, Christian Brothers, Redemptorists, Piarists, Benedictines, Augustinian Recollects and Jesus Divino Obrero.

During the Liberal revolt led by President Zelaya from 1894 to 1908, the Nicaraguan government outlawed Catholic religious orders and put many restrictions on priests. However, these policies were rescinded after Zelaya was expelled from power. Many new religious orders arrived during the 20th century.

Today, of the 304 priests in the country belonging to Catholic religious orders, few are Nicaraguans. Spain, Italy, Germany and the United States rank as the major sending countries for Catholic missionary organizations in Nicaragua. At present, a total of four orders and 42 priests come from the United States: Capuchins (32), Maryknoll Fathers (2), Brothers of the Christian Schools (3), Monfort Fathers (4) and one lay brother. The Capuchin Fathers maintain churches, schools and a seminary on the Atlantic coast, which is administered as a missionary area (vicarate apostolic). Significant ministries being carried out by missionaries include education, community development, medical and public health and social welfare. The National Seminary in Managua is operated by priests from Canada. In 1960, the Jesuits founded in Managua the first Catholic University in Central America, "La Universidad Centroamericana."

Presently, there are a number of U.S. religious orders for women that are serving in Nicaragua: St. Agnes (12), Maryknoll (9), St. Teresa of Jesus (5), St. Francis of the Holy Cross (5), Missionary Sisters of the Sacred Heart (1), Carmelite Sisters of the Divine Heart (1), Dominican/Adrian (1) and a lay sister; a total of 34 workers. These orders mainly serve in primary and secondary schools, but they also care for a seminary, an orphanage, a sanitarium and most of the hospitals and clinics in the country. Community development is carried out by the Sisters of St. Agnes and the Maryknoll Sisters in Managua, Condega and Puerto Cabezas. Among other foreign missionary orders of women serving in Nicaragua are the following: Sisters of the Assumption, Josephites, Sisters of Charity of the Blessed Virgin Mary, Oblate Sisters of Divine Love, Oblates of the Sacred Heart and Franciscans.

Catholic Relief Services, which operates under the auspices of the US Catholic Conference, has assisted its counterpart in Nicaragua, Caritas, in food distribution programs, disaster relief and refugee work during the 1970s, especially after the 1972 Managua earthquake and the 1979 civil war.

### MAJOR CHRISTIAN ACTIVITIES

#### EVANGELISM

The first known evangelistic effort on the interdenominational level was conducted in Managua by Harry Strachan and Roberto Elphick in 1924. Strachan was the founder of the Latin American Evangelization Campaign, later known as the Latin America Mission (LAM). Several other efforts under Strachan's leadership were held during the 1920s and 1930s.

In the 1950s, several more evangelistic campaigns were conducted with encouraging results. In 1950 and 1952, the LAM conducted two evangelistic crusades in Managua. The first crusade lasted two weeks and the average nightly attendance was 1,000-1,500. The second crusade lasted 19 days and reached over 2,000 people nightly. The LAM also sponsored an evangelistic crusade in Bluefields in 1951. Hundreds of converts resulted from these crusades.

Crusades sponsored by the Assemblies of God in Managua resulted in many conversions and the formation of a number of new churches. In 1956, a crusade caused significant growth among the Assemblies of God churches. A decade later, the Evangelistic Center of the Assemblies of God sponsored a campaign with evangelist Richard Jeffrey; it lasted for about seven months and was occasionally covered by television. As a result of this crusade, the Assemblies of God formed two new churches: the Christian Cathedral in Colonia Morazan, and another church in Barrio Quinta Nina, both in Managua. The Evangelistic Center reported 100% increase in its attendance due to the special meetings.

The most notable crusade in the 1960s was the Evangelism-in-Depth program, sponsored by the LAM, that involved scores of churches in training and mobilization for mass evangelism, house-to-house visitation, prayer cells and many special activities. Nicaragua, for five months in 1960, became the test run for a similar series of Evangelism-in-Depth programs, held in dozens of Latin American and Caribbean countries in the 1960s. The program began with the formation of 500 prayer cells, where believers joined together to pray for the conversion and spiritual growth of their neighbors and friends. Special training classes were held for preparing Christian workers in personal evangelism and discipleship, with the participation of over 2,000 people. During the following house visitation phase, over 65,000 homes were contacted where the gospel was shared and invitations extended for special city-wide evangelistic meetings in 14 towns and cities. The Rev. Ruben Lores, a Cuban on the LAM staff, was the principal evangelist for these regional campaigns which culminated in a large crusade in Managua.

Evangelism-in-Depth inspired new evangelistic efforts for years to come in Nicaragua, building on over 2,500 professions of faith and on intensified lay training and mobilization during this significant interdenominational effort. As never before, Nicaraguans were aware of the growing evangelical presence in their midst.

However, since eastern Nicaragua was largely left out of the earlier Evangelism-in-Depth program in 1960, a special five-month effort was launched along the Caribbean coast in 1967, centered in the towns of Bluefields and Puerto Cabezas. The people mainly affected by this campaign were the Creole population, but special efforts were also directed toward the Miskitos. There were 13 local evangelistic crusades and two city-wide campaigns, resulting in hundreds of professions of faith.

More recently, crusades were held by "Hermano Pablo" (Assemblies of God evangelist Paul Finkenbinder) and Argentinian evangelist Luis Palau in 1969 and 1975, respectively. The Hermano Pablo crusade, co-sponsored by many denominations, culminated in a parade by thousands of evangelicals, who marched from the Plaza de la Republica through the streets of Managua and terminated in a final rally in the National Stadium with more than 6,000 in attendance. The Palau crusade was held in the National Stadium where 30,000 people attended and 6,000 conversions were reported. Palau also appeared on a nightly television talk-show, answering questions phoned in by listeners This resulted in wide popular support for the meetings. The crusade was sponsored by over 125 evangelical churches in Managua and the surrounding areas.

At the same time that the Palau crusade was being conducted in Managua, another campaign was occurring along the Caribbean coast in the port towns of Bluefields and Puerto Cabezas, under the joint sponsorship of the Institute of In-Depth Evangelism (INDEPTH) and African Enterprise (AE). INDEPTH provided advisors to help the local committees in preparations for the crusades, and AE provided the evangelists: Episcopal Bishop Festo Kivengere of Uganda, Michael Cassidy of South Africa, Ebenezer Sikakane of the Zulu tribe in South Africa and Ernie Wilson, a black evangelist from the U.S. who had been born in Colon, Republic of Panama.

Practically all of the local churches in Puerto Cabezas and Bluefields cooperated in the crusades, which were sponsored locally by interdenominational church councils. Since the parish priests of the Catholic Church in these two towns were members of the local councils, they also participated in the campaigns. In fact, the campaign in Puerto Cabezas was finally held in St. Peter's Catholic Cathedral after a rainstorm threatened the scheduled open-air meeting. The Cathedral, the largest building in town, was packed each night with over 3,000 individuals. Additional people listened to the meetings by loudspeakers outside. In a town of only 8,000-10,000 people, the attendance was by far the largest audience that had ever heard the gospel at one time in the history of Puerto Cabezas. In Bluefields, the crusade drew some 2,000 individuals nightly.

During 1978 and 1979, Rafael Baltodano of the INDEPTH team served as advisor and promoter for a number of evangelistic programs, some denominational and others interdenominational in character. Examples of the latter were city-wide crusades sponsored by several denominations in Leon, Rivas and Managua, coordinated by NICAFONDO (Evangelism-in-Depth in Nicaragua), with very good attendance and hundreds of conversions. New converts and other interested persons were incorporated into a number of discipleship cell groups, led by trained leaders under the supervision of their local pastors, using discipleship materials prepared and distributed by INDEPTH. A number of special evangelistic crusades were also conducted under denominational sponsorship, aided by Baltodano and other members of the INDEPTH team, among churches of the Central American Mission, the Church of the Nazarene, the Baptist Convention and other groups. Baltodano also worked with the Socio-pastoral Department of CEPAD (Evangelical Committee for Relief and Development), sponsoring and teaching a number of regional pastoral seminars in various parts of Nicaragua, mainly among Latinos. Although Baltodano relocated in San Jose, Costa Rica in early 1980, NICAFONDO continues to provide help to Nicaraguan churches. Evangelistic efforts aided by INDEPTH were conducted during 1980 in Rivas, the Island of Omotepe in Lake Nicaragua, Managua and other locations.

A united campaign in Managua was aided jointly by NICAFONDO and Campus Crusade for Christ in 1980. A series of training and mobilization activities were sponsored under the banner "Renuevo de Cristo," culminating in local evangelistic campaigns in many neighborhoods. Materials used were provided by INDEPTH and Campus Crusade.

## BROADCASTING

In 1957, the Baptist Convention asked the Latin America Mission, who operated TIFC in San Jose, Costa Rica, to assist them in establishing a similar station in Managua. However, the Baptists wanted the station to represent all evangelicals, and promoted the formation of the Nicaraguan Cultural Association to sponsor Radio YNOL, "Ondas de Luz" (Waves of Light), administered by an interdenominational group. Broadcasting began with the dedication of Ondas de Luz in 1958, and the station has continuously improved its programming and facilities and increased its power, so that it is now making a significant contribution to the spreading of the gospel in Nicaragua. However,

financial problems and technical difficulties, especially during the recent civil war, have hampered its operations.

Although many evangelical pastors and denominations produce programs that are aired on Radio YNOL, other evangelicals also utilize commercial stations throughout Nicaragua to broadcast the gospel. Television broadcasting has not been used frequently, but a few such efforts are noteworthy. During an evangelistic crusade in Managua in 1970-1971, with the Assemblies of God, a television program was produced. It was later continued by David Spencer, pastor of the Centro Evangelistico, after the crusade ended. This TV program, along with a radio broadcast called "Problems and Solutions," gave Spencer wide exposure to the public. Spencer began to sponsor meetings with Catholic Charismatics, which reached many middle and upper class Nicaraguans with the gospel. The Charismatic movement was encouraged by favorable exposure via mass media on Spencer's broadcasts. However, Spencer left Nicaragua in the mid-1970s.

Luis Palau's Crusade "Continente 1975" was accompanied by a late-night TV talk-show, where testimonies were given by some who had been transformed by the gospel during the campaign. Palau's program enjoyed a wide viewing audience during the week-long crusade, which also included a regional radio hook-up via satellite. This increased the potential listening audience to about 100 million in Central, South and North America, as well as the Caribbean. Technical assistance was provided by Interamerican Communications (DIA) of San Jose, Costa Rica, a ministry affiliated with the Latin America Mission.

More recently, the popular "700 Club" and "PTL Club" programs have been offered on local television stations in Managua. Follow-up work is done by local Christian workers with those who call or write in for counseling. These programs have had a special appeal to middle and upper income Nicaraguans, who are often reluctant to attend local evangelical churches because of pressure from their Catholic relatives and friends.

## LITERATURE

During the early 1960s, compelled by the 70-80% illiteracy rate among Nicaragua's rural poor, a national evangelical literacy program was launched. The program was related to ALFALIT International of Alajuela, Costa Rica. In addition to teaching people to read and write, ALFALIT workers offer training and assistance in nutrition, cooking, sewing, handcrafts and community development. ALFALIT, by coordinating its efforts with CEPAD's literacy, basic education and community development departments, now operates 70 training centers in Nicaragua, serving more than 1,600 people.

Christian literature is available to the general public through Christian bookstores in Managua (4), Jinotepe (1), Bluefields (1) and Puerto Cabezas (1). Other distribution services are provided by Southern Baptist missionaries, who work with the Nicaraguan Baptist Convention (related to the American Baptist Convention) and have a bookmobile ministry that offers literature from the Baptist Publishing House (Casa Bautista) in El Paso, Texas. The Adventists have traditionally done a large volume of literature work in Nicaragua, using local colporteurs, with a central office in Managua. The Assemblies of God also provide literature produced by their own publishing house, Editorial Vida. The Nicaraguan Bible Society is the main source for Bible distribution, and ALFALIT provides literacy materials.

The Baptist Convention publishes a magazine for the Christian public, called "La Antorcha," and CEPAD's Socio-Pastoral Department also publishes an occasional evangelical newspaper, entitled "Refleccion." Christian films are available from the Baptist Convention, the Baptist International Mission and CEPAD's Department of Communications and Audio-visuals. At least four evangelical groups offer Bible correspondence courses for new converts and inquirers.

## BIBLE TRANSLATION AND DISTRIBUTION

Distribution of the Spanish Bible did not begin in western Nicaragua until the mid-1850s, during occasional visits by representatives of the British and Foreign Bible Society (BFBS), or in the late 1800s by colporteurs of the American Bible Society (ABS). After 1914, with the opening of the Panama Canal, Bible distribution for Central America and Nicaragua was handled by the new regional office of the ABS in Cristobal, in the Canal Zone.

German United Brethren (Moravian) missionaries in eastern Nicaragua made a significant contribution to linguistic and Bible translation work, through their determined efforts in the Miskito and Sumo languages, beginning in 1857. The Four Gospels and Acts in Miskito were published in 1899 by the Herrnhut Bible Society, and the entire New Testament was made available in 1905, with financial assistance from the BFBS. A new Miskito

translation of the New Testament was completed and published in 1925, also by the Herrnhut Bible Society.

Today, in addition to several editions of the Spanish and English Bible, a more recent version of the New Testament in Miskito was made available (5,000 copies) in 1975, through the combined efforts of the Moravian Church, the Roman Catholic Church and the United Bible Societies. Also available in Miskito are Old Testament portions, various Bible stories, a hymnbook and a devotional manual. Translation work is also desired by the Sumos.

Since 1974, the United Bible Societies have had a national office in Managua. Many Protestant groups, as well as a growing number of Catholics, are active in Bible distribution work throughout Nicaragua. Especially useful in this important stage of Nicaraguan history has been the New Reader materials, now used widely in literacy efforts by many groups, along with ALFALIT materials. The United Bible Societies reported the following distribution for 1979, excluding commercial publishers:

| | |
|---|---:|
| Bibles | 15,869 |
| New Testaments | 15,600 |
| Portions | 75,358 |
| New Reader Portions | 51,000 |
| Selections | 565,701 |
| New Reader Selections | 100,000 |
| | ------- |
| Total (1979) | 823,528 |
| Total (1978) | 1,443,196 |

The Reconstruction government has recently requested 800,000 popular language New Testaments from Christian groups to be distributed through the churches to those who have completed literacy training. The Minister of the Interior, Tomas Borge Martinez, requested the Bibles, realizing that "if the new readers don't get material to read, they will lose what they've learned." The first 100,000 Bibles entered Nicaragua in June, 1980, largely through funds provided by the Full Gospel Businessmen's Fellowship International. The version being sent is Dios Llega al Hombre and is the Spanish equivalent of Good News for Modern Man.

## EDUCATION

Christian. Many Protestant churches, responding to the basic education needs of the children of Nicaragua, have established several primary and secondary schools, all fully recognized by the government. Six primary schools and a kindergarten are operated in Managua, while 10 are located in outlying areas, principally in the Department of Zelaya. The Adventists administer five primary schools, and the Moravians, three. There are 13 secondary schools, mainly operated by the Adventists (6), Moravians (2), Baptist Convention (2) and AMEN (2). Five of these high schools are located in Managua.

The Polytechnical University, founded by the Baptist Convention in 1968, is now an independent educational institution, which also includes a School of Nursing that was founded earlier at the Baptist Hospital in Managua.

Theological. Formal programs of theological education were established in Nicaragua by the Moravian Church and the Baptist Convention about 1940. The Moravian Bible Institute was founded at Bilwaskarma in 1938. The Baptist Convention operated a theological institute in Masaya between 1941 and 1958, while the present Baptist Seminary was founded at Managua in 1965. In 1960, the Adventists and the International Church of the Foursquare Gospel also established Bible institutes in Nicaragua. Today, there are eight Bible institute programs (six in Managua, and one each at Condega and Bilwaskarma), along with three seminary programs for resident students operated by the Baptist Convention, the Moravians and the Episcopal Church. Programs of Theological Education by Extension (TEE) are offered by two small Mennonite groups and the Baptist Seminary.

## SOCIAL CONCERN

In the area of agricultural, rural and community development, most work is being done through programs sponsored by CEPAD (The Evangelical Committee for Relief and Development), including integrated rural-urban community development, cooperatives and housing. In addition, the Adventists operate a program called OFASA, providing technical training and assistance to their churches throughout Nicaragua. The Federation of Central American Churches, affiliated with the Central American Mission (now, CAM International), maintains an agricultural project in Nueva Guinea, Department of Zelaya.

In the area of medicine and public health, about 20 clinics are operated by Protestant denominations, mostly in rural areas, although there are three clinics in Managua. AMEN maintains a medical launch in Zelaya Department, and there are several comprehensive programs of medical assistance provided by CAMEN (Committee of Evangelical Medical Agencies), PROVADENIC

(Vaccination and Community Development Project) and CEPAD's Public Health Department. In-patient care is provided by four evangelical hospitals, which were established by the Moravians in Bilwaskarma and Puerto Cabezas, the Adventists in La Trinidad de Esteli and the Baptist Convention in Managua. Recent reports indicate that the Moravian hospitals have been taken over by the Government of National Reconstruction, which has placed Nicaraguan doctors as chief administrators, while continuing to allow Moravian participation. The Baptist and Moravian hospitals both have schools of nursing that provide many evangelical women with an opportunity for vocational training. The Baptist Convention also operates an Old People's Home in Managua.

Christian camping programs have provided many children and adults with varied recreational activities, often in conjunction with annual meetings of their respective denominational assemblies. At least ten Christian campgrounds are maintained by evangelical groups in Nicaragua, located in widely scattered areas of the country. However, only a few of these sites, such as the Mount of Olives Baptist Camp, are campgrounds with improved facilities; some are quite primitive in their accommodations.

Children's ministries are provided for by CEPAD's Childcare Department, along with three homes for orphans or abandoned children operated by various groups in Nicaragua.

Vocational training, in addition to the nursing schools already mentioned, is provided by the Salvation Army, the Adventists, ALFALIT, CEPAD and NICAFONDO (through its Extended Hands Program).

After the 1972 earthquake in Managua, and during the recent civil war, numerous Protestant and Catholic organizations aided victims by providing food, clothing, shelter and medical care. Counselling was also offered to victims for their psychological, social and spiritual rehabilitation and development. Similar services have been offered to disaster victims of hurricanes, floods, volcanic eruptions, etc., since evangelical work began in Nicaragua.

## GENERAL SERVICE ORGANIZATIONS

In 1973, about 40 Protestant denominations and service organizations formed a new service agency called CEPAD, the Evangelical Committee for Relief and Development, as a response to the recent powerful earthquake that destroyed the entire central district of Managua.

CEPAD's handling of international aid from churches and relief organizations in other countries following the earthquake, together with its role during the civil war, have earned CEPAD the respect of the international Christian community and the confidence of the general public in Nicaragua.

CEPAD's overall aim is to contribute to the total development of the Nicaraguan people, principally by ensuring for all inhabitants the full enjoyment of human rights, dignity and social justice, regardless of race, religion or socio-economic status. In order to promote and fulfill this goal, CEPAD maintains fourteen service departments which work through eight regional offices. These programs include literacy, basic education, child welfare, cooperatives, community development, public health, housing, integrated rural-urban development, socio-pastoral action and human rights. Cooperating with CEPAD are many international Christian service organizations which channel funds, personnel and materials through CEPAD to help the evangelical community in Nicaragua serve those in need.

NICAFONDO (Evangelism-in-Depth in Nicaragua), is a national project of the Institute of In-Depth Evangelization (INDEPTH), an interdenominational service organization of evangelical character, with international offices in San Jose, Costa Rica. INDEPTH advisors provide assistance to individual denominations, to interdenominational efforts and to local congregations and pastors in activities designed to promote evangelism, discipleship, integral church growth and unity among and by evangelicals. One of the departments of NICAFONDO is Manos Extendidas (Extended Hands), which works mainly with women in a variety of activities designed to teach vocational skills, to develp small industries, to build stronger Christian families and to help women fulfill their role in the Christian community.

**NATION AND ITS PEOPLE**

## POPULATION

In 1980, Nicaragua's population was estimated at 2.5 million people, up from 2.2 million in 1976. The population is growing at an annual rate of 3.4 percent. Population density varies considerably from region to region. The Pacific, Central and Atlantic Regions have respective densities of 62.4, 18.0 and 2.6 inhabitants per square kilometer (162, 47 and 17 per square mile).

Urban centers, Managua being the largest, are zones of attraction. Managua's 582,000 residents are concentrated in an area of 30 square kilometers (12 square miles). From 1950-1976, Managua's population quadrupled. Leon, Granada and Masaya, cities located in the Pacific Region, have also shown rapid growth. Altogether, it is estimated that 53% of the population is urban and 47% is rural.

Another area that has shown rapid growth is the zone that divides the Central Region from the Atlantic Region. This zone experiences almost continuous rainfall, making it possible for cleared forests to be turned into permanently green pastures for cattle grazing. This is the reason behind the increase in population of the Department of Zelaya, which grew 68% in eight years.

Almost half (48%) of the population of Nicaragua is under 15 years of age. Of these, 650,000 persons, or more than half (54%), are under ten years old.

## COMPOSITION

The majority of Nicaraguans can be classified as mestizos (mixed Spanish and Indian), and as bearers of Spanish heritage. The term "Latino" is a cultural, rather than a racial label and refers to the traditions of the Hispanic population. According to the 1971 census, 86% of the population considered themselves Latinos. They are racially about 70% mestizo and 16% white. The Latino population predominates in the Pacific and Central Mountain Regions.

The Negro population forms the second largest racial group (about 9%) in Nicaragua. This group is ethnically diverse and difficult to classify. Ethnically, the English-speaking Negroes (mostly mulattoes) are descendants of West Indians from British colonies in the Caribbean, are predominantly Protestant and are called Creoles or "Costenos" (coast-dwellers). However, the Spanish-speaking Negroes, who are Hispanicized and Roman Catholic, may sometimes be referred to by local custom as mestizos rather than Negroes. The French-speaking Negroes are generally called "patois," but not much is known about their contemporary local customs or acculturation patterns, although they are predominantly Roman Catholic by heritage. A large number of Negroes are culturally Indian and speak either Miskito, Sumo or Rama, due to geographic isolation and intermarriage with Indian groups. The Black Caribs are an example of this group.

Amerindians, according to the 1971 Census, constitute about 3-4% of the population. Indian groups in western Nicaragua are largely Hispanicized and Roman Catholic: the Matagalpa (20,000) in the Central Highlands, the Sutiaba (5,000) of Leon and the Monimbo (10,000) of Masaya. Historically, however, the Indians of eastern Nicaragua have, resisted Spanish conquest and Hispanicization although the Miskitos in particular have freely intermarried with other nationalities and races. The Indian groups in eastern Nicaragua have more strongly retained their native customs and dialects, whereas the Indians in western Nicaragua have been largely assimilated into the Hispanic culture and are usually considered mestizos.

The unassimilated Indian groups on the Mosquito Coast are the Miskito (40,000), Sumo (3,000), Black Carib (2,000) and Rama (600-1,000).

## LANGUAGE AND LITERACY

The official language is Spanish, spoken by nearly 96% of the population. The percentage of non-Spanish speaking people has been declining. Most of them live on the east coast in the Department of Zelaya, where the Sumo and Miskito Indians live and speak their own languages. English is also spoken in this region by the Creoles.

Education is free and compulsory. The Sandinista government is making a concerted effort to raise the literacy rate from its present 52%. It was estimated that by 1981, 88% of the population was literate.

## RELIGION

Historically, there has been no constitutional provision for an official religion in Nicaragua since independence from Spain, although the government has normally granted Roman Catholicism certain privileges. Official diplomatic ties were usually maintained with the Vatican. During the Somoza dynasty, all churches had the right to own and acquire property, and the clergy could even participate in politics. The principal of religious freedom existing under the Somozas has been continued by the Sandinista Front of National Liberation (FSLN) since its rise to power in July, 1979.

The FSLN has continued to affirm that religion is an inalienable right of the Nicaraguan people, and that no one will be discriminated against in the new Nicaragua for publicly professing or propagating his or her religious beliefs. However, those who do not profess a religious faith also have this freedom, meaning that the teaching of atheism is a right guaranteed by the new government. The FSLN recognizes that many Christians supported the Sandinista cause either directly or indirectly, although others were politically opposed to the rebellion, and some adopted a wait-and-see attitude. However, the FSLN has called upon church leaders to expand the dialogue between the Christian Faith and the revolutionary cause, and to participate in reconstruction activities designed to build a new and free society in Nicaragua. Although a majority of Christians now support the National Reconstruction Government, a minority hold opposing viewpoints, which may bring them into conflict with the FSLN.

## GEOGRAPHY AND CLIMATE

Nicaragua is the largest and least populated republic of Central America. Two mountain ranges, one of them volcanic, separate the coastal plains of the Pacific and the Caribbean.

Two large, freshwater lakes dominate the west coast: Lake Nicaragua and Lake Managua. Lake Nicaragua is connected to the Mosquito Coast on the Caribbean by the San Juan River and only a narrow strip of land separates it from the Pacific. This condition, favorable to the creation of an interoceanic canal, has made Nicaragua the object of international interest.

The Pacific coast is an area composed of lowland plains. Here, more than half the population live in a geographic area which amounts to approximately one-sixth of the total land area of the country. It is endowed with naturally fertile volcanic soils and moderate, consistent rainfall.

The Central Mountain Region constitutes almost a third of the country and contains over a third of the population. Here, a rugged topography, with peaks around 1,500 meters (5,000 feet), alternates with comparatively small plateaus and lowland valleys. An exception is provided by the plains that exist in Matagalpa and Jinotega.

Extending from the lower slopes of the Central Highlands to the Mosquito Coast is the Caribbean Region, covering half the land area but containing less than 10% of the population. This region is geographically isolated from the rest of Nicaragua and is relatively underdeveloped.

Along the Pacific coast, the rainy season extends from May to November and the dry season from December to April. The average annual temperature is 25 degrees C. (78 degrees F.) and an annual rainfall of 200 centimeters (80 inches) is registered. The climate is slightly cooler and far more humid on the East coast. The rainy season lasts nine months and the dry season is not as clearly defined. An annual rainfall of 400 centimeters (160 inches) is recorded. In the Central Mountain Region the temperatures are lower, with an average of 15 degrees C. (60 degrees F.).

## HISTORY

Discovered by Columbus on his fourth voyage to the New World (1502), Nicaragua was the home of several Indian tribes. After founding the cities of Granada and Leon, Spain developed Nicaragua as an agricultural colony. A separate history developed on the Caribbean coast, where Negro immigrants intermarried with Indians (Miskito and Sumo) and Europeans to form a mixed race of mulatos and Creoles. Britain formed an alliance with the Miskito chief, making the region a British dependency until Nicaragua became independent from Spain in 1821.

North American intervention began in 1910 and ended with the withdrawal of the U.S. Marines in 1933. The closing years of this period were marked by the activities of the guerrilla leader, Sandino. However, it was General Anastasio Somoza who became president in 1937. The Somoza family, backed by the National Guard, governed Nicaragua from 1937-1979. The rise in national income experienced during this period generally benefitted Somoza family holdings but did little to improve the condition of the general public. Civil discontent flared up in 1978, leading to all-out civil war. Somoza was ousted in July, 1979 and the victorious Sandinista Front of National Liberation (FSLN) set up a new government known as the National Reconstruction Government.

## GOVERNMENT AND POLITICAL CONDITIONS

Since the Sandinista Revolution, Nicaragua has been ruled by the National Reconstruction Government. Acting as a cabinet to the Government is the Council of Ministers. Popular representation is expressed in the Council of State, a fifty member "sounding board" for the Government. Membership in the Council is pluralistic. Included are such diverse representatives as those of political parties, the churches and private enterprise. However, the Sandinista

Liberation Front is the dominating force.

From the onset, the Reconstruction Government has placed great emphasis on programs aimed at reactivating the economy. Businesses and landholdings belonging to the Somozas have been taken over. In the case of these businesses, many are now state owned or owned jointly by the state and private shareholders. In order to stimulate agricultural production three forms of land ownership and production are being practiced: state, private and cooperative. The latter type is especially favored. A government sponsored credit institution called PROCAMPO has alloted 320 million cordobas in loans to 1,470 agricultural associations during the past year. Another move toward increasing production has been the nationalization of the country's mineral wealth. It is expected that gold and silver mining will produce 45 million dollars in 1980.

Other programs undertaken by the Reconstruction Government include a massive literacy campaign and an integrated public health program. Approximately 900,000 people are presently attending literacy classes taught by thousands of volunteers.

The National Guard has been dismantled. In its place the Sandinista Police and the Sandinista Popular Army now function. Their members receive literacy training or primary education, as well as instruction in their specialized skills.

## ECONOMY

Agriculture forms the base of the economy of Nicaragua. In fact, 47% of the "economically active" population is engaged in agriculture. Most other sectors of Nicaragua's economy, such as industry, commerce and services are related to the processing and distribution of agricultural products.

The importance of agriculture is also seen in the fact that 42% of the total national territory is given over to agricultural activities. One fourth of the GNP comes from agriculture. Nicaragua produces coffee, cotton, tobacco and sugar as export crops and is virtually self-sufficient in the production of corn, beans and rice; elements basic to the diet of the population.

Industrial development got underway in 1950, when Nicaragua initiated its cotton processing industry. Industrialization of other agricultural products followed immediately. At the same time, efforts were made to build and improve roads, increase electrical output, expand seaports and create protective laws. Today, industry accounts for 20% of the GNP and industrial exports constitute 55% of the total exports. Nicaragua's major manufactured products include food processing, chemicals, chemical products, shoes, textiles, clothing, beverages, tobacco and metal products. Most industries are located in the Pacific Region, with the heaviest concentration being in Managua, with 60% of the national production.

Of the total land area, 42% is dedicated to agriculture, 18% consists mainly of mountains and swamps and 40% is covered by forests. Land distribution in Nicaragua is unequal. Approximately half of all farms are under 17.3 acres and together they account for only 3.5% of the total occupied area. Farms of over 863.5 acres represent only 1.5% of the total number, but include over 40% of the land in use. The gravity of this situation is recognized by the new government and land reform will be implemented in the near future.

## CHURCH STATISTICS FOR NICARAGUA

NOTE: Statistics are from the 1979 PROCADES survey of Protestant Churches and are based on official denominational reports or estimates. Although definitions of membership vary slightly among churches, the data is highly comparable and reliable. All known churches are included in this list.

| Church or Mission Name | Number of Congregations | Membership | % of Total |
|---|---|---|---|
| PROTESTANT | | | |
| Liturgical | 19 | 1,841 | 2.4% |
| Anglican | 16 | 1,800 | |
| Fed. of Evang. Lutherans | 3 | 41 | |
| Evangelical Non-Pentecostal | 682 | 34,681 | 44.2% |
| Assoc. of Churches of Christ | 61 | 1,877 | |
| Bapt. Conv. (Amer. Bapt.) | 174 | 4,659 | |
| Bapt. International Mission | 21 | 3,040 | |
| Church of Christ | 11 | 1,500 | |
| Churches of the Nazarene (2 groups) | 72 | 2,382 | |
| Conv. of C.A. Churches | 13 | 647 | |
| Federation of C.A. Churches (CAM) | 66 | 1,437 | |
| Good Samaritan Baptist Churches | 15 | 765 | |
| Mennonites (4 groups) | 46 | 1,720 | |
| Moravian Church | 123 | 12,950 | |
| National Evangelical Missionary Assoc. | 27 | 2,000 | |
| Other Baptists (7 groups) | 40 | 1,218 | |
| Misc. groups | 13 | 486 | |
| Pentecostal | 740 | 35,273 | 45.0% |
| Apostolic Church | 60 | 3,600 | |
| Assemblies of God | 186 | 8,500 | |
| Assembly of Christ. Churches | 43 | 1,027 | |
| Christian Mission (Indep.) | 14 | 895 | |
| Church of God - Cleveland | 116 | 5,250 | |
| Church of God of Prophecy | 32 | 1,100 | |
| Fraternity of Pentecostal Evangelical Churches | 6 | 600 | |
| Free Apostolic Church | 43 | 2,995 | |
| Foursquare Church (2 groups) | 19 | 900 | |
| Pentecostal Church of God | 10 | 650 | |
| Pentecostal Free Will Bapt. | 13 | 520 | |
| Pent. Mission of Christian Churches | 31 | 1,815 | |
| United Pent. Evan. Mission | 49 | 3,004 | |
| Other "Jesus Only" Churches (8 groups) | 43 | 1,105 | |
| Adventist | 84 | 6,073 | 7.7% |
| All Adventists (2 groups) | 84 | 6,073 | |
| Miscellaneous/Non-classified | 6 | 519 | 0.7% |
| All Miscellaneous (3 groups) | 6 | 519 | |
| TOTALS (1979) | 1,531 | 78,387 | 100.0% |

## SELECTED BIBLIOGRAPHY AND INFORMATION SOURCES

The sources listed below are to help the reader find additional information on this country and Christian ministries there. This list does not try to be comprehensive or complete.

DOCUMENTS

General

Cozean, Jon D., Latin America, 1980, Washington, D.C.: Stryker-Post Publications, 1980.

Herring, Hubert, A History of Latin America, New York: Alfred A. Knopf, 1968.

Ryan, John Morris, et al, Area Handbook for Nicaragua, Washington, D.C.: U.S. Government Printing Office, 1970.

Woodward, Ralph Lee, Jr., Central America: A Divided Nation, New York: Oxford University Press, 1976.

Christian

"Directorio Geografico de las Iglesias y Misiones Evangelicas de El Salvador," San Jose, Costa Rica: INDEPTH/PROCADES, 1980.

Good, Thelma A. "Now What? 125 Years of Moravian Missions in Bluefields, 1849-1974," Bluefields, Nicaragua: Moravian Church, 1974.

Grimes, Barbara F., ed., Ethnologue, Huntington Beach, CA: Wycliffe Bible Translators, 1978.

Grubb, Kenneth G., Religion in Central America, London:World Dominion Press, 1937.

"Sandinist Government States Policy on Religion in Nicaragua," Latinamerica Press, Part I in Vol. 12, No. 41 (6 Nov., 1980), Part II in Vol. 12, No. 42 (13 Nov., 1980).

Orr, J. Edwin, Evangelical Awakenings in Latin America, Minneapolis, MN: Bethany Fellowship, 1978.

Read, William P., et al, Latin American Church Growth, Grand Rapids: Eerdmans, 1970.

Taylor, Clyde W. and Wade T. Coggins, eds., Protestant Missions in Latin America: A Statistical Survey, Washington, D.C.: EFMA, 1961.

## ACKNOWLEDGMENTS

The information in this profile was taken from many sources which were the best available to the editors at the time of preparation. However, the accuracy of the information cannot be guaranteed. Views expressed or implied in this publication are not necessarily those of World Vision. The editors have tried to present the ministries of various organizations in an objective manner, without undue bias or emphasis. Where we have failed, we apologize for erroneous impressions that may result and request that comments and corrections be sent to MARC, 919 West Huntington Drive, Monrovia, California, 91016, USA. We appreciate and acknowledge the comments and contributions of various organizations and individuals in the preparation of this publication.

# STATUS OF CHRISTIANITY COUNTRY PROFILE

# PANAMA

### SUMMARY

AREA — 75,650 square kilometers (28,745 square miles.)
POPULATION — 1,830,175 (1980 Census)
RELIGION — 86% Roman Catholic 12% Protestant, 2% Other

Because of its strategic location at the narrowest point between the Atlantic and Pacific Oceans, Panama has historically been the center of international attention. Panama became the staging area for the Spanish conquest of South America. During the California Gold Rush of 1849, Panama was a major route of travel. The increase of trade and travel between the east and west coasts of the American continents pointed out the need for an interoceanic canal. The Republic of Panama was formed as a direct result of American interest in the building of this canal.

The Panama Canal has profoundly affected the nation's life in other ways. Its population is the most heterogeneous in all Central America due to the immigration of various peoples to work on and service the Canal. Furthermore, due to its control over the Canal Zone, American influence has been keenly felt in the Panamanian government and economy. The Carter-Torrijos Treaty of 1977/1978 will give Panama complete ownership of the Canal by the year 2000.

One of the other effects of building the Panama Canal was the introduction of Protestantism into Panama. Although originally limited to the West Indians and Americans in the Canal Zone, Protestant Christianity has spread to the surrounding mestizo community. Today, some 86% of the total Panamanian population are considered Roman Catholic while 12% are now Protestant. Over two-thirds of all Protestants are mestizos. The Protestant Church grew at an overal annual rate of 4.7% between 1960 and 1978.

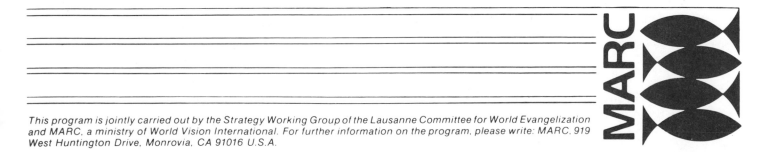

*This program is jointly carried out by the Strategy Working Group of the Lausanne Committee for World Evangelization and MARC, a ministry of World Vision International. For further information on the program, please write: MARC, 919 West Huntington Drive, Monrovia, CA 91016 U.S.A.*

## Mestizos (70% of all Panamanians)

Although the presence of the Catholic faith is felt in most aspects of Panamanian life, its impact is relatively weak on most Panamenos. While birth, marriage and death are generally marked by religious rites and many of the national holidays are religious celebrations, a style of renewed life and signs of a redeemed community are largely absent. Only 20% of the people regularly attend Mass. Those who attend regularly, mostly women and children, frequently are only complying with expected social norms and are not acting from deep religious convictions.

Few men attend Mass regularly and even fewer take an active part in the religious life of the community. Church teachings, particularly its restrictive morality and emphasis on humility and abnegation, are at direct variance with the most important features of Panamanian "machismo." While subscribing to Catholicism and recognizing it as part of their heritage, most mestizo men feel that religious matters fall more properly within the realm of feminine interest. Their lack of participation is reflected in the small number of Panamenos who enter the priesthood.

The Catholic Archbishop, Monsignor McGrath, has denounced the attitude of nominal Panamanian Catholics who see in Catholicism no more than an exterior quality lending decorum and order to life. Even so, it is doubtful that even this function of religion is taken seriously. Many Catholic precepts and proscriptions are ignored or violated, rarely drawing public censure.

As in other Latin American countries, many Catholic mestizos approach the treatment of disease and illness on the basis of folk cures and remedies. Treatment of such ills can be either by physical or herbal means, or by techniques that involve supernatural cures. There is a common belief that supernatural forces, either impersonal or purposefully directed, can cause serious illness. Numerous ailments are attributed to these forces, and many supernatural or magical cures are used as antidotes by "curanderos" (folk medicine specialists), "comadronas" (midwives) or "brujas" (witches). The bruja is considered especially valuable for fortune telling, interpretation of dreams, determining one's love life or folk psychiatry. These folk specialists are considered to be

especially gifted by God, and the total belief system is an integration of indigenous Animism and Catholicism.

These weaknesses within Panamanian Catholicism, sometimes referred to as Christo-paganism or Popular Catholicism, help to explain why a growing number of mestizos are turning to evangelical churches in search of a more dynamic and relevant faith. Mestizos form the majority of Protestant adherents in Panama, especially in areas where evangelicals are growing rapidly, such as Chiriqui Province. It can no longer be said that the relatively large Protestant Community in Panama (12%) is composed mainly of West Indians and Anglo-American residents of the Canal Zone. Now, about 69% of all Panamanian Protestants are mestizos, but only about 11.4% of all mestizos are Protestants - up from 5.1% in 1960. Nevertheless, Mestizos are still an unreached people in many regions throughout Panama.

## White Upper Class (9%)

Although not all wealthy Panamanians are Caucasians, most whites in Panamanian society are members of the upper class. This class, centered mainly in the capital, is formed by old families of Spanish descent, augmented to a slight degree by newer European or North American immigrants. The upper class is composed of large landowning families and those who have acquired wealth through commerce or industry. It also includes government leaders and some who have achieved success as professionals. This is a small, close-knit group that has developed strong ties of association and kinship over the years. It is necessary to view Panama's upper class as largely unreached, due to the fact that Catholic religious practice is seen merely as an aspect of their Spanish heritage. However, during the 1970s, the Catholic Charismatic movement had considerable impact among members of the upper class, although few became members of evangelical churches. But a growing receptivity among the upper class is evidenced by attendance during the past few years at meetings sponsored by the Full Gospel Businessmen's Association and Women's Aglow.

## Antillean Negroes (8%)

The term Antillean (West Indian Islanders) refers to English-speaking Negroes who immigrated to Panama from the Caribbean Islands formerly controlled by the British. Large scale immigration of West Indians took place in the second half of the nineteenth and the beginning of the twentieth centuries. The distribution of

West Indians in the country still reflects the circumstances of their arrival. With the exception of a sizeable concentration of Antilleans (or "Antillanos") around Puerto Armuelles in the banana zone of Chiriqui Province, most reside in the Interoceanic Region: Panama City, Colon and the Canal Zone.

While most Panamanians of West Indian origin call themselves Protestants, relatively few take their religion seriously. Although a dozen or more Protestant denominations can be found among them, most of these local congregations have low attendance at their services except on special occasions, just like the nominal Catholics. More than ever before, West Indian young people prefer to worship in Spanish-speaking mestizo churches, if they choose to attend church at all. Most Antillean Protestant churches have a ghetto mentality, exhibiting a strong desire to preserve cherished traditions based on their British Caribbean heritage and to resist acculturation to Hispanic norms. Consequently, the West Indian population is a declining ethnic group, with little hope of being strengthened by large numbers of new arrivals from the Caribbean islands. Instead, growing numbers of West Indians are emigrating from Panama and are seeking employment opportunities in the United States or in neighboring Latin American countries.

Nominal Protestantism being the norm among the Antilleans, this minority ethnic group comprises a significant segment of unreached people in Panama. Since few Protestant churches are communicating a vital Christian faith among West Indians, some Antilleans are turning to revitalization movements that take the form of African spiritism. Several spiritist sects are active in the black neighborhoods of Panama City, Colon and surrounding areas. Today the choice among West Indians seems to be between the spiritists or the more active Spanish-speaking Protestant churches that have experienced significant growth among the mestizo population, especially Pentecostal denominations in Panama City and Colon.

## Amerindians (6%)

Panama's Amerindian population numbers about 76,500. The three major groups: the Guaymi, the Kuna and the Choco, are concentrated in three distinct and widely separated localities, where they are exposed to varying degrees of contact with rural Panamanians. Most of the Indians have chosen to remain in their own semiautonomous communities, subject to tribal government, and to live according to centuries-old traditions.

Guaymi (40,000). The largest Amerindian group in Panama comprises about 50% of the indigenous population and is chiefly located in the western provinces of Bocas del Toro, Veraguas and Chiriqui. The Guaymi are descended from various preconquest tribes and are generally subdivided into two groups: the Valientes in Bocas del Toro and the northern part of Veraguas, and the Sabaneros in Chiriqui and the southern part of Veraguas. Government statistics on language usage among the indigenous population indicate that in Bocas del Toro and Chiriqui provinces, approximately 97% speak their native language at home, 55% also speak Spanish and 3% use Spanish exclusively. In Veraguas Province, on the other hand, 69% use their dialect at home, 21% know Spanish as a second language and 31% speak Spanish as their first language. Naturally, the degree of Hispanization is closely associated with the use of Spanish; as Spanish fluency increases, Guaymi cultural traits become less apparent in this region.

However, there are two distinct cultural worlds among the Guaymi in western Panama, in addition to language variables caused by Hispanization. On the Atlantic watershed, north of the continental divide, the Valiente Guaymi cultivate their crops in the well-watered highlands or sell their labor on large banana plantations in Bocas del Toro Province. But on the southern slope of the mountains, the Sabanero Guaymi often see drought destroy their struggling corn fields, or have to travel long distances over dry ground to work as herdsmen or miners in Chiriqui and Veraguas provinces. The Wesleyan Methodists pioneered among the Valiente Indians in the early 1900s, but most Protestant groups among the Guaymi date from the 1950s. During a recent survey, the following groups reported congregations among the Guaymi: the Foursquare Church, Church of God - Cleveland, New Tribes Mission, Seventh-day Adventists, Gospel Missionary Union, Central American Mission, Southern Baptists and the Wesleyan Methodists.

Wycliffe Bible Translators reported that Scripture portions in Guaymi (Ngobere) were available prior to 1950. A rough translation of the New Testament was done in Guaymi in the 1970s, but a reliable version will not be available until the mid-1980s. However, the Gospel of John has been published by the United Bible Societies.

The Kuna (26,000). The most highly organized and economically active Indians in Panama, the Kuna preserve their native customs with relative ease in their isolated habitat. Most Kuna live on the San Blas Islands off the northeastern coast (Kuna-San Blas). Several mainland Kuna groups also have little contact with Panamenos because the tribal people (Kuna-Colombia) live in remote regions of the provinces of Panama and Darien. The latter group number only about 300 in Panama, but 600 or more live in neighboring Colombia.

The Kuna constitute 42% of the Indian population of Panama. They engage in considerable trade with surrounding Panamanians and speak Spanish extensively. Local surveys indicate that almost 37% are bilingual, and about 20% speak Spanish in the home. Nevertheless, the Kuna maintain a close-knit internal organization that tends to shield them from the eroding effects of exposure to alien influences. However, some Kuna have found employment in the Canal Zone, or aboard ships passing through the canal, while others have left the islands to live and work in Colon or Panama City. Some have attained a university education. Most of the public school teachers in the San Blas Islands are Kuna.

The Kuna economy depends upon coconut production, fishing, subsistence farming and native handcrafts. Coconuts are cultivated in large quantities on the San Blas Islands and sold to Colombian traders. However, little farming is done on the islands. Many national and foreign tourists have been drawn to the San Blas Islands, largely due to the scenic beauty of the palm-covered islands and to the handcrafts made by Kuna women. Hand-sewn Molas and other fine items are famous for both quality and design.

Protestant work began among the Kuna in the early 1900s. Thousands of islanders have been converted over the years and are members of numerous Baptist, Church of God - Anderson or Adventist congregations. A strong national church exists among the Kuna on the San Blas Islands, as well as among Kuna migrants in Panama City and Colon, where several congregations have been formed using both Kuna and Spanish. The New Testament in Kuna was translated during the 1960s, but it needs revision. Much of the translation work has been done by capable Kuna linguists.

The Chocoes (7,000). Two tribes now dwelling in the jungles of Darien Province originally came from the Province of Choco in Colombia. The Waunana number about 1,000 in Panama and 2,000 in Colombia,

whereas the Embera total 4,000 in Panama and 2,000 in Colombia. The Chocoes, comprising 8% of the indigenous population of Panama, occupy a region that stretches from the Colombian border in the southeast, to the Provinces of Panama and Colon in the northwest, close to Kuna territory along the north coast. The Chocoes tend to have weak tribal organization, with most Chocoes living in houses separated by great distances. Recognizable villages are few. They are not as strongly opposed to assimilation as the Kuna or Guaymi, and most Chocoes speak Spanish as well as their native language. Numerous Spanish-speaking Negroes from Colombia, who fled political disturbances in their own country, have settled in the Darien region and have intermarried freely with the Chocoes. Acculturation is common among the Waunana and Embera. Most Chocoes engage in hunting and subsistence agriculture for survival in this remote area of Panama.

Protestant efforts among the Chocoes began in the late 1950s when the Mennonite Brethren sent linguists and teachers into the region. The first congregation of Choco believers was formed in 1961, and there are now about 1,000 adherents in 10 or more congregations. An indigenous national church organization has been formed by the Mennonite Brethren. The New Tribes Mission and the Church of the Foursquare Gospel also have churches among the Chocoes. Scripture portions are now available in Waunana and Embera through the efforts of several workers, but the New Testament will not be completed until the mid-1980s.

Smaller Tribes in Western Panama (3,500). The small Buglere tribe, now integrated among the Valiente Guaymi, speak Monana Sabanero and live among the coastal mountains of Veraguas and Bocas del Toro Provinces. This group, also known as the Bokota Indians, number about 2,000. Approximately 50% speak some Spanish, but only 25% are functionally bilingual in Buglere and Spanish, although most also speak Ngobere. Wycliffe reports that some Scripture portions are now available in Buglere. The New Tribes Mission is the only Protestant group known to have congregations among them.

Another small tribe in western Panama, the Teribe, number about 1,000 and live in the Teribe Valley on the Caribbean coast, near Changuinola in Bocas del Toro. In this region the United Fruit Company has large banana plantations, which provide occasional employment for the Teribe. They are related to a similar tribe in the mountains of Costa Rica, called the Terrabas, who number only a few dozen families. Portions of the New Testament are available in Naso, the language of the Teribe. However, this group is extremely bilingual; perhaps 95% speak some Spanish. The Adventists have worked among the Teribe for about 50 years, but the number of converts among them is unknown.

## Chinese (30,000).

The Chinese population of Panama is the largest in Central America. But only about 6,000 are considered "pure" Chinese; i.e., those who are least Hispanicized. Members of this group tend to keep to themselves, mostly speaking Hakka or Cantonese, and adhering to traditional Chinese customs and values.

The present Chinese population in Panama has resulted from several waves of immigration: the older Chinese, who came to Panama as railroad or canal workers prior to 1910; other Chinese who fled from China after the Communist revolution; and younger Chinese who arrived during the 1960s and 1970s from Hong Kong. Added to these immigrant groups are their descendants who are Panamanian-born and predominantly Spanish-speaking.

Most Chinese live in Panama City and Colon, although many reside in the larger towns of the interior. The Chinese are said to hold a virtual monopoly on the retail grocery business in the capital, while others operate shops and restaurants along the Pan-American Highway. Four small Chinese newspapers are published in Panama.

Many of the earlier Chinese immigrants have intermarried and adopted mestizo culture, including nominal Roman Catholicism. Apparently there is no intense non-Christian religious life, although most of the "pure" Chinese families still maintain Buddhist or ancestral shrines in their homes. However, for many Chinese in Panama, materialism provides the main competition for the Christian faith.

Few efforts have been made by Protestants to reach the Chinese in Panama. The Methodist Episcopal Church sponsored work among the 3,000 Chinese in Panama City during 1918 and 1919, by means of a day school and Sunday school operated by missionaries. However, this outreach was soon discontinued, and no known attempts were made by other Protestant groups until the 1970s.

Two Chinese Protestant churches were established a few years ago, not as a formal denominational thrust, but rather through the sincere efforts of a small group of Chinese Christian women who began to pray for their relatives and friends and organized a Bible study group. Now, a Chinese Christian Mission of about 50 members meets in Panama City, along with a smaller group of about 15 in Colon. For a few years, these small congregations were assisted by a Spanish-speaking Panamanian pastor and were loosely related to the Southern Baptist Convention of Panama. More recently, however, they have been aided and encouraged by the Chinese Christian Mission of Petaluma, California, who have sent Chinese workers to Panama from the United States during 1979-1980. Obviously, more intensified efforts must be made to reach the Chinese of Panama.

## Jews (2,500-3,000).

Today there are about 3,000 Jews in Panama, most of whom live in the capital city. The first Jews to enter Panama did so in the nineteenth century, coming mainly from Spain and Portugal and arriving prior to 1850. Then, during the 1930s, hundreds of Jews relocated in Panama from Central and Eastern Europe. The most recent arrivals came from the Middle East.

Jewish community life is reportedly strong. A Jewish school, the Albert Einstein Institute, was founded in 1955 in Panama City. In 1970 this school had nearly 50 teachers and offered preschool, primary and secondary education. Hebrew and Jewish traditions were taught and many graduates went off to Israel for a year or two of advanced studies. Several other Jewish organizations also exist: the Cultural Center of Panama, the B'nai B'rith Benevolence Society and the Central Council.

However, Jews have tended to integrate into Panamanian social, political and cultural life, while preserving some important aspects of their Jewish heritage, especially its religious values. There are seven Jewish synagogues in Panama, but only three had their own rabbis in 1970. Most of the Jewish population are members of the middle and upper classes of Panamanian society. Few are known to have become Christians, thus they can be considered one of Panama's unreached peoples.

## Other Unreached Peoples.

Several smaller ethnic groups can be found in Panama, especially in Panama City and Colon. Although their size is unknown, groups of East Indian Hindus and Middle Eastern Muslims are reportedly quite active in the import-export business and in retail trade stores that cater to tourists. Some Eastern Mediterranean peoples have also migrated to Panama, as evidenced by the appearance of two Greek Orthodox Churches in the two major port cities. None of these smaller ethnic groups are known to have Protestant believers, which indicates that they should be considered unreached peoples.

Adventists (11,735), Baptist Convention (6,245), Assemblies of God (5,500) and the Episcopal Church (4,738 communicants).

RELIGIOUS COMPOSITION OF PANAMA

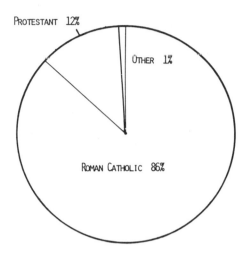

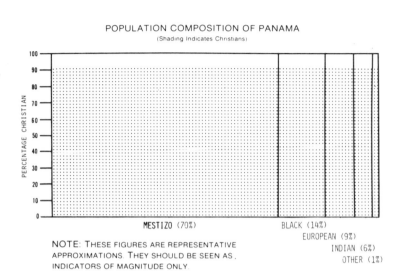

POPULATION COMPOSITION OF PANAMA
(Shading Indicates Christians)

NOTE: These figures are representative approximations. They should be seen as indicators of magnitude only.

**NATIONAL CHURCHES**

## CURRENT STATUS OF CHRISTIANITY

About 98% of the people of Panama consider themselves Christian with the Roman Catholic Church representing over 86% of the population. However, nominality continues to plague the Catholic Church.

While Protestant growth among West Indians and North Americans has been relatively static since the 1950s, notable increases were recorded among Hispanics and, to a lesser degree, among Amerindians since 1960. In fact, prior to 1960, only the Foursquare Church, Adventists and the Baptists showed much increase among Hispanics, with the Foursquare Church dominating the scene. Since 1960, Protestant growth among Hispanics has been significant: from 14,102 in 1960 to 49,943 in 1978 (7.3% AAGR). The number of Protestant Amerindians increased at a slower rate: from 3,752 in 1960 to 6,751 in 1978 (3.3% AAGR).

Today the largest Protestant denominations in Panama are the Foursquare Church (21,700 baptized members), Seventh-day

PROTESTANT CHURCHES

Data on Protestantism in Panama can be confusing and misleading if distinctions are not made between the Panama Canal Zone and the Republic of Panama, between church statistics on various ethnic groups within the general population and between denominational families of churches.

Protestantism has traditionally had a large following among the English-speaking Canal Zone population, predominantly West Indians and North Americans. However, by 1935 the proportion of Protestants in the Republic of Panama had increased to 48% of the total Protestant Community in Panama and the Canal Zone. Panama had only 38 organized congregations while the Canal Zone had 52. But by 1960, Panama accounted for 90% of all Protestants and the Canal Zone accounted for only 10%. By 1978, 95% of the total Protestant Community lived in the Republic of Panama and only 5% lived in the old Canal Zone.

It is often assumed that the majority of Protestants in Panama are Negroes who brought their Protestant faith with them from the British West Indies. Although this was true prior to 1940, by 1960 only

33.4% of the Protestant population were West Indians. Moreover, the Hispanic population (white-mestizo and Spanish-speaking) constituted 44.3% of all Protestants in 1960, while Amerindians were 11.9% and North Americans were 10.5%. The ethnic distribution of Protestants in 1978 was: Hispanic 68.7%, West Indian 17.5%, Amerindian 9.3% and North American 4.6%.

An overview of Protestant membership in Panama by families of denominational types between 1935 and 1978 reveals that the Liturgical family declined, proportionately, while the Pentecostal family greatly increased. Although the Adventist family has remained about the same, the Evangelical non-Pentecostal family has decreased proportionately in size. In 1935, the Liturgical family accounted for 40.6% of all Protestant communicants, the Evangelical non-Pentecostals 40.2%, the Adventists 17.9% and the Pentecostals 1.3%. However, by 1960, the Liturgical family had declined to 15.1% and, in 1978, represented only 6.7% of all communicant members. The Evangelical non-Pentecostals declined to 33.3% in 1960 and 27% in 1978. The Adventist family changed little proportionately: 14.8% in 1960 and 16.1% in 1978. The Pentecostals, on the other hand, increased notably from 1.3% in 1935, to 36.9% in 1960 and to 50.2% in 1978.

Regionally, the Evangelical non-Pentecostals predominate in the Western Atlantic and Eastern Regions, whereas the Pentecostals constitute the majority of churches in the Western Pacific, Central Pacific and Interoceanic Regions. The Adventists are strongest in the Western Pacific Region and the Liturgical groups in the Interoceanic Region.

Overall, Protestant communicant membership increased more rapidly between 1935 and 1960 (7.2% AAGR) than between 1960 and 1978 (4.7% AAGR). This is due to several principal factors: (1) a large proportion of Protestants prior to 1960 were English-speaking West Indians, but since 1960 that population has had relatively lttle growth due to emigration and acculturation; (2) the high number of North American Protestants in the Canal Zone prior to the 1950s constituted a large proportion of all Protestants in Panama; and (3) the rapid growth of the large Foursquare Church prior to 1960 (11.9% AAGR) slowed down between 1960 and 1978 (4.6% AAGR).

The total Protestant population of the Republic of Panama and the Canal Zone increased from 4.6% in 1935 to 6.7% in 1950. By 1960, the Protestant community accounted for 8.5% of the population and increased to 12% by 1980 (about 228,000).

## CATHOLIC CHURCHES

The Roman Catholic Church holds a respected, though not powerful, position in Panamanian society and is a familiar facet of daily life. The Constitution of 1946 recognizes that the Catholic faith is the country's predominant religion and Catholicism is taught in the public schools. Such instruction or other religious activity is not compulsory, however.

In 1980 approximately 86% of the population was considered Roman Catholic. Virtually every town has its Catholic Church, although many do not have a resident priest. Due to the small number of Catholic clergy in Panama, only one priest for every 6,299 inhabitants in 1980, many rural dwellers receive only an occasional visit from a busy priest who travels among a number of parishes. While Catholicism permeates the environment of most Panamanians, its impact is not as pronounced as in many other Catholic countries of Latin America.

The Catholic Church in Panama consists of one archdiocese, three dioceses, a vicar apostolic in Darien and a nullius prelate in Bocas del Toro. A papal nuncio also represents the Vatican. The archbishop of Panama is Monsignor Marcos Gregorio McGrath. Panama is organized into 133 parishes, served by 79 diocesan priests, and was supported by the efforts of 209 religious priests, 490 sisters and 58 lay brothers. Catholic institutions include 70 schools, a Catholic university, a seminary for training diocesan priests and numerous charitable programs.

In recent years the Catholic Church has attempted to revive active interest in religious affairs, raise church attendance and increase the number of church marriages. This has been a continuing effort since 1958, when a lay mission group, La Santa Mision Catolica (The Holy Catholic Mission), arrived from Rome to stimulate and support the local clergy. Focusing first on the lower classes in the capital, the campaign soon spread throughout the country. It helped introduce Church-sponsored social welfare projects, and served to rouse Catholics from the lethargy that has traditionally plagued the Church in Panama. However, the Panamanian Church continues to confront obstacles: a shortage of priests, the indifference of nominal Catholics and the secular attitudes of a growing urban population.

Today, the Catholic Church receives moderate public support, bolstered at times by militant Catholic action groups, such as federations of Catholic doctors and lawyers, who have campaigned for a more dynamic role for the Church in community life. A growing number of priests and nuns have taken a more active role in labor movements, formation of cooperatives, concern for the poor and in activities that seek to produce moderate reform within Panamanian society.

An added dimension during the 1970s has been the growth of the Catholic Charismatic Movement. Numerous Bible study, prayer and fellowship groups were organized in the early 1970s, along with Charismatic Masses and rallies. Soon, Protestant pastors and laymen were participating in the movement, which then took on an ecumenical flavor. More recently, however, the Catholic hierarchy has attempted to place restrictions on the Charismatic Movement and to direct its course in order to avoid losing members to evangelical groups.

### FOREIGN MISSIONS

PROTESTANT MISSIONS

Protestantism is a newcomer to the Isthmus of Panama and occupies ground traditionally held by Roman Catholicism. The heterogeneous character of Protestantism is related to the ethnic divisions peculiar to the Panamanian population. Whereas Protestantism was first introduced to Panama by immigrant groups, its impact and development among Spanish-speaking Panamanians, various Indian groups and newer ethnic minorities deserves special attention.

The Wesleyan Methodists were the first known Protestants to arrive in present-day Panama. Mother Abel, a mulatto, landed at Careening Cay in western Panama with a party of English and Jamaican settlers, about 1815-1825. Under her direction, a Methodist society was established. This work was later developed by the United Methodist Free Churches of England, who sent ministers and teachers to organize churches and schools about 1879. However, this pioneer work was eventually passed to the care of the Wesleyan Methodists.

Most Wesleyan Methodist work was centered in the Interoceanic Region among West Indians in Panama City and Colon, and in the segregated West Indian towns in the Canal Zone. In 1936, fourteen Wesleyan Methodist Congregations were in existence, with 1,869 communicants and about 2,700 adherents. In 1979, the Wesleyan Methodists reported 16 congregations and 1,794 members in the provinces of Panama, Colon and Bocas del Toro.

The Protestant Episcopal Church was apparently the first Protestant Church to be formally organized with a resident minister in present-day Panama, with the founding of Christ Church By-the-Sea in 1864 at Aspinwall, Colombia (now Colon, Panama). This church was the second non-Roman Catholic church built in Central America; the oldest is St. John's Cathedral in Belize City, founded in 1825.

Anglican work in Panama was begun in 1883 among West Indian laborers on the French-sponsored canal. As new towns were developed in the Canal Zone, the Episcopal Church established missions in Ancon, La Boca, Gatun, Paraiso, Empire and Las Cascades, as well as maintaining work in the cities of Panama and Colon. By 1919, there were about 7,500 adherents and 1,400 communicants in Panama.

In 1947, Anglican work in western Panama was transferred to the American Episcopal Church in the Canal Zone. After 1947, the Episcopal Church in Panama was divided into two archdeaconries. The archdeaconry of Western Panama included many missions in a large area that extended from Bocas del Toro on the Atlantic side to Puerto Armuelles on the Pacific Coast. The Archdeaconry of Panama and Colon comprised the terminal cities on the canal route, as well as other organized churches in the Interoceanic region.

The constituency of the Episcopal Church in Panama reflects the heterogenous character of the population in general, but its work among the Spanish-speaking inhabitants has been somewhat limited. Statistics on the Episcopal Church in Panama reflect the changing patterns of West Indian and Canal Zone population fluctuations over the years. Beginning in 1920 with 1,435 communicants and 9,763 adherents, growth increased to 3,465 communicants and 14,404 adherents in 1950. Communicant membership peaked in 1960 with 5,039, and has continued to maintain this level; 4,738 communicants were reported in 1978. From 18 churches and missions in 1920, Episcopal work increased to 29 congregations in 1960, with 23 congregations reported in 1978. The total Episcopal Community was estimated at 13,000. In 1950 about half of all Episcopalians were located in the Canal Zone, but by 1960 60% were located in the western provinces of Bocas del Toro and Chiriqui, mainly among West Indian workers in the banana zones.

Methodist Episcopal work was begun in 1905. Statistically, Methodist work in Panama shows very slow membership growth since its origin. Membership peaked at 239 full members in 1925, declined to 102 in 1940 and rose to 211 in 1950. By 1960, there were 490 full members among 11 organized congregations and 16 preaching points. Only about 500 members were reported in 1970, but by 1978 the Evangelical Methodist Church of Panama had increased to 695 members among five churches and five missions, composed predominantly of Spanish-speaking Panamanians.

The Seventh-day Adventist Church began work among West Indians in Panama in the 1890s. By 1960 the Adventist Church reported 3,898 members and almost 7,000 adherents. About half of their 44 congregations and 15 preaching points were located in Chiriqui Province, which accounted for 1,113 members and 2,145 adherents. Adventists were also well represented in the provinces of Colon and Bocas del Toro, in addition to the Canal Zone.

Continued Adventist growth since 1960 produced a membership of 6,210 in 1967 and 11,735 in 1978. The period of most rapid growth was between 1960 and 1967 when Adventist membership increased 6.9% (AAGR). The proportion of Adventists who are Hispanic increased from 40% in 1967 to 60% in 1978, while West Indians decreased from 40% to 35%. The proportion of Amerindians decreased from 20% to about 4%. North Americans accounted for the remaining 1% of Adventist membership in 1978. Adventist work is

The Southern Baptist Convention, through its Home Mission Board, began work among North Americans in the Canal Zone in 1905. Work among West Indians was added in 1908 when the Jamaican Baptist Missionary Society invited the Home Mission Board to assume responsibility for its work in Panama along the canal route. In the same year, the First Baptist Church of Balboa was established by North Americans in the Canal Zone. Five other Baptist churches were formed in the Zone among Americans.

Prior to the 1940s, Southern Baptist work was largely limited to the Canal Zone and the port cities of Colon and Panama, among North Americans and West Indians. Overall, Baptist growth was slow. Only 125 members were reported in 1925, but by 1935 membership totaled 1,250. However, only a slight gain was recorded during the next 20 years; in 1955, there were 1,845 members.

In the 1940s increased efforts were made by the Home Mission Board to evangelize and plant churches in Spanish-speaking communities. Two Hispanic churches were soon organized: the First Baptist Church of Panama City (1943) and La Chorrera Baptist Church (1946). Independent mission work among the Kuna Indians on the San Blas Islands was incorporated into the Home Mission Board in the 1950s. The Panama Baptist Convention was organized in 1959 representing four different cultures: West Indian, North American, Kuna and Hispanic Panamenos.

Between 1955 and 1967, Baptist work increased from 1,845 to 5,568 members. The membership increase between 1955 and 1960, from 1,845 to 4,464, was largely due to the addition of six Kuna congregations and six West Indian churches in Bocas del Toro region. In the mid-1960s, one-third of Baptist membership was West Indian, one-third was Amerindian (Kuna) and the other one-third was distributed among Americans in the Canal Zone and Hispanics in Panama.

The total membership of the Baptist Convention of Panama reached 6,245 in 1979 among 57 churches and 66 missions. However, the membership has been somewhat static since 1971, when 6,114 were reported. In 1979, Baptist membership by ethnic groups was 24% Kuna, 35% West Indian, 28% Hispanic and 13% North American.

About 7,000 Choco Indians are scattered throughout the jungles of Darien Province in eastern Panama. Since 1956, the Mennonite Brethren, New Tribes Mission and the Foursquare Church have combined efforts to learn the Choco dialects (Waunana and Embera) and to direct joint literacy work. Denominational differences have apparently been minimized and a scientific understanding of anthropology has been employed; a conscious waiting on guidance from the Holy Spirit has also been practiced.

The beginnings of a "people movement" have reportedly occurred among the Chocoes, and Protestant church life has increasingly taken on indigenous forms. From the beginning, Chocoes themselves have carried the initiative for teaching and evangelizing among their people. A new work is usually started in a neighboring village only after an invitation has been received from their leaders. After the Gospel is explained, the new community leaders are given several months or even years to consider their response to the message. If they decide to follow the Lord, the pastor of the visiting congregation baptizes the new believers and organizes a new congregation in that village.

The Choco congregations were organized in 1971 as the United Evangelical Church, but the structure was very informal. In 1977, ten congregations reported a membership of 700 and a Christian community of about 1,000, of which only about 300 were active members. Many of those who have been baptized have migrated in search of more fertile farmland in isolated areas where they are outside the reach of local congregations. Nevertheless, new converts are continually being added to the congregations, and new villages are being reached through Choco evangelists and teachers. A roving Bible school functions among the churches. The translation of the New Testament into Waunana is in progress.

The Churches of Christ began work in the Canal Zone in 1945 and organized their first church at Balboa that same year. Although progress was slow during the early years, by 1979 the work of the Churches of Christ had increased to 26 churches and 18 missions, with a total membership of about 3,000. The membership is largely Hispanic (37 congregations and 2,500 members), but there are also six congregations among the West Indians (about 400 members) and one among the North Americans at Balboa.

Other small non-Pentecostal denominations in Panama include: the Central America Mission, the Gospel Missionary Union, the Free Will Baptist Church, the Church of the Nazarene, the National Baptist Church, the Evangelical Mission of Panama, the Lutheran Church, Missouri Synod, the United Gospel Church, the Society of Bible Churches and the Christian Mission of Panama. None of these groups have more than 500 members each. Other larger groups in Panama, for which there is little historical data, are the Salvation Army and the Church of God (Anderson).

The rapid growth of the International Church of the Foursquare Gospel in Panama, prior to 1960, resulted in its becoming the largest Protestant denomination in the country, and it remains so to the present. The Foursquare Church, in 1960, accounted for approximately one-third of the total Protestant constituency in Panama and the Canal Zone, and more than 70% of all Spanish-speaking Protestant church members. Not surprisingly, the Foursquare Church in Panama has become synonomous with Protestantism - evangelicals are often referred to as "los Salvacuatro" (meaning Foursquare church members).

Soon after its introduction into the country in 1928, active lay workers carried the Pentecostal message to outlying areas of Panama. There were few Protestant churches in any of these Spanish-speaking areas, consequently the Foursquare work grew without much competition, especially in Chiriqui Province. In the 1940s, Foursquare work experienced rapid growth: from 1,000 members in 1940 to 7,000 in 1950 (21.6% AAGR). However, the growth rate slowed during the 1950s; by 1960, membership had increased only slightly to 9,173 (2.6% AAGR).

By 1950, scores of Foursquare congregations had been formed throughout Panama; by 1961 there were 128 churches and 65 preaching points with 10,276 members. Institutions included two Bible institutes with 65 students and 17 teachers, and one day school with 60 students and three teachers. There were 163 national workers, only fifteen of whom were fully ordained; three missionary couples also supported Foursquare ministries. Ninety-five percent of membership was Spanish-speaking. Foursquare work prior to 1960 grew with little administrative control, since it was largely a spontaneous expansion led by gifted lay workers without much formal education. Since the early 1960s, the Foursquare Church in Panama has entered into a period of consolidating previous efforts, constructing church buildings and increasing pastoral salaries.

Although the Foursquare Church has not suffered a major division in Panama, several leaders have left the denomination because of doctrinal differences, and have started their own movements. About 1940, the Evangelistic Doctrinal Church of Puerto Pilon was started in Colon Province. This group now has 11 organized churches and 17 missions in Panama with about 1,800 members. This movement believes strongly in visions, dreams and prophecy as means of discerning the Lord's will, while maintaining a highly critical attitude towards other churches.

Because of these and other reasons, several pastors of the Evangelistic Doctrinal Church of Puerto Pilon left the movement in 1970 to start another one under a similar name: the Evangelistic Doctrinal Church. With its mother church located in Puerto Armuelles, this group now has a total of 14 churches and 14 missions with 1,070 members. The new movement is considered less dogmatic and more evangelical than the former one.

The New Life Evangelical Church came into existence in 1967 under the leadership of a group of pastors who left the Foursquare Church in the Province of Chiriqui. It maintains a strong holiness emphasis and only members of their churches may take part in the Lord's Supper. Ten churches and eight missions have been organized with about 460 members.

The work of the Church of God - Cleveland began in Panama in 1935. A period of rapid growth took place between 1955 and 1964, resulting from a revival among the Church of God congregations. In 1964 there were 18 organized churches and 15 missions with 920 members. Fourteen of these were Spanish-speaking congregations with about 200 members (22%), 13 were Guaymi congregations with 460 members (50%), four were West Indian congregations with 175 members (19%) and two churches were among US servicemen with 85 members (9%).

By 1979, the total membership had increased to 1,657 among 39 churches and 19 missions. Latins represented 40.4% of the total membership, while West Indians totaled 39%, Guaymi 19.3% and US servicemen and their families accounted for 1.4%.

The Church of God operates a Bible Institute and a Theological Seminary in Ciudad Radial near Panama City. A more informal Bible Institute for laymen is maintained in Colon.

The Assemblies of God entered Panama in 1967. Most of the 22 churches and 28 missions organized since that time have been the result of extended evangelistic campaigns. As of February 1980, there were 13 such campaigns in process in many parts of Panama. The total membership of the Assemblies of God was estimated at 5,500 in late 1979.

In addition to three Christian bookstores operated by the Assemblies of God, many of their pastors had local radio programs throughout the country. The Assemblies of God Bible Institute, with 231 full-time students and 25 professors, trains pastors and lay leaders for service among the growing work in Panama.

Other Pentecostal denominations for which historical data is missing are: the Apostolic Assembly, Ebenezer Christian Association, Pentecostal Christian Church of the World Missionary Movement of Puerto Rico, Church of God in Christ, Pentecostal Church of God, Church of God of Prophecy, the International Evangelical Church and the Soldiers of the Cross of Christ.

The largest mission agency in terms of personnel is the New Tribes Mission. Since their work began in 1952 among the Amerindians, they have formed 46 congregations under national leadership, with a total membership of about 3,000. Thirty-five congregations are located among the Guaymi and one among the Buglere in Bocas del Toro Province, whereas there are nine Choco congregations and one among the Kuna in eastern Panama.

When churches are formed, local leaders are free to evangelize on their own, and no membership records are normally kept. All are independent local congregations with no official ties, but each one has a nucleus of baptized believers and several ordained elders. This reflects the non-denominational character of the New Tribes Mission and something of its Baptist church polity.

In 1979, the New Tribes Mission had a staff of 60 US missionaries, half of whom were working in church planting and discipleship training. Other ministries include Bible translation and literature, teaching, medicine, aviation and administration. The Mission operates a language school for teaching Spanish to missionaries.

Other large agencies working in Panama include Campus Crusade for Christ (with 29 missionaries), the Southern Baptists (18 missionaries), Wycliffe Bible Translators (16), Gospel Missionary Union (15) and the Assemblies of God (12). There are a total of 314 Protestant missionaries from 33 North American agencies working in Panama during 1979.

ROMAN CATHOLIC MISSIONS

Members of the Catholic clergy accompanied the Spanish Conquistadores from the earliest days of exploration in the New World. The first Catholic Church established in Panama was called Santa Maria la Antigua del Darien, built in 1510. It became the seat of the first diocese to be formed on the mainland of the Western Hemisphere. The Church had the responsibility for Christian instruction and conversion of the Indians and, in general, did much to protect them.

Under Spanish rule, both the Church and religious orders acquired considerable wealth. The orders, in particular, profitted from banking activities in the absence of organized commercial houses on the Isthmus of Panama. The Catholic Church acquired the resources to build schools and other institutions, in addition to elaborate churches in the old City of Panama. Public education was provided by priests, friars and nuns.

However, with the expulsion of the Jesuit Order in 1767, a long period of religious apathy followed, during which the Church lost much of its power and wealth. Although the Church did not experience the strong surge of anti-clericalism that swept through Latin America, there was (and still is) a widespread lack of interest and support for the Catholic Church.

Panama's Constitution of 1904 provided for complete religious freedom, claimed no government jurisdiction in the appointment of Church officials and specified no restrictions on Church management of internal religious affairs. Although the Catholic religion was recognized as the faith of the majority, the state itself does not support the Church monetarily. From the early years of independence up until the late 1960s, the Catholic Church continued to emphasize its spiritual role and generally avoided involvement in secular affairs. However, since the Second Vatican Council and the Conference of Latin American Bishops in Medellin in 1969, the Catholic Church has become more active in temporal matters, due to its increasing concern for and commitment to improving the social conditions of the impoverished masses in Panama and elsewhere.

Traditionally, Panama has had a very low percentage of native-born priests and nuns within the religious orders. In 1970, more than 75% of Catholic missionaries in Panama were foreigners, mostly coming from Spain, Italy, the United States or from other Latin American countries. Present in Panama are religious orders and personnel from Catholic missions in North America that include: the Vencentians (21), Benedictines (1), Holy Cross Fathers (1), Sulpicians (1) and three diocesan priests and one lay worker. In addition, there are ten female religious workers representing the Maryknolls (6), Mercy of Brooklin (1), Franciscans of Mary Immaculate (1) and St. Joseph of Medaille (1) and one lay worker. Also the Scarboro Foreign Mission Society of Canada has one priest in Panama.

However, these religious orders and missionaries from North America represent a small part of the total number of Catholic mission workers in Panama during 1980. Most of the 209 religious priests, 490 sisters and 58 lay brothers were from Europe or other Latin American countries.

## EVANGELISM

Although evangelistic activities have been an important part of organized Protestant church work in Panama since the 1850s, most evangelism prior to 1930 was concentrated in the West Indian population, and to a lesser extent among North American residents in the Canal Zone. However, these early efforts were aimed at immigrant groups of Protestant heritage, rather than towards the Spanish-speaking population. The exceptions were the Wesleyan Methodist work among the Guaymi Indians in Bocas del Toro, the independent San Blas Mission among the Kuna Indians, and the Methodist Episcopal and Adventist outreach among the Hispanics.

The founding of the International Church of the Foursquare Gospel in 1928 was the first concentrated effort to evangelize and plant churches among the Hispanic population. By 1960, the Foursquare church reported over 10,000 Spanish-speaking members, whereas other Protestant churches were noticeably less successful: Adventists, 1,700; Southern Baptists 800; Church of God - Cleveland, 800; Methodist Episcopal, 500; and Pan American Mission, 300. Since the 1960s, only a few Protestant groups have maintained strong evangelistic efforts among Hispanics: Assemblies of God, Adventists, Southern Baptists and the Foursquare Church. The New Tribes Mission has had notable success among Amerindians (Guaymi and Choco), also the Mennonites (Choco) and Southern Baptists (Kuna).

In mass evangelism, the Assemblies of God stands out during the 1970s in much the same way as the Foursquare Church did in an earlier period (1930s and 1940s). Divine healing campaigns sponsored by the Assemblies of God have drawn large crowds, especially in Panama City and along the Pan American Highway where a string of new congregations have now been formed.

Interdenominational evangelistic campaigns are relatively new to Panama. Evangelist T.L. Osborn of Tulsa, Oklahoma, held a campaign in Colon during the early 1950s, which had a great impact on the West Indian population. Also during the 1950s, a similar campaign among the Spanish-speaking population in Panama City, led by an evangelist named Espinosa, and supported by the Foursquare Church and the Church of God - Cleveland, resulted in hundreds of professions of faith. Evangelists Leighton Ford and Grady Wilson held a crusade in Panama City in 1958, as part of Billy Graham's Caribbean Crusade. Graham himself spoke at the conclusion of the campaign in PanamaIn spite of newspaper and bus strikes, large crowds attended and there was good response: an aggregate attendance of 59,680 and 1,877 professions of faith.

Earlier crusades were organized by the Latin America Mission of Costa Rica in 1951, with Wesleyan Methodist preacher Efraim Alphonse leading the meetings among Afro-Americans, and LAM-evangelist Victor Monterroso among Spanish-speaking Panamanians. However, LAM-sponsored Evangelism-in-Depth Campaigns, held during the 1960s in many countries of Latin America, by-passed Panama due to a lack of local support and cooperation. The Southern Baptists, participating in their denomination's Crusade of the Americas during the late 1960s, reported 1,200 professions of faith and 644 new church members during 1969.

Several Protestant organizations worked together during 1977 and 1978 to awaken believers, train laymen and mobilize local congregations in a series of activities leading to interdenominational evangelistic crusades in Panama City, Balboa (Canal Zone) and Colon. A local Panamanian committee, aided by missionaries of the Latin America Mission, coordinated efforts with African Enterprise to sponsor the Africa-Panama Crusade. African Enterprise team members, led by Bishop Festo Kivengere of Uganda and Michael Cassidy of South Africa, made several visits to Panama during the period 1976-1978 to help the local committee plan, promote and conduct pre-crusade meetings in late 1977 and the crusade itself in January, 1978. Most of the pre-crusade activities, however, were concentrated among West Indians and North Americans, with little participation from the Spanish-speaking churches. Consequently, the crusade meetings were attended largely by West Indians in Panama City and Colon, and by North Americans in Balboa. The results of the bilingual crusade, interestingly enough, showed that 55% of the inquirers were Spanish-speaking. However, of the 823 inquirers, only 111 were professions of faith, 89 were rededications and the rest came for general counselling or obtaining booklets written by Kivengere and Cassidy.

Moreover, the crusade meetings had a poor turnout with an aggregate attendance of 14,235 - an average of only 1,080 nightly. The crusade was principally supported by traditional, mainline denominations and by small, independent churches. Pentecostal backing was lacking, but the crusade had strong support from the Episcopal Church, no doubt reflecting the fact that the chairman of the local committee and the leading evangelist, Kivengere, were both Anglicans.

Many Pentecostal groups in Panama City joined forces during mid-1979 to support a campaign by Domingo Pilarte, a noted evangelist of the Pentecostal Holiness Church from the Dominican Republic. Eyewitnesses report that this crusade drew larger crowds (about 4,000 nightly) than the Africa-Panama Crusade, and that Pilarte's meetings were conducted only in Spanish.

A city-wide crusade held in David, Chiriqui in late 1978, was sponsored by Alfa y Omega (Campus Crusade for Christ) and ten local congregations, representing both Pentecostals and non-Pentecostals. This crusade, which had a significant impact on the growing city of David, was similar in strategy to the "I Found It!" campaigns conducted by Campus Crusade in the United States. More than 550 laymen received special training in evangelism and discipleship during pre-campaign meetings. Attendance at the city-wide campaign averaged about 700-800 nightly.

Since the beginning of the Charismatic renewal in Panama during the mid-1970s, a new openness and receptivity to the gospel have been apparent among the middle and upper strata of Panamanian society. Several new Charismatic churches have emerged in Panama City, mainly among the upper classes, where barriers between Protestants and Catholics have become less important. This spirit of unity among Christians, regardless of their church affiliation, has been evidenced in scores of small groups that have developed spontaneously to meet the growing need for fellowship, prayer and Bible study among new converts and revitalized older believers. Recently, chapters of the Full Gospel Businessmen's Fellowship and Women's Aglow have been established in Panama City among the growing Charismatic community, especially among business and professional people.

BROADCASTING

Radio HOXO, "The Voice of the Isthmus," was founded in 1949 when a group of evangelicals in Panama and the Canal Zone purchased a small radio station in Panama City. The power of the station has increased over the years from 500 to 5,000 watts so that the gospel can be heard throughout Panama, in Spanish and English. Financial help and technical assistance have been provided by the Latin America Mission of Costa Rica (until 1963) and the

World Radio Missionary Fellowship of Ecuador. This has enabled HOXO to effectively serve the Christian public in Panama and to win many to faith in Christ. In 1971, HOXO added an FM/Stereo station, Radio Vida, to complement AM broadcasting, and in 1974 these two stations were incorporated as the Tropical Broadcasting Association, under a Panamanian board of directors.

Although many Protestant denominations and local pastors cooperate with and support the ministry of HOXO and Radio Vida, dozens of evangelical programs are also broadcast on local commercial stations throughout Panama. Recently, evangelical pastors who produce their own programs formed the Christian Association of Radio Pastors, with technical assistance from the HOXO staff.

Only a few Christian television programs have been produced by evangelicals in Panama, but the PTL Club and the 700 Club are both aired regularly in Spanish. The PTL Club has a regional office in Panama which handles program distribution throughout Latin America as well as the correspondence with viewers.

## LITERATURE AND FILMS

A variety of Christian literature is available in Panama and the Canal Zone through about a dozen Christian bookstores: four in Panama City, four in the Canal Zone and one each in Colon, David and La Concepcion de Boqueron. Literacy materials are distributed by Alfalit of Panama. At least five evangelical groups offer the use of Christian films or other audio-visual aids.

## BIBLE TRANSLATION AND DISTRIBUTION

In addition to the Spanish Bible the New Testament has been published in Kuna-San Blas, and Scripture portions are available in Guaymi, Embera and Waunana. In 1978, Wycliffe Bible Translators were working on translations of the scriptures into the following languages: Buglere, Embera, Kuna-Paya, Ngobere (Guaymi), Teribe (Naso) and Waunana. Other Protestant missions who have worked with Wycliffe or have done their own translation work are New Tribes Mission, the Mennonite Brethren, Central American Mission, Southern Baptists, Foursquare Church, Adventist Church and the Wesleyan Methodists.

In mid-1981, the government of Panama asked Wycliffe to leave the country. The government had allowed Wycliffe to work two years beyond their expired contract, which was not renewed.

Since 1917, when the American Bible Society established its regional headquarters in the Canal Zone, the Bible House in Cristobal has been the major distribution center for Bibles throughout Central America. A national office of the United Bible Societies was established in Panama in 1974.

The latest distribution reports for Panama reveal the following:

| | |
|---|---:|
| Bibles | 22,817 |
| New Testaments | 17,018 |
| Portions | 17,986 |
| Selections | 528,813 |
| New Reader Portions | 127,217 |
| New Reader Selections | 65 |
| | --------- |
| Total 1979 | 713,916 |
| Total 1978 | 1,672,627 |

## EDUCATION

Christian. Great progress had been made in education by a number of Protestant denominations in Panama by 1960. The Methodist Episcopal Church continued to offer primary and secondary education at their Pan American Institute (IPA) in Panama City; the Episcopal Church operated two primary schools, in Colon and Panama City, and the Foursquare Church had a new school in Darien Province. However, the Adventist church, apparently placing a high priority on Christian education, operated eleven primary schools and one secondary school.

Today, Protestants are responsible for at least ten kindergartens (mainly the Southern Baptists, Salvation Army and Episcopal Church), 16 primary schools (the Adventists have ten) and four secondary schools (two Episcopal, one Adventist and one United Methodist). The Salvation Army also operates a school for the blind in Panama City. New Tribes Mission has a school for missionary's children and a language school for teaching Spanish to missionaries.

Theological. Theological education had a slow development among Protestant denominations. The only known programs to be established prior to 1960 were by the Adventists in 1921 (the West Caribbean Training School) and the Foursquare Church in 1938 (the Foursquare Bible Institute). Today, there are at least four programs of Theological Education by Extension (TEE), eleven Bible institutes (the Foursquare Church and the Church of God - Cleveland, each have two), and two formal seminary programs are operated by the Southern Baptists (the Baptist Theological Seminary) and the Church of God -

Cleveland (the International Latin American Seminary). Some Protestant denominations in Panama send their ministerial candidates to other countries for theological education.

SOCIAL CONCERNS

Community and Rural Development. Several agricultural and rural development projects are sponsored by the Wesleyan Methodists, Episcopals, Adventists and the Lutheran Church of Panama. The Salvation Army is the only group known to be working in community development in urban areas (Colon and Panama City).

Medicine and Public Health. Medical assistance programs were developed by the Adventists and Wesleyan Methodists among the Creoles Guaymi in Bocas del Toro and by the independent San Blas Mission among the Kuna during the 1910s, but no other programs are known to exist prior to the 1950s. The Gospel Missionary Union began medical work at El Amanecer soon after their arrival in Panama in 1952. More recently, medical and health assistance programs have been developed by the Mennonite Brethren among the Choco in Darien, the New Tribes Mission among the Guaymi in Bocas del Toro, the Southern Baptists and the Church of God - Anderson among the Kuna in the San Blas Islands and the Gospel Missionary Union among the Guaymi in Veraguas.

Other Social Ministries. The Salvation Army operates several social ministries in Colon and Panama City: childcare centers, a school for the blind, a home for the elderly and an orphanage. The Episcopal Church maintains a home for young girls in Panama City. Several denominations also provide spiritual care to patients of the Palo Seco Leper Colony, and to inmates in jails and prisons in Panama and the Canal Zone. The Women's Christian Temperance Union also has a chapter in Panama City.

Christian camping programs and facilities have been developed by at least eight Protestant denominations, mainly in western Panama along the Pacific coast. However, only a few of these facilities are improved campgrounds that could be utilized by other Protestant groups on a rental basis. The Southern Baptist camp at Santa Clara, known as "Cresta del Mar," is the best example of an improved campground.

Several evangelical groups have specialized programs for high school or university students. The United Methodists, Episcopals and Adventists offer special activities for youth through their secondary schools. Youth for Christ has recently sent workers to Panama to develop high school ministries, particularly in the Canal Zone among North American youth. University students are being served by Campus Crusade for Christ, the Episcopal Church and MINAMUNDO (Ministry to the Student World, an international and interdenominational student ministry related to the Latin American Mission). The Mennonite Brethren have established a student center in Juan Diaz, near Panama City, where Choco students can live and receive help while attending public schools in the capital.

General Service Organizations. The Republic of Panama has never had a broad-based interdenominational service organization like those in Nicaragua (CEPAD), Honduras (CEDEN), Guatemala (CEPA/CEDI) or Costa Rica (Goodwill Caravans). But, in recent years, concerned evangelicals in Panama have begun to discuss the need for such an organization. In January, 1980, the Evangelical Association for Development (AEPAD), patterned after CEPAD, was formally constituted under the laws of Panama as a non-profit benevolent organization. AEPAD is now developing its staff and expanding its departments to offer valuable new services to the evangelical public and to the people of Panama in several key areas: administration, community development, education and human development, social services, public health, housing loans for developing small businesses, relief assistance, emergency aid, communications and pastoral concerns.

The Institute of In-Depth Evangelization (INDEPTH), based in Costa Rica and related to the Latin America Mission, has assisted evangelical leaders in Panama for a number of years. INDEPTH now has resident advisors in Panama - one in Panama City and another in Chiriqui Province. Both are Panamanian pastors who help coordinate activities designed to promote evangelism, discipleship, integral church growth and unity among evangelical churches. INDEPTH advisors provide assistance to individual denominations, to interdenominational efforts and to local congregations and pastors. One of INDEPTH's recent projects in Panama has been to coordinate a church growth study of the Protestant movement in Panama, and to publish a geographical directory of churches as well as other reports on the status of evangelical work in Panama. Several church growth seminars and workshops were held in Panama during 1980-1981 sponsored jointly by INDEPTH and AEPAD.

## NATION AND ITS PEOPLE

### POPULATION

The population of Panama was 1,830,175 in 1980, up from 1,428,000 in 1970. The annual growth rate was 3.2%. According to the 1970 Census, 43% of the population was under 15 years of age, 53% were between 15 and 64 and only 3.7% were over 65 years.

Geographically, the Interoceanic Region has 50% of the total population, which includes the major cities of Panama City and Colon. The Central Pacific Region accounts for 28% of the population; the Western Pacific Region (Chiriqui Province), 15.5%; the Western Atlantic Region, 3.8%; and the Eastern Region 3.2%. The average national density is 22.1 inhabitants per square kilometer (57.1 per square mile).

Panama's urban population is now 49.6%, whereas in 1950 it was only 36%. The most heavily urbanized provinces are Panama (77.7%) and Colon (56.5%). Panama City (642,600) dominates the urban scene to such an extent that Panamanians refer to two Panamas: the capital and the rest of the country, called the "interior." The urban growth rate is estimated at 5% annually. The main area of attraction is Panama City and its buffer zones. In spite of government efforts to curb rural-urban migration, by the establishment of schools and health centers and the implementation of an agricultural development program, every period of drought in the interior produces a new migratory wave to the larger cities. However, it is important to note that this migratory influx is comprised primarily of middle and upper income families, rather than of the poor.

Emigration totals 25,000 to 50,000 yearly, mainly to the United States. The proportion of foreign born has declined from 11.6% in 1911 to 4.4% in 1960, and it now stands at about 1%. The new canal treaty has caused more West Indians to emigrate to U.S. cities.

### COMPOSITION

Panama has one of the most racially mixed populations in the Central American region. The people of Panama spring from three major components: the indigenous Indians, the Spanish colonialists and the Negro slaves brought from Africa. Added to these basic components have been several immigrant groups, including West Indian Negroes, Chinese, East Indians, Jews and other eastern Mediterranean peoples. Today, the population of Panama includes 70% mestizo, 13% Negro, 10% Caucasian, 6% Indian and about 1% Oriental and Middle Eastern.

The term "Panameno" is commonly used to describe the mestizo population - Spanish-speaking, largely Roman Catholic and culturally Hispanic - regardless of racial origins. The term technically refers to all Panamanian citizens. Although "mestizo" normally distinguishes the white-Indian mixture, in Panama the term is used for any racial combination within the Hispanic population. The mestizo component of the population is growing due to the high rates of acculturation among the Indian and Negro populations, who are becoming increasingly Hispanicized through intermarriage with mestizos.

The Negro population includes two ethnic groups: the Hispanicized Negroes and the West Indian Negroes. Approximately 5% of the population are Spanish-speaking blacks, descendants of African slaves, who are completely Hispanicized and culturally accepted as Panamenos. Because of their cultural distinctives, most Hispanicized blacks usually resent being confused with West Indians. By contrast, the West Indians speak an English-based Creole, are mostly Protestant and show preference for urban settlements. The term "antillano" refers to Negroes who came to Panama from the Caribbean to work on railroad construction and building the canal. The size of the West Indian population in Panama has declined from 11% in 1950 to 5% in 1970, due largely to emigration or assimilation as mestizos.

The majority of the Caucasian population are descendants of the old landed and wealthy Spanish aristocracy, who have maintained political and economic control of Panama for more than 400 years. Most members of the upper class are of unmixed blood and tend to marry within their group. The old Spanish families are largely urbanized. Small numbers of North Americans and Europeans are also present in the larger cities. The present white civilian population of the Canal Zone includes about 20,000 North Americans who are either employees of the Panama Canal Company or are civilian dependents of military personnel.

The Amerindians were the origianl inhabitants of present-day Panama. Today, there are three major Indian groups: the Kuna (26,000) along the northeastern Caribbean coast, the Choco (7,000) in the southeastern lowland jungle of Darien Province and the Guaymi (46,000) in western Panama. Smaller tribes include the Teribe (1,000) and the Buglere (2,500) in the mountains of western Panama, near the Costa Rican border. The proportion of Amerindians in the Panamanian population has declined over the years as the mestizo component has increased.

The Indian groups in Panama have chosen to maintain their own semi-autonomous communities, subject to tribal government, and to live according to their own traditions. Assistance is given to the tribes by the government, especially in the areas of public health and welfare. Although the tribal communities have a separate and largely autonomous political status, this does not deprive their members of full voting rights nor are they restricted to their own tribal areas. Most Indians remain in their isolated communities by choice, which reflects their longstanding resistance to assimilation.

Several small ethnic minorities can be found within the Panamanian population. Members of these groups are mainly urban dwellers, are principally engaged in commerce and are largely bilingual in Spanish and their native tongue, although they tend to preserve their separate communities. The largest groups are the Chinese (30,000) and the Jews (3,000), who reside primarily in Panama City and Colon. Smaller groups include East Indians and Middle Easterners.

## LANGUAGE AND LITERACY

In 1970, the number of illiterates in Panama totalled to 21% of the population. Illiteracy was high in remote areas. Panama's national language is Spanish, which is spoken by the majority of the population. However, the West Indian Negroes traditionally speak a Caribbean English-based Creole, which is apparently intelligible to Jamaican and other Central American creoles. Standard English is also spoken by many West Indians, especially residents of the old Canal Zone and of Panama City and Colon. English was the official language of the Canal Zone, but a dual language system is now being established.

In addition, many minority languages are spoken. Among the Amerindians, many speak no Spanish and others have only recently become bilingual. Indian dialects include Buglere (Bokota), Kuna-Paya, Kuna-San Blas, Embera, Guaymi (Ngobere), Teribe and Waunana. The Chinese population is largely Cantonese-speaking, especially those who live in Panama City and Colon, while smaller numbers speak Mandarin or Hakka. However, most older Chinese immigrants or native-born Panamanians of

Chinese descent are bilingual in Spanish.

## RELIGION

The 1970 Census reported 93% of the population as Roman Catholic, 6% Protestant and 1% smaller religious groups - Jews, Chinese, Hindus and Muslims. However, these statistics do not include the nation's Amerindian peoples, many of whom have resisted centuries of proselytizing efforts and few have become Christians. These tribal peoples are predominantly Animists, although a growing number of Protestant churches are located among them. In mid 1979, the Protestant population numbered 218,000 people, or 11.6% of the population.

## GEOGRAPHY AND CLIMATE

Panama is a narrow, "S"-shaped country lying between Costa Rica and Colombia. Its boundary with Colombia marks the division between Central and South America. The Panama Canal, crossing the lowest and narrowest point of land between the Atlantic and the Pacific, bisects the republic from ocean to ocean. Panama's two largest cities, Panama City and Colon, are situated alongside the canal's Pacific and Atlantic entrances. Three-fifths of Panama consist of rolling hills to rough mountains. In the rugged Sierra de Chiriqui and Cordillera de Veraguas are several volcanic peaks, the highest being Chiriqui (11,410 feet). Eastward the rough Cordillera de San Blas with summits nearly 3,600 feet high, borders the Caribbean to Colombia.

Lowlands have temperatures of 27 degrees C.(80 degrees F.) with little monthly variation. Mean annual temperatures decrease from 23 degrees C.(74 degrees F.) at 3,000 feet to 16 degrees C.(60 degrees F.) at 5,000 feet and to 7 degrees C.(45 degrees F.) in the high Sierra de Chiriqui. The Caribbean coast, with no distinct dry season, receives from 317 to 400 centimeters (127 to 160 inches) of rain per year. Annual precipitation at Santa Clara, on the Pacific coast, is 127 centimeters (51 inches), with January to April almost rainless. The western Chiriqui plains receive 240 centimeters (96 inches) per year and the southern Darien receives 240 centimeters (96 inches) per year, with no distinct dry season.

## HISTORY

The northern coast of the Isthmus of Panama was discovered by Spanish explorers in 1501 and a small, successful colony was subsequently established by Balboa. In 1531, Francisco Pizarro sailed from the fishing village of Panama, located on the Pacific side of the Isthmus, for Peru. Thereafter the importance of Panama was in its location. The riches of the Spanish possessions to the south and north were brought to it for transhipment, while in the opposite direction merchandise of the mother country was distributed to the colonies. Panama City became the third richest colonial center of the New World.

The considerable Indian population of the Isthmus declined abruptly during these early years. Tens of thousands were killed in the conquest, many were worked to death as slaves and thousands more died of diseases brought by the Spaniards. The rapid depletion of the Indian population prompted the importation of slaves from Africa. Panama experienced great economic decline when Spain started to permit direct and intercolonial trade in her American colonies. Furthermore, Panama's monopolistic trade center had been under continual maritime assaults, staged primarily by the English. Political subordination followed this decline, and in 1751 the Isthmus was demoted to a dependency of Colombia.

Panama proclaimed its independence from Spain in 1821, after Bolivar liberated New Granada, and voluntarily joined the Colombia Union. In 1826, Panama was the seat of the assembly of representatives of Latin America states, and enjoyed considerable local autonomy.

The migration of thousands of people to California during the Gold Rush of 1849 provided the impetus for building a railroad across the Isthmus of Panama from north to south. The railroad did much to restore Panama's prosperity and created a new city and port on the northern terminus of the line, Aspinwall (now Colon).

Construction of an interoceanic canal was begun in 1880 by the Universal Interoceanic Canal Company headed by the Frenchman, Ferdinand de Lesseps. Legal entanglements, fraudulent financial arrangements and disease brought about the collapse of the company in 1889.

Meanwhile, Panama experienced considerable political instability. Whether it had status of a state or a department, it was continually beset by civil strife. When Panama seceded from Colombia in 1903, she did so as a protectorate of the United States, a status defined by the Hay-Bunau Varilla Treaty.

The United States was given possession in perpetuity of a ten-mile wide strip across the Isthmus, as well as other concessions highly favorable to the construction of the canal. A government was duly installed under the Constitution of 1904, with the usual delegation of powers between the executive, legislative and judicial branches. But these representative principles proved meaningless, for a handful of principal families assumed control of public affairs.

Construction of the Panama Canal was initiated in 1907. The success of the undertaking was beyond debate. A major triumph was the eradication of yellow fever and malaria. Less convincing was the resultant existence of a state dominated politically and economically by a foreign-controlled canal.

Despite the benefits, the presence of the Canal and the Canal Zone under American control occasioned prolonged and bitter controversy, as well as demonstrations and bloodshed. As a result, several revisions were put into effect. These culminated in the adoption of the Carter-Torrijos Treaty (1977/1978) which contemplates American withdrawal in the year 2000.

GOVERNMENT AND POLITICAL CONDITIONS

Until the coup d'etat of 1968, which resulted in a moratorium on traditional party politics, power had been wielded almost exclusively by a small number of wealthy, educated families. The military coup that brought the Provisional Junta to power in 1968 seemed to be motivated by gross electoral impurity and the overt attempts of President Arnulfo Arias to dominate the National Guard. The Provisional Junta, drawn from the middle class, consolidated its control of the government and General Omar Torrijos became the undisputed head. Undertaking a program of urban and agrarian development and with a highly nationalistic policy, this government was able to gain widespread support.

Popular elections took place in August, 1972, when Panamanians turned out to vote for representatives for their neighborhood councils (corregimientos). Today, the base of the government is formed by the 505 representatives to the National Assembly of Neighborhood Councils. The Constitution promulgated by this National Assembly makes provisions for three types of political power structures. One is traditional: it defines the executive, legislative and judicial branches. The other is the popular power structure: it legitimizes popular control over the National Assembly of Neighborhood Councils, Municipal Councils and Village Councils. A third power is exercised by a mediating figure called the "Chief of

Government."

Today, Aristides Royo, elected by the National Assembly of Neighborhood Councils, is President of Panama. General Omar Torrijos prescinded some of his powers as "Chief of Government," turning more and more to his functions as head of the National Guard. However, Torrijos was killed in a plane crash in July, 1981. The Panamanian government, described as center-leftist, is bent on an independent foreign policy. It has recently signed important agreements with Japan, including a study by that nation of the construction of another sea-level canal.

## ECONOMY

Two different economic systems exist side by side in Panama. One is the highly sophisticated urban economy of Panama city, Colon and their environs that provides a relatively high standard of living for most of their residents. The urban economy is based upon domestic and foreign trade and services. The other is an agriculture-based economy that provides a subsistence or low-income standard of living for the majority of the population.

Mainly because of the highly advanced urban economy, Panama has one of the highest per capita incomes in Latin America, the equivalent of US $660. The distribution, however, is highly unequal. About 10% of the population receive 48% of the country's wealth while 35% receive only 5% of it.

After a decline in the GNP in 1976, the Panamanian economy is now showing signs of growth with a 5% increase in the GNP in 1979. The increased control of some of the Canal Zone facilities is expected to generate more revenues. Four products account for 90% of all exports. Bananas are the major export. Panama usually contributes between 6 and 7 percent to the total world banana market. Petroleum products, shrimp and sugar follow in importance as exports.

## CHURCH STATISTICS FOR PANAMA

NOTE: Statistics are from the 1978 PROCADES survey of Protestant Churches and are based on official denominational reports or estimates. Although definitions of membership vary slightly among churches, the data is highly comparable and reliable. All known churches are included in this list.

| Church or Mission Name | Number of Congregations | Membership | % of Total |
|---|---|---|---|
| PROTESTANT | | | |
| Liturgical | 25 | 4,848 | 6.7% |
|   Episcopal Church | 23 | 4,738 | |
|   Redeemer Lutheran Church | 2 | 110 | |
| Evangelical Non-Pentecostal | 391 | 19,657 | 27.0% |
|   Church of God - Anderson | 24 | 600 | |
|   Church of Christ | 44 | 3,000 | |
|   New Tribes Mission | 46 | 3,000 | |
|   Salvation Army | 6 | 851 | |
|   Southern Baptist Conv. | 123 | 6,245 | |
|   United Methodist | 10 | 695 | |
|   Wesleyan Methodist | 17 | 1,795 | |
|   Misc. | 121 | 3,472 | |
| Pentecostal | 498 | 36,460 | 50.2% |
|   Apostolic Assembly | 16 | 786 | |
|   Assemblies of God | 50 | 5,500 | |
|   Church of God - Cleveland | 57 | 1,657 | |
|   Church of God of Prophecy | 23 | 572 | |
|   Doctrinal Evangelistic Church of Puerto Pilon | 28 | 1,882 | |
|   Doctrinal Evangelistic Church (Independent) | 28 | 1,070 | |
|   Ebenezer Christian Assoc. | 2 | 700 | |
|   Foursquare Church | 218 | 21,700 | |
|   Pentecostal Church of God | 14 | 941 | |
|   Misc. | 62 | 1,652 | |
| Adventist | 120 | 11,735 | 16.1% |
|   Seventh-day Adventist | 120 | 11,735 | |
| TOTALS (1978) | 1,034 | 72,700 | 100.0% |
| ESTIMATED PROTESTANT COMMUNITY | | 218,000 | |
| ROMAN CATHOLIC | 130 parishes | 1,520,000 | |

# SELECTED BIBLIOGRAPHY AND INFORMATION SOURCES

The sources listed below are to help the reader find additional information on this country and Christian ministries there. This list does not try to be comprehensive or complete.

## DOCUMENTS

### General

Cozean, Jon D., Latin America, 1980, Washington, D.C.: Stryker-Post Publications, 1980.

Helms, Mary W., and Franklin O. Loveland, eds., Frontier Adaptations in Lower Central America, Philadelphia: Institute for the Study of Human Issues, 1976.

Herring, Hubert, A History of Latin America, New York: Alfred A. Knopf, 1968.

Weil, Thomas E., et al, Area Handbook for Panama, Washington, D.C.: U.S. Government Printing Office, 1972.

### Christian

Butler, Charles, "Protestant Growth and a Changing Panama: A Study of Foursquare Gospel and Methodist Patterns," Unpublished M.A. Thesis, Dallas: Perkins School of Theology, 1964.

PROCADES, "directorio de Iglesias y Organizaciones y Ministerios del Movimiento Protestantes: Panama," San Jose, Costa Rica: PROCADES/INDEPTH, 1980.

Grimes, Barbara F., ed., Ethnologue, Huntington Beach, CA: Wycliffe Bible Translators, 1978.

Grubb, Kenneth G., Religion in Central America, London: World Dominion Press, 1937.

Hall, David R., "Radio HOXO: A Critical History of an Overseas Christian Radio Station," M.A. Thesis, Billy Graham Communications Program, Wheaton College Graduate School, 1978.

Orr, J. Edwin, Evangelical Awakenings in Latin America, Minneapolis, MN: Bethany Fellowship, 1978.

Read, William R., et al, Latin American Church Growth, Grand Rapids, MI: Eerdmans, 1969.

## ORGANIZATIONS

The Evangelical Association for Development (AEPAD), Apartado 1792, Balboa, The Republic of Panama.

Bible Society of Panama, Apartado 3316, Panama 4, Republic of Panama.

Evangelical Radio Station HOXO, Apartado 3269, Panama 3, Republic of Panama.

## ACKNOWLEDGMENTS

The information in this profile was taken from many sources which were the best available to the editors at the time of preparation. However, the accuracy of the information cannot be guaranteed. Views expressed or implied in this publication are not necessarily those of World Vision. The editors have tried to present the ministries of various organizations in an objective manner, without undue bias or emphasis. Where we have failed, we apologize for erroneous impressions that may result and request that comments and corrections be sent to MARC, 919 West Huntington Drive, Monrovia, California, 91016, USA. We appreciate and acknowledge the comments and contributions of various organizations and individuals in the preparation of this publication.

# II
# STATUS OF CHRISTIANITY
# COUNTRY PROFILES
# THE CARIBBEAN

This program is jointly carried out by the Strategy Working Group of the Lausanne Committee for World Evangelization and MARC, a ministry of World Vision International. For further information on the program, please write: MARC, 919 West Huntington Drive, Monrovia, CA 91016 U.S.A.

# STATUS OF CHRISTIANITY COUNTRY PROFILE

# THE BAHAMAS

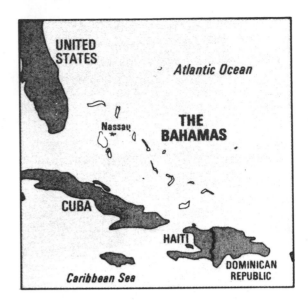

## SUMMARY

AREA - 11,396 sq. km. (5,389 sq. miles)
POPULATION - 216,000 (1977 est.)
RELIGION - 95% Christian (83% Protestant,
    12% Roman Catholic)

Scattered over the sun-drenched Caribbean waters between Cuba and Florida are more than 700 islands and cays which are collectively known as the Bahama Islands. It was here where Columbus first glimpsed the New World. The Bahamas got their name from the Spanish words, "baja" and "mar," meaning "shallow sea" - a good description of the area. The Spanish, however, did not colonize the islands, but left them for the English to settle. The first English in the islands were buccaneers and pirates who preyed upon Spanish ships. They were followed by planters and their slaves. Today, the majority of the people are the descendants of those slaves.

Tourism has become the mainstay of the Bahamian economy. North Americans enjoy its beautiful beaches, warm waters and balmy climate.

Christianity is well established as the religion of the people. However, a great many are nominal Christians.

## PEOPLE GROUPS

Christianity has always been the only recognized religion in the Bahamas. Churches abound; religious knowledge is even taught in the public schools. In this respect, there are few people groups who are truly unreached. There are small communities of Jews, Chinese and Muslims who are still unreached, but the vast majority of the people would claim to be Christian. The West Indies Mission reports church planting among the Haitian immigrants. By broadcasting the gospel in Haitian Creole, a bridge was built for effective ministry, resulting in new churches among this people group.

However, according to some reports, as much as 90% of the Christianity in the Bahamas is nominal. The Obeah worship (an African witchcraft and ancestor worship) is practiced extensively by the average Bahamian. Bahamians, in general, are evangelized to the extent that they have a knowledge of Christianity, but in the more narrow sense, the Bahamians are unevangelized since a great number do not understand what it means to be spiritually reborn.

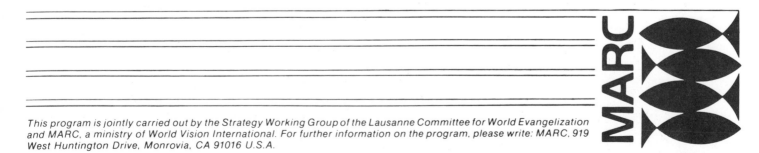

*This program is jointly carried out by the Strategy Working Group of the Lausanne Committee for World Evangelization and MARC, a ministry of World Vision International. For further information on the program, please write: MARC, 919 West Huntington Drive, Monrovia, CA 91016 U.S.A.*

The first recorded church worship in the Bahamas was by the Eleutheran Adventurers who were Puritans from England and came seeking freedom of worship. They landed on an island in 1648 which they named Eleuthera and worshipped in a cave, presumably building a chapel later. An Anglican chapel was built in Nassau in 1724, and the Anglican Church became the established church from 1734 to 1869. The Methodist Church was started by a free black in 1786 and effective missionary work was begun by this Church in 1800. No permanent Catholic work was started until 1866. Other groups present in the islands now include the Brethren, Seventh-day Adventist, Church of God - Anderson, Church of God of Prophecy, Church of God - Cleveland, Assemblies of God, Salvation Army, Church of Christ, Lutheran, Presbyterian and the Baptist International Mission. Other Baptists, with about 50,000 members and adherents, are the largest denomination.

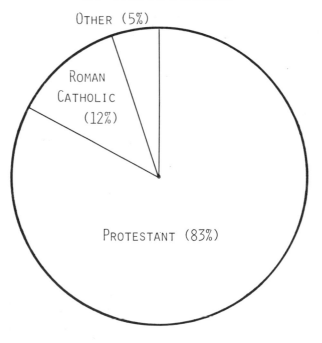

## RELIGIOUS COMPOSITION OF THE BAHAMAS

OTHER (5%)

ROMAN CATHOLIC (12%)

PROTESTANT (83%)

## PROTESTANT

The initial missionary effort was made by the Church of England in the early eighteenth century. Prior to this time, the only Christian presence was the Eleutheran Puritan colony and the Anglican chaplains on the British men-of-war which occasionally called upon the islands. For many years progress was very slow. Toward the end of the eighteenth century, the Anglican Church was reinforced by the Loyalists who fled from the American Revolution. During the nineteenth and twentieth centuries the work became strong. Today, there are over 41,000 adherents and 40 priests in the Anglican Diocese of Nassau and the Bahamas.

In 1786, Joseph Paul, an ex-slave from the Carolinas, arrived. He is recognized as the founder of Methodism in the Bahamas. In 1800, Rev. William Turton of Barbados came as the first Methodist minister. The Bahamas came under the jurisdiction of the British Methodist Church through the Methodist Missionary Society, which sent its first missionary to the Bahamas in 1848. In 1968, they joined the Conference of the Methodist Church in the Caribbean and the Americas. In 1973, the church listed over 3,300 members and an estimated community of 7,400.

Baptist work started in 1780 with the preaching of Frank Spence, a former slave. In 1790, a group of free slaves, including one Prince Williams, came in an open boat from St. Augustine, Florida, and started preaching. They built a small chapel and started what is known as Bethel Baptist Church in 1801. Sambo Scriven was its first pastor and Prince Williams was his assistant. Williams later began another church. In 1833, Mr. and Mrs. Joseph Burton were sent as missionaries of the Baptist Missionary Society. They began almost one hundred churches in the islands. There are now eight different Baptist associations and several independent Baptist churches. Together, their numbers constitute the largest denomination in the Bahamas.

Pentecostal influence began in 1909 when a Negro couple from the Bahamas were converted in Florida and brought back the Pentecostal message. Along with a retired Methodist minister, they were the founders of the Church of God - Cleveland in the Bahamas. Today, there are 57 Church of God congregations in the Bahamas. In 1928, the first Assemblies of God church was founded in the city of Nassau. The Bahamian Council of the Assemblies of God was organized in 1955. There are now 17 Assemblies of God churches with over 2,400 adherents.

## CATHOLIC CHURCHES

Roman Catholic ministry started in 1866. The Bahamas were organized as a Diocese in 1960. The 1980 Catholic Almanac counts 26,340 Catholics (or 12% of the population) in the Bahamas. This figure is considerably below the 34,000 Catholics (28% of the population) reported in 1968. There are 32 parishes overseen by 47 priests.

## FOREIGN MISSIONS

### PROTESTANT MISSIONS

In 1969 there were ten North American Protestant mission agencies with a total of 64 missionaries laboring in the islands. The largest sending agencies at that time were the Southern Baptists and the Gospel Missionary Union. Since then, six other agencies began work in the islands. The largest agency is now the Baptist International Mission (a fundamentalist group) with 47 missionaries. Next in size are the Southern Baptists and the Gospel Missionary Union, both with 18. Worldteam (formerly the West Indies Mission) is working among the Haitian immigrants. There are 96 North American missionaries now working in the Bahamas.

In 1979, there were four career missionaries and ten short-termers serving in the Bahamas from the United Kingdom. The United Society for the Propagation of the Gospel sent two career missionaries and three short-termers. The Methodist Church also sent two career missionaries but sent six short-termers. The Church of Scotland sent one short-termer.

### ROMAN CATHOLIC MISSIONS

The Roman Catholics list four brothers and 66 sisters from North America serving in the Bahamas. Most are serving in Catholic schools.

## MAJOR CHRISTIAN ACTIVITIES

### BROADCASTING

There are two broadcasting services in the Bahamas, station ZNS (Bahamas Broadcasting and Television) and station ZNS II, a smaller station with a more limited range. A number of American networks give coverage to the area, but the signals are weak as far as television reception is concerned. Several Christian programs can be heard. "The Baptist Hour" and the Assemblies of God "Revivaltime" are both heard over Bahamian airwaves.

### BIBLE TRANSLATION AND DISTRIBUTION

The Bahamas is under the jurisdiction of the West Indies District of the United Bible Society. This area includes Jamaica and the Turks and Caicos Islands. In 1979, the anticipated scripture distribution for the entire area was as follows:

| | |
|---|---|
| Bibles | 60,165 |
| New Testaments | 13,629 |
| Portions | 36,728 |
| Selections | 825,042 |
| | ------ |
| TOTAL 1979 | 935,564 |
| TOTAL 1978 | 738,681 |

### EDUCATION

#### Christian

The Roman Catholics have historically stressed education as a way to evangelize and nurture their church members. They operate eighteen schools in the Bahamas. The Anglicans operate five day-care centers, three primary schools and two secondary schools. The Baptists run the combined primary and secondary school: the Jordon-Prince Williams Baptist School.

#### Theological

Two schools with a combined enrollment of 52 students are taught by the Assemblies of God. One of them is located in Nassau, the other is a four-year Bible Institute on Great Abaco Island. The Southern Baptists saw a need for leadership training and theological education and opened the Bahamas Baptist Institute in 1953. It closed temporarily in 1967 but was reopened as a night school in 1973 under the name Bahamas Baptist Bible Institute.

## SOCIAL CONCERN

Several denominations minister to the social needs of the Bahamians. The Salvation Army entered the Bahamas as a field of service in 1931. They now operate an institute for the blind and a welfare office in Nassau. The Methodist Church runs a home for the aged, a day-care center and has a job training program in a prison.

## NATION AND ITS PEOPLE

## POPULATION

Only 40 of the 700 islands and cays of the Bahamas are inhabited. Of the total population of 216,000 (1977 est.), over 75% of the people live on either New Providence or Grand Bahama Islands. The 1977 population estimate for New Providence - containing Nassau and Paradise Island - was 122,000 people. The capital city, Nassau, had 120,000 inhabitants. The 1970 populations of the other main islands were: Grand Bahamas, including the second largest city, Freeport (25,850); Eleuthera (9,470); Andros (8,845); Abaco (6,500); Long Island (3,860); Exuma and Cays (3,770); and Cat Island (2,650).

## COMPOSITION

About 16% of the population of the Bahamas are foreign born. Included in this figure are Haitian immigrants and North Americans. Over 85% of the people are blacks while the remainder are the descendants of English settlers.

## RELIGION

The largest Christian groups represented in the Bahamas are Baptist (29%), Anglican (23%) and Roman Catholic (12%). The remaining Christian population is divided among Pentecostal groups, Methodists, Seventh-day Adventists and others. The Bahamaian population is reported to be 95% Christian.

## LANGUAGE AND LITERACY

The official language is English. The Haitian immigrants speak Haitian Creole. Education is free and compulsory between the ages of five and fourteen. Over 80% of the 228 schools are government owned and operated while the remainder are private. About 90% of the Bahamians are literate.

## GEOGRAPHY AND CLIMATE

The Bahamas consist of 700 islands and cays with a total land area of 13,935 square kilometers (5,380 square miles). The islands are coral formations and the highest point on any of them is only 120 meters (400 feet) above sea level. The Bahamians enjoy a semitropical climate and have only two seasons. Winter extends from December through April and summer is from May through November. Temperatures are subtropical, ranging from 21 to 34 degrees C. (70 to 94 degrees F.) in mid summer and 15 to 24 degrees C. (60 to 75 degrees F.) in winter. Yearly rainfall averages 132 centimeters (52 inches), largely concentrated in the periods of May to June and September to October. Trade winds temper the effects of high humidity. The islands are vulnerable to hurricanes between June and November.

## HISTORY

Christopher Columbus' first sight of land on his first voyage to the New World was San Salvador Island of the Bahamas. The islanders of that time, the Arawak Indians, were soon exterminated through slavery and disease. The Spanish, however, did not establish any permanent settlements. England first staked a claim on the Bahamas in the form of a land grant in 1578; however, no attempt was made to colonize the islands until they were granted to Sir Robert Heath in 1629. The first settlement was on Santa Catalina, now called New Providence, in 1630. Other settlers came in gradually, among them the Puritan Eleutheran Adventurers who settled in 1647. Many buccaneers used Santa Catalina Island as a base. They so harrassed Spanish ships that, in 1641, the Spanish raided Santa Catalina Island, retaining possession until 1666 when the English regained control. In 1717 the Bahamas became a British Crown Colony. The buccaneers were brought under control by the first British governor, Captain Woodes Rogers, a former pirate himself.

The economy was based principally on fishing and salvaging the remains of the numerous shipwrecks which occurred in the shallow Bahamian waters. Poor soil brought failure to any large-scale plantation operation. The Bahamas had periods of prosperity as a center of Confederate blockade running during the American Civil War and as a base for American Prohibition rum-runners. Since World War II, the Bahamas have become an attractive tourist resort area.

## GOVERNMENT AND POLITICAL CONDITIONS

The Bahamas became independent from Great Britain on July 10, 1973 but have remained part of the British Commonwealth. The head of state is Queen Elizabeth II, who is represented by a Governor-General whom she appoints. The Head of Government is Prime Minister Lyndon O. Pindling. Legislative powers are vested in the Parliament, consisting of an elected 38 member House of Assembly and an appointed 16 member Senate.

The Progressive Labor Party (PLP) controls the politically stable Bahamian government. It won 30 of the 38 seats of the House of Assembly in the July, 1977 elections. The PLP was formed in 1953 by blacks discontented with the policies of white businessmen and politicians. The PLP first came to power in 1967. The opposition party is the Bahamian Democratic Party. The year following its formation in 1976, it won six seats.

## ECONOMY

In the past, the Bahamian economy has experienced long periods of stagnation interspersed with short periods of large influxes of wealth (the periods of the American Civil War and Prohibition). Following World War II, Americans discovered the pleasant qualities of Bahamian beaches and climate. Tourism soon became the mainstay of the economy. Americans account for over 75% of foreign visitors.

Banking and finance constitute the economy's second most important sector. The Bahamas status as a tax haven and its system of banking regulations have led to its growth as an international banking center.

The Bahamas have become an important transhipment point for oil going to North America. Other industries include pharmaceuticals, cement, rum and liquor distilleries.

## SELECTED BIBLIOGRAPHY AND INFORMATION SOURCES

The sources listed below are to help the reader find additional information on this country and Christian ministries there. This list does not try to be comprehensive or complete.

DOCUMENTS

General

"The Bahamas," Background Notes, Washington, D.C.: U.S. Department of State, November, 1978.

Christian

"Bahamas," Field Focus, Springfield, MO: Assemblies of God, Division of Foreign Missions, 1977.

## ACKNOWLEDGMENTS

The information in this profile was taken from many sources which were the best available to the editors at the time of preparation. However, the accuracy of the information cannot be guaranteed. Views expressed or implied in this publication are not necessarily those of World Vision. The editors have tried to present the ministries of various organizations in an objective manner, without undue bias or emphasis. Where we have failed, we apologize for erroneous impressions that may result and request that comments or corrections be sent to MARC, 919 West Huntington Drive, Monrovia, California, USA, 91016. We appreciate and acknowledge the comments and contributions of various organizations and individuals in the preparation of this publication.

# STATUS OF CHRISTIANITY COUNTRY PROFILE

# CUBA

### SUMMARY

AREA - 114,478 square kilometers (44,217 square miles)

POPULATION - 9.9 million (1979)

RELIGION - 51% Christian (49% Roman Catholic, 2% Protestant), 49% Secular

The Republic of Cuba, known as the "Pearl of the Antilles," is comprised of some 3,715 islands, islets and cays of which the island of Cuba is by far the largest island in the Caribbean. Cuba was so centrally located and had such good natural harbors that it soon became one of Spain's most valuable possessions after its discovery by Columbus in 1492. Strategically, it was used as the staging area for the Spanish expeditions of discovery and conquest in the New World. Commercially, its central location put it on the crossroads of Spanish trade to and from Spain's colonies.

Cuba's colonial history profoundly influenced its society. Spanish culture and values are dominant. However, African, Chinese and American influences have also helped shape Cuban society. African slaves, and later, Chinese laborers were imported to work in the rich sugar cane and tobacco fields. Each group has contributed much to Cuban life, including art, literature and religion. U.S. influence began after Cuba's War of Independence in 1898. American business, culture and religion soon made their way into Cuban society.

The Marxist government of Fidel Castro has done much to reshape Cuban life. In his attempts to make the "New Man," Castro has outlawed racial and class distinctions, improved the health and educational level of the people and reshaped the Cuban economy. Cuba has become the outpost of communist doctrine in the Western Hemisphere.

Numerically, most Christian churches have fared poorly under Communist rule. The Catholic Church has declined from 85% to 49% of the population. The Protestant Churches have declined also, though some are now beginning to grow once more.

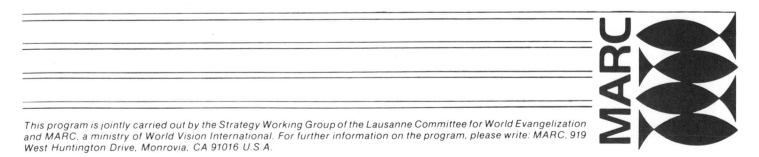

*This program is jointly carried out by the Strategy Working Group of the Lausanne Committee for World Evangelization and MARC, a ministry of World Vision International. For further information on the program, please write: MARC, 919 West Huntington Drive, Monrovia, CA 91016 U.S.A.*

## PEOPLE GROUPS

The Cuban Revolution in 1959 profoundly affected the social system which Cuba inherited from the days of Spanish colonialism. Prior to the Revolution, Spanish immigrants to Cuba set the character of society. Spanish values, language, lifestyles and cultural traits were highly regarded. The Spaniards were divided into two sub-groups: those who married white Cubans and adopted a Cuban identity were called "Criollos"; and those who maintained a European outlook still considered themselves Spanish.

Generally, the Spaniards and the Criollos occupied the upper class positions in society. They were the business and military leaders, large land owners and politicians. It is interesting that the children of these upper class Spaniards and Criollos often associated with nationalistic movements in opposition to their parents. This was true in both Cuba's War of Independence in 1898 and in the Revolution of 1959.

Because of the shortage of female Spanish immigrants, Spanish men often intermixed with blacks and Indians. The descendants of Criollos and Spanish who intermarried were called "mestizos." In Cuba, the term "mestizo" is used interchangeably to describe any person with mixed parentage. Generally, mestizos have held a higher social status than blacks, though not as high a position as the Spanish.

Beginning in 1517, the Spanish began importing black slaves. By the time the slave trade was finally halted in 1865 there were more blacks than Spanish in Cuba. Blacks from Haiti and Jamaica also were brought to Cuba to work in the cane fields.

From these various elements of the black population there evolved a cohesive Afro-Cuban tradition that has permeated several aspects of Cuban life, including the arts and religions. Afro-Cuban music and a style of writing called "negrismo" have profoundly influenced Cuban society at all levels. The principal Afro-Cuban religion is known as "Santeria" (things of the saints) and is a blending of African animism and Roman Catholic rituals.

There are several versions of Santeria, each originating from a different tribal region of Africa. However, almost all practitioners of Santeria consider themselves Roman Catholics and believe that the names of the saints are translations into Spanish of the African names of the spirits. These spirits are called "santos" (Spanish word for saint) or "orishas" (Nigerian Yoruba tribe's word for spirit). The "orishas" are supposedly the spirits of important men who have died.

Santeria worship ritual varies but is usually an imitation of Roman Catholic ritual, complete with the Lord's Prayer, Hail Mary, candles and gestures. Singing, dancing and drumming are important aspects of Santeria meetings. Usually such a meeting culminates in the spirit possession of the "santero" or leader by the "orishas" of the dead. Under the control of the "orisha," the "santero" takes on the character and voice of the dead person.

Since the Revolution, Santeria worship has declined. It is still practiced, though mostly in rural areas.

When slave trading was abolished in 1865, Chinese laborers were contracted to work in the cane fields in conditions which were little better than slavery. By 1899, they accounted for about one percent of the total population. There were virtually no Chinese women in Cuba at that time. Consequently, the Chinese intermarried and the proportion of pure Chinese steadily decreased. Only 0.3 percent of the population was considered Chinese in the 1953 Census (although many more people of part-Chinese ancestry considered themselves part of the Chinese community).

Another people group is the small Jewish community. Prior to the Revolution there were over 12,000 Jews in Cuba. Since many of them were owners of businesses, most of the Jews fled Cuba after the Revolution. Today, only about 1,000 remain.

Although the Revolution has attempted to minimize the significance of ethnic distinctions, such differences are still considered important by Cubans today. Little scholarly work has been devoted to the categorization of ethnic groups since the Revolution, but several trends have been noted. Among the most important of these is the increased ethnic homogenization of the society as a result of emmigration. Most emmigrants have been upper or middle class families (although the 1979 exodus was noted for its many lower class peoples) who were usually white Criollo, Spanish and some mestizos, as well as Chinese, Jews and English-speaking people. Recent estimates now put the black population at about 40 percent of the total.

Another result of the Revolution is the government's attempts to legislate racial equality. These attempts have not been met with particular success. Increased educational opportunities have been very important for the blacks, who constituted the largest group of illiterates prior to 1959. Nevertheless, blacks charge that levels of educational differences still exist between whites and blacks. Furthermore, prejudice still appears to be present. Blacks are conspicuously absent from proportional representation in high levels of the government, the military and the Communist Party. Many Cubans believe that such discrepancies will correct themselves within a generaton.

## CURRENT STATUS OF CHRISTIANITY

The Constitution of Cuba, adopted in February, 1976 states that "the Socialist state, which bases its activity on and educates the people in the scientific materialist concept of the universe, recognizes and guarantees freedom of conscience, the right of each person to profess whatever religion he pleases and to practice, within legal limits, the worship of his choice." The Cuban Communist Party has stated that one of the "tasks of the ideological struggle" in Cuba is "the gradual conquest of religious beliefs." This is to be done "by adusting scientific materialist propaganda to the cultural level of workers." The party further stated that it rejects "antireligious campaigns and coercive...measures against religion." Instead, believers must not be "isolated from the Revolution but drawn into its concrete tasks."

The status of Christianity in Cuba today is a reflection of these stated goals and principles of the Cuban rulership. Churches in Cuba are numerically weaker than in pre-Revolution times and have little impact upon society. Christian activities such as evangelism and Christian education must be confined to church buildings. Government permits are necessary for Christian camps and conferences. Although there is no overt persecution, Christians are looked down upon and the government is often suspicious of their motives and activities.

In order to understand the present situation, it is helpful to study Cuba's religious history. Cuba was never as "Catholic" a country as were most others in Latin America. Cuba was dominated by the Spanish until 1898 and most of the Cuban clergy before and after that time were Spanish.

Furthermore, the Catholic Church was concentrated more in the cities than in the countryside and more among the middle and upper classes than among the poor. Many of the clergy supported the government and the aristocracy in Cuba's War of Independence in 1898 and in the Revolution of 1959. Hence, the Catholic Church was never viewed with trust or acceptance by the victors of the struggles.

The situation at the eve of the Revolution reflected the Catholic Church's problem of assimilation in Cuba. In 1957 the ratio of priests to the population was one to every 8,145. Of the 514 priests in Cuba in 1946, only 82 were born in Cuba; 432 were from other countries, mostly Spain, the United States and Canada.

Although the overwhelming majority of people (85%) were Roman Catholic, few men went to church. One estimate put the number of practicing Catholics in 1960 at only two percent of the population. In one Cuban city there were more centers of Santeria worship than Catholic and Protestant churches combined. A sudden surge occurred in Catholic worship attendance and devotion in the years just prior to and just after the Revolution. This was seen by observers to be a demonstration against Communism rather than loyalty to Christ.

Consequently, the course of the Cuban Catholic Church could be predicted following the Revolution. Some Catholics at first thought they would be favored under the Castro regime. He had graduated from a prestigious Jesuit high school and, in 1953, had been saved from execution by Archbishop Enrique Perez Serantes of Santiago. Furthermore, a priest had travelled with Castro's guerrillas and Castro himself was godfather at many baptisms. However, as Castro lead Cuba toward socialism, the historic mistrust between the Catholic Church and the goverment began to grow again. This situation was further exacerbated when Castro nationalized all religious schools in 1961 and when it was discovered that many prominent Catholics, including three priests, were involved in the Bay of Pigs invasion fiasco sponsored by J.F. Kennedy and the CIA. The ensuing power struggle resulted in the revocation of permits for most foreign clergy and the loss of Catholic media sources.

In the years that followed, all Christian denominations declined in numbers and influence. Between 1959 and 1980, over 850,000 Cubans left, most for the United States. Many of these were middle and upper class Catholics. As religion was discouraged in Cuba, many already nominal Catholics left the Church. Today, only 49 percent of the Cubans still claim to be Catholic and less than one percent worship regularly.

The Protestant churches have generally fared no better. Following the War of Independence in 1898, U.S. Protestant denominations sent many missionaries. This created a tension between Catholics and Protestants and it also helped identify Protestant denominations with U.S. influence in Cuban affairs.

Furthermore, the process of indigenization was very slow, with most Cuban Protestant churches relying heavily on American dollars and personnel for their operations. With the exception of the Pentecostals and some other evangelical groups, the Protestants had the greatest influence on the middle and upper classes.

Therefore, when the opportunity arose for Cubans to leave Castro's socialist program, most Protestant leaders and laity emmigrated to the U.S. Thus, those who remained were left leaderless and without resources. By 1970, about half of the Episcopal, Methodist and Presbyterian congregations had left Cuba. It was not until recently that some of the remaining Protestant churches have begun to report growth.

Despite the absence of open persecution, a subtle discrimination is practiced against those who openly profess their religious faith. A young person who attends church regularly will probably not be recommended for the university, be promoted at work, or be eligible for Communist Party membership. Even if one wanted to cooperate with the regime from a high level position, one would not be able to if active at church.

Many churches are now attempting to cooperate with the government. Instead of attacking the revolution, many evangelical churches are working under its laws and programs. This has been successful for those churches who preach both the need for personal conversion and for its outworking in society. The Catholic Church has also tried to come to terms with the government. After years of silence, the Catholics issued a pastoral letter in 1969 calling for an end to illiteracy, condemning the U.S. economic blockade and calling on Catholics to recognize the dignity of work in Cuba. This was quite a step considering that earlier letters condemned the government's Marxist stance. Cuba has never severed diplomatic relations with the Vatican.

All in all, however, the Cuban anti-religious program has never been as severe as in most Communist countries. No priest or minister has been killed in Cuba since Castro, although several have been arrested. Nevertheless, many people in both Catholic and Protestant churches still see the Church as the only institution to survive the Revolution. Suspician of the government's anti-religious stance makes Christians nervous about their status in Cuba's future.

RELIGIOUS COMPOSITION OF CUBA

PROTESTANT (2%)

SECULARISTS (49%)   ROMAN CATHOLIC (49%)

**NATIONAL CHURCHES**

PROTESTANT CHURCHES

In 1878, a revolution broke out in Spain, and in October the Cubans took up arms and declared their independence. Captain of one of the rebel bands was Alberto J. Diaz. Forced by Spanish soldiers to flee to sea, he was rescued by a passing ship and taken to New York City. There, he enrolled in medical school and then became a Christian while seriously ill in a hospital. After graduation, he took his practice back to Cuba where he also began evangelizing his countrymen. Despite persecution by ecclesiastical anthorities, Diaz was able to establish a Bible society. Diaz's work was later combined with the Southern Baptists through the efforts of a Baptist missionary from Florida. By 1959 there were over 200 Southern Baptist churches with over 7,000 members in Cuba. Northern Baptists were represented at this time by more than 120 congregations.

Following the Revolution, Baptist churches were subjected to two major challenges: 1) approximately 4,000 members, including 50 pastors, left the country, 2) some of the pastors were arrested. Both of these factors combined to create an acute shortage of leadership within the churches. However, Baptists have weathered the crisis fairly well, compared to some other denominations. A small number of Baptist churches have been founded since 1959. The Baptists are generally part of the Eastern (formerly the Northern Baptist) or Western (the former Southern Baptist) Conventions or the major independent group known as Bautista Libres. In 1969, it was reported by an American missionary who had just been released from a Cuban jail, that there were about 90 Baptist churches in the Western Conference with more than 8,000 members. In 1976 the Western Conference reported 102 churches and 75 Cuban pastors. By 1981, the Baptist Convention of Western Cuba, an affiliate of the Southern Baptist Convention, represented 105 churches with 6,300 members. There were 24 Baptist Churches in Havana alone. The largest church in Cuba is Calvary Baptist Church in Havana with more than 1,500 members.

The Eastern Baptist Convention had 125 churches, 15 missions and 55 pastors in 1976. Their total membership in that year was reported to be about 6,200. It is notable that they have missions aimed at reaching Haitian immigrants. Overall membership has remained stable in the last few years. The Independent Baptists were reported to have 4,000 members in 1981.

Other early Protestant denominations in Cuba were the Methodists, Anglicans and Presbyterians. In 1883 the Methodist Church began work in Cuba. By 1958 they had a membership of 7,600 but by 1971 this had dwindled to 2,700. Of the 120-130 Methodist ministers in 1958, all but six left the country. Episcopalian services for foreign residents were begun in 1871 but it was not until after 1880 that there were Cuban Anglicans. By 1959, there were 85 congregations ministered to by more than twenty national pastors. It had some 2,000 members. It has been reported that at least half of the leaders and members have since left the country. The same fact is true of the Presbyterians. They

had an entirely indigenous ministry and over 3,000 members in 1959 but now record only half that number. About two-thirds of the 50 Presbyterian ministers left after the Revolution. Today there are only 15 Presbyterian ministers.

Generally, the evangelical churches initially declined in membership following 1959 but have since recouped their losses. One of the denominations which is now beginning to grow again is that of the West Indies Mission (now Worldteam). Founded in 1928 by Elmer Thompson and B.G. Lavastida, the West Indies Mission work in Cuba sought to evangelize the neglected rural areas. By 1958 they had some 200 congregations with 2,000 members, a Bible School, a Christian bookstore and regular radio broadcasts. In 1976 they reported only 63 churches but their attendance was increasing.

The Assemblies of God has shown the most remarkable growth. Assemblies work started in 1920 and by 1929 the denomination was well established. By 1958 there were 25 organized churches, 143 outstations and 130 Cuban leaders. There were 2,600 members and a Christian community of 6,500 people. By 1978 the Assemblies of God had more than 115 churches in Cuba.

Today, the largest Protestant denomination in Cuba is the Seventh-day Adventists with over 9,000 members. Their evangelistic zeal often gets them in trouble with Cuban authorities.

There are about 46 Protestant denominations in Cuba, with approximately 1,000 congregations. In 1975 it was estimated that Protestants number 160,000 or about 2% of the population. This number is down from the 360,000 Protestants in 1952. Among some of the other denominations are the Friends Church, Christian Church, Church of God - Cleveland, Free Will Baptists and the Church of the Nazarene.

The greatest need evident among churches in Cuba is trained pastors, teachers and leaders. A severe shortage of qualified leadership is one factor which has limited the growth of the Church in Cuba.

CATHOLIC CHURCHES

Today, only 49 percent of the Cubans still claim to be Catholic - a drop of 42 percent from 1959. Less than one percent of these attend Mass regularly.

In 1960, there were 723 priests and 2,225 religious women working in Cuba. Today, with a highly increased population Cuba has only 215 priests (down from 228 in 1970) and a like number of nuns. Today Cuba has a ratio of one priest for every 21,554 Catholics.

Two seminaries are open in Cuba with a total of 110 students studying for the priesthood. This is down from 128 students in 1970. Religious education is permitted in Cuba, but only within the church buildings. The Church is no longer involved in the regular education process or in social concerns. These limitations, however, release the Church from many financial worries and time commitments.

The Catholic Church in all of Cuba prints only two tiny liturgical bulletins each week, nothing else is allowed.

## FOREIGN MISSIONS

### PROTESTANT MISSIONS

There are no longer any Protestant missionaries in Cuba. There is one American working under appointment of the Presbyterian Church of Cuba. She directs music education for the church and teaches music in Christian education at the interdenominational Protestant seminary at Matanzas.

### ROMAN CATHOLIC MISSIONS

There are still several expatriate priests working in Cuba. However only one Catholic worker is from the U.S. There are 34 Canadian Catholics (14 priests, 20 sisters) working in Cuba.

## MAJOR CHRISTIAN ACTIVITIES

### EVANGELISM

Christians are not officially permitted to proselytize. All religious functions must be held within the churches. Those groups that engage in public witnessing, such as the Seventh-day Adventists, are persecuted. Nevertheless, personal evangelism is still carried out.

### BROADCASTING

There are no Christian broadcasts originating from Cuba. However, Cubans can listen to the Trans World Radio broadcasts from Bonaire in the Caribbean and to Worldteam's Radio Lumiere from Haiti. Cuba is also within range of Christian broadcasts originating in Florida.

### LITERATURE

There is a shortage of Christian literature. Small amounts are permitted to be imported but nothing is printed in Cuba except for two small Catholic liturgical bulletins. Two men working for a Christian ministry to people in Communist countries were recently released from a Cuban prison where they had served sentences for dropping Christian literature from an airplane.

### BIBLE TRANSLATION AND DISTRIBUTION

The Cuban Bible Society was closed down in 1968 as a result of government legislation affecting private businesses. Since then there have been only occasional imports of Scriptures. These have been in small quantities and do not satisfy demand. The most recent imports took place in 1977, when the Bible Society in the West Indies was able to send in 2,500 Reina Valera Spanish Bibles and 2,500 Spanish "Popular Version" New Testaments, and in 1979, when 10,000 "Popular Version" Bibles were dispatched at the request of the Ecumenical Council.

### EDUCATION

The Castro government nationalized all the religious schools in 1961 so today there are no church-sponsored primary and secondary schools. However, a number of seminaries still operate on the island. One is a union seminary for Methodist, Episcopalian, Presbyterian and Pentecostal students in Las Villas province known as Mantanzas Evangelical Seminary. It has 65 to 75 students and is "very progressive" in that the faculty supports the Revolution. It holds night extension courses in Havana, Matanzas, Las Villas and Camaguey provinces as well.

Three different seminaries are operated by the Baptists each with about 30 students. The "Oriental Convention" (North American Baptists) is at Santiago de Cuba; the "Occidental Convention" (Southern Baptists) is in Havana and has some women studying Christian education; the indigenous Baptists, whose ranks include Puerto Ricans and other West Indians, are at Loss Pinos Nuevos in Las Villas province.

There is a Nazarene seminary ("very conservative") with about 10 students in a Havana suburb, and a Seventh-day Adventist seminary near Havana airport.

A Catholic seminary with 50 students operates in Santiago de Cuba, and another with 60 students operates in Havana.

## SOCIAL CONCERNS

Except for promoting Revolutionary reforms and programs (such as supporting literacy training and volunteering to work in the cane fields) churches are not allowed to contribute to social concerns.

## NATION AND ITS PEOPLE

## POPULATION

In 1979 Cuba had a population of approximately 9.9 million people. About 60% of these people live in urban areas. The capital, Havana, is the nation's largest city with over 1.8 million residents. It is also known for its deep water port, the best in the Caribbean. Other large cities in Cuba are Santiago de Cuba, Camaguez and Santa Clara. The average population density of Cuba is 83 people per square kilometer (215 per square mile). The annual population growth rate averages 1.7% but the exodus of 1% of the population to America in 1980 makes this figure temporarily lower.

## COMPOSITION

The population of Cuba is composed largely of people with Spanish and African backgrounds. Indians have long since been absorbed into other ethnic groups. Some 30-40 percent of the population is black, the descendants of slaves brought to Cuba by the Spanish. The intermixture of the Spanish with blacks and the Spanish with Indians produced those who are known in Cuba as mestizos. Except for small handfuls of Chinese and Jews, they and the Spanish constitute the rest of the population.

## LANGUAGE AND LITERACY

The official language of Cuba is Spanish. Virtually all the people speak it. Cuban Spanish is basically Castilian although in its spoken forms it varies greatly from the Spanish of Spain. Several English and African words along with local idioms have found their place in accepted usage.

The Cuban government launched an all-out drive in 1961 to achieve full adult literacy. Since that time, they have achieved a literacy rate of 96%.

## RELIGION

Just over half of Cuba's population consider themselves Christian. However, most of these people do not regularly attend church. Roman Catholics comprise 49% of the population while some 2% are Protestant. Many practice the Afro-Christian cult known as Santeria.

## GEOGRAPHY AND CLIMATE

Cuba is the largest island in the Caribbean. It stretches 1,200 kilometers (745 miles) long and varies between 35-200 kilometers (22-125 miles) in width. Cuba's coastline is indented with hundreds of small bays and inlets. The harbors at Havana, Guantanamo and Bakia Honda are among the best deep water harbors in the world. Cuba also has some 1,600 adjacent keys and islands, the largest of which is the Isle of Pines off the south west coast.

Three-fifths of Cuba's area is flat or gently rolling hills. The main group of mountains is located in the eastern, central and western areas of the island. The highest elevation is the eastern Sierra Maestra range with peaks over 1,829 meters (6,000 feet) above sea level.

Cuba enjoys a semi-tropical climate because of its position in the tradewind belt. There are two seasons: the dry, lasting from November to April; and the wet, lasting from May to October. The average yearly rainfall is 137 centimeters (54 inches) with 75% of the rain occurring in the wet season. The average temperature is about 21 degrees Celcius (70 degrees Fahrenheit) in the winter and 27 degrees Celcius (81 degrees Fahrenheit) in the summer.

## HISTORY

Christopher Columbus discovered Cuba during his first voyage on October 27, 1492. He made two other trips, returning to Spain with some gold objects given him by the native Arawak Indians. The Spanish, under Diego Valasquez, conquered the island in 1511. By 1515 seven towns had been established, including Havana. Havana became important as a commercial seaport between Spain and its colonies in the New World.

The Spanish colonists moved inland, establishing sugar plantations and using Indians as slave labor. As the Indians died out, African slaves were imported to work in the fields.

The independence movement in Cuba began in 1850 when Cuban planters led several expeditions against Spanish troops on the island. On October 10, 1868 under the leadership of Carlos Manuel de Cespedes, the Ten Years War broke out. The final struggle began in 1895 when Jose Marti began another full scale uprising against the Spanish. This time, the United States was drawn into the conflict when the U.S.S. Maine was sunk in Havana harbor by an explosion. On December 10, 1898 Spain gave up Cuba. Three years of U.S. administration followed and in 1902 Cuba proclaimed her independence.

Political conditions remained unstable, leading to a reintroduction of U.S. rule between 1906-1909. In 1933, Fulgencio Batista led a popular army and student revolt that put him into the forefront of Cuban politics. After ruling through a series of presidents, Bautista was elected President in 1940. In 1952, Bautista, having been succeeded by two other presidents, seized power in a bloodless coup. His rule was toppled in January, 1959 by a communist inspired revolution led by Fidel Castro. All political activity in opposition was abolished. Thousands of political refugees have since fled the country, mostly to the U.S.

## GOVERNMENT AND POLITICAL CONDITIONS

Until the adoption of a Constitution in 1976, Cuba was ruled by decree of the Castro government. The Constitution organized a government based on that of the Soviet Union. Executive power is vested in the Council of Ministers. Legislative power resides in the National Assembly, which is headed by the Council of State. Fidel Castro presides over the Council of Ministers and the Council of State, and is First Secretary of the Cuban Communist Party. His brother Raul is Second Secretary. The government employs an elaborate and extensive security system to prevent the rise of any opposition.

## ECONOMY

Cuba's economy is primarily based upon the sugar industry which accounts for a total of 86% of its export earnings and 25% of its GNP. Therefore, Cuba's economy fares well or badly, depending on the worldwide price of sugar. The economy is slowly being diversified. Among the major ventures of the Cuban government are in the mining of the island's nickel reserves (which accounts for 10% of Cuba's exports) and the development of the island's fishing industry. Since 1970, the yearly catch has nearly doubled.

There is a considerable amount of small industry. Cigar production constitutes the largest part of Cuba's tobacco exports. Cement production has doubled. Other industries include food processing, beverage manufacturing, meat packing and canning.

Since the 1960s Cuba's economy has been centrally planned. All farms and businesses are under the control of the government. Due to several factors, including poor management, adverse weather and lower sugar and nickel prices, Cuba's economy has stagnated. The Soviet Union has subsidized the Castro government to the amount of $8.3 billion since the revolution. In recent years the Soviet Union's aid to Cuba has amounted to $3 million per day. Although there have been improvements in social security, health and education under the Castro regime, the economy is characterized by low productivity and shortages of consumer goods.

## SELECTED BIBLIOGRAPHY AND INFORMATION SOURCES

The sources listed below are to help the reader find additional information on this country and Christian ministries there. This list does not try to be comprehensive or complete.

DOCUMENTS

General

Black, Jan Knippers, et al., Area Handbook for Cuba. Washington, D.C.: US Government Printing Office, 1976.

Cozen, John D., Latin America 1980. World Today Series, Washington D.C.: Stryker-Post Publication, 1980.

Goff, James E., Latin America Press. Weekly News Bulletin, Lima, Peru: Noticias Aliadas.

Kurian, George Thomas, Encyclopedia of the Third World. New York: Facts on File, 1978.

Christian

Canadian Catholic Missionaries. Ottowa, Canada: Canadian Religious Conference, 1979.

Frei, Pauline, editor, Latin America Documentation LADOC. Washington, D.C.,: Office of International Justice and Peace U.S. Catholic Conferences.

Kane, J. Herbert, A Global View of Christian Mission. Grand Rapids, MI: Baker Book House, 1971.

Mission Handbook, Washington D.C.: United States Catholic Mission Council, 1980.

Orr, J. Edwin, Evangelical Awakenings in Latin America. Minneapolis, MN: Bethany Fellowship, 1978.

United Bible Society, Program ´80. Stuttgart, West Germany: 1980.

Wilson, Sam, Mission Handbook: North American Protestant Ministries Overseas. Monrovia, CA: MARC, 1981.


## ACKNOWLEDGMENTS

The information in this profile was taken from many sources which were the best available to the editors at the time of preparation. However, the accuracy of the information cannot be guaranteed. Views expressed or implied in this publication are not necessarily those of World Vision. The editors have tried to present the ministries of various organizations in an objective manner, without undue bias or emphasis. Where we have failed, we apologize for erroneous impressions that may result and request that comments and corrections be made to MARC, 919 West Huntington Drive, Monrovia, California, USA, 91016. We appreciate and acknowledge the comments and contributions of various organizations and individuals in the preparation of this publication.

# STATUS OF CHRISTIANITY COUNTRY PROFILE

# DOMINICAN REPUBLIC

### SUMMARY

AREA - 48,692 square kilometers (18,811
    square miles)
POPULATION - 5.6 million (1981 est.)
RELIGION - 98% Nominal Roman Catholic
            1% Protestant 1% Other

Though the people of the Dominican Republic share the island of Hispaniola with Haitians, they have little in common. A brief look at history reveals the impact of colonialism on the lives of the people and on the development of their present culture. The citizens of the Dominican Republic retained the language, religion and cultural patterns of the Spanish. Haitians had a French colonial background. Thus socio-political conflicts have prevailed for the last 300 years and are unlikely to diminish rapidly in effect or intensity.

Contrasts between the Dominican Republic and Haiti are particularly evident in the economic realm. The growth rate of the Dominican Republic's gross national product has increased significantly and is higher than that of most Latin American countries. Natural disasters are among the few things Haiti and the Dominican Republic have in common. Hurricane David and tropical storm Frederick wrought

physical destruction and severe economic setbacks in both nations. The Dominican Republic was able to apply redevelopment funds successfully and the economy grew during 1980 despite the major losses. Christian individuals, agencies and church groups in both countries were able to respond to the immediate needs of thousands of homeless and injured victims of the storms. When Christians lived out the gospel in action, the people were willing to listen and respond to the scriptural message shared verbally. A renewed interest and commitment to Christian principles has become evident.

*This program is jointly carried out by the Strategy Working Group of the Lausanne Committee for World Evangelization and MARC, a ministry of World Vision International. For further information on the program, please write: MARC, 919 West Huntington Drive, Monrovia, CA 91016 U.S.A.*

## PEOPLE GROUPS

Statistics are not readily available concerning ethnic backgrounds as few publications within the country reveal such information. It is a sensitive issue which is better not ignited. That policy is helpful when considering particular people groups since numerous subgroups comprise a single racial group. The terms mulatto and mestizo refer to descendants of blacks, whites or Indians who have intermarried. A particular mulatto family may attend Roman Catholic churches and schools, may live in a spacious home in an urban area and may be quite wealthy. Another mulatto family may be agnostic and attend no church, may be uneducated, may live on a rural farm and have no money at all. Significantly different evangelistic strategies are needed for each family.

Western ethnographers who deem it necessary to record racial deliniations report that 73% to 75% of the total population of the Dominican Republic is mulatto. Estimates of the number of whites, referring to anyone of pure Spanish (Castilian), Lebanese, German Jew or other European background, vary from 10% to 16%. The number of resident blacks and whites is disputed because generalities prevail regarding nationalities. Blacks are assumed to be Haitians or descendants of Haitians. Historically, many Haitians have entered the Dominican Republic both legally and illegally. They have been despised, misunderstood and mistrusted because they spoke French or French Creole, were uneducated, had no status and reflected Haitian cultural traditions, including Vodun. For these reasons they were disliked by the Spanish-oriented mulattoes, whites or other blacks. Haitians were usually trying to escape unemployment and destitute poverty. In desperation, nearly 300,000 have accepted low paying jobs as cane cutters in sugar plantations. Thus many citizens of the Dominican Republic have viewed them as poor migrants and they have become a downtrodden minority. Many live in cramped, temporary sugar mill towns which lack health care facilities or proper sanitation and water systems. Even national Christians and churches have had a difficult time reaching out to Haitians in any culturally appropriate manner.

Blacks of American ancestry trace their roots to families of Baltimore or Philadelphia who immigrated in the 1800's and formed their own isolated, Protestant English speaking community along a peninsula in the northeast.

Other small groups of ethnic distinction include German Jews who responded to Trujillo's invitation for persecuted Jews to immigrate during World War II. Here again double standards based on racial prejudice are evident since Trujillo had just finished eradicating thousands of unwanted black Haitians by ordering his military troops to slaughter them. Many Jews were professionals who either moved to some other country or learned to farm the rich and fertile soil. Chinese immigrants numbered from 2,500 to 4,500 in 1979. Those of employment age have been involved in trade or commerce and most now own or are involved in operating the nation's bars and restaurants. A small number of Japanese immigrants operate a successful agricultural colony in the central highlands. Virtually no information is available on these people and it is unlikely that they have been reached by any Christians.

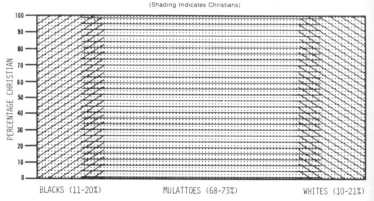

POPULATION COMPOSITION OF DOMINICAN REPUBLIC
(Shading Indicates Christians)

PERCENTAGE CHRISTIAN

BLACKS (11-20%)     MULATTOES (68-73%)     WHITES (10-21%)

NOTE: THESE FIGURES ARE REPRESENTATIVE APPROXIMATIONS. THEY SHOULD BE SEEN AS INDICATORS OF MAGNITUDE ONLY.

## CURRENT STATUS OF CHRISTIANITY

Christianity accompanied explorers and immigrants who settled the island of Hispaniola in the 16th century. The Roman Catholic Church was the major source of transfer of Spanish culture to the people. Thus Christianity has been entwined with the evolving culture of the Dominican Republic.

Because Protestants have been regarded as helpful to the development of the nations infra-structure, there has not been overt discrimination or severe persecution.

Christian principles have been verbally acclaimed but political policies and social crimes have provided grounds for judgment because of overt hypocrisy. This was true in the case Trujillo (authoritarian ruler from 1930 to 1961) who catered to the desires of the church heirarchy. It was he who prevented church property from being sold for any reason and it was he who instituted Roman Catholicism as the official state religion. He also ordered the destruction of thousands of black Haitians. Thus social justice within the context of Christianity is a new principle. Liberation theology is being accepted by many nominal Catholics because it addresses issues that affect their lives. The interpretation of Scripture, doctrines held and lifestyles expressed by missionaries and pastors of evangelical traditions provide creative alternatives to traditional forms of Christianity. The people need sound teaching with relevant explanations of Scripture in culturally appropriate ways and they need to see that those who teach and disciple are genuine servants with lives of good repute.

Church growth within most denominational groups is hindered by a shortage of qualified teachers and pastors who devote themselves totally to the ministries of the church. Training programs in Bible colleges and seminaries are essential for development of leadership which can challenge church members to reach the residents of cities, towns, villages and farms of the Dominican Republic.

RELIGIOUS COMPOSITION
OF DOMINICAN REPUBLIC

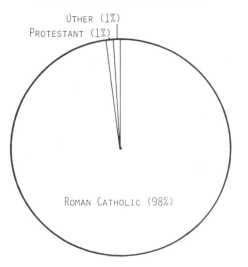

OTHER (1%)
PROTESTANT (1%)

ROMAN CATHOLIC (98%)

PROTESTANT CHURCHES

Congregations in the Dominican Republic which adhere to protestant principles are relatively new. Receptivity is increasing as both felt and real needs of the people are being addressed. The latest available information indicates that 79,821 individuals are members of 941 churches which belong to 32 denominations. The total Protestant community is estimated at 300,000, which constitutes 2% of the total population. Seventh-day Adventists report the largest number of members and the largest community with 18,000 and 72,000 respectively.

Independent churches who compile their statistics report 235 separate churches with 10,000 members and a community of 40,000 constituents. The Assemblies of God have the greatest number of churches with 260 different congregations. The 10,584 Baptist members are part of a community of 17,694. Approximately 200 national workers assist 100 credentialed ministers. Most of the congregations are totally, or at least partially, self-supporting. Eighty congregations affiliated with the Church of God denomination have a community of 24,000 with 6,000 members.

The Dominican Evangelical Church is sponsored by the United Methodist, the Moravian and the United Presbyterian Church. In slightly more than 50 years, 62 congregations have been formed and membership has grown to 6,000. Fourteen ordained ministers and eight lay pastors minister in 30 organized churches of which six are completely self-supporting in all aspects of congregational life and mission outreach. Twenty are churches affiliated with the Christian and Missionary Alliance. Nearly 100 students enroll in their Sunday schools each year.

CATHOLIC CHURCHES

The Roman Catholic Church has long been the central religious institution in the Dominican Republic. Colonial powers introduced it, ruling factions upheld it and even under the dictatorship of Trujillo it prevailed as a major influential force. Within the context of the socio-political changes of the 1980s a major source of change is arising within the Church, expressed by proponents of Liberation Theology. People need solutions to contemporary problems and thus many are leaving the church without bothering to remove their names from membership roles, or they are joining with those who offer constructive explanations of Christian social principles. The present church hierarchy consists of one archdiocese, seven dioceses and 197 parishes under the direction of one cardinal, 499 priests, 63 brothers and 1,380 sisters. Official church statisticians report that 94.2% of the population are at least nominally Catholic.

## FOREIGN MISSIONS

### PROTESTANT MISSIONS

Protestant missionaries were not able to minister effectively in the Dominican Republic until the early part of the 20th century. Seventh-day Adventist personnel have been particularly successful in their endeavors and have established over 80 churches with over 18,000 members. Protestant missionaries associated with United Brethren, Methodist and Presbyterian missions societies determined from the beginning of their partnership in 1919 that all permanent congregations formed by their efforts should be part of an indigenous church affiliation. In 1922 the first permanent congregation of the Iglesia Evangelica Dominicana was established with 48 members. By 1972 there were 40 congregations with 8,000 members under the direction of 30 pastors.

West Indies Mission, now Worldteam, established ministries in the Dominican Republic in 1939 following the pioneer outreach and survey of a Cuban who received Christian education in Jamaica. A training center for Bible students was one of the first projects of missionaries who believed in the importance of training young people to teach Scripture accurately and effectively among their own people. Worldteam reported nine career missionaries working among members of 34 churches in 1979.

The ministries of the Assemblies of God were initiated by a Puerto Rican evangelist who had already established several churches by the time North American expatriates arrived. Thus the cooperation of national workers has always been strong. Eight missionaries assisting 99 pastors and 196 national workers are able to minister to the 10,584 members and 17,700 constituents of 260 organized churches and 635 outstations.

The Dominican Republic has been for the Southern Baptists, and many other Protestant mission agencies, one of the last areas in which they have established ministries. The first Southern Baptist missionaries were a husband and wife team transferred from Ecuador in 1962. Missions personnel increased to 23 in 1977 working among 700 church members in eight churches. By 1979, 26 missionaries, including 20 career staff members, four journeymen and two associate personnel were involved in ministries of nine churches, five of which were self-supporting. They assisted nine national pastors who ministered to 800 members and 700 other constituents. The Baptist Student Center and the University of Santo Domingo provide opportunities for students to discover the claims of Christ and the challenge of biblical Christianity. Young people facing the conflicts of the 1980s are particularly interested, open and receptive, according to Campus Crusade for Christ, who sent its first personnel to the Dominican Republic in 1977 and now supports 15 active staff members.

A total of 31 North American Protestant agencies were involved in some type of ministry in the Dominican Republic in 1979. Of the 21 agencies who had resident career personnel, the Southern Baptist Convention had the largest number (20).

Brethren Assemblies, a conglomerate of churches, chapels and assemblies in North America, reported 18 missionaries; Unevangelized Fields Mission (UFM), 17; Campus Crusade for Christ, 15; and Baptist Mid Missions, 14.

Ministries of missionaries vary widely with many involved in support services, church planting, theological education or evangelistic outreach, particularly among young people in urban areas.

### ROMAN CATHOLIC MISSIONS

The number of personnel sent by the United States Catholic Mission Council fluctuated between 24 and 34 from 1976 to 1980. The lowest figure reported was 24 in 1979, but the number increased to 30 by 1980. This latest figure includes 10 men of the Missionhurst order. Nine Redemptorists, four diocesan and four of the Dominican order were active in 1980. Canadian Catholic missionaries comprise the largest single missions force with 89 individuals reported in 1979. This includes 29 priests and seven brothers of the Sacred Heart Missions Society and 13 priests of the Scarboro Foreign Missions Society.

## MAJOR CHRISTIAN ACTIVITIES

### SOCIAL CONCERNS

Many ministries of Protestant missionaries are directed toward meeting the immediate physical needs of the poverty stricken residents in rural areas of the Dominican Republic. The Southern Baptists maintain outpatient clinics in cooperation with M.A.P. (Medical Assistance Programs). Emergency disaster relief assistance was provided by several agencies in response to the destruction caused by hurricane David and tropical storm Frederick. The Mennonite Central Committee responded to requests for assistance of the Evangelical Mennonite Church and sent a rehabilitation team to initiate a short term program for reconstruction of 600 houses, and adult education programs in health, family-planning, agriculture and Bible. Catholic Relief Services provided emergency aid to thousands of homeless and injured victims. Many grass-roots level projects had been underway prior to the storms including a help program in which 59,500 volunteer workers participated. They helped build an irrigation system, constructed schools and health centers and provided education in nutrition and methods of agriculture. Over 3 million dollars were available for relief and development. Medical clinics provided opportunities for missionaries to reach out to people in need. The Free Methodists have established eight clinics; the Southern Baptists, six; and the Plymouth Brethren, Seventh-day Adventists, Mennonite Church and Christian and Missionary Alliance one each.

A medical center has been constructed by the Plymouth Brethren, and the Free Methodists sponsor the Dominican Christian Medical Association.

### EDUCATION

The Free Methodists were the first to open a coeducational boarding school in the Dominican Republic. Since then education and establishment of educational facilities have become important facets of missionary outreach. The Dominican Evangelical Church operates 10 schools which serve nearly 2,500 primary and secondary schools. The Seventh-day Adventists operate four schools; the Free Methodists, three; Worldteam, two; Mennonite Church, two; Plymouth Brethren and Missionary Evangelical Church, one each.

Worldteam provides educational courses through the Radio Bible School and the Assemblies of God operates a Bible Institute. The Baptist Theological Institute, which was opened in 1972, has extension courses at three training centers in Santo Domingo, Santiago, Bonao and one in San Pedro de Macoris. Nine seminaries provide graduate level courses for students seeking professions as pastors and Bible teachers.

Catholic institutions are well staffed and provide primary, secondary, undergraduate and graduate level courses for students in a variety of fields. The Universidad Catolica Madre y Maestra has a large student body. Thirteen seminaries provide graduate studies in theology for 499 seminarians.

## NATION AND ITS PEOPLE

### POPULATION

The population of the Dominican Republic was estimated in 1981 to be 5.6 million. It has an average annual growth rate of 2.8%, one of the highest growth rates in the Caribbean. In 1970, the official census put the population at 4,006,405 people. The nationwide population density is about 96 people per square kilometer (250 per square mile). In agricultural areas the average is 166 people per square kilometer (430 per sqare mile).

About half the people are concentrated in urban areas. During the Trujillo regime (1930-1961) internal migration was restricted. In 1950, only 23.8% of the people lived in urban centers but migration to urban centers increased rapidly after his death. Santo Domingo, the oldest European settlement in the New World had a 1975 population of 922,528, more than 40% of the nation's urban population. Other urban centers include Santiago de los Caballeros (209,179), San Pedro de Macoris (61,944), San Francisco de Macoris (58,174) and Barahona (51,109).

### COMPOSITION

Mulattoes are considered a separate race in the official census. They form the largest group and account for 73% of the population. Whites account for 16% of the population and blacks make up the remaining 11%. Blacks have come from Africa, Haiti and the United States. Emigrants from Spain, Lebanon and Germany are regarded as whites. There are also small numbers of Chinese, Japanese and other Asians.

Race is an important determinant of social status. Mulattoes have dominated the government and armed forces since the time of Trujillo. Generally, blacks occupy the lowest social class, particularly the black migrant workers from Haiti.

## LANGUAGE AND LITERACY

Spanish is the official langue of the Dominican Republic, spoken by 98% of the people. The other 2% speak Haitian Creole, especially those who live along the Haitian border. The Spanish spoken has changed little in the past few hundred years. English is widely spoken, as a second language, particularly in commercial circles.

Primary education is free and compulsory for children between the ages of seven and fourteen years. In spite of this, the literacy rate is low, particularly among the older generation and in rural areas, where it is only 68%.

## RELIGION

By the Concordat of 1954, Roman Catholicism became the official religion of the Dominican Republic. The overwhelming majority (98%) of the people consider themselves to be at least nominally Roman Catholic. During the Trujillo regime the Roman Catholic Church was openly favored by the government. More recently, the Church has come out in favor of social change.

Religious freedom is protected by law. There is a growing Protestant community. There are also practitioners of Haitian Vodun (Vodoo) among the Haitian immigrants. There is also a small Jewish community comprised of descendants of Jews who settled in the Dominican Republic after fleeing German persecution before World War II.

## GEOGRAPHY AND CLIMATE

The Dominican Republic, located on the eastern two-thirds of the island of Hispaniola, has a land area of 48,442 square kilometers (18,703 square miles). It shares a 290 kilometer (180 mile) border with Haiti. Four mountain ranges run parallel to each other in the western half of the country. The largest of these, the Cordillera Central, extends the length of the country and into Haiti. The largest mountain in the Caribbean is located in this range: Pico Duarte, 3,174 meters (10,414 feet) in elevation. The lowlands consist of several long parallel valleys lying generally in a southwesterly direction. The largest and most productive in agricultural products is the Cibao. Fast moving and unnavigable rivers flow down through these valleys, providing irrigation water. The Cibao Valley contains two of the largest rivers, the Yaque del Norte flowing west and the Yuna flowing east. The largest of many lakes is Lake Euriquillo in the Neiba Valley. With its waters 43 meters (140 feet) below sea level, it is the lowest point in the Caribbean.

The climate can be described as tropical, tempered by sea breezes and elevation variations. Temperature ranges are not great though there is a difference between summer and winter. During the period from June through October temperatures rise to between 34 degrees and 37 degrees Celsius (93 to 98 degrees Fahrenheit) with high humidity. From late November to April, the dry season, temperatures are around 29 to 30 degrees Celsius (80 to 85 degrees Fahrenheit). The rainy seasons are between May and July, and October through November. The nationwide mean rainfall is between 139 and 152 centimeters (55 to 60 inches). Hurricanes frequently pass to the east or the west of the country, but sometimes hit the Dominican Republic with full intensity.

## HISTORY

In 1492 Columbus discovered the island of Hispaniola (now Haiti and the Dominican Republic), which became the staging point for further Spanish exploration of the New World. Santo Domingo was established in 1502, becoming the oldest European settlement in the Western Hemisphere. The French began settlements in the western end of Hispaniola during the beginning of the 17th century, and in 1697 Spain ceded that portion to France. In 1801, General Toussaint L'Ouverture led Haitian slaves in revolt and occupied the Spanish part of the island. In 1808, the Spanish inhabitants rebelled and their territory became reincorporated with Spain.

In November of 1821, the colony proclaimed its independence from Spain. However, Haiti soon invaded and conquered the entire island in 1822. After 22 years of Haitian rule, the Spanish colonists rose in arms under the leadership of Juan Pablo Duarte and proclaimed their independence on February 27, 1844. The Dominican Republic was returned to Spanish rule in 1861, but the country regained its independence after another rebellion in 1865.

For the next 50 years, the Dominican Republic saw 28 revolutions and 35 governments. Finally, in order to protect American interests, the United States occupied the country in November, 1916.

This occupation lasted eight years, terminating in 1924.

Civilian rule lasted until a coup in 1930 put the military in power. Under their auspices, an election was held and Rafael Leonidas Trujillo Molina, the commander of the army, took power. He established a dictatorship and ruled until he was assassinated in 1961. During his authoritarian rule the nation experienced considerable economic development and severe repression of human rights.

After Trujillo, Juan Bosch was elected President. He was deposed in a military coup in 1963 and a civilian junta was set up. The army rebelled against the ruling junta in 1965, setting off fighting between pro-Bosch forces and those who proposed a military junta. The fighting resulted in the intervention of U.S. military forces and, later, an inter-American peace force composed of troops from other Latin American countries was formed to stop the fighting. By the spring of 1966, sufficient order was established to permit elections and Dr. Joaquin Balaguer was elected President for a four-year term.

President Balaguer, leader of the Reformist Party, was reelected to office twice, both times after the major opposition parties withdrew late in the election. During his presidency, the Dominican Republic enjoyed sustained economic growth. In 1978, Balaguer was defeated by Antonio Guzman of the Partido Revolutionario Dominicans. During the election it became clear that the armed forces would stage a coup when it appeared that Guzman would win. Pressure from the United States helped eliminate military interference from the election.

## GOVERNMENT POLITICAL CONDITIONS

According to the Constitution of 1966, executive power is vested in a president directly elected for four-year terms. There is a bicameral Congress: the Senate, formed by one representative from each province and the Distrito Nacional, and the Chamber of Deputies, with one representative for each 50,000 inhabitants.

Antonio Guzman of the Partido Revolucionario Dominicano (PRD) was elected President in 1978. The PRD defines itself as "social democratic." The Partido Reformista of former President Balaguer still controls the Senate.

## ECONOMY

During the early 1970's, the Dominican Republic enjoyed one of the highest economic growth rates in Latin America. More recently, however, the country has experienced a slowdown brought about by the fall in sugar prices and the increase in oil prices. Agriculture dominates the economic picture. Sugar and sugar by-products account for nearly one-third of the export income. Coffee and cocoa together account for another one-third, and mineral products amount to 22% of the export total. The main customer of Dominican exports is the United States with 80% of the exports going there. The Dominican Republic imports 50% of its overseas products from the U.S.

The Dominican Republic has been promoting industrialization by offering incentives to foreign investment. Major industries deal with sugar refining and processing, mining of gold, silver, nickel and bauxite, cement manufacturing, soft drinks, clothing and furniture.

Exchange rate (1981): 1 peso = 1 dollar (U.S.)

## CHURCH STATISTICS FOR DOMINICAN REPUBLIC

Note: Statistics have been taken from different sources and are the most current data available. Definitions of "membership" vary among churches and may not always be comparable. Not all known churches have been included in this list.

| Church or Mission Name | Communicants (Full Members) | Community (Estimate) |
| --- | --- | --- |
| PROTESTANT | | |
| African Methodist Church | 2,366 | 4,732 |
| Apostolic Faith Church | 420 | 840 |
| Arca de Salvacion | 2,000 | 8,000 |
| Assembly of God | 7,000 | 14,325 |
| Baptist Convention | 340 | 1,020 |
| Baptist International | | |
| Baptist Mid-Missions | - | - |
| Bautista Bethel | 325 | 975 |
| Child Evangelism Fellowship | - | - |
| Christian Assembly | 3,270 | 32,000 |
| Christian Biblical Church | 450 | 1,800 |
| Christian Medical Society, Medical Group | - | - |
| Christian & Missionary Alliance | 450 | 2,000 |
| Church of God | 6,000 | 24,000 |
| Church of God of the Prophecy | 3,000 | 9,000 |
| Church of the Nazarene | - | - |
| Defenders of the Christian Faith | 3,000 | 12,000 |
| Dominican Baptist | 360 | 1,440 |
| Dominican Border Church | 450 | 1,800 |
| Dominican Episcopal Church | 3,000 | 6,000 |
| Dominican Evangelical Church | 4,201 | 26,804 |
| Evangelical Mennonite Church | 975 | 3,00 |
| Free Methodist Church | 6,180 | 18,540 |
| Haitian Baptist | 620 | 1,240 |
| Independents | 10,000 | 40,000 |
| MAP | - | - |
| Pentecostal Church of God | 1,340 | 5,360 |
| Plymouth Brethren | 4,000 | 16,000 |
| Seventh-day Adventist | 18,000 | 72,000 |
| Southern Baptist | 449 | 1,347 |
| Tabernaculo Evangelistico | 800 | 2,400 |
| Templos Evangelicos | 800 | 3,000 |
| World Missions (Cleveland) | | |
| Unevangelized Field Missions | - | - |
| TOTALS | 79,821 | 298,923 |

Sources: Estadistica de la obra evangelica en la R.D., Mar 1974

## SELECTED BIBLIOGRAPHY AND INFORMATION SOURCES

The sources listed below are to help the reader find additional information on this country and Christian ministries there. This list does not try to be comprehensive or complete.

DOCUMENTS

General

Cozen, John D., Latin America 1980, World Today Series, Washington D.C.: Stryker-Post Publication, 1980.

Kurian, George Thomas, Encyclopedia of the Third World, New York: Facts on File, 1978.

Olien, Michael D., Latin Americans, Contemporary Peoples and Their Cultural Traditions, New York: Holt, Rinehard and Winston, 1973.

Christian

Brierly, Peter, U.K. Christian Handbook, Vol. 1; London: Overseas Evangelical Missionary Alliance, 1981.

Canadian Catholic Missionaries, Ottawa, Canada: Canadian Religious Conference, 1979.

Kane, J. Herbert, A Global View of Christian Mission, Grand Rapids, MI: Baker Book House, 1971.

Mennonite Central Committee Workbook, Akron, PA: Mennonite Central Committee, 1979.

Mission Handbook, Washington D.C.: United States Catholic Mission Council, 1980.

Orr, J. Edwin, Evangelical Awakenings in Latin America, Minneapolis, MN: Bethany Fellowship, 1978.

The Caribbean, Richmond, VA: Dept. of Communication Foreign Mission Board SBC, 1977.

Thiesen, John Caldwell, A Survey of World Mission, Chicago: Moody Press, 1961.

## ACKNOWLEDGMENTS

The information in this profile was taken from many sources which were the best available to the editors at the time of preparation. However, the accuracy of the information cannot be guaranteed. Views expressed or implied in this publication are not necessarily those of World Vision. The editors have tried to present the ministries of various organizations in an objective manner, without undue bias or emphasis. Where we have failed, we apologize for erroneous impressions that may result and request that comments and corrections be sent to MARC, 919 West Huntington Drive, Monrovia, California, 91016, USA. We appreciate and acknowledge the comments and contributions of various organizations and individuals in the preparation of this publication.

# STATUS OF CHRISTIANITY COUNTRY PROFILE

# HAITI

### SUMMARY

AREA - 27,713 square kilometers (10,714 square miles)
POPULATION - 6 million (1981 est.)
RELIGION - 80% Catholic, 90% Vodun, 10%-20% Protestant
(SEE: Religion)

Economic depression and social repression are factors which render Haiti the poorest country in the Western Hemisphere. The people, in general, have a conscious awareness of spiritual battles within everyday affairs. Many individuals have not been given a valid opportunity to respond to a culturally appropriate explanation of Christianity, and many others have not made commitments accompanied by changes in lifestyles or the alleviation of habits and patterns of the "old nature." Meager subsistence level farming is prevalent for most families though some do produce crafts for tourists or goods for export. Forces of nature, politics, society and the spiritual realm are all elements creating and maintaining socio-cultural tensions and political pressures.

The people struggle for financial and social improvements but feel trapped.

They preserve random religious beliefs and cling to Vodun (Voodoo), an informal but established religion with no defined theology or writings but with a full set of rituals for propitiation and control of supernatural powers.

Numerous Christian organizations have sought to fill voids in the lives of Haitians by providing educational opportunities and various social reform programs. Resulting church growth has been an issue of extensive debate since many individuals simply add the new teachings to previously held superstitions without expressing clear commitments or significantly changing their ways of life.

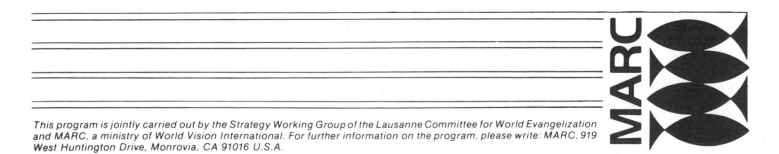

*This program is jointly carried out by the Strategy Working Group of the Lausanne Committee for World Evangelization and MARC, a ministry of World Vision International. For further information on the program, please write: MARC, 919 West Huntington Drive, Monrovia, CA 91016 U.S.A.*

## PEOPLE GROUPS

The majority (90%) of Haitians are blacks. Mulattoes (mestizos) comprise the remaining 10% of the population. Significant distinctions result from differences in educational backgrounds, status levels, wealth and familial ties.

At the top of the socio-economic structure is a small group of elite mulattoes totaling perhaps 2% of the population. They are wealthy, well-educated persons with purely French values, language, and cultural interests. Physical labor is looked down on as menial and only professional positions are held in high regard. Few elite ever assume positions in education or the clergy since they would need to be involved with the masses.

A small middle class is emerging which includes those willing to be involved with the general public. Many individuals who are able to secure savings choose to leave the country rather than stay on and confront the problems and struggles of politics and poverty. This group has its own unique needs which must be addressed by Christians in a special way.

Approximately 88% of all Haitians are part of families who have traditionally been peasant farmers on very small plots of land. Population density affects land cultivation since more than 400 Haitians try to farm an average square mile of land. Resources are eroding as fast as the population is increasing. Some farmers have turned to cash crops, some raise supplemental livestock and others have become rural tradesmen or artisans.

A growing number of people are part of a group identified as the urban lower class. By 1973, nearly 6% of the population belonged to this group. Those who succeed in business and industrial jobs move up to the middle class or emigrate. For every individual that does move up or leaves, however, one or more people move in from rural areas to fill tenements, slums or shanties.

Most Haitians speak Creole, a language which reflects the socio-cultural changes of Haiti. It is a mixture of French, Spanish, English and words of various African dialects.

Although 80% of Haiti's rural workers are reported to be Catholics, a much smaller percentage regularly practice their faith. Most adhere to some form of Vodun with fear and superstition holding tight control over their minds and hearts.

Of those who proclaim to be Protestants, as many as 30% to 40% also engage in Vodun. The mixture of Christo-pagan beliefs manifests itself in syncretistic Vodun, which is the most widespread influence. Many individuals who are thus entangled have never really been given a chance to respond to Christ with a clear understanding of the implications and commitments necessary within their cultural context.

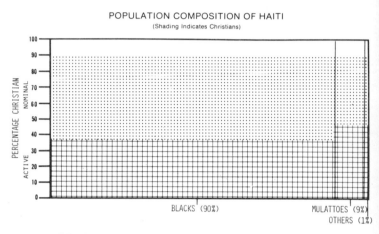

POPULATION COMPOSITION OF HAITI
(Shading Indicates Christians)

NOTE: THESE FIGURES ARE REPRESENTATIVE APPROXIMATIONS. THEY SHOULD BE SEEN AS INDICATORS OF MAGNITUDE ONLY.

## CURRENT STATUS OF CHRISTIANITY

The percentage of Haitians who claim to be Christians is reported by secular sources to be as high as 90%. Statistics are misleading since 90-95% of the population are also actively practicing Vodun and heed occult principles. The people have been conditioned to regard themselves as Christian. The Roman Catholic Church itself has identified over 4.6 million people, 80% of the total population, who are nominally Catholic.

Some strife has developed as disillusioned rural Haitians resist changes. Such was the case of the residents in one mountain village who ousted their priest when he advocated a particular social reform program. Otherwise, there is little overt discrimination against Christians or even Protestants engaging in missionary or evangelistic activities. Many Protestant church leaders report substantial growth in community constituencies, to the degree that there often is not enough national or expatriate leadership to effectively train and nurture the individuals interested in Christianity. Some Christian leaders have become frustrated with the apparent lack of commitment to Christian lives and values by many who attend church.

## RELIGIOUS COMPOSITION OF HAITI

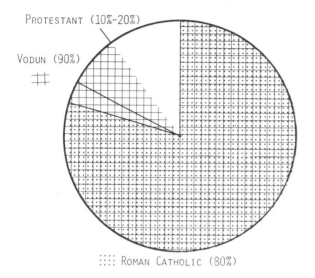

PROTESTANT (10%-20%)

VODUN (90%)

ROMAN CATHOLIC (80%)

**NATIONAL CHURCHES**

PROTESTANT CHURCHES

The Protestant community, including church members, children and non-members, is estimated to be between 600,000 and 1 million or 10 to 20% of the total population. Actual church membership is 275,000 to 300,000 or approximately 5% of the population.

Protestant churches were formed in Haiti in the early 1800's as a result of missionary work initiated in Great Britain and the United States. Baptist churches have the largest constituency among Protestants with a community numbering more than 200,000 distributed among five major mission-related Baptist conventions. The largest single group is the Convencion Baptiste d'Haiti (Baptist Convention of Haiti) which is affiliated with the American Baptist Convention. It is by far the largest single group with 80,000 individuals, of which 38,000 are members. They are under the direction of 58 national pastors and gather in 86 church meeting centers, only one of which is self-supporting.

The Seventh-day Adventists reportedly have 55,000 constituents with church growth at approximately 9% per year. The churches associated with Worldteam report nearly 40,000 constituents, of which approximately 50% are members.

The Church of the Nazarene has over 21,000 constituents including 8,000 members. Ministries include 117 churches, 56 primary schools and 219 mission stations with 10 related medical facility centers.

The Assemblies of God report a community of 30,500 with 6,300 baptized members. They list 67 credentialed ministers with assistance from 78 national workers.

Other large churches include the Evangelical Church of Haiti, Churches of God and the Episcopal Church. There are more than 1,600 Protestant congregations, 4,000 mission stations and 5,600 meeting places. Ordained national workers work alongside expatriates and part-time lay church workers.

Studies of church growth in Haiti reveal that Protestant churches in rural areas have been growing more rapidly than those in cities and towns. Conversions have been primarily among individuals of lower social and economic levels who have turned from the entangling forces of Vodun. Often, entire families have become involved in churches within a short period of time. There are many paradoxes, as large numbers of individuals identify themselves as Protestants, yet have little contact with a local congregation. They are generally not interested in renouncing Vodun superstitions and rituals. As many as 750,000 persons may need culturally appropriate forms of evangelistic outreach combined with unique strategies to incorporate them into local churches and discipleship programs in which they can receive training in Biblical principles.

CATHOLIC CHURCHES

Catholicism was established in Haiti by colonists as early as the 16th century. It was designated the official religion from 1860 until 1960. French Capuchin and Jesuit priests were involved in missionary activities throughout the 18th century. Many Catholic leaders were of French origin or received religious training in France. Political upheavals in the early 1960's accompanied by the resurgence of African-oriented cultural practices proved to be a major hindrance for Roman Catholic leaders. Church hierarchy includes 398 priests, 201 brothers and 660 sisters who serve in 185 parishes of the six dioceses within the archdiocese.

## COOPERATIVE AGENCIES

The Council of Evangelical Churches in Haiti, which is an indigeneous fellowship of 18 church organizations, seeks to promote coordination and exchange of information among various churches and missions in Haiti. Related to the Council of Evangelical Churches is the Center of Information and Evangelical Statistics. The Center provides information to help church leaders understand and evaluate the growth and development of churches in Haiti.

## FOREIGN MISSIONS

### PROTESTANT

Shortly after national independence, Protestant missionaries from the Church of God visited Haiti at the request of the Haitian president. In the 1820´s, Rev. James Holly, a black priest, emigrated with over 100 black Americans and ambitious plans for a colonial community. The church established by Rev. Holly eventually came under the jurisdiction of the Protestant Episcopal Church of the U.S.A. Numerous Baptist mission groups are active in Haiti including the American Baptists. They sent workers to assist and eventually replace English Baptists in the 1920´s. The Lott Carey Baptist Foreign Mission, Baptist Haiti Mission, Baptist International Missions, Baptist Mid-Missions, Maranatha Baptist Mission, National Baptist Convention of America and Southern Baptist Convention each have ministries of their own as well as cooperative ventures. Salvation Army workers (soldiers) are engaged in ministries throughout Haiti including three medical centers, two homes and two workshops for the blind and handicapped, an orphanage, primary and secondary schools and one "Home Science" school. There are 18 known mission and service groups relating to Mennonite and Brethren in Christ churches. Radio programs are aired on Radio Lumiere. Nutrition programs include new training materials for six-week basic nutrition courses. Agricultural development and related training materials are of great importance to the Mennonite Central Committee as are a variety of health and health education programs.

Many mission groups operate within distinct regional areas. For example, Worldteam has many of its ministries in the southern region; OMS International is primarily represented in the northern and central areas; UFM concentrates its efforts in the western end of the northern peninsula; the Wesleyan Church has ministries in the southern and northern peninsulas and particularly Gonave Island. Most denominations have churches in and around the capital of Port-au-Prince. Over 450 foreign missionaries from 75 North American Protestant sending agencies are assigned to projects in Haiti. Four agencies from the United Kingdom and one from Australia send personnel. The largest Protestant mission agencies include Unevangelized Fields Mission (UFM), Worldteam, OMS International and the Wesleyan Church.

### ROMAN CATHOLIC

The number of Canadian Catholic missionaries increased significantly from 436 in 1975 to 457 in 1980. Ministries were quite diverse with 20 priests, 48 brothers and 152 sisters involved in education; one brother and 87 sisters involved in medical treatment and patient care; one priest, three brothers and 24 sisters in social services and 14 priests, five brothers and 29 sisters involved in pastoral care and counseling. The total number of Catholic missionaries from the United States has remained consistent since 1975 with approximately 50 each year.

## MAJOR CHRISTIAN ACTIVITIES

### EVANGELISM

Churches and missions have carried out a variety of evangelistic ministries in most areas of Haiti. Several groups have conducted regional saturation evangelism campaigns. The Baptist Haiti Mission and Conservative Baptists offer youth retreats which provide a variety of learning experiences in Christian living with a stress on personal salvation for each individual. The Wesleyan Church has extensive ministries including evangelistic church planting work in the rural areas of the southern mountainous region and La Gonave.

Preaching, home visitation and personal witnessing are supported by literature and broadcasting ministries with intercooperation among many agencies.

## BROADCASTING

Christian broadcasting is a widely known activity and is carried on by two major missionary radio networks: Radio 4VEH, operated by OMS International ; and Radio Lumiere, a cooperative effort sponsored by Worldteam and national groups. These stations operate in conjunction with the Trans-Haiti Network. Radio Lumiere has grown to a network of five AM stations reaching areas of Haiti in which 94% of the people live. During the hurricane David crisis, Radio Lumiere was tied in with the national radio stations and served as the emergency broadcasting network station with up to the minute reports on weather conditions, damage estimates and injuries. Radio is an important link among churches in Haiti and is utilized by many denominations and mission groups. Attempts to coordinate evangelism campaigns, outreach ministries and Bible correspondence courses by radio announcement and on-going programming are proving beneficial to local churches and mission agencies. Haitians were able to assume more than 25% of the financial responsibilities related to operating expenses of Radio Lumiere by 1980.

## LITERATURE

Literature ministries are limited because of the widespread illiteracy among Haitians.

## BIBLE TRANSLATION

Distribution increased noticeably from 1972 to 1979 for both New Testaments and selections of Scripture, but not for complete Bibles. This pattern will most likely change with the introduction of the complete Bible in Haitian Creole. It is expected to receive widespread acceptance and distribution. Bible reading is being encourged by numerous speakers on radio programs. Distribution campaigns are particulary successful on festival days, such as Day of the Dead, when people are consciously aware of spiritual battles. The Bible Society of Haiti reports the following distibution:

|                | 1972    | 1978      |
| -------------- | ------- | --------- |
| Bibles         | 34,469  | 19,491    |
| New Testaments | 16,421  | 44,031    |
| Portions       | 88,451  | 479,581   |
| Selections     | 52,921  | 2,730,234 |
| TOTALS         | 192,262 | 3,315,239 |

## SOCIAL CONCERN

Natural disasters, economic hardships and social conditions in Haiti have provided extensive opportunities for Christian organizations to assist the physical as well as spiritual needs of the people. At least seven hospitals, and 23 dispensaries are operated by mission groups in addition to hundreds of health clinics, first aid stations and nutrition centers. Agencies are involved in a variety of ministries ranging from health education programs to specialized care centers for the handicapped and from short term well digging projects to rural agricultural development and self-help programs. Over 30 different agencies were sponsoring development assistance programs by 1977.

Catholic Relief Services reported expenditures of over 1 million dollars. Worldteam allocated $750,000 for construction of Hospital Lumiere (Hospital of Light) including $100,000 for development of a hydroelectric plant in 1977 alone. Emergency aid poured in from individuals, agencies and church groups throughout North America and other Caribbean Islands for relief of victims of hurricane David and tropical storm Frederic.

Opinions vary regarding the value of several social concern projects. Some Christian leaders have been extremely disappointed with programs which meet only physical needs but lack involvement by trained Christians who effectively share the gospel and emphasise discipleship and commitment to a local church. Problems have resulted when individuals have called themselves "Christian" in order to receive the benefits of social ministries, but lacked true commitment to Christ. The individual is hurt as much as anyone because he never learns the complete challenge of biblical Christianity. Haitian Christians are grateful for the good social programs, but want to work with the expatriate benefactors so that new converts are incorporated into local congregations.

The newly formed Association des Ingenieurs Chretiens D'Haiti (L'AICH) is attempting to coordinate the efforts of agencies involved in development projects and also insure a clear Christian testimony. L'AICH has been designed to reinforce the concept that moral and spiritual problems must be considered as important as immediate economic and social needs.

## NATION AND ITS PEOPLE

### POPULATION

Haiti's population in 1981 was estimated at 6 million and was growing at an annual rate of 2.6%. If that rate continues, Haiti's population will be 10 million by the year 2000. Arable land and per capita productivity have nearly reached their limits. Overall population density is 165 per square kilometer (428 per square mile). The density in agricultural areas is as high as 486 per square kilometer (1,259 per square mile). Nearly 80% of the total population live in rural areas and migration to urban areas is limited to the availability of jobs and housing, both of which have been scarce in recent years. The largest cities are Port-au-Prince, the capital, with 306,000 people, Cap Haitien with 30,000, Les Cayes with 14,000, Gonaives with 14,000 and Jeremie with 12,000.

Haiti is experiencing such a high rate of emigration that some secular sources report that Haiti's major export is people. Several factors contribute to this migration, specifically: extreme poverty, periodic droughts and other natural disasters, population density and the promise of affluence in other countries. Legal and illegal immigrants are arriving almost daily in the United States, Puerto Rico, Bahamas and the Dominican Republic. During the late 1970s and early 1980s, the tide of emigrants became a flood and created a particularly accute political problem since most Haitians are regarded as economic refugees, not political refugees and thus must be subject to quota limitation statutes. Numerous ethical problems have arisen as governments attempt to cooperate, implement social justice and guarantee human rights. Extreme poverty compels many Haitians to risk their lives and board leaky boats which they hope will take them to a better life. For many, these attempts have only led to death.

### COMPOSITION

Haiti's population is relatively homogeneous with blacks constituting approximately 90% of the population and mulattoes (mestizos) more than 9%. The small community of whites is concentrated in Port-au-Prince and includes emigrants from France, Holland, Germany, Syria, Lebanon, Corsica and the United States. After driving out colonial landlords during Haiti's revolution for independence in 1804, the mulattoes (mestizos) held elite positions of power and wealth.

Since 1946, blacks have become predominant in politics, but mulattoes (mestizos) and whites have retained their status as the wealthy elite.

### LANGUAGE AND LITERACY

Haiti is the only republic in the Western hemisphere in which French is an official language. Most Haitians speak Creole, a separate language which evolved among immigrants who retained words of African tribal languages, added French and Spanish words and changed others to form new words. Pure French is the first language of only 10% of the population. In 1969 a law was passed which gave Creole formal legal status, thus permitting its use in congress and lower courts. The national literacy rate of Haiti is 10% and is unlikely to change rapidly since only 27% of the children of primary age attend school in spite of free and compulsory education. Over half the primary school enrollment and 75% of the secondary school enrollment is in private Catholic or Protestant schools who have taught students in Creole rather than French. As a result, the entire educational system is undergoing rapid change.

### RELIGION

The official religion of Haiti is Roman Catholicism, which is practiced nominally by 80% of the population. However, its influence in the hearts and lives of most Haitians is nil. Vodun (or Voodoo) is the popular religion of the people. Practitioners of Vodun do not see any contradiction between their Catholic religion and the Vodun system. A popular proverb of Haiti states, "Haiti is 90% Catholic and 100% Voodoo." Vodun is based on the Dahomean religions brought to Haiti by the African slaves. The word Vodun is based on the Dahomean word meaning god or spirits. Worshippers meet together at the local cult temple (known as a "hounfor") under the direction of a houngan (priest). Because of his knowledge of the rituals of Vodun, his experience in dealing with the spirits, and his ability to practice magic, the houngan posseses great community status and respect. Possession is the most important aspect of the cult. The god or spirit is said to "mount his horse" when the worshipper is possessed. Sacrifice to the gods, the cult of the dead, and the practice of magic are also important aspects of Vodun.

Vodun is primarily the religion of the masses, although a great many of the elite engage in some of its practices. The former President-for-life Francois Duvalier, openly encouraged and reputedly practiced Vodun, retained Vodun houngans as advisors and had numerous clashes with the Roman Catholic Church.

Most Haitians think of Protestantism as the option to Vodun. Whenever men wish to be free of the fears of Vodun, they turn to Protestantism. Whereas there is much syncretism between Vodun and Roman Catholicism, both Protestants and followers of Vodun agree that none can be a follower of Vodun and a committed Protestant. Protestants now make up almost 20% of Haiti's population.

## GEOGRAPHY AND CLIMATE

Situated on the western third of the island of Hispaniola, Haiti occupies 27,750 square kilometers (10,714 square miles) of land. It shares its 360 kilometer (224 mile) border with its eastern neighbor, the Dominican Republic. Three-fourths of the land area is covered by five mountain ranges which meet one another to form a continuous highland. The highest peak is the Morne de la Selle (2,680 meters, 8,793 feet). Lowlands cover only one-fourth of the area. There are four major flatlands and 16 smaller valleys and plains. Over one hundred rivers flow from the mountains. None are navigable but they serve for irrigation. Due to population pressures, all available land, even marginal hilly land, is used for farming.

The climate is tropical but the mountains cut off the interior from the moist trade winds. Hence, the country is semiarid and warm. Temperatures range between 20 and 34 degrees Celsius (68 and 94 degrees F) and are hottest from June through September and coolest between February and April. The heaviest rainfall occurs on the north coast with an average of 254 centimeters (100 inches) falling annually. In Port-au-Prince, rainfall drops to 137 centimeters (54 inches). Haiti lies in the hurricane belt. Although most hurricanes pass to the north or south of the island, they occasionally strike the south coast of Haiti with destructive force.

## HISTORY

On December 6, 1492, Christopher Columbus discovered the island which now includes the Dominican Republic and Haiti. He named it La Isla Espaniola. By the end of the 16th century most of the island's native Arawak Indians had died as a result of disease, conquest or slave labor. The Spanish settled primarily on the eastern end of the island. The unpopulated western end became the lair of French pirates and planters. By 1664, they had established the settlement, Port-de Pais,

in the northwest and the French West India Company took possession. In 1697, the western third of the island was ceded to the French and called Saint-Dominique. The French colonists rapidly developed Haiti's resources, using slave labor. The colony became extraordinarily rich, making it France's richest possession. Within a few years, the slave population greatly outnumbered the French settlers. By the end of the 18th century all of the island of Hispaniola was ceded to France by Spain.

In 1789, the population of Saint-Dominique was 556,000. Of this, 500,000 were black slaves; 32,000 were whites; and 24,000 were free blacks or mulattoes. On August 24, 1789, the slaves revolted. In order to keep the island as a French possession, slavery was abolished in 1794. A former slave, Toussaint-Louverture, became governor general in 1801. Although he did not sever official colonial ties with France, Napolean Bonaparte sent General Charles de Clerc to restore the old regime.

With the rumor that Napolean would restore slavery, the blacks, led by Jean-Jacques Dessalines and Henri Christophe, rebelled in 1802. By late 1803, the French were defeated. On January 1, 1804, the island was declared independent with the name of Haiti.

The economy was left in shambles by the war with France and the disruption caused by the shift from slave labor to freedom. Dessalines declared himself Emperor Jacques I in 1804 but he was killed during a revolt in 1806 and Henri Christophe took power. A civil war in 1808 left Christophe in power in the western end of the island but the Spanish rule was restored in the east (now the Dominican Republic). Christophe became Emperor Henri I but was overthrown by mutinous soldiers in 1820.

Jean-Pierre Boyer became president and in 1822 he invaded the newly independent Santo Domingo in the east. It was not until 1844 that the Haitians were expelled. Boyer was overthrown in 1843. Twenty rulers governed Haiti between 1843 and 1915, 16 of whom were overthrown or assassinated.

From 1915 to 1934, Haiti was occupied by the United States. During this time, schools, hospitals and roads were built but the Haitians still resented foreign occupation. In 1934 direct U.S. control ended, but direct fiscal control lasted until 1941.

Political instability continued until 1957 when Francois ("Papa Doc") Duvalier was elected to office. After consolidating his power (through the use of men hired to intimidate or kill opponents), Duvalier proclaimed himself President-for-Life. Duvalier's reigns saw the exodus of many educated Haitians, fleeing persecution and death. Poverty and starvation are prompting rural dwellers to become economic refugees, fleeing to the Dominican Republic, Puerto Rico, the Bahamas and to the United States.

## GOVERNMENT AND POLITICAL CONDITIONS

Haiti is the second oldest republic in the Western Hemisphere. The country has had more than 20 constitutions since its independence in 1804, the latest in 1964. Haitian politicians, however, often ignore constitutional laws and safeguards. For instance, the present constitution calls for individual freedoms, due process of law and direct elections of presidents, all of which have been ignored by the Duvaliers. The President-for-Life has abolute powers, including the right to nominate his successor, govern by decree and to dismiss the National Assembly and Cabinet. He controls the military, the secret police, the civil militia and an elite unit known as the Presidential Guard.

Haiti is divided into five departments for local administration. Each of these is headed by a prefect who is appointed by the central government. On a secondary level there are 27 arrondissements and at the third level there are 112 communes. Each commune elects its own mayor.

## ECONOMY

Haiti is the poorest country in the Western hemisphere. The average per capita gross national product in 1981 was $261 (U.S.). More than 80% of the Haitian population are subsistence farm families and urban poor with an annual per capita income of less than $100. Between 1960 and 1977, the Haitian GNP grew at an annual rate of 1.7%, less than the rate of population growth.

Agriculture employs 80% of the work force and accounts for over 60% of the foreign exchange. However, Haitian agriculture is unable to feed the population. While the population growth is over 2.6%, the annual growth in agricultural output is only one percent. Only one-third of the total land area is available for cultivation due to the mountainous terrain. Frequent droughts, poor irrigation, small farm plots and excessive soil erosion cut agricultural output.

The government is offering tax incentives in order to lure foreign businessmen to open plants there. A number of manufacturing plants have opened as a result. Many of these industries import unassembled parts to be assembled and re-exported. Electronic components and sewing assembly lead the field in these types of industries. The main cash crops for export are coffee, sugar and sisal. Bauxite is mined in quantity and copper has been found in the northern part of the country.

The 1981 exchange rate was five gourdes per $1 (U.S.).

# CHURCH STATISTICS FOR HAITI

Note: Statistics have been taken from different sources and are the most current data available. Definitions of "membership" very among churches and may not always be comparable. Not all known churches have been included in this list.

| Church or Mission Name | Communicants Full Members | Estimated Community |
|---|---|---|
| American Wesleyan Mission | 3,500 | 11,250 |
| Assemblies of God | 5,500 | 19,800 |
| Baptist Mid-Missions | 500 | 1,100 |
| Church of God (Cleveland) | 18,800 | 56,500 |
| Church of God of Prophecy | 16,800 | 33,700 |
| Church of God in North America | 400 | NA |
| Church of the Nazarene | 8,000 | 25,400 |
| Conservative Baptists | 8,000 | 40,000 |
| Convencion Baptiste d'Haiti | 38,000 | 80,000 |
| Eglise Episcopale | 15,658 | 39,091 |
| Eglise Evangelique d'Haiti | 2,000 | 7,100 |
| Faith Holiness Mission | 255 | 1,240 |
| Free Methodist Church | 1,000 | 1,900 |
| Methodist Church | 2,757 | NA |
| Missionary Church Association | 4,400 | 7,700 |
| Mission Evangelique Baptiste d'Haiti | 10,700 | 35,000 |
| Mission Evangelique Baptiste du Sud Haiti | 20,500 | 38,800 |
| Pentecostal Church of God | 4,500 | 13,300 |
| Seventh-day Adventists | 30,500 | 55,000 |
| World-wide Mission of Haiti | 15,000 | NA |
| Various independents (several thousand) | | |
| TOTAL PROTESTANT | 180-185,000 | 300,000 |
| TOTAL ROMAN CATHOLIC | | 4,613,690 |

NA = Information Not Available

The sources listed below are to help the reader find additional information on this country and Christian ministries there.  This list does not try to be comprehensive or complete.

DOCUMENTS

General

Cozen, John D., Latin America 1980, World Today Series, Washington D.C.: Stryker-Post Publication, 1980.

Grosvenor, Gilbert Hovey, editor, National Geographic, The Caribbean: Sun, Sea, and Seething", Vol. 159 No. 2, Washington D.C.: National Geographic Society, Feb. 1981.

Kurian, George Thomas, Encyclopedia of the Third World, New York: Facts on File, 1978.

Weil, Thomas E. et al, Area Handbook for Haiti, Washington D.C. : U.S. Government Printing Office, 1973.

Christian

Brierly, Peter, U.K. Christian Handbook, Vol. 1, London: Overseas Evangelical Missionary Alliance, 1981.

Canadian Catholic Missionaries, Ottowa, Canada: Canadian Religious Conference, 1979.

Kane, J. Herbert, A Global View of Christian Mission, Grand Rapids, MI: Baker Book House, 1971.

Mennonite Central Committee Workbook, Akron, PA: Mennonite Central Committee, 1979.

Mission Handbook, Washington D.C.: United States Catholic Mission Council, 1980.

Orr, J. Edwin, Evangelical Awakenings in Latin America, Minneapolis, MN: Bethany Fellowship, 1978.

The Caribbean, Richmond, VA: Dept. of Communication Foreign Mission Board SBC, 1977.

Thiesen, John Caldwell, A Survey of World Mission, Chicago: Moody Press, 1961.

Wilson, Sam, editor, Mission Handbook: North American Protestant Ministries

## ACKNOWLEDGMENTS

The information in this profile was taken from many sources which were the best available at the time of preparation.  However, the accuracy of the information cannot be guaranteed.  Views expressed or implied in this publication are not necessarily those of World Vision.  The editors have tried to present the ministries of various organizations in an objective manner, without undue bias or emphasis.  Where we have failed, we apologize for erroneous impressions that may result and request that comments and corrections be sent to MARC, 919 West Huntington Drive, Monrovia, California, 91016, USA.  We appreciate and acknowledge the comments and contributions of various organizations and individuals in the preparation of this publication, particularly Rev. Robert C. Gordon and Mr. George Fune.

# STATUS OF CHRISTIANITY COUNTRY PROFILE

# JAMAICA

### SUMMARY

AREA - 11,422 square kilometers (4,411
     square miles)
POPULATION - 2.2 million
RELIGION - 76% Protestant 8% Catholic
           16% Other

Over the years, Jamaicans have acclimated themselves to diverse cultures, dialects of English and hybrid religious beliefs. Colonialism, nationalism and socialism have all affected the lives of the people. Christianity, the Rastafarian movement and a wide variety of religious rituals and occult practices have developed among the people. Displaced Africans who were subjected to Spanish and British colonialism originated their own patterns of speech, art, music and social values. While other Caribbean nations have slid towards socialism, Jamaica, which until recently was led by socialists, has experienced a major change in direction as the people chose to seek relief in free enterprise. Economic recession and suffocating inflation have been severe. The people are well acquainted with poverty, natural disasters, inflation and materialism. Within this context, Christianity has survived as a religion, but in few situations have Christians been able to effectively address the felt needs and struggles of the public in general. Church institutions have been in Jamaica as long as the ancestors of the people, and for many there is no real distinction between Christian and secular values.

Reports indicate that nearly 70% of the children born each year do not have a father and mother who are married and living together. The challenge to the church is great as it attempts to confront contemporary problems and deal with real needs in such a hurting and complex society.

*This program is jointly carried out by the Strategy Working Group of the Lausanne Committee for World Evangelization and MARC, a ministry of World Vision International. For further information on the program, please write: MARC, 919 West Huntington Drive, Monrovia, CA 91016 U.S.A.*

## PEOPLE GROUPS

Identification of specific people groups in Jamaica is challenging because many social, economic, linguistic, religious and ethnic differences exist. Numerous combinations of these differences are incorporated by individuals within various groups. For instance, the ethnic background of one family may be West African; their language, English; their religion, Roman Catholicism; and their financial status, upper-middle class. Another family of West African ethnicity, who appear to be similar, may speak Jamaican (English) Creole, go to a small Pentecostal church and have little money or social status, while yet another black family of West African descent, who have little money and speaks Jamaican Creole, may be devout adherents of the Rastafarian movement which, in and of itself, affects their conduct and attitudes. There is no single specific characteristic which sets people apart. Rather, many characteristics must be considered in combination in order to describe particular people groups.

Specific statistical information is of limited value when one considers such a complex society of immigrants. The following figures must be considered as guidelines in defining combinations of characteristics common to particular people groups.

Secular sources report that 76.3% of the total population are descendents of black groups from West Africa. Most families are in Jamaica because their ancestors were transported from Africa to slave markets by the British. Jamaica was one of the largest slave trade centers with more than 3 million residents by the end of the 1700's. Most individuals worked on one of the 230 plantations where Jamaican (English) Creole evolved.

Prior to British colonization, a small number of blacks related to Ashanti tribes of Africa were taken to Jamaica by the Spanish. These slaves, known as Maroons, fled to the mountains when the Spanish were expelled. Their descendents consistently resisted British control and preserved their own mixtures of Spanish, Ashanti and Fanti cultural traditions.

With the introduction of African slaves into the British West Indies, especially Jamaica, several African religious practices became widespread. Many of the slaves were from the Ashanti-Fanti and Ibo peoples of West Africa, who continued to practice their own brands of African animism. These practices became somewhat modified in the context of the New World through contact with other religious beliefs. In Jamaica, two similar belief systems emerged: Obeah and Myalism. The "obeah-man" is a private practitioner, sometimes called a witch or wizard (Shaman). He has a tendency toward the use of "black magic;" whereas the "Myal-man" is a leader of a cult group that is devoted to organized religious life, with a tendency toward the practice of "white magic."

Large numbers of blacks own or lease small plots of land on which they raise food and cash crops without mechanization. Only traditional methods are utilized and life is difficult, with little opportunity for potential expansion or for saving money. Plantations, though on the decline, still employ significant numbers of lower-class blacks. Religious practices of fundamentalist, Pentecostal or other diverse denominational groups from North America were particularly attractive to blacks of lower socio-economic backgrounds. Many have adopted patterns taught by North American missionaries who emphasized prohibition of alcohol, any form of dancing, rock music or smoking. Churches, sects and cults, which strongly emphasize issues and practices appealing to the emotions, have been particularly successful.

The blending of African animism with Christian beliefs and practices occured over the course of many centuries in the Caribbean. The acceptance of the Christian faith by Africans was a slow process, which resulted in varying leveels of syncretism. Converts to Protestantism often retained lingering elements of their old animistic belief system.

Several Afro-Christian sects emerged in this context. Revivalism or Pocomania (sometimes called Zion Revivalism) became a strong religious movement between the 1840s and 1860s, then declined in importance. However, Pocomania experienced a resurgence during the 1880s and again in the 1910s. Bedwardism, which emerged in Jamaica during the 1930s, apparently had its roots in Pocomania and Myalism.

The Rastafarian movement is of particular interest since it has widespread influence in Jamaican society. It also began during the 1930s in Jamaica. Many of the underlying premises appeal to the felt needs of individuals who may be bitter or critical of the "establishment." Political, social and religious issues are addressed by Rastafarian philosophies which have often provided impetus for counter revolutionary activities. To the devout, man is divine, and any gods, rules or regulations become subject to the desires of man. Anything suggesting the establishment, including tidy clothing, styled haircuts, shoes, or even baths, are rejected by the most radical members. Particular portions of Scripture are readily used if they express a Rastafarian principle. One example is long hair. One passage in Ezekiel prohibits any razor from touching one's hair until the people return to their homeland. For the Rastafarians this was originally Ethiopia. Marijuana (ganja) is liberally used to raise the individual's level of consciousness and increase self awareness. It is indeed a challenging task to reach the Rastafarians with the gospel and it requires a unique strategy.

Many Jamaicans are descendants of blacks and Europeans. Several descriptive words have been coined, including Mulatto, colored and Afro-European, to describe members of this particular group which comprise 14.6% of the population. Again, financial and religious differences are important in accurately identifying sub-groups. Most Mulattoes more readily accepted the religious and cultural traditions of the British. They preserved more traditional forms of English, though many understood some form of Creole but dared not use it lest they lose respect. Anglican, Presbyterian, Methodist or Roman Catholic church doctrines and traditions have been closely adhered to as more elite forms of Christianity.

Two specific groups identified primarily by ethnic distinction are the 10,000 to 20,000 Chinese and the 30,000 East Indians. Each group has preserved selected cultural traditions and has historically held specific jobs and played a particular role in the social structure. Descendants of hard labor slaves who once gathered bird fertilizer have now risen to positions as import-export middlemen. Chinese have generaly remained separate by marriage, but East Indians have been more willing to intermarry and adapt themselves to other lifestyles. Most Chinese and East Indians have been exposed to the superficial Christianity of the general public, but many have not understood the distinctive claims which bring about commitments.

Jamaicans who have become interested in socialist philosophies have formulated unique blends of religious doctrines and political persuasions. They have mixed Marxism with superstitious beliefs and pagan practices which have accompanied the revival of African cultural traditions.

Christianity is a facade for some who accept as part of their cultural heritage the spirit worship or pagan rituals which now characterize cult practices and even some church activities.

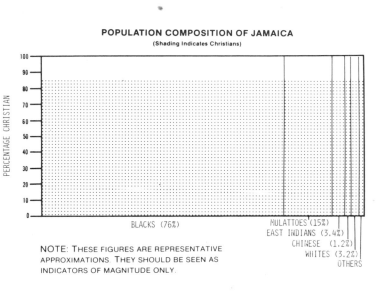

**POPULATION COMPOSITION OF JAMAICA**
(Shading Indicates Christians)

PERCENTAGE CHRISTIAN

BLACKS (76%)    MULATTOES (15%)
EAST INDIANS (3.4%)
CHINESE (1.2%)
WHITES (3.2%)
OTHERS

NOTE: THESE FIGURES ARE REPRESENTATIVE APPROXIMATIONS. THEY SHOULD BE SEEN AS INDICATORS OF MAGNITUDE ONLY.

## CURRENT STATUS OF CHRISTIANITY

Christianity was introduced to slaves in Jamaica by Christians from nations in which slavery was permitted. Thus one can easily observe the dichotomy between what was taught and what was done. Those who were disrupted and displaced from their homes and lifestyles accepted Christianity as part of the new life given them.

Emancipation from slavery provided the opportunity for each individual to consider the role and importance of Christianity. For those who were bitter, angry or judgmental, Christianity was one more institution of the imperial colonialists to be thrown out. Cults arose to fill the spiritual vacuum. African messiahs were identified and false teachings proliferated. Others chose simply to ignore or reject their spiritual natures.

Many Jamaicans have been disillusioned by the hypocritical practices of some churches and are frustrated with financial systems based on exploitation. Socialists have been trying to convince them to shun imperialism, capitalism and religion. Many Jamaicans have been exposed to Christianity without culturally appropriate methods or messages. Thus many have not been given the opportunity to study the message of Christ for themselves, nor have they been confronted with the Biblical principles regarding poverty, justice and value. Materialism has also become a motivating force for many who strive to succeed and accrue savings to spend on themselves. Christianity is often viewed as an unimportant force that has little to do with business or profit. For others who understood and/or accepted the teachings of Christ, salvation by grace became a living reality. Churches developed their own worship services with forms and expressions of the heart common to their culture. Students of the Scriptures listened to missionaries explain the Bible and they sought to serve their people even as Christ would.

## RELIGIOUS COMPOSITION OF JAMAICA

OTHER (16%)

ROMAN CATHOLIC (9%)

PROTESTANT (75%)

**NATIONAL CHURCHES**

## PROTESTANT CHURCHES

Protestant churches in Jamaica are self-sufficient as well as self-propagating and they have historically been an important center of national attention and influence. Church members and leaders, dissatisfied with the socialist government and humanist teaching of the 1970's, were part of a movement which ousted socialist leaders from office

in 1980 and replaced them with more conservative leaders who upheld Christian principles, rather than despising them.

The Anglican Church has been in Jamaica for over 200 years and remains the largest single denomination with approximately 73,000 members, and 317,000 adherents, comprising nearly 15% of the total national population. Church leadership includes two Bishops, 54 priests, 14 curates and 24 other clergy.

The Jamaica Baptist Union is comprised of 270 churches who have significant outreach ministries, including radio broadcasts and training centers in electronics, music, drama and creative writing. Many Baptist lay workers are involved in evangelistic outreach programs, and have welcomed assistance from itinerant teachers offering seminars and training courses in Bible and evangelistic practices and methods.

National pastors are each usually responsible for at least two, and sometimes four churches since there are only 80 full time ordained ministers for the 270 churches which have a combined community of 35,000.

The Assemblies of God has a community of more than 7,000, of which approximately 2,000 are baptized members. They receive training from 44 credentialed ministers and 28 national workers who minister in the 35 churches and five Bible schools.

The Disciples of Christ in Jamaica have five ministers. The African Methodist Episcopal Church (A.M.E.) maintains three conferences for administrative purposes, and operates a kindergarten.

The Disciples of Christ maintain several mission and preaching stations and three community churches. Sixteen ministers are assisted by one Christian education worker and two lay pastors among the 5,000 members.

The Jamaica District of the Methodist Church provides leadership for 18,600 members who attend 162 churches. Only 43 ministers are ordained, but nearly 600 local preachers provide capable leadership.

A very active ministry sponsored by the Brethren, is conducted by the Chinese Christian Fellowship. Programs are geared to all age groups, utilizing either English or Chinese, depending on what is appropriate. Sunday morning services are conducted entirely by Christian Chinese church leaders. Programs designed for youth include game nights, camps and retreats. Regular Sunday evening visitation provides opportunity for evangelistic teams to reach Chinese living in outlying areas. Small groups of Chinese Christians and non-Christians meet in cottages to sing, listen to choirs, contemplate messages of lay preachers and share needs and concerns of the various families.

## CATHOLIC CHURCHES

A vicariate apostolic was organized for Jamaica in 1837. The prevailing hierarchy was established in 1967 with one Archdiocese, one diocese and 18 parishes served by 105 priests, 215 sisters and nine brothers among 3,700 baptized Catholics who were part of a community of 187,200. Official church estimates report that nearly 9% of the total population are nominally Catholic.

## COOPERATIVE AGENCIES

The Caribbean Conference of Churches administered $332,200 for 11 projects in 1977, $318,600 for 15 projects in 1978 but only $149,000 for three projects in 1979. The churches are apparently experiencing the severe economic pressures created by recession and inflation. One multipurpose community center, a small business development center and a single institute were the only recipients of financial assistance in Jamaica.

The Social Action Centre was established as the extension school of St. George's College. It provides basic seminars on development of a Christian social conscience; conducts summer camps and provides courses in community development and designing self-help programs.

The United Bible Society maintains an office with an executive secretary who oversees the production and distribution of Bibles, New Testaments and abbreviated Scripture portions. The staff depends on close cooperation with members of all denominations and groups.

## FOREIGN MISSIONS

## PROTESTANT MISSIONS

Missionaries of the Society for the Propagation of the Gospel in Foreign Parts, sponsored by the Church of England, began ministries in Jamaica by 1665. Evangelism and church planting followed patterns established in England, and for nearly 100 years no other mission agencies or groups sent personnel to Jamaica.

Moravian missionaries responded to invitations of plantation owners who willingly gave small subdivisions of land on which the Moravians could raise their own food. Ministries were focused primarily on slaves of large estates but responses were initially limited. British Methodist missionaries, who observed little outreach on the part of the Church of England, were able to initiate effective ministries among plantation slaves.

An American black emigrated in 1783 and began a preaching ministry during the hours he wasn't working. A small congregation of friends formed the first Baptist church in Jamaica. Three British Baptist missionaries entered in 1814 and were pleased to find a solid base on which to extend their ministries. Tensions between small church groups opposing slavery, including the Baptists, Moravians and Methodists and leaders in the Church of England, prevented many missionaries from entering Jamaica until emancipation of all slaves in 1834. Numerous mission groups encountered great openness and receptivity to new forms of worship and biblical lifestyles when they were allowed to enter and minister among the freed Jamaicans. The Baptist Missionary Society was able to establish a self-propagating fellowship in a little more than 10 years, with national believers carrying on many of the ministries. Such was the case for ministries initiated by the London Missionary Society and the American Missionary Association, though the time was slightly longer until self-sufficiency was attained. Numerous other agencies sent personnel in the 1800's.

An evangelical awakening began in a Moravian chapel in 1860 which touched all segments of Jamaican society. It rapidly spread to parishes, churches and cottage congregations everywhere. Conversions were numerous and revival was extensive among church members who had lost their vitality in dead formality vitality in dead formality. Christians became motivated to reach unchurched areas and mission stations were soon opened in most outlying regions. The total population became at least aware of, if not directly involved in, changes in conduct and attitudes.

In the early 1900's a significant increase in missionaries occurred when five North American groups of Pentecostal and Holiness tradition sent personnel to begin ministries. A third wave of missionaries entered during and after World War II, including many who were affiliated with independent and interdenominational para-church agencies, rather than a specific denominational sending board.

Mennonite Central Committee ministries were begun in 1954 by a retired Canadian couple. Within one year a Sunday school and cottage meetings were held each week and the stress of expanded ministries required more expatriate assistance. The Virginia Mission Board sent personnel, and by 1957 the first church building was constructed. All foreign personnel left in 1977 leaving behind a small, well-built, established and growing Mennonite community. The Baptist Union, in particular, grew rapidly. The 60 Baptist and 20 unaffiliated-member churches reported that 6,000 individuals were baptized or restored to fellowship and 6,000 others were interested in becoming baptized members. The Union of Churches, which had been losing members from 1840-1860, realized an increase of 5,000 during the awakening. The United Presbyterian Church of Scotland was extremely encouraged by the maturity and growth of member churches who reported over 1,300 conversions and a total community of 10,420 in 26 congregations. Baptist, Congregational, Methodist, Moravian and Presbyterian churches all shared in the revival among black Jamaicans who wanted to be free from spiritual slavery, even as they had obtained freedom from physical slavery.

By 1979, 56 North American Protestant agencies were sending a total of 121 career missionaries to work with members of 1,534 churches. They were joined by 27 career missionaries, 11 associates and three short-termers from 13 agencies in the United Kingdom. Three Australians affiliated with the Salvation Army were also ministering in Jamaica. The Church of the Nazarene sent the largest number of North Americans (22). International Evangelism Crusades had 10 people active, as did the General Conference of Seventh-day Adventists, who reported that its personnel ministered among 235 related churches. The Salvation Army has territorial headquarters in Kingston, Jamaica. The Church of Scotland, with seven career personnel, reported the largest number from the United Kingdom. They were followed by the Overseas Council of Methodists and United Society for the Propagation of the Gospel, each with four.

## ROMAN CATHOLIC MISSIONS

Dominican and Franciscan Catholic missionaries engaged in evangelistic ministries within Jamaica from 1512 until 1655 when they were requested to leave by British colonial officials who replaced the Spanish rulers. Jesuits were allowed to enter in the early 1800's. By 1979, 56 Jesuits worked alongside members of four other orders of priests and brothers as well as seven orders of sisters, including the Franciscans of Allegany who had 21 sisters. The number of Jesuits decreased significantly from 75 in 1976 to 56 in 1979. The total number of overseas personnel declined from 164 in 1976 to 128 in 1980.

## INDIGENOUS MISSIONS

The church in Jamaica was able to send more than 15 missions personnel to other countries by 1978. The International Missionary Fellowship, an interdenominational cooperative group, operates the School of Mission Training which sent over 27 graduates into pastoral and missionary ministries by 1979.

## MAJOR CHRISTIAN ACTIVITIES

## SOCIAL CONCERN

The Salvation Army has numerous social service programs, including homes and workshops for the handicapped.

Short-termers from Salvation Army centers in the U.S.A. regularly work with national workers. Such was the case in a 10 day cadets' campaign in which 126 individuals accepted Christ as Savior. Of these, 66% did so as a result of personal contacts. Other ministries include evangelism training seminars, workshops for the handicapped, welfare programs, community centers, a medical clinic, prison and probation counselling, homes for the blind, an agricultural training center, daycare centers, a men's hospital, a thrift shop and a training college.

## CHRISTIAN EDUCATION

The Jamaican Methodist district shares responsibility for 32 primary schools and has full control of 19 preparatory schools, high schools and vocational training schools. The Salvation Army operates 15 primary and secondary schools with 920 students, and one training college.

Several Christian agencies initiated activities in Jamaica by opening schools and thereby gaining the respect and attention of the people.

## THEOLOGICAL EDUCATION

United Theological College of the West Indies provides higher level education for students primarily of Presbyterian, Methodist and Anglican backgrounds. The Jamaica Theological Seminary, sponsored by the Missionary Church, caters to students of contemporary evangelical denominations.

Fairview Baptist College, operated by Baptist Mid-Missions, serves the diverse Baptist communities. Jamaica Bible College offers three-year programs for rural pastors who seek intensive Bible education which can be applied in forms culturally appropriate for the people. Jamaican students who desire further Christian education are free to attend any of the 43 Bible schools.

## BIBLE TRANSLATION AND DISTRIBUTION

The Bible Society headquarters for the West Indies are in Kingston, Jamaica.

All figures listed are combined totals for Windward Islands, Leeward Islands, Guyana, Belize, Barbados, Trinidad and Tobago, Bahamas and Jamaica. Costs have soared for production of materials as inflation has jumped rapidly within Jamaica and the overall distribution rate has been dropping. Though contributions have increased, the value of the funds have decreased.

Combined totals for the West Indies region in 1976 and 1979:

|  | 1976 | 1979 |
|---|---|---|
| Bibles | 92,859 | 85,446 |
| New Testaments | 16,785 | 13,629 |
| Portions | 63,556 | 36,728 |
| Selections | 797,241 | 825,042 |
| New Reader | 131,935 | 62,910 |
| TOTALS | 1,102,376 | 1,023,755 |

## NATION AND ITS PEOPLE

## POPULATION

The 1970 Census listed 1,938,000 people in Jamaica. By 1981 the population had grown to 2,200,000. A high rate of emigration kept the annual population growth rate to a low 1.5% in the 1960's. However, a decline in emigration resulted in a higher growth rate in the 1970's. It is now estimated to be at 2.1%. The population is relatively young: 43% are under the age of 15.

Jamaica is one of the most densely populated countries in the world with an average of over 185 per square kilometer (429 people per square mile) and over 330 per square kilometer (855 people per square mile) in areas with arable land. In 1981, about 50% of Jamaica's people lived in urban areas. The largest population center is the Kingston-St. Andrew metropolitan area; over 28% of Jamaica's people live there.

## COMPOSITION

By the time the British settled in Jamaica in 1655, the indigenous Arawak Indians had died out. The present population is now composed of the descendants of British colonialists and their slaves. Nearly 91.4% of the population is of African descent with 76.3% of pure Negro origin and 15.1% of mixed Negro and white origin. Chinese and Afro-Chinese constitute 1.2%, East Indians and Afro-East Indians constitute 3.4%, whites constitute about 4%.

## LANGUAGE AND LITERACY

English is the official language, although different forms of English are spoken by the various social classes. British English is spoken by British expatriates and those Jamaicans educated in England. Jamaican English is similar to British English but it has its own particular pronunciation, idiomatic expressions and loan words from Jamaican Creole. Jamaican Creole, the language of the lower classes, is a mixture of English and West African influences. Chinese and Hindi are spoken by the Chinese and Indian communities.

The literacy rate for adults was reported at 82% in 1970 but the functional literacy rate was estimated at about 40%.

## RELIGION

Christianity is the major religion adhered to by most Jamaicans. Over 100 denominations are represented with the Anglican Church being the largest. It is followed by the Baptist, Church of God, Roman Catholic, Methodist, Presbyterian, Seventh-Day Adventist, Moravian, Congregational, Pentecostal, Plymouth Brethren and Salvation Army churches.

Several cults with African backgrounds have arisen, mainly among the poor of Jamaica. The Afro-Christian cults of Pocomania (Revivalism) and Rastafarianism are two of the most popular. The Rastafarian cult supports repatriation of black people to Africa and advocates that the late Emporer Haile Selassie of Ethopia is divine.

There are several Muslim and Hindu groups and a very small Jewish community.

## GEOGRAPHY AND CLIMATE

Jamaica is located in the Caribbean Sea south of Cuba and west of Haiti. It has a total land area of 11,424 square kilometers (4,411 square miles) and it stretches 235 kilometers (146 miles) in length and 82 kilometers (51 miles) at its widest point.

The topography consists mostly of coastal plains divided by the Blue Mountain range in the east. Hills and plateaus predominate in the central and western regions of the interior. The average height of the Blue Mountains is 1,800 meters (6,000 feet) with the Blue Mountain peak being the highest point on the island at 2,256 meters (7,402 feet). Several rivers begin in the mountains, including the Black River, which is the largest.

The island of Jamaica has a tropical climate in the coastal lowlands and a temperate climate in the higher elevations. There are four seasons: two rainy seasons, one from May to June and one from September to November; and two dry seasons, one from December to April and one from July to August. Average annual rainfall measures 195 centimeters (77 inches) with the greatest rainfall, 503 centimeters (200 inches), recorded along the northeast coast and in the Blue Mountains, and the least rainfall, 84 centimeters (33 inches), falling in the Kingston area. Temperatures remain fairly constant. From the lowest average of 24 degrees Celsius (75 degrees Fahrenheit) in January and February, the temperature only rises to an average of 27 degrees Celsius (80 degrees Fahrenheit) in July and August.

## HISTORY

Jamaica was discovered by Christopher Columbus in 1494 and was settled by the Spanish in the 16th century. By the 17th century, the native Arawak Indians had died out. The British took control of the island in 1655 and Spain formally ceded it to them in 1670. The British continued importing slaves from Africa and developed an economy based upon sugar plantations. The abolition of slavery in 1834 brought about the destruction of this economy.

The following year the British Parliament established Jamaica as a Crown Colony and the economy was gradually rebuilt. Jamaica achieved a measure of self-government in 1944. It joined the

Federation of the West Indies in 1958 but withdrew just three years later. On August 6, 1962, Jamaica became an independent nation.

## GOVERNMENT AND POLITICAL CONDITIONS

The Jamaican government is patterned after the British parliamentary system. The executive power is vested in the cabinet, led by the Prime Minister. The parliament consists of an appointed senate and an elected house of representatives. Thirteen senate members are appointed by the Prime Minister and eight by the leader of the opposition. House elections are held at the discretion of the Governor General by the advice of the Prime Minister, but at intervals no longer than five years. The Prime Minister and members of the cabinet are selected from the parliament.

There are two major political parties in Jamaica. The Jamaica Labor Party (JLP) supports a platform of "Nationalism." During the years it was predominant in Jamaican politics (1962-1972), it encouraged foreign investment in the Jamaican economy but it endorsed the policy of Jamaican ownership of financial institutions and of some foreign owned businesses. The People's National Party (PNP), which assumed power in 1972 under the leadership of Michael Manley, embraces a philosophy of "Democratic Socialism." Manley's government took an active role in managing the economy. However, due to a high unemployment rate (over 25%), inflation and its close ties with Cuba, Jamaican voters turned the PNP out of office and installed Seaga of the JLP as Prime Minister in 1980. The election was bitterly fought and violence between the party supporters reflects the intense differences between the two parties.

## ECONOMY

The Jamaican economy was based on large scale plantation agriculture with sugar and bananas being the primary crops. The discovery of huge bauxite reserves in the 1950's led to the development of the bauxite/aluminum industry. During the 1960's, tourism became a major factor in the island's economy. The economy expanded rapidly in all areas in 1965-1971 but, beginning in 1972, the economic growth leveled. In 1976, a severe economic slump, coupled with increased government spending, forced the Jamaican government to seek help from the International Monetary Fund. Continued high unemployment (over 25%) and high inflation (over 50%) were primary factors in the defeat of the PNP in 1980.

# CHURCH STATISTICS FOR JAMAICA

Note: Statistics have been taken from different sources and are the most current data available. Definitions of "membership" vary among churches and may not always be comparable. Not all known churches have been included in this list.

| | Adult Members | Total Community |
|---|---|---|
| Apostolic Church | | |
| Assemblies of God | 1,798 | 2,720 |
| Associated Gospel Assemblies | 1,800 | |
| Brethren Assemblies | | |
| Church of God | | 17,130 |
| Church of God (Anderson, IN) | 2,421 | |
| Church of God of Prophecy | 11,200 | |
| Church of the Nazarene | 86 | 633 |
| Church of the Province of the West Indies (Anglican) | 52,600 | 73,000 |
| Church of the United Brethren in Christ | 1,009 | |
| Disciples of Christ/Christian Church | 5,500 | 12,000 |
| Ethiopian Orthodox Church (Holy Trinity) | 2,000 | 3,000 |
| International Church of the Foursquare Gospel | 291 | 591 |
| Jamaica Baptist Union | 34,000 | 306,037 |
| Jamaica Mennonite Church | 318 | |
| Methodist Church in the Caribbean and Americas | 19,479 | 120,000 |
| Moravian Church in Jamaica | 8,500 | 23,298 |
| Open Bible Standard Churches of Jamaica | 1,000 | 2,000 |
| Pentecostal Church of God of America, Jamaica Branch | 701 | |
| Religious Society of Friends Jamaica Yearly Meeting | 750 | 1,300 |
| Seventh-day Adventist Church | 53,865 | |
| Seventh-day Baptist Church, Jamaica Conference | 965 | |
| United Church of Jamaica and Grand Cayman | | |
| Wesleyan Holiness Church | 1,549 | 4,015 |

# SELECTED BIBLIOGRAPHY AND INFORMATION SOURCES

The sources listed below are to help the reader find additional information on this country and Christian ministries there. This list does not try to be comprehensive or complete.

DOCUMENTS

General

Cozen, John D., Latin America 1980, World Today Series, Washington D.C.: Stryker-Post Publication, 1980.

Grosvenor, Gilbert Hovey, editor, National Geographic, "The Caribbean, Sun, Sea, and Seething", Vol 159 No. 2, Washington D.C.: National Geographic Society, Feb. 1981.

Kaplan, Irving, et al, Area Handbook for Jamaica, Washington D.C.,: U.S. Government Printing Office, 1975.

Olien, Michael D., Latin Americans, Contemporary Peoples and Their Cultural Traditions, New York: Holt, Rinehart and Winston, 1973.

Christian

Brathwaite, Joan, Handbook of Churches in the Caribbean, Bridgetown, Barbados: CADEC (Christian Action for Development in the Caribbean), 1973.

Brierly, Peter, U.K. Christian Handbook, Vol. 1; London: Overseas Evangelical Missionary Alliance, 1981.

Canadian Catholic Missionaries, Ottawa, Canada: Canadian Religious Conference, 1979.

Kane, J. Herbert, A Global View of Christian Mission, Grand Rapids, MI: Baker Book House, 1971.

Mission Handbook, Washington, D.C.: United States Catholic Mission Council, 1980.

Orr, J. Edwin, Evangelical Awakenings in Latin America, Minneapolis, MN: Bethany Fellowship, 1978.

The Caribbean, Richmond, VA: Dept. of Communication Foreign Mission Board, SBC, 1977.

## ACKNOWLEDGMENTS

The information in this profile was taken from many sources which were the best available to the editors at the time of preparation. However, the accuracy of the information cannot be guaranteed. Views expressed or implied in this publication are not necessarily those of World Vision. The editors have tried to present the ministries of various organizations in an objective manner, without undue bias or emphasis. Where we have failed, we apologize for erroneous impressions that may result and request that comments be directed to MARC, 919 West Huntington Drive, Monrovia, California, 91016, USA. We appreciate and acknowledge the comments and contributions of various organizations and individuals in the preparation of this publication.

# STATUS OF CHRISTIANITY COUNTRY PROFILE

# LEEWARD ISLANDS

## SUMMARY

AREA - The islands of:
      Antigua, Guadeloupe, St. Kitts-Nevis
      and Anguilla
POPULATION - 450,000
RELIGION - See Nation and People section

The Leeward Islands are a group of small islands south east of Puerto Rico. The largest island is the butterfly-shaped island of Guadeloupe, while the smallest is Redonda (less than one square kilometer). The islands were controlled by the French and English at various times. Those islands which were influenced by the English are today primarily Anglican in their religion, while the French island of Guadeloupe is primarily Roman Catholic. Today, Anguilla, Antigua, Nevis and St. Kitts remain British while Guadeloupe is a French possession.

## PEOPLE GROUPS

Most people of the Leeward Islands consider themselves to be Christians. Nevertheless, the faith of many is only nominal. It is estimated that over half the population of Antigua, for instance, does not attend church. A great need prevails for spiritual renewal among the people.

Many of the residents of the Leeward Islands are descendants of Negro slaves who were transported to slave markets and plantations throughout the West Indies. A few residents are expatriates from the U.S., Canada and the United Kingdom.

*This program is jointly carried out by the Strategy Working Group of the Lausanne Committee for World Evangelization and MARC, a ministry of World Vision International. For further information on the program, please write: MARC, 919 West Huntington Drive, Monrovia, CA 91016 U.S.A.*

## CURRENT STATUS OF CHRISTIANITY

As is typical of other Caribbean Islands, those Leewards which were controlled by, or heavily influenced by, the French or Spanish presently preserve traditional patterns of Roman Catholicism. The French island of Guadeloupe is reportedly 94% Roman Catholic. The Anglican and Methodist Churches are dominant in the British Islands of Antigua, St. Kitts, Nevis and Anguilla. Only 10% of the people of Antigua and only 8% of the residents of St. Kitts, Nevis, and Anguilla are Roman Catholic. Four other major Protestant church groups are also represented.

## NATIONAL CHURCHES

### PROTESTANT CHURCHES

The largest Protestant church in the Leeward Islands is the Anglican Church. Gilbert Ramsey, the first Anglican priest to the Leeward Islands, entered Antigua in 1634. His work came under the jurisdiction of the Bishop of London. The Leeward Islands became a part of the Bishopric of Barbados which was established in 1824. The Bishopric of Antigua was established in 1842. It assumes responsibility for church matters in Antigua, Aruba, Barbuda, Dominica, Montserrat, Nevis, Saba, St. Barts, St. Eustatuis, St. Martin and St. Kitts. By 1973, the Diocese of Antigua included 68 registered churches, directed by 28 priests and deacons who were assisted by 45 lay readers among a total membership which exceeded 60,000 individuals.

The Methodist Church in the Caribbean and the Americas had its beginning with the preaching of Nathaniel Gilbert who preached to his slaves in Antigua. John Baxter continued the work and established a Methodist Society. On December 25,1789, the first Methodist minister was brought to the Leeward Islands by Dr. Thomas Coke who was the first Methodist missionary to the Leewards. Dr. Coke made several visits to other islands and did begin a work on Dominica. He visited St. Eustatius and left responsibilites for ongoing ministries to Black Henry, a Negro slave, who became the first church leader. Dr. Coke, Mr. Baxter and Mr. William Hammett went to St. Kitts and Nevis, and Mr. Hammett stayed on as the first Methodist missionary. Work in Anguilla began in 1813 and in Montserrat in 1820. In 1973, the Leeward Islands District of the Methodist Church in the Caribbean and America reported 74 churches, 25 ministers, 170 local preachers and a membership of nearly 16,000 individuals.

Some of the other denominations active in the Leeward Islands are: Seventh-day Adventists, with 50 churches and 10,600 members; the Church of God - Cleveland, with 12 churches; Worldteam, formerly West Indies Mission, with 24 churches and a community of 5,000 belivers on Guadeloupe; Church of God - Anderson with seven churches on St. Kitts and Nevis; Southern Baptists, with four churches and a community of 160 people on Guadeloupe, three churches on Antigua and three on St. Kitts; the Salvation Army; and Moravians. French Pentecostal Churches have 18 congregations and 1,000 members in Guadeloupe.

### CATHOLIC CHURCHES

Approximately 7,000 individuals, 10% of the total population residing in Antigua, are nominally Roman Catholic. One diocese is comprised of two parishes under the direction of three priests who are assisted by six brothers and eight sisters. Guadeloupe is considered part of the French overseas department. Of the total population, 300,000 or 92%, are reported to be nominally Catholic. One diocese is comprised of 46 parishes under the direction of 85 priests assisted by seven brothers and 205 sisters. St. Kitts and Nevis are under ecclesiastical jurisdiction of St. John's diocese in Antigua. Eight parishes are directed by four priests assisted by nine sisters. Catholics comprise 8% of the population.

### FOREIGN MISSIONS

### PROTESTANT

The Church of England established congregations on the islands of Antigua and St. Kitts soon after the British assumed control of the area. Significant ministries to non-whites, however, did not begin until Moravian missionaries entered Antigua in 1756 and St. Kitts in 1777. Activities of the Moravians have continued since that time.

Doctrines maintained by Methodists were first taught in Antigua by Nathaniel Gilbert, a plantation owner who was converted in England through the teaching of John Wesley. When he returned to Antigua from England in 1760, he became a lay preacher. By 1774, the year of his death, a Methodist community of 200 had been established.  In 1778, John Baxter, a shipwright who devoted his spare time to preaching, continued the ministries initiated by Nathaniel Gilbert.  By 1786 there were nearly 2,000 Methodists on the island.  From the strong base established in Antigua, Methodism spread to neighboring islands.  Methodist Churches in the Leeward area became part of an autonomous conference in May, 1967.

The Salvation Army sent representatives to Antigua in 1904 and ministries have continued since that time.  The ministries of North American Protestant missionaries to Caribbean nations and territories increased significantly during the 1940's.  The Church of God - Cleveland, a Pentecostal group, started work in St. Kitts in 1943, Guadeloupe in 1946 and Antigua in 1954.  By 1980, they sponsored 12 churches in these islands.  Worldteam, originally known as the West Indies Mission, began ministries within Guadeloupe in 1947.  Nine missionaries assisting in the ministries of 24 churches were active in 1980.  The Church of God (Anderson, IN), which inititated ministries in 1946, reported seven churches and two missionaries in St. Kitts-Nevis in 1980.

The Southern Baptists are the newest and largest missionary force.  They started work in 1964 in Guadeloupe (now part of their French West Indies mission).  In 1968, the Baptist mission in Trinidad sent assistance to Baptists on Antigua in the form of temporary workers.  The following year a Southern Baptist missionary couple moved permanently to Antigua in order to assist with leadership training and church development.  The same year, the Trinidad mission began to assist Baptists on St. Kitts.  The work on Antigua grew and several mission points developed into churches.  In 1976 the Southern Baptists sent an agricultural missionary to Antigua.

Pentecostal churches in France have sent four missionaries to Guadeloupe where they are involved with the growing Pentecostal churches on the island.

## ROMAN CATHOLIC MISSIONS

Historically, Catholic missionaries accompanied Spanish and French colonists who founded early settlements.

Until recently, the vast majority of priests were expatriates, but the local Catholic seminaries on Trinidad and Jamaica are now training national priests.  Nevertheless, the need for Catholic missionaries is still apparent.  Guadeloupe, for instance, has seven

brothers from the U.S. and seven brothers from Canada, along with over 200 sisters working on the island.  Antigua, with a much smaller Catholic constituency, has nine brothers (three U.S. and six Canadian) and one sister.

### MAJOR CHRISTIAN ACTIVITIES

## BROADCASTING

The Southern Baptists have broadcast radio programs on the government radio station in Guadeloupe.  All the islands are within range of the Trans World Radio station located on Bonaire.

## LITERATURE

Christian Literature Crusade works out of Antigua, supplying Christian literature and correspondence courses to the area.

## BIBLE TRANSLATION DISTRIBUTION

Bibles are available in all the major languages of the area.  The Leeward Islands are part of the United Bible Society's Eastern Caribbean District.

## EDUCATION

One of the primary emphases of the Catholic Church is on education.  They operate 22 schools on the island of Guadeloupe.  There are six schools scattered among the islands of Antigua, Anguilla, Nevis and St. Kitts.

Of the Protestant schools, it is known that the Anglicans operate one primary school on Antigua.  The Methodists partially control three primary schools and fully control one prep. school and one high school.

## SOCIAL CONCERNS

The Southern Baptist mission sponsors short term medical and dental teams in the islands.  They report that over 10,000 people have received medical and dental care through their efforts.

The Caribbean Council of Churches is active through the Christian Action for Development in the Caribbean (CADEC), trying to make people aware of social concerns and issues.  Some of the projects CADEC supports are an education and training program in Guadeloupe, construction of a community center in Anguilla and maintaining a preschool in Anguilla.

## NATION AND ITS PEOPLE

### ANTIGUA

POPULATION. In 1970 the census numbered 65,525 people in Antigua. The population in 1978 was estimated to be 73,000. The annual growth rate is between 1.2 and 1.3 percent. About 34% of the population lives in urban areas. The town of St. John's has a population of 24,000. The population density averages 412 persons per square mile.

COMPOSITION. Nearly all Antiguans are of African descent.

LANGUAGE AND LITERACY. English is the official and commercial language although English Creole is widely spoken. About 80% of the people are literate.

RELIGION. The largest body is the Anglican Church with 60,000 members reported. Roman Catholics and other Protestant bodies are represented.

GEOGRAPHY AND CLIMATE. Antigua and its dependencies, Barbuda and Redonda, are low-lying islands on the outside of the Leeward Island chain. They are small in size - Antigua is 281 square kilometers (108 square miles), Barbuda is 161 square kilometers (62 square miles) and Redonda is slightly more than one square kilometer (less than one-half square mile). Antigua is mountainous and has its highest elevation at Boggy Peak (400 meters, 1,330 feet). Barbuda is a flat coral island 25 miles north of Antigua.

The tropical climate is tempered by sea breezes, averaging between 24 and 29 degrees C. (75 and 85 degrees F.). An average of 115 centimeters (46 inches) of rain falls annually. Antigua experiences hurricanes, usually in early Autumn.

HISTORY. Christopher Columbus discovered the island on his second voyage. Several attempts to colonize by the Spanish and French failed. The English finally established a successful settlement after 1632. The island's early economy was based on tobacco farming but this soon gave way to sugar plantations which were maintained by slave labor. Antigua emancipated the slave population in 1834, four years before the general emancipation in the British Empire.

Antigua became a State in Association with the United Kingdom in 1967. Antigua became independent in 1981.

GOVERNMENT AND POLITICAL CONDITIONS. As an Associated State, Antigua was ruled by a Crown-appointed Governor, assisted by a Cabinet responsible to Parliament. There is a Senate formed by 10 nominated members and a 17 member elected House of Representatives. The new island nation has adapted a Parliamentary system of government.

ECONOMY. Sugar production, once the mainstay of the economy, was discontinued in 1972, but is now being restarted. Tourism now accounts for the greatest percentage of income. The government has been encouraging industrialization. A large oil refinery is now in operation.

### GUADELOUPE

POPULATION. The population of Guadeloupe is estimated to be 318,000 people. The largest city is Pointe-a-Pitre with over 60,000 people. Basse-Tarre, the capital, has a population of 26,000.

COMPOSITION. The population is composed mainly of Creoles of European extraction, blacks and East Indians.

LANGUAGE AND LITERACY. French is the official language but most people speak a Creole language based on French. Nearly 98% of the children between the ages of six and sixteen attend school.

RELIGION. The Constitution provides for freedom of religion. Roman Catholicism is dominant, but several Protestant denominations are active.

GEOGRAPHY AND CLIMATE. Known as the "Emerald of the Caribbean," Guadeloupe is a butterfly shaped pair of islands divided by a narrow tongue of ocean. The two islands, Basse-Terre and Grande-Terre have a total area of 1,513 square kilometers (584 square miles). The western island, Basse-Terre, is heavily forested. Grande-Terre is low lying with rolling hills.

The climate is tropical, with three seasons: a cool season from November to April; a warm dry season from April to July; and a warm rainy season from July to November. The most rain falls on Basse-Terre. Guadeloupe lies in the hurricane path.

HISTORY. Christopher Columbus discovered Guadeloupe in November, 1493 but Spaniards did not settle it. The French took possession in 1635. Native Carib Indians departed for Dominica. The production of sugar and slave importation were begun in 1644. Although the British occupied the island four times, the French maintained their control. Since 1871, Guadeloupe has been represented in the French Parliament. In 1946, Guadeloupe was made into an "Overseas Department" of France.

GOVERNMENT AND POLITICAL CONDITIONS. Guadeloupe is an Overseas Department of France. As such the island is represented in the French legislature by three Deputies in the National Assembly and two Senators in the Senate. The island is governed by a Prefect who presides over the General Council, comprised of 36 members elected to office for a period of six years.

ECONOMY. Sugar and sugar refining are still the most important sector industries. The chief exports are bananas and sugar and its by-products. Tourism is becoming increasingly important. France must subsidize the island's economy as its balance of trade is consistently in the red.

## ST. KITTS, NEVIS, ANGUILLA

POPULATION. The 1970 Census listed the population of the three islands at 64,000. However, in 1973, St. Kitts' population was estimated at 36,000 and Nevis' population was estimated at 11,900. In 1977, Anguilla's population was only 6,500. These numbers indicate the effects of emigration from the islands.

COMPOSITION. The people of all three islands are mainly of Negro descent. Some Anguillans have a trace of Irish blood, their ancestors having been members of an Irish settlement in 1698.

LANGUAGE AND LITERACY. English is the official and commercial language. Literacy is about 80%.

RELIGION. The major religious bodies present in the islands are the Anglicans (36%), Methodists (32%), Moravians (10%), Roman Catholics (8%) and several smaller groups.

GEOGRAPHY AND CLIMATE. St. Kitts (169 square kilometers or 65 square miles in area) and Nevis (94 square kilometers or 36 square miles in area) are approximately three kilometers (two miles) apart by sea. Both are volcanic in origin. St. Kitts' highest peak is Mt. Misery (1138 meters, 3,792 feet) and Nevis' highest point is Nevis Peak (1050 meters, 3,500 feet). Scientists feel that these volcanos are dormant but not extinct. Anguilla is located 106 kilometers (70 miles) northwest of St. Kitts and has an area of 91 square kilometers (35 square miles).

It is a relatively flat, coral limestone island which is surrounded by reefs.

The average annual temperature is about 26 degrees C. (79 degrees F.). Anguilla has an annual average of 27 degrees C. (81 degrees F.). St. Kitts and Nevis receive more rainfall than Anguilla but both have experienced droughts in recent years.

HISTORY. St. Kitts was the first Caribbean island to be settled by the British when a group of colonists settled there in 1623. From this base, several other islands were colonized by the British. Although two French settlements were made on the island, it remained in British hands.

Under a new constitution, approved in 1966, St. Kitts, Nevis and Anguilla became a State in Voluntary Association with Great Britain in 1967. However, in the same year Anguilla rebelled against the association, necessitating the formation of a separate government for that island.

GOVERNMENT AND POLITICAL CONDITIONS. Although still formally a part of the State in Association with Great Britain, Anguilla has had a separate administration shortly after the Association was formed in 1967. St. Kitts and Nevis are governed by a Premier and his cabinet and a 13 member House of Assembly. Anguilla is governed by an Executive Council, consisting of a Chief Minister and four other members, and a 12 member Legislative Assembly.

St. Kitts and Nevis are pushing for independence but a large number of Nevisians are demanding that Nevis secede from the Association as Anguilla has done.

ECONOMY. St. Kitts and Nevis have been striving to diversify their sugar-based economies. About 12 new industries, including the assembly of electronic goods and garment factories, have been started. The tourist industry has also been growing.

Anguilla exports sea salt and lobsters. It must rely on finances from the British government for half of the government budget. It does not have a tourist industry.

## SELECTED BIBLIOGRAPHY AND INFORMATION SOURCES

The sources listed below are to help the reader find additional information on these islands and the Christian ministries there. This list does not try to be comprehensive or complete.

### DOCUMENTS

#### General

Crawley, Eduardo, ed., Latin American and Caribbean, 1980. Essex, England: World of Information, 1980.

#### Christian

Brathwaite, Joan, ed., Handbook of Churches in the Caribbean. Bridgetown, Barbados: CADEC, 1973.

Foy, Felican A. O.F.M.,ed., 1980 Catholic Almanac. Huntington, Indiana: Our Sunday Visitor, Inc., 1979.

### ACKNOWLEDGMENTS

The information in this profile was taken from many sources which were the best available to the editors at the time of preparation. However, the accuracy of the information cannot be guaranteed. Views expressed or implied in this publication are not necessarily those of World Vision. The editors have tried to present the ministries of various organizations in an objective manner, without undue bias or emphasis. Where we have failed, we apologize for erroneous impressions that may result and request that comments and corrections be sent to MARC, 919 West Huntington Drive, Monrovia, California, USA, 91016. We appreciate and acknowledge the comments and contributions of various organizations and individuals in the preparation of this publication.

# STATUS OF CHRISTIANITY COUNTRY PROFILE

# PUERTO RICO

## SUMMARY

AREA - 8,768 square kilometers
      (3,507 square miles)
POPULATION - 3.2 million (1981 estimate)
RELIGION - 90% Catholic, 8% Protestant
        2% Other

All Puerto Ricans are American citizens and receive full benefits guaranteed therein. Most speak Spanish and many are bilingual. As citizens of a commonwealth of the United States, residents are free to travel freely and emigrate to any of the fifty states. Federal income tax, however, is not required.

Roman Catholicism has long been a part of the cultural traditions of the people. Secularism and materialism are rapidly increasing, however, and are drowning out the voice of the church. Comparatively few individuals are committed to ministries in local parishes or congregations.

## PEOPLE GROUPS

People groups within Puerto Rico can be readily identified because of significant socio-economic differences. Few ethnic distinctions exist and those that do are not important since members of various ethnic groups are found in most socio-economic groups. Wealthy San Juan families of Castillian Spanish origin have historically been the elite upper class who predominated in government, commerce and the preferable professions. Some have chosen to associate with large American corporate concerns and have thus adopted elements of other cultures. Their wealth is often conspicuous, evidenced by luxurious summer homes in the mountains, extravagant homes on the beaches and exclusive clubs which cater to the elite. Children of these families usually receive their education at private institutions in other countries.

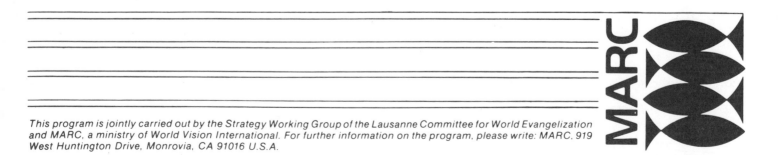

*This program is jointly carried out by the Strategy Working Group of the Lausanne Committee for World Evangelization and MARC, a ministry of World Vision International. For further information on the program, please write: MARC, 919 West Huntington Drive, Monrovia, CA 91016 U.S.A.*

In contrast, however, many Puerto Ricans dwell in shantytowns or slums. They seek employment in large cities such as San Juan, but they live in poverty. Those who live in slums find tenement quarters in the center of the city close to business districts. Shantytowns are usually at the edge of town on marginal public lands. Residents gather wood, tin or other scrap materials to construct a makeshift shanty as shelter. They are set apart physically and socially from prosperous areas and each area becomes a barrio with outdoor water faucets, limited sanitation, few electric systems and virtually no recreational facilities. Though many shantytowns have reportedly disappeared, thousands of Puerto Ricans remain in poverty with little more than four walls and a roof, which they call a house. Young people in the barrios often find little interest in school so they turn to the streets or industrial centers for employment and recreation. Special evangelistic strategies are needed for each of the groups within the barrios. Young street people need a significantly different approach than busy housewives struggling to meet the needs of the household.

Another people group in Puerto Rico is the "Neoricans;" these are individuals who have returned from the United States, perhaps as many as 150,000 per year during the '70's. They are distinct from others and are esteemed by some, but regarded with resentment by others. Education for them has certainly been different, be it the streets of New York City, a university or a job.

The high literacy rate in Puerto Rico, along with extensive economic aid and industrial development, have provided the opportunity for the formation of a large middle class. In 1977, 45% of the families received only 15% of the income produced. Yet many families shared what wealth they had and thus utilized and strengthened family ties.

The middle class in particular expresses the dichotomies of culture in Puerto Rico. Spanish and English, each as important as the other; movies from Madrid, Mexico City and Hollywood; meals of black beans and rice or hotdogs and coke; refrigerators and televisions; wrought iron and icons; macho men and liberated women.

One small specific ethnic group is comprised of the 2,000 Chinese living in Puerto Rico. A small informal church gathers each week for worship but most Chinese are as yet unreached.

Needless to say, the number of people groups in Puerto Rico is quite large and each has unique spiritual needs of its own.

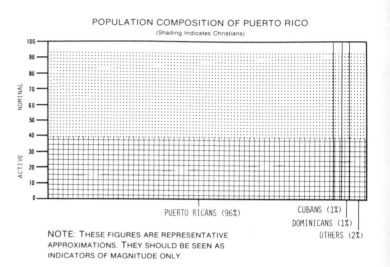

POPULATION COMPOSITION OF PUERTO RICO
(Shading Indicates Christians)

PUERTO RICANS (96%)   CUBANS (1%)
DOMINICANS (1%)
OTHERS (2%)

NOTE: THESE FIGURES ARE REPRESENTATIVE APPROXIMATIONS. THEY SHOULD BE SEEN AS INDICATORS OF MAGNITUDE ONLY.

## CURRENT STATUS OF CHRISTIANITY

Like most Latin American countries, Puerto Rico has long been predominantly Catholic. Roman Catholicism was the official religion beginning with the colonization of Puerto Rico by Spain from the late part of the 15th century until 1898. The only Protestant church permitted was the English-speaking Anglican congregation serving the British city of Ponce. Religious freedom is now guaranteed with complete separation of church and state for each Puerto Rican (U.S.) citizen.

The percentage of Protestants is significantly higher in the cities than the overall percentage. Whereas estimates have placed the total Protestant community at about 8.8% of the population, recent surveys show that approximately 15% of those who live in San Juan claim to be Protestant. Numerical growth is reported on the rolls of the Protestant churches, but, even more importantly, analysis indicates that they are also growing in relation to the overall population.

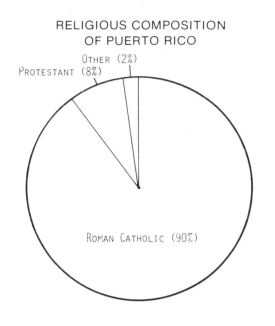

RELIGIOUS COMPOSITION
OF PUERTO RICO

Other (2%)
Protestant (8%)

Roman Catholic (90%)

**NATIONAL CHURCHES**

PROTESTANT CHURCHES

The largest Protestant denomination in Puerto Rico is the Pentecostal Church of God. It is only one of several Pentecostal bodies. The first Pentecostal missionaries were Puerto Ricans who had been converted in Hawaii and Los Angeles, California. They returned to the southern part of the island in 1916 and formed loose ties with the newly-organized Assemblies of God. Following this, congregations were formed in the northern and central sectors of the island. Within two years the first Pentecostal periodical was published and shortly afterwards the Puerto Rican church officially defined its indigenous approach to missions. This was the only Pentecostal body until the 1930's, when divisions began to appear. Some of the larger divisions included the Church of God - Cleveland, Iglesia de Cristo Misionera; the Defenders of the Faith and the Assemblies of God. The Pentecostal Church of God became a national church in 1956 and almost immediately began an active missions program in the United States, other Latin American countries and Europe.

Among the historical denominations from the United States, the American Baptists, the United Methodists, Disciples of Christ, United Presbyterians, and United Evangelicals make up the largest church bodies, each having over 5,000 members. All five bodies entered the island in 1899, and a comity agreement was worked out to prevent overlapping of mission territory. Generally these groups have remained within these same comity areas, except for ministries in the larger towns and metropolitan areas. Cooperative efforts include joint work in seminary training, publications and ecumenical councils.

The Seventh-day Adventists began with a small mission in 1901 in the western sector of the island. Today they are expanding their missionary tasks throughout the entire island through church planting, religious schools, conferences, medical work and publications.

By 1979, a total of 765 members among a community of 1,200 were constituents of Mennonite and Brethren in Christ churches. Congregations were meeting in 10 cities and three areas within San Juan plus two in rural locations. Strong national leadership has developed as 11 pastors and six full time lay workers are assisted by expatriates. A wide variety of outreach ministries includes radio broadcasting, Bible correspondence courses, youth clubs, women's societies and overall education programs.

The fastest growing denominations in Puerto Rico are the Assemblies of God with a reported average growth per year of 35%, the Southern Baptist with over 12%, Church of God - Cleveland with 9%, Seventh-day Adventists with 8%, Wesleyan Methodist with 8%, American Baptist with 6% and Church of the Nazarene with 5%.

The second fastest growing denomination, the Puerto Rico Baptist Association (Southern Baptists), originally entered the island in 1956 to assist the English-speaking North American members of their denomination. However, they soon seized the opportunity to evangelize the Puerto Rican people also. They also have been successful in reaching Cuban immigrants. At present, they have 2,308 members in 22 congregations. Ministerial training is conducted mainly by the extension method in five strategically located centers around the island.

Third in growth is the Church of God - Cleveland. In its initial efforts on the island this Pentecostal denomination was able to bring together several independent Pentecostal groups. In 1971 they reported 6,104 members in 97 churches. Their ministerial training is conducted at the Instituto Biblico Interamericano in Saint Just, Rio Piedras.

Fourth is the Seventh-day Adventist Church. This group ministers through hospitals, schools, intensive literature promotion, tent meetings, and other means of evangelization. In 1970 they reported 12,207 members in 139 congregations. They had at that time 31 ordained ministers and 233 total active workers.

## FASTEST GROWING DENOMINATIONS
Average growth per year

| | |
|---|---|
| Assemblies of God | 35.00% |
| Southern Baptist | 12.65% |
| Church of God - Cleveland | 9.45% |
| Seventh-day Adventist | 8.25% |
| Wesleyan Methodist | 8.17% |
| American Baptist | 5.90% |
| Church of the Nazarene | 4.72% |
| United Methodist | 3.94% |
| United Presbyterian | 3.43% |
| Church of God of Prophecy | 3.30% |
| Pentecostal Church of God | 3.02% |
| United Lutheran | 2.92% |
| Disciples of Christ | 2.80% |

## OTHER GROUPS

The Jehovah's Witnesses are reporting growth at the rate of 16% per year. A charismatic movement under Juanita Garcia Peraza (known as the Mita) gained very rapidly until the death of their leader in 1970. Since she claimed to be the incarnation of the Holy Spirit, it was expected that she would not die. With no successor able to command the loyalty of the group, the results remain to be seen. Reports showed a following of approximately 8,000 at the time of her death.

## CATHOLIC CHURCHES

From the time of the discovery of the island and its evangelization by Spanish missionaries, the Roman Catholic Church was the only official church on the island. A diocese in San Juan was formed in 1511. Roman Catholicism continued as the recognized religion of Puerto Rico, though not the official religion, after the island became a U.S. commonwealth in 1898. The present hierarchy was established in 1960 with an apostolic delegate. One archdiocese and four dioceses consisting of 256 parishes (an increase of 63 since 1974) are under the direction of one cardinal and eight bishops who are assisted by 712 priests (one per 3,800 Catholics), 123 brothers and 1,490 sisters.

## COOPERATIVE AGENCIES

The Evangelical Council of Puerto Rico was formed in 1954 and affiliated with the National Council of Churches of Christ in the U.S.A and with the World Council of Churches. The member bodies are the American Baptist, the United Methodist, United Presbyterian, United Evangelical, Disciples of Christ, Church of the Nazarene, Salvation Army, Mennonite and the Union Church. Its objectives are to carry out interdenominational projects assigned to it, to stimulate all possible denominational cooperation, and to represent the member denominations and local churches before governmental agencies and the general public. It represents less than 50% of the evangelical populace. Other inter-faith organizations include the Association of Evangelical Men of Puerto Rico, the Commission of the Puerto Rican Evangelical Child and the Bible Society of Puerto Rico and the Virgin Islands.

## FOREIGN MISSIONS

The termination of the Spanish-American War resulted in the acquisition of Puerto Rico as a commonwealth territory by the United States. It was not long until Protestant missionaries arrived with a variety of backgrounds, doctrines and strategies. The first Lutheran service was held in November of 1898. An American Baptist pioneer missionary arrived in 1899 and a Methodist Episcopal church pastor preached his first sermon in Puerto Rico in early 1900. In many cases, the first pastor of early congregations also served as an instructor, teaching the people to read and write. Missionaries of the Presbyterian Church of the U.S.A. were surprised when they arrived and were greeted by a group of indigeneous believers. A comity agreement was informally recognized at an early date. Baptists had ministries in San Juan and Ponce, Presbyterians in Mayaguez and Aguadilla, Methodists in Arecilo and Guayana, Congregationalists in Fajardo and Hamacado and Disciples of Christ in Bayamon. As the complexity of the work became more evident, less attention was paid to comity, more to cooperation in the overwhelming task at hand.

Evangelical efforts in Puerto Rico thrived and the people responded favorably. By 1920, 13,000 individuals had become members of evangelical churches and nearly 22,000 were attending Sunday School. In 1924 Harry Strachan, a Lutheran missionary, conducted extensive evangelistic campaigns with support of young pastors in numerous cities. Churches grew rapidly as personal commitments increased.

The Pentecostals became interested and active in evangelistic ministries in the early 1900's. Early ministries were initiated by migrant Puerto Rican workers who returned from Hawaii where they had been converted. They began open air evangelistic services outside Ponce. Expatriate Pentecostal missionaries joined them in 1921 and by 1946 church membership exceeded 9,000.

A Christian Puerto Rican with the Assemblies of God in New York began ministries in Puerto Rico in 1918 and by 1960 Assemblies of God church membership surpassed 10,000 making it the largest single denomination.

A host of other mission groups sent missionaries during and after the Second World War. Several men preparing for missionary service with the Mennonite Central Committee in China were redirected to Puerto Rico because of political conditions and changes in 1943. They established the groundwork for community service centers, medical and agricultural programs including the well-known Mennonite Hospital in La Plata. The first Mennonite church began in Pulguillas with seven baptized believers meeting on land donated with the understanding that a clinic, school and church would be established. All of this did come to pass. Mennonite and Brethren in Christ church ministries developed in several rural communities and small towns of the interior.

Other mission boards which sent personnel during the 1940's included the Church of the Nazarene, Wesleyan Methodist, Southern Baptist, Assemblies of God, Conservative Baptist and the Salvation Army. Many of the missions which began ministries prior to the 1940's have concentrated on development of educational facilities and programs. For some of these groups, the funds formerly allocated for support of foreign missionaries are now applied to the salaries of national workers.

The total number of Protestant foreign missionaries has not declined despite these changes. On the contrary, recent statistics indicate that there are now 296 North American Protestant missionaries alone, an increase of 30 since 1976. There are also a smaller number of evangelical agencies sending more personnel. Many of these particular agencies are involved in church planting ministries.

The list of sending agencies at the end of this chapter supplies information about the beginning date of ministries for each agency and the number of missionaries now active. It is difficult to report accurate figures since Puerto Rico is included as a "home" mission by a number of agencies. For example, the Southern Baptist Convention, which has 18 missionaries in language programs and four in church extension, includes Puerto Rico as a "home" mission.

## ROMAN CATHOLIC MISSIONS

From the time of the Spanish colonization in the early 1600's, the Roman Catholic Church sent its emissaries to the island. During the period of Spanish Catholic supremacy (1493-1898), all non-Catholic religions and literature were prohibited. The legal union of Church and state meant that almost 100% of the Puerto Ricans claimed to be Catholic. In 1898 the Catholic Church suddenly lost its official position, state financial support ceased and the church came under the direction of an American bishop. The most significant missionary activity was the establishment of a system of private and parochial schools within the larger towns. Elementary schools, high schools and one university were established and other institutions include homes for the elderly, poor and orphans; clinics, hospitals, health centers and medical dispensaries. The Catholic forces represent eight religious and missionary men's orders and 20 women's congregations.

Catholic missionaries from North America totaled 252 in 1980 including 251 from the United States and one from Canada. The number from the United States decreased by 10 from 1979 and by 35 from 1977.

## MAJOR CHRISTIAN ACTIVITIES

The following descriptions are intended to make readers aware of the potential for various types of ministries. Not all church agencies are specifically mentioned.

## EVANGELISM

The different churches and denominations maintain continuing evangelistic programs and at times conduct special evangelistic campaigns throughout the island. The last united effort was the Billy Graham Crusade in 1965, for which the largest stadium in the capital of San Juan was used. Other large centers were used in other major cities. The Pentecostal denominations frequently hold preaching services in the streets, public plazas and amphitheaters throughout the island.

## BROADCASTING

The radio and television stations usually confine Christian programs to Sundays. Many of these programs are scheduled on free public time. While most of the programs are prepared by a denominational recording center outside Puerto Rico, a number of them are prepared and transmitted locally on a weekly basis. The number of Spanish Christian television programs is very small. The Evangelical Council transmits a 30-minute program weekly with the cooperation of several denominations, agencies and organizations. Others are produced outside the island and transmitted either in English or dubbed with Spanish voices. There are 49 radio stations and 25 television stations on the island.

In 1973 the Seventh-day Adventists broadcast a weekly radio program over 32 stations. The Southern Baptists broadcast a program in Spanish during a period of 31 weeks and in English for a period of 16 weeks. They also carried two weekly television programs transmitted over 11 stations.

There are two evangelical radio stations in Puerto Rico, WCGB and WIVV. The former limits itself almost entirely to Spanish broadcasting, and divides its time between religious and non-religious programs. The latter broadcasts predominantly in English, beaming programs from Puerto Rico to the adjacent English-speaking islands of the Caribbean.

The Roman Catholic Church has a radio station in Ponce which operates on a commercial basis.

## LITERATURE

Most of the Christian literature produced in Puerto Rico is in the form of magazines and tracts. Several denominations maintain official church publications produced on the island. These include the American Baptists, Disciples of Christ, Pentecostal Church of God and Church of God, Inc. Several other denominations use publications which are multinational in scope.

The publication of evangelical books is very limited. Several Puerto Rican writers prefer to use publishing houses located outside the island, in the United States, the Dominican Republic or Spain. These publications by Puerto Rican writers are mostly sermons, sermon outlines, hymns, biographies and evangelical history.

Bible correspondence courses are readily available thoughout the island. Many radio programs offer free Bible correspondence courses to the listening audience.

Since the 1950's, the number of evangelical book stores which sell a wide variety of evangelical publications has increased. The metropolitan area of San Juan, with a population of approximately 1 million, has at least five Christian book stores. Other cities on the island have at least one. Two of the book stores have colporteur projects, either for local church members to distribute or for young people to sell from door to door.

## BIBLE TRANSLATION AND DISTRIBUTION

The Bible has been translated into Spanish and English, and thus has been available in the two dominant languages spoken on the island. The Bible Societies of Puerto Rico and the Virgin Islands distribute Bibles and Bible portions primarily through local churches and church organizations. Each year Penzotti courses are given to instruct members of various denominations as to the best way to distribute the Bibles. The number of Bibles distributed annually in Puerto Rico is one of the highest in the Spanish world.

In 1973 the International Organization of the Gideons had a special Bible distribution campaign entitled "Christ in the Police." Approximately 1,000 New Testaments were distributed to the San Juan metropolitan police.

The United Bible Societies report shows the following distribution:

|                | 1975      | 1978      |
|----------------|-----------|-----------|
| Bibles         | 55,025    | 57,017    |
| New Testaments | 44,745    | 24,666    |
| Portions       | 138,713   | 163,524   |
| Selections     | 1,250,475 | 2,247,362 |
| TOTAL          | 1,488,958 | 2,492,569 |

## EDUCATION

Theological. To provide theological and biblical preparation for their leaders, evangelical churches and missions have set up Bible institutes and theological seminaries. There has been more concern for residential institutions than for extension programs. The historical denominations which arrived about 1900 cooperate with the Evangelical Seminary of Puerto Rico. It is the oldest educational institution for ministers on the island. The Pentecostal denominations maintain at least six ministerial training programs. Some of these are experimenting effectively with seminary by extension programs.

Christian. Evangelical missions in Puerto Rico have been associated with basic education since 1899. In the early years when illiteracy was prevalent, most local churches became centers where the pastor-teacher taught people to read. As the public schools expanded, and as the literacy level of the general public increased, the need decreased proportionately for the churches to work in this area. The churches concern themselves primarily with the young in church academies, elementary and high schools. Although they exist in many parts of the island in conjunction with local churches, these schools are found mostly in the larger cities. The first rural high school in the interior was a church-sponsored school. Some of the denominations who have been active in education are the Episcopal, the United Methodist, the United Presbyterian, the American Baptist, the Congregationalist and the Seventh-day Adventist.

The Evangelical Council has been influential in encouraging the member churches to take advantage of the government-sponsored education programs for persons in lower economic classes.

On the post-high school level, evangelicals have also been active in providing educational facilities. The oldest and largest is the Inter-American University which has campuses in several inner cities. It has its roots in Presbyterianism. A second college is sponsored by the Seventh-day Adventists in Mayaguez and a third by the American Baptists in Carolina.

## SOCIAL CONCERN

Evangelical missions in Puerto Rico have a continuous history of social concern. Today four hospitals are directed by the evangelicals, and two others were initiated by them. Evangelical missions have operated several orphanages and medical clinics, ministered to the leprosy colony, provided agricultural assistance and development programs, maintained literacy programs, youth hostels and homes for the aged, and sponsored camps and civic youth organizations.

The social concern of the Pentecostals has been demonstrated in their rehabilitation centers for drug addicts. At least one church is making efforts to help provide housing. All evangelicals have aided by sending clothes and other needed items to disaster areas outside the island. On the island one denomination has a mobile medical unit to be used for on-the-spot relief in disaster areas.

## NATION AND ITS PEOPLE

### POPULATION

In 1981 there were 3.2 million people on the island of Puerto Rico. Its growth rate is 1.7% per year and 34% of its population is under 15 years of age and only 6% is over 64.

The island is becoming more and more urban; the number of people living in urban areas has increased by over 50% from 1960 to 1970. In contrast, the rural population decreased by 13% during the same period. At present nearly 70% of the population live in urban areas.

The population density is 369 inhabitants per square kilometer (955 per square mile), even higher than Japan. Puerto Rico is therefore more densely populated than most of the Caribbean islands.

### COMPOSITION

The people of Puerto Rico are basically one homogeneous ethnic unit. During the time of Spanish rule over the island, there were two social classes: the upper and the lower. These classes were based on wealth and the ownership of land. It is now generally recognized that a middle class has come into being. As the middle class emerges, American-type cultural practices are adopted. Puerto Ricans recognize that the process of Americanization is still going on and a few are resisting the change. Indicative of the American influence is the fact that English words are making their way into everyday conversation.

### LANGUAGE AND LITERACY

Spanish is the primary language for residents of Puerto Rico, but it is a distinctive Spanish, differing from that of Spain and other areas of Spanish speaking Latin America. Several English words and other "Americanisms" have contributed to the distinctive Spanish spoken. Many residents are bilingual. English is taught as a second language in schools and adult education centers, and is utilized in many businesses. Literacy is steadily increasing with approximately 90% of the people literate in 1980, a very high rate for the Caribbean region.

Education is free and compulsory, although there are many private and religious schools.

## RELIGION

The reported religion of 90% of the population is Roman Catholicism. Approximately 8% profess to be Protestants.

## GEOGRAPHY AND CLIMATE

Puerto Rico is one of a chain of semi-tropical islands stretching from the tip of Florida to the northeast coast of Venezuela, separating the Atlantic Ocean from the Caribbean Sea. It is roughly rectangular in shape. Its length from east to west is 161 kilometers (100 miles) and its width 56 kilometers (35 miles). Its rugged terrain of broken mountain ranges prohibits cultivation of more than 50% of the land.

It is a well watered island with a great number of rivers, mostly small. They are not navigable, but many of them have been dammed for irrigation and hydro-electric power.

Puerto Rico enjoys a tropical climate tempered by almost constant trade winds and by high altitudes. Temperature ranges are not great. In the summer the average daily maximum is 30 degrees Celsius (86 F) and in the winter approximately 28 degrees Celsius (82-84 F). Rainfall is heaviest between May and December and it is generally heavier in the north than in the south, ranging from 140 to 190 centimeters (55-75 inches) per year in the former and 71 to 127 centimeters (28-50 inches) in the latter. Hurricanes rarely strike the island with enough intensity to do great damage.

## HISTORY

The island of Puerto Rico was first visited by Columbus in 1493. He named the island San Juan Bautista. The island was settled by colonists under the command of Ponce de Leon. They settled near the present site of the city of San Juan, then named Puerto Rico. Over the years, the name of the city and island were interchanged. The Indian population either died or were absorbed into the new culture. African slaves were imported to replace Indian labor. They were later emancipated in 1873. The three races fused into the present Puerto Rican population.

Spain controlled the island until 1898, when it was ceded to the United States at the close of the Spanish-American War. In 1900, free trade with the United States was introduced, and in 1917 the populace became U.S. citizens. The Constitutional freedoms of the United States were guaranteed, including that of freedom of religion.

In 1952 a new constitution for Puerto Rico created a unique relationship with the United States, called a commonwealth (Estado Libre Asociado). No longer termed a territory, the island began a new voluntary relationship with the U.S. through the bonds of free choice, affection and common citizenship. In a referendum in 1967, 60% of the voters reaffirmed their desire to retain the prevailing political status between statehood and independence.

## GOVERNMENT AND POLITICAL CONDITIONS

As a commonwealth, Puerto Rico is neither a state nor a territory, although it has attributes of both. The "Commonwealth" constitution provides for a republican form of government with executive, legislative and judicial branches. The governor is directly elected by the people for a term of four years and is advised by a Cabinet of 14 Secretaries who are appointed by the governor. The legislature is bicameral and consists of a Senate comprising 27 members and a House of Representatives with 51 members.

Puerto Ricans have no vote in U.S. Presidential elections. Nor do they elect representatives to the U.S. Senate or House of Representatives. Puerto Rico does, however, have a voice in the U.S. Congress through a Resident Commissioner who is elected to a four year term. Puerto Ricans do not pay United States federal income taxes. Nevertheless, their own tax rate is high.

The island's politics often center around the issue of Puerto Rico's status. Four main political parties represent differing viewpoints. In the 1980 elections, Governor Carlos Romero Barcelo, of the New Progressive Party, advocated that Puerto Rico be incorporated into the United States as a state. In a close election; Rafael Hernandez Colon of the Popular Democratic Party (which advocates maintaining Puerto Rico's current commonwealth status) was narrowly defeated by Romero. The two other parties, the Puerto Rican Independence Party and the Puerto Rican Socialist Party, both favor independence. Their popular support is small.

## ECONOMY

During the last two decades Puerto Rico has been moving from an agricultural to an industrial economy. The major agricultural products are sugar, coffee and tobacco. The thrust in recent economic growth has been toward diversified manufacturing, including clothing, textiles, electrical and electronic equipment, plastics and petrochemical industries. Tourism continues to play a vital part in the economy, along with its related service personnel and construction industries. The World Bank has now classified Puerto Rico among the rich nations, although the island continues to struggle with conditions of poverty.

## CHURCH STATISTICS FOR PUERTO RICO

Note: Statistics have been taken from different sources and are the most current data available. Definitions of "membership" vary among churches and may not always be comparable. Not all known churches have been included in this list.

| Church or Mission name | Communicants |
|---|---|
| Pentecostal Church of God | 22,667 |
| Seventh-day Adventist Church | 12,207 |
| United Methodist Church | 12,062 |
| Disciples of Christ | 10,014 |
| American Baptist Church | 9,501 |
| Assemblies of God | 7,892 |
| United Presbyterian | 7,578 |
| United Evangelical Church | 5,348 |
| Church of God - Cleveland | 4,654 |
| Iglesia de Cristo Misionera | 4,245 |
| Episcopal Church | 4,243 |
| Defenders of the Faith | 3,834 |
| Iglesia de Dios, Inc. | 3,250 |
| Iglesia Pentecostal de Jesuscristo | 2,509 |
| United Lutheran Church | 2,448 |
| Southern Baptist | 2,308 |
| Iglesia de Cristo en las Antillas | 1,672 |
| Christian and Missionary Alliance | 935 |
| Church of the Nazarene | 800 |
| Samaria Iglesia Evangelica | 750 |
| Mennonite Church | 672 |
| Church of God of Prophecy | 473 |
| Wesleyan Methodist Church | 385 |
| Church of Christ | 327 |
| Brethren | 100 |
| Salvation Army | 60 |
| TOTAL | 120,934 |
| Roman Catholic | 2,726,570 |

The sources listed below are to help the reader find additional information on this country and Christian ministries there. This list does not try to be comprehensive or complete.

<u>DOCUMENTS</u>

<u>General</u>

Cozen, John D., <u>Latin America 1980</u>, World Today Series, Washington D.C.: Stryker-Post Publication, 1980.

<u>Economic and Social Progress in Latin America</u>, Weekly News Bulletin, Lima, Peru: Noticias Aliadas.

Goff, James E., <u>Latin America Press</u>, Weekly News Bulletin, Lima, Peru: Noticias Aliadas.

Grosvenor, Gilbert Hovey, editor, <u>National Geographic</u>, "The Caribbean: Sun, Sea, and Seething" Vol. 159 No. 2, Washington D.C.: National Geographic Society, Feb. 1981.

Olien, Michael D., <u>Latin Americans, Contemporary Peoples and Their Cultural Traditions</u>, New York: Holt, Rinehard and Winston, 1973.

<u>Christian</u>

Brathwaite, Joan, <u>Handbook of Churches in the Caribbean</u>, Bridgetown, Barbados: CADEC (Christian Action for Development in the Caribbean), 1973.

Brierly, Peter, <u>U.K. Christian Handbook</u>, Vol. 1; London: Overseas Evangelical Missionary Alliance, 1981.

Carver, E. Earl, <u>Showcase for God: A Study of Evangelical Church Growth in Puerto Rico</u>, (unpublished thesis), Pasadena: Fuller Theological Seminary, 1972.

Frei, Pauline, editor, <u>Latin America Documentation LADOC</u>, Washington D.C.,: Office of International Justice and Peace U.S. Catholic Conferences, Monthly publication.

Kane, J. Herbert, <u>A Global View of Christian Mission</u>, Grand Rapids, MI: Baker Book House, 1971.

<u>Mennonite Central Committee Workbook</u>, Akron, PA: Mennonite Central Committee, 1979.

<u>Mission Handbook</u>, Washington D.C.: United States Catholic Mission Council, 1980.

Moore, Donald T., <u>Puerto Rico para Cristo: A History of the Progress of the Evangelical Missions on the Island of Puerto Rico</u> Cuernavaca: Centro Intercultural de Documentacion, (Sondeos, Num. 43), 1969.

Orr, J. Edwin, <u>Evangelical Awakenings in Latin America</u>, Minneapolis, MN: Bethany Fellowship, 1978.

<u>The Caribbean</u>, Richmond, VA: Dept. of Communication Foreign Mission Board SBC, 1977.

Thiesen, John Caldwell, <u>A Survey of World Mission</u>, Chicago: Moody Press, 1961.

United Bible Society, <u>Program '80</u>, Stuttgart, West Germany: United Bible Society, 1980.

Wilson, Sam, editor, <u>Mission Handbook: North American Protestant Ministries Overseas</u>, Monrovia, CA: MARC, 1981.

ORGANIZATIONS

Bible Society of Puerto Rico and Virgin Islands,

Carver, E. Earl 1140 Lawrence St. Houston, Tx. 77008

Evangelical Council of Puerto Rico

## ACKNOWLEDGMENTS

The information in this profile was taken from many sources which were the best available to the editors at the time of preparation. However, the accuracy of the information cannot be guaranteed. Views expressed or implied in this publication are not necessarily those of World Vision. The editors have tried to present the ministries of various organizations in an objective manner, without undue bias or emphasis. Where we have failed, we apologize for erroneous impressions that may result and request that comments and corrections be sent to MARC, 919 West Huntington Drive, Monrovia, California, USA, 91016. We appreciate and acknowledge the comments and contributions of various organizations and individuals in the preparation of this publication.

# STATUS OF CHRISTIANITY COUNTRY PROFILE

# TRINIDAD and TOBAGO

## SUMMARY

AREA - 5,128 square kilometers (1,980
    square miles)
POPULATION - 1,150,000 (1980 est.)
RELIGION - 63% Christian, 25% Hindu, 6%
    Muslim, 6% Other

Trinidad was named by its discoverer,
Columbus, in honor of the Trinity.
However, the Spanish never gave much
attention to either Trinidad or nearby
Tobago and they even encouraged French
colonists to settle there.  The British
took over in 1797 and ruled until Trinidad
and Tobago gained independence in 1962.

The ethnic and religious mixture on the
islands reflects their colonial past.
First Africans, then East Indians, were
imported to work as laborers.  These two
ethnic groups now constitute the largest
proportion of the population.  Although
most blacks were converted to
Christianity, the influence of African
religions is still strong.  Although some
East Indians became Christians, most are
still Hindu or Muslim.

Due to its oil reserves, Trinidad and
Tobago has one of the higest per capita
Gross National Products in the Caribbean.
Nevertheless, a high population density
and a high unemployment rate have put
severe presures on the government.

## UNREACHED PEOPLES

Whereas the majority of Caribbean peoples
are by-and-large Christian, Trinidad and
Tobago presents quite a different
situation.  Over 30% of its people are
Hindu, Muslim or Buddhist.  Most of the
followers of these religions are East
Indians.

When the Negroes were freed from slavery
in the West Indies, East Indians were
brought into Trinidad and Tobago as
indentured workers for canefield labor.
They remained and today make up over 40
percent of the 1.1 million people of this
nation.  Today they do most of the farming
and have penetrated almost every area of
economic and political life.

The East Indians have retained much of
their culture along with their Hindu or
Muslim religion in the 125 years they have
been in Trinidad.  Though living in a

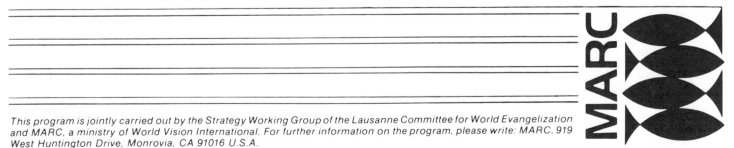

*This program is jointly carried out by the Strategy Working Group of the Lausanne Committee for World Evangelization
and MARC, a ministry of World Vision International. For further information on the program, please write: MARC, 919
West Huntington Drive, Monrovia, CA 91016 U.S.A.*

pluralistic society, intermarriage has been minimal. The Presbyterians reached a number of these East Indians in the late 19th century through educational programs but they have been largely ineffective in reaching these people in recent years. Worldteam has also been evangelizing the East Indians.

There has been some softening in their attitudes toward Christianity because of prolonged contact with Christians, and a people movement could possibly be precipitated if the gospel were preached and churches planted which utilized forms more familiar to them. Past evangelism has been foreign or otherwise ineffective, and approximately 250,000 Hindus and 70,000 Muslim East Indians have yet to see Christianity as a viable option. About 12% claim to be Christian.

A small but important unreached people group are the Chinese. They constitute only 0.86% of the total population. Upon their arrival in the Caribbean in the 19th century they were able to fulfill an important social position as shopkeepers. Some have become quite wealthy in this profession. So completely do Chinese monopolize the commercial sector that the "Chinese shop" has become synonymous for little store.

The Chinese are mostly urban dwellers. More than one-third live in the capital, Port-of-Spain. However, they do not live in separate neighborhoods but rather are spread relatively evenly throughout the city. Although most Chinese are still Buddhists, they seem to be becoming more and more aculturated into the Creole segment of Trinidad society.

## CURRENT STATUS OF CHRISTIANITY

The 1970 Census listed about 63 percent of the population as belonging to various Christian denominations. The majority of Christians were either Roman Catholic (53%) or Anglican (29%), reflecting the influence of colonial powers. A number of other denominations are present, including Presbyterians, Methodists, Baptists, Seventh-day Adventists, Moravians, Nazarenes and several Pentecostal groups. The fastest growing churches are the Pentecostals (Pentecostal Assemblies, Open Bible Standard and several independent churches) and the Seventh-day Adventists.

Upper class religion, as well as family life and values, continue to be European oriented. Members attend church more as a sign of social solidarity with their class than as a genuine profession of religious belief. Middle class Christians are usually more serious in their religious belief. Whereas upper class attitudes are perfunctory, middle class attitudes are literal and rigid, and they see Christian teaching as a guide to public as well as private moral behavior. Generally, except among Roman Catholics, doctrine is more fundamentalist, church attendance is more regular, and religion is more important to middle class than to upper class Trinidadians.

The belief systems of lower class Christians and the institutional structures and emotional significance of their services reflect both the fundamental, evangelical, and revival forms of Christianity and the spiritism of their African ancestors.

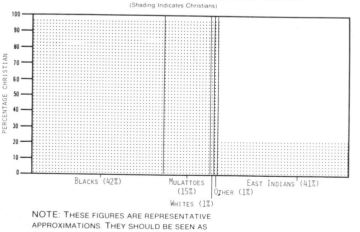

POPULATION COMPOSITION OF TRINIDAD and TOBAGO
(Shading Indicates Christians)

NOTE: THESE FIGURES ARE REPRESENTATIVE APPROXIMATIONS. THEY SHOULD BE SEEN AS INDICATORS OF MAGNITUDE ONLY.

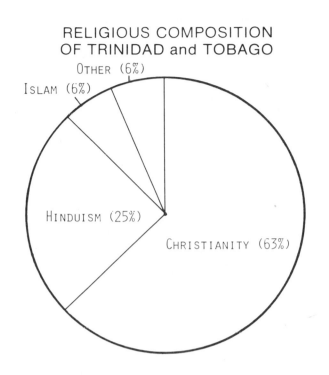

RELIGIOUS COMPOSITION
OF TRINIDAD and TOBAGO

OTHER (6%)
ISLAM (6%)
HINDUISM (25%)
CHRISTIANITY (63%)

**NATIONAL CHURCHES**

## PROTESTANT

Roman Catholicism was already strongly rooted in Trinidad when the British took control in 1797. In the early 19th century missionaries of the Society for the Propogation of the Gospel and the Church Missionary Society began working on the islands. Today the Anglican Church is the largest Protestant body in Trinidad and Tobago. In 1960 there were 86 Anglican churches with a Christian community of 150,000. They grew to 90 churches with over 175,000 people in its community by 1973, reflecting a biological rate of increase.

The Methodist Missionary Society placed its first missionary in Trinidad in 1809. They had a reported community of 50,000 people in 1978. The Canadian Presbyterian Church began a ministry in Trinidad in 1865. A strong evangelistic and educational program was begun among the East Indian community by the Presbyterian Church. In 1968 there were 32,400 people in the Presbyterian community. This number grew biologically to about 40,000 people in 1973, and worshipped in 60 churches.

The fastest growing denominations are the Seventh-day Adventists and the Pentecostals. The Adventists had 61 churches in 1960 with almost 13,000 people

attending them. In 1979 they recorded 117 churches. The Pentecostal denominations have shown the most phenomenal growth. Beginning their ministry in 1954, the Open Bible Standard missionaries established a growing work and quickly trained local leadership. By 1960 they had eight churches, a membership of 522 people and a Christian community of nearly 1,600. By 1973 they had grown to 30 churches, 70 preaching points, 1,500 members and an estimated community of 5,000. By 1979 they recorded 65 churches. They have experienced an annual growth rate of 20%.

Similar outstanding growth was recorded by the Pentecostal Assemblies. Canadian Pentecostal missionaries started the work in 1920 and it is now largely indigenous. Having 43 churches and 2,500 members in 1960, the Pentecostal Assemblies grew to 60 churches with 6,162 members in 1973. In 1979, it was estimated that the Pentecostal Assemblies ministered to a Christian community of 30,000 people. One of the major reasons for their growth is the Pentecostal emphasis on the ability of the Holy Spirit's power to minister to people's needs. In this area of the world, where occult practices such as spirit possession and magic are so prevalent through the influence of the Shango and Rada cults, the forces in the spiritual realm are much more keenly felt. Although the upper class Trinidadians generally view the occultic practices of Shango and Rada worship as superstition, those who are involved in it recognize the power of spiritual beings. The Pentecostals recognize the validity of the spiritual realm and are therefore, through the power of Christ, able to deal effectively with those who are trapped or oppressed by demonic forces. For instance, the Curepe Pentecostal Church in Trinidad began holding evangelistic services with an emphasis on deliverance from demonic forces. In a four-year period the congregation grew from 100 members to the point where they had to build a 1,200 seat sanctuary.

There are several other denominations present in Trinidad and Tobago. These include the Baptists, Moravians (mainly on Tobago), Church of the Nazarene (20 churches, 1979), Church of God - Cleveland, Pentecostal Church of God, Church of God of Prophecy, Evangelical Alliance Mission and Worldteam. Unfortunately membership and Christian community figures are not available for these churches.

## CATHOLIC CHURCHES

The first Catholic church in Trinidad was built in 1591, years after several missionary ventures had been launched and a number of missionaries had been killed by Indians. Capuchins were there from 1618 until about 1802. Missionary work continued after the British gained full control early in the nineteenth century. Cordial relations have existed between the Church and state, both of which have manifested their desire for the development of native clergy. Trinidad and Tobago established diplomatic relations with Vatican City in 1978.

There is an estimated Catholic community of 370,000, which is 33% of the total population. There are 61 parishes and 116 priests ministering in the country.

### FOREIGN MISSIONS

## PROTESTANT MISSIONS

There was a total of 66 missionaries serving in Trinidad and Tobago from 23 North American agencies in 1979. Great Britain sent an additional 23 missionaries from five agencies. The Protestant agency with the most personnel is the Evangelical Alliance Mission (TEAM) with 14 missionaries who are engaged in church planting and evangelism among the East Indians. They have established 10 churches in the islands. Second in the number of missionaries is the General Council of the Seventh-day Adventists with 11. They are followed by Worldteam with 10, ministering to 12 churches.

The United Society for the Propogation of the Gospel still sends missionaries to Trinidad and Tobago. They have eight men working among the Anglicans. Among the other missionary sending agencies involved in Trinidad and Tobago are: the Baptist Missionary Society (7 missionaries), the Nazarenes (7), the Southern Baptists (6) and the Mennonites (4).

## ROMAN CATHOLIC MISSIONS

North American Catholic missionaries are few in number. It is reported that there was one Canadian priest, one Carmelite sister and one layperson ministering in Trinidad and Tobago in 1979.

## EVANGELISM

About six percent of the population could be considered evangelical Christians. The number of evangelicals is greater on Tobago than Trinidad. A variety of methods of evangelism are used, with varying degrees of success. Many churches rely largely on Sunday schools and preaching to evangelize those who come to church. Home Bible studies have met with greater degrees of success. Pentecostals have seen the greatest growth by taking the gospel to the people through street meetings and open air preaching. Their emphasis on God's power to work miracles also attracts crowds to healing and deliverance services.

## BIBLE TRANSLATION AND DISTRIBUTION

Bible distribution is carried out by the East Caribbean Bible Society, organized in 1979. Previously, distribution was overseen by the West Indies Bible Society. No distribution figures are available for Trinidad and Tobago yet.

## EDUCATION

The Roman Catholics operate a number of schools and training institutions on Trinidad and Tobago. These include a teachers' training college and a vocational school in addition to 134 primary schools and 31 secondary schools.

There are several seminaries and Bible schools in Trinidad and Tobago. The Catholic seminary of St. John Viannez was established in December of 1942. This seminary was originally cared for and taught by the Benedictine Monks. It soon acquired the responsibility of training students from other West Indies islands. In 1969 the seminary was changed from an Archdiocesan Seminary to the Regional Seminary. There were nine Trinidadian students studying for ministry in 1979.

St. Andrew's Theological College, formerly Presbyterian Theological College, was founded in 1892 by the Presbyterian Church of Trinidad to train catechists for Christian ministry. In 1960, the college changed its name and opened its doors to other Christian denominations in the region. Today it provides theological training to students desiring to go on to the United Theological College in the West Indies, located in Jamaica.

The Seventh-day Adventists founded the Caribbean Union College as a small training school. It now offers College level courses in minsterial and teacher training. It draws students from all over the Caribbean.

Three Bible schools are operated by evangelical churches: Baptist International Missions, Church of God – Cleveland and Open Bible Standard: each run a school to train people for Christian ministry.

## SOCIAL CONCERNS

Churches attempt to meet the social needs of the people in varieties of ways. The Catholics run three hospitals and the Seventh-day Adventists operate one. The Baptists conduct medical clinics using volunteers from the United States. Catholic social work also includes the operation of two orphanages, eight children's homes and eight homes for the aged. The Christian Action for Development in the Caribbean (CADEC) has sponsored several development projects in Trinidad and Tobago.

## NATION AND ITS PEOPLE

## POPULATION

The official census in 1970 listed the population of Trinidad and Tobago at 945,210. Since then, the government admitted that this figure was inaccurate and should be revised to 1,025,000. The population in 1980 is estimated at 1,150,000 with an average annual growth rate of 1.8%. The growth rate had been as high as 4.2% in the mid-1950's but a combination of emigration and family planning measures reduced it to a low 1.3% in 1972.

Just under 50% of Trinidad and Tobago's people are urban dwellers. This number is decreasing rather than increasing, however. Many people from the cities are moving into the country for several reasons: to take advantage of the government's sale of low cost state land, the development of urban satellite towns where housing costs are lower than in the city, an industrial diversification program which provides jobs in rural areas and a policy of providing low interest credits for those who want to begin farms. As a result, the largest city of Port-of-Spain had a population of 94,000 in 1960 but by 1973 it had plunged to 60,000. However, the exodus of city dwellers out of Port-of-Spain has boosted the population of the nearby area to some 250,000.

According to the official 1970 census, the population of the island of Trinidad was 906,200, giving it a population density of 1,263 per square kilometer (486 per square mile). The smaller island of Tobago had only 39,000 people in 1970, giving it a density of 873 per square kilometer (336 per square mile).

## COMPOSITION

The official census lists five main ethnic groups in Trinidad and Tobago: Negro, 42.83%; East Indian, 40.12%; mixed (or colored), 14.7%; white, 1.0%; Chinese, 0.86%; and the remainder include the indigenous Arawak Indians and other minor ethnic immigrant groups. However, East Indians claim that the 1970 census was inaccurate and that, in reality, there are now more East Indians than blacks. Since 1970, the government conceded that the census was inaccurate and it is commonly held that East Indians now outnumber blacks.

Ethnic backgrounds do not form the only boundaries for social groups. Such factors as color, religion and wealth diversify Trinidad and Tobago's already complex social composition. Generally, lighter skinned, wealthier people with a Christian background occupy the elite strata of society while poorer, darker skinned Negores and East Indian people occupy the lowest social strata.

Although the different races mix, living side by side, they have little in common and do not integrate or intermarry.

## LANGUAGE AND LITERACY

The official language of Trinidad and Tobago is English. However, three Creole languages and some Indian languages are spoken also. The Creole languages are based on English, French and Spanish with some input from African languages. The English Creole, called Trinidad English, is the language of most common people. It is not so different from standard English as to make it unintelligible. Standard English is given a higher status than Trinidad English and it is the language of the upper and middle classes. The popular music form, Calypso, uses Trinidad English in its lyrics.

French and Spanish Creole are spoken in the northern parts of Trinidad. French and Spanish languages underwent the same type of change that English did after its contact with Caribbean culture. Today,

Creolized French and Spanish are both unintelligible to those who speak the mother tongues from which they evolved.

The literacy rate for adults in Trinidad and Tobago is one of the world's highest. It increased from 88% in 1960 to 95% in 1970. Nearly all children of primary age are enrolled in schools.

## RELIGION

Christianity is the dominant religion in Trinidad and Tobago with an estimated 63% of the population professing this faith. The next largest religious group is the Hindu religion of the East Indians with 25% of the people. This is followed by the Muslims with 6%.

Hinduism in Trinidad is a synthesis of various traditions and beliefs. Hindu beliefs are much simpler and more homogeneous than the various Hindu systems of belief found in India. This is due to two major reasons: 1) the caste system did not survive the transplantation of East Indian migrants to Trinidad; 2) these immigrants were very quiet about their beliefs, not holding public festivals, and building no temples until the 1860's.

In general, the remaining characteristics of Hindu belief are known by older members of the East Indian community but are less familiar to the younger generation. These beliefs still include the ordained duties of the four "varnas" (or classes) of people, the four stages of life and the four goals in life (righteousness, vocation, fulfillment of desires and the release from cyclical birth and death), as well as the beliefs in reincarnation and the transmigration of the soul. Hinduism still serves to unite the East Indian community with its ethnic identity.

The vast majority of Muslims in Trinidad are also the descendants of East Indian immigrants. A number of Muslims are prominent in business and the community.

Although most Negroes and mulattoes (called Creoles) on Trinidad and Tobago consider themselves Christians a great number also participate in Afro-Christian cults, including Shouter, Shango and Rada (whose practices are similar to Shango). The Shouters (who are also called Spiritual Baptists) are called a cult but they believe in the inerrancy of the bible, the virgin birth of Christ, life after death, the physical resurrection of Jesus and the authenticity of miracles. Because of their emotional services which were similar in some respects to the emotional Shango worship, their churches were banned until 1951. Since that time

they have become more accepted. Nevertheless, they are still looked down upon by middle and upper class Trinidadians.

The Shango cult originated in the nineteenth century when people of African descent -- mainly Yorubas of Nigeria -- combined their traditional beliefs with rituals and elements of Catholicism. The saints of Roman Catholicism are identified with the dozen Shango deities. Among the most imporant features are animal sacrifices, dancing, drumming and spirit possession.

It has been noted that a great deal of religious syncretization has occurred among the lower classes. It is not uncommon for people to cross over religious lines in order to participate in festivals or rituals. For instance, some Roman Catholics also participate in African-based rituals and some Christian East Indians might celebrate the Hindu festivals of Diwali and Phagawa.

## GEOGRAPHY AND CLIMATE

Trinidad and Tobago are the southernmost islands of the Lesser Antilles chain. Trinidad is located just 11 kilometers (seven miles) off the coast of Venezuela. Trinidad is the largest island of the chain, with an area of 4,830 square kilometers (1,864 square miles). Tobago is located 30 kilometers (19 miles) northeast of Trinidad and has an area of 300 square kilometers (116 square miles).

Three low mountain ranges traverse Trinidad from east to west. The highest mountains are in the Northern range with a maximum elevation of 940 meters (3,085 feet). The northern valley is flat and well watered while the southern valley is rolling and water often fails in the dry season. Tropical forests cover half the island and swamps are found along the east and west coasts. Tobago, known as the "Robinson Crusoe Island," has miles of scenic and deserted beaches. A mountain ridge runs the length of the island, reaching a maximum height of 549 meters (1,800 feet).

The climate of both islands is tropical but pleasant. Both islands are out of the hurricane path. The average maximum temperature of Trinidad is 33 degrees Celcius (92 degrees Fahrenheit) but the climate of Tobago is cooler because of its exposure to trade winds.

216

## HISTORY

Trinidad and Tobago were discovered by Columbus on his third voyage to America in 1498. The first successful attempt to colonize Trinidad was made in 1592 by the Spanish. No mineral deposits were found and the colony suffered several attacks by the English, French and Dutch. The chief export, cocoa, was struck by disease. By 1733 only 150 colonists remained. As part of the island's recovery, the Spanish urged foreigners to settle there. Many French colonists came after 1783, bringing with them coffee, sugar cane and cotton cultivation. The British took the island in 1797. Tobago was ceded to them in 1814. Slaves were brought in to work on sugar plantations and by 1834, the year of their emancipation, there were 21,000 slaves on Trinidad and 11,000 on Tobago. This caused a labor shortage for the large plantations which was solved after 1846 by the policy of importing indentured Indian laborers. The descendents of the slaves and the Indians now form the bulk of the populace.

Trinidad and Tobago merged in 1888 to form a single colony. In 1958, Port-of-Spain, Trinidad, became the capital of the newly formed Federation of the West Indies, comprising Trinidad and Tobago, Jamaica, Barbadoes and the Leeward and Windward Islands. This federation was short-lived, breaking up in 1961. Trinidad and Tobago gained full independence in 1962.

## GOVERNMENT AND POLITICAL CONDITIONS

A new Constitution enacted in August, 1976 changed the status of Trinidad and Tobago from a British Commonwealth nation to a republic. A president, elected by the two houses of the Trinidad and Tobago Parliament, replaced the Queen of England as the head of state.

Executive power resides in the office of Prime Minister, who is responsible to the Parliament. The supreme judicial authority is the Court of Appeal whose Chief Justice is appointed by the President on the advice of the Prime Minister. The final appellate court, however, is the Privy Council in London.

In the most recent national election, Prime Minister Dr. Eric Williams of the People's National Movement (PNM) party was re-elected to his fifth term. The PNM also won 24 of the 36 seats in Parliament. However, Williams passed away in March, 1981.

## ECONOMY

Because of Trinidad and Tobago's oil reserves, the country has one of the highest per capita gross national products in the Caribbean, exceeded only by the Bahamas. New discoveries have boosted the daily production of crude oil to over 220,000 barrels. The industrial sector is primarily devoted to the refining of both domestic and imported crude oil. The world's largest pitch lake (100 acreas) is mined for its asphalt in southwest Trinidad. Light industrial manufacturing and tourism are two other important sources of revenue. Tobago's pleasant climate and beautiful beaches make it a prime tourist resort in the Caribbean.

Trinidad and Tobago also export several agricultural and forest products. Among the major ones are: sugar, cocoa, coffee, citrus, bananas, coconuts, teak and mahogany.

Economic problems facing the nation include a high population density and high unemployment.

Exchange rate TT$ 2.3 = U.S.$ 1

The sources listed below are to help the reader find additional information on this country and Christian ministries there.  This list does not try to be comprehensive or complete

DOCUMENTS

General

Black, Jan Knippers, et al., Area Handbook for Trinidad and Tobago. Washington, D.C.: U.S. Government Printing Office, 1976.

Christian

Brathwaite, Joan, ed., Handbook of Churches in the Caribbean, Bridgetown, Barbados: CADEC, 1973.

Erskine, Noel Leo, Decolonizing Theology, Maryknoll, New York: Orbis Books, 1981.

Foy, Felican A., O.F.M., ed., 1980 Catholic Almanac, Huntington, Indiana: Our Sunday Visitor, 1980.

Ratcliff, Herbert, and Dollar, Harold, "A Church Growth Study of Six Denominations in Trinidad and Tobago," research paper on file, Monrovia, CA: MARC, 1973.

## ACKNOWLEDGMENTS

The information in this profile was taken from many sources which were the best available to the editors at the time of preparation.  However, the accuracy of the information cannot be guaranteed.  Views expressed or implied in this publication are not necessarily those of World Vision.  The editors have tried to present the ministries of various organizations in an objective manner, without undue bias or emphasis.  Where we have failed, we apologize for erroneous impressions that may result and request that comments and corrections be sent to MARC, 919 West Huntington Drive, Monrovia, California, USA, 91016.  We appreciate and acknowledge the comments and contributions of various organizations and individuals in the preparation of this publication.

# STATUS OF CHRISTIANITY COUNTRY PROFILE

# WINDWARD ISLANDS

## SUMMARY

AREA - The islands of:
     Barbados, Dominica, Grenada
     Martinique, St. Lucia, St. Vincent
POPULATION - 1,007,000 (1980 estimate)
RELIGION - SEE: Nation and its People

Located at the southern end of the Antilles chain, the Windward Islands are made up of some of the smallest nations in the world. With the exception of the French island of Martinique, the islands of Barbados, Dominica, Grenada, St. Lucia and St. Vincent are sovereign nations. They are still largely dependent on their former ruler, Great Britain, for economic aid. Their economies are mainly based on agricultural products; tourism has not yet been fully developed.

Most of the people of these islands are descendants of the African slaves who were imported to work in the sugarcane fields. The legacy of the colonial era is apparent in their religious life. The dominant religion of each island depends on how much influence the Roman Catholic French or the Anglican British had on each island.

## PEOPLE GROUPS

The vast majority of people in the Windward Islands consider themselves Christian. However, among the major denominations, many members are nominal. Renewal is needed among these people. The Christian witness has been largely neglected on the smaller islands and cays, due in large part to their inaccessibility. They are rarely visited by priests, pastors or missionaries. An interdenominational group is attempting to minister to the people of the Grenadines (a group of islands between Grenada and Trinidad) on a regular basis by means of a boat.

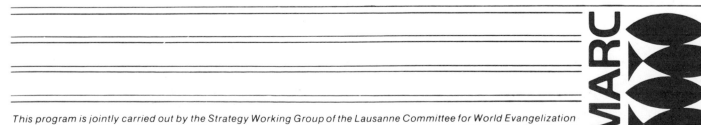

This program is jointly carried out by the Strategy Working Group of the Lausanne Committee for World Evangelization and MARC, a ministry of World Vision International. For further information on the program, please write: MARC, 919 West Huntington Drive, Monrovia, CA 91016 U.S.A.

## CURRENT STATUS OF CHRISTIANITY

Christianity was introduced in the Windward Islands by the various colonial powers. Generally, those islands settled or influenced by the Spanish or French remain predominantly Roman Catholic, while those islands colonized by the British have large Protestant churches. On the whole, the number of professing Catholics is greater in the Windward Island group, representing 54% of the population.

Barbados, a former British colony, has the largest Protestant population: some 53% of its people claim to be Anglican while only 4% are Roman Catholic. The Church of the Nazarene, the Church of God - Cleveland and the Methodist Church are also represented on Barbados. Several Protestant churches are represented in the country of St. Vincent. The Anglicans are largest with 47% of the population, while the Methodists account for 27%. The Roman Catholics total only 13,000 members or 12% of St. Vincent's population. The Roman Catholic Church forms the major Christian body in the islands of Grenada (64% of the population), Martinique (81%), St. Lucia (90%) and Dominica (87%). Both the Roman Catholics and the main-line Protestant denominations count as members those people who should be considered nominal Christians.

Many syncretistic cults have arisen in the Caribbean due largely to African influences. On St. Vincent, for instance, a thriving syncretistic cult known as the Shakers (or Spiritual Baptists) developed in the early 20th century and it has a conglomeration of Christian and pagan beliefs. It is now a recognized religion that has gained respectability with its growth. On the island of St. Lucia the Catholic Church is plagued with the practice of Obeah, a traditional African religion practiced by the early slaves. Spirits of the dead are believed to aid in healing and telling the future. Catholic clergy have interpreted this practice as the work of the devil and have unsuccessfully tried to stamp it out.

### NATIONAL CHURCHES

PROTESTANT CHURCHES

The first Protestant activity in the Windward Islands came as an outgrowth of Anglican work on Barbados begun in 1626. By 1637, six churches and ten chapels had been built. Originally, the West Indies was under the jurisdiction of the Bishop of London. In 1824, the Windward Islands, along with the Leewards, Trinidad and Guyana, were formed into the Diocese of Barbados. Not until 1878 was the separate Diocese of the Windward Islands created. These two dioceses shared the same Bishop with Barbados until 1930.

Throughout the Caribbean, the early Anglican Church remained predominantly a white man's church and, in most cases, even the whites gave it only nominal allegiance. Very few efforts were made to attempt to convert the numerous slaves on these islands. Several influential plantation owners were afraid of educating their slaves. Therefore, most slaves continued in their own African beliefs. Even when some Protestant missionaries tried to evangelize the slaves, they faced persecution from slave owners and opposition from the slaves themselves. The slaves' opposition stemmed from two sources: Sunday was their market day and was therefore their only day off, and the slaves had marriage practices which were totally misunderstood and unacceptable to early missionaries.

Nevertheless, as early as 1678, several Anglican missionaries continued to defend the right of the slaves to hear the gospel, despite fines and opposition from the planters. It was not until 1784 that the first baptisms of slaves took place in Barbados under the auspices of the Anglican Church. The 19th century saw further increase in the Anglican Church's influence among the black population. Tremendous efforts were made to incorporate slaves into Anglican Churches and provide secular and Christian education.

With the rise of the non-conformist denominations, missionaries and adherents from these groups began to arrive in the Caribbean. The Moravians were the first-comers. Beginning in the Danish West Indies in 1732, their work expanded to Barbados in 1765, but this work did not last. Another attempt was made in 1770 which was more successful. Today, the Eastern West Indies Province of the Moravian Church is headquartered in Barbados.

The Methodist Church began its work in the Caribbean in 1760 on the island of Antigua. Work in the Windward Islands began on St. Vincent in 1787. Methodism soon spread to Barbados, Grenada and St. Lucia. The Methodist Church in the Caribbean and the Americas became an autonomous conference in 1967 with seven districts. The South Caribbean District comprises the Windward Islands.

Some of the newer denominations include the Baptists and the Pentecostals. The Church of God - Cleveland accepted four small congregations in 1936 in Barbados. They grew to 48 churches and 2,500 members by 1973. The Southern Baptists entered Barbados in 1972, Dominica and Grenada in 1975 and St. Vincent in 1977. They report over 10 churches and have founded the Barbados Baptist College.

Current statistics for the individual churches in each island are not yet available. The larger denominations represented are the Anglicans, Methodists, Moravians, Plymouth Brethren, Salvation Army, Seventh-day Adventists, Baptists, Pentecostals and numerous independent groups.

## CATHOLIC CHURCHES

Territories colonized by the French or Spanish in the Caribbean are predominantly Roman Catholic today. In territories which were colonized by the British, but had French or Spanish influence before they became British lands, Roman Catholic influence is still dominant. This is true of Dominica (87% Roman Catholic), Grenada (64%), Martinique (81%) and St. Lucia (90%). The Catholic Church has had to find missionary priests to labor among its believers, even on islands where the Catholic population is dominant. English Jesuits have worked in Barbados for over 100 years. English Dominicans have worked in Grenada and Barbados. Canadian Scarboro Fathers have worked in St. Vincent and in St. Lucia. Also there are the French "Sons of Mary Immaculate," who help the Belgian Redemptorists in Dominica. There are now two Catholic seminaries in the Caribbean which are training local candidates.

The Windward Islands are administered by the Archdiocese of Port-of-Spain (Trinidad) and by the Dioceses of Castries (St. Lucia), Roseau (Dominica), St. George's (Grenada), Bridgetown-Kingstown (Barbados) and the Archdiocese of Fort-de-France (Guadeloupe).

Barbados has the smallest number of Catholics (10,000), with six parishes, nine priests and five schools. St. Vincent has only 13,000 Catholics, six parishes, six priests and five schools.

French influence gives Grenada a higher percentage of Catholics (64%) with a total number of 68,000 members in 20 parishes with 22 priests and 34 schools. The highest numbers of Catholics are found in Dominica with 67,000 or 87% of the population, St. Lucia with 96,000 or 87% and Martinique with 300,000 or 81%. There are 16 parishes, 24 priests and six Catholic schools in Dominica; 22 parishes, 31 priests and 88 schools in St. Lucia; and 47 parishes, 97 priests and 10 schools in Martinique.

### FOREIGN MISSIONS

## PROTESTANT MISSIONS

A total of 133 missionaries were working in the Windward Islands in 1979 according to the 12th edition of the Mission Handbook. Grenada listed 33 missionaries working wih six agencies. St. Lucia counted 29 missionaries from four groups and Barbados had 22 from 17 mission agencies. St. Vincent was next with 19 missionaries and eight agencies. Both Dominica and Martinique listed 15 missionaries each from six and three agencies, respectively.

The newest missionary sending agency represented is the Southern Baptist Board of Foreign Missions, beginning in 1964 in Martinique and 1972 in Barbados. They are already the largest missionary sending agency in the area in terms of personnel (31).

## ROMAN CATHOLIC MISSIONS

Many of the priests and members of religious orders in the Caribbean are expatriates. Although the number of local priests is rising due to the presence of two Catholic seminaries in the Caribbean, foreigners still are responsible for a large proportion of work. In addition to the expatriate priests, a total of 33 Roman Catholic missionaries (brothers, sisters and laymen) from the United States and Canada are active. Barbados accounts for eleven of these.

### MAJOR CHRISTIAN ACTIVITIES

## EVANGELISM

Evangelistic efforts in the Windward Islands have usually followed a pattern of individual denominational or church efforts. A coordinated effort made by the Latin American Mission in 1958 brought the Billy Graham evangelistic team to the Caribbean. When the team arrived in

Barbados, Graham preached to an audience of 60,000, a quarter of the island's population. Nearly 1,200 made decisions for Christ during the meeting.

Another example of a cooperative evangelistic effort was the New Life Crusade held in St. Vincent in 1969-1970 and approved by the West Indies Mission. For the first time, six of the island's denominations worked together to bring renewal and revival. Over 180 prayer cells were formed, out of which a strong desire was born for the salvation of the lost. As a result of personal witnessing and New Life Crusade rallies, over 500 people met Christ.

## BIBLE TRANSLATION AND DISTRIBUTION

Bibles are readily available in the major languages of the region, English and French. According to the United Bible Societies' report for 1980, the Windward Islands came under the jurisdiction of the newly formed Bible Society in the East Caribbean. This area includes the Leeward Islands, Trinidad and Tobago, Guyana and French Guiana. Scripture distribution for 1980 was planned to reach 29,590 Bibles; 7,700 New Testaments; 7,000 portions and 60,000 selections.

## EDUCATION

### Theological

Founded in 1745 by the Anglicans, Codrington College was the only institution for higher education in the Caribbean for some time. Codrington offers a B.A.(theology) degree along with the L.Th. degree and an Advanced Ministerial Course. Among other centers for Biblical learning are the Bible colleges located in Barbados which are sponsored by the New Testament Church of God - Cleveland and the Wesleyan Church.

### Christian

Protestant churches sponsor wholly or partially 107 primary schools and eight secondary schools along with several vocational training and preparatory schools in the Windward Islands. The Roman Catholic Church sponsors over 108 schools.

## SOCIAL CONCERN

The larger and older denominations in the Caribbean are vitally concerned with the social dimensions of the gospel. The ecumenically oriented Caribbean Council of Churches sponsors the Christian Action for Development in the Caribbean islands. Their work includes the support of

hospitals, orphanages, day care centers, feeding programs, housing, co-ops, agriculture, fishing and education.

## NATION AND ITS PEOPLE

### BARBADOS

POPULATION. The population of Barbados in 1980 was estimated to be 270,000 people. Bridgeton, the capital and largest city, had 9,000 people in 1970.

COMPOSITION. The majority of the people are descendants of slaves. The 1970 Census lists 224,318 blacks, 9,354 whites, 9,305 mixed and 675 East Indians.

LANGUAGE AND LITERACY. The official language is English. Free education is provided in all government primary and secondary schools. The literacy rate is estimated at 98%.

RELIGION. The Anglican Church is dominant in Barbados, representing 53% of the population. Next in size is the Methodist Church with 9%. Various Pentecostal groups account for 9% of the people. Only 4% of the people are Roman Catholics. More than 17% of the population do not claim a religious preference.

GEOGRAPHY AND CLIMATE. Barbados is a fairly small island lying well out in the Atlantic to the east of the lower end of the Antilles chain. It has a total land area of only 432 square kilometers (166 square miles). The highest point is Mount Hillaby at 332 meters (1,105 feet), located toward the center of the island. There are no rivers, as rainwater percolates quickly through the soil to form underground channels. Temperatures range from 24 to 30 degrees C. (72 to 86 degrees F.). The rainy season is from June to November.

HISTORY. Barbados was discovered by the Portuguese in 1536 and named after the "bearded" fig trees found there. The island was settled in 1627 by the British and it has remained in British hands ever since. On November 30, 1966 it became independent.

GOVERNMENT AND POLITICAL CONDITIONS. The Head of State is the British monarch, represented by a governor-general. There is a bicameral Parliament: a 21 member designated Senate, and a 24 member elected House of Assembly (which elects the Prime Minister).

ECONOMY. Sugarcane, which provides the basis for the economy and is the main source of employment, has been cultivated since 1640. It is a suitable crop for this type of area, providing more work per acre than any other, can be grown economically, provides its own fuel for processing, is resistant to climatic variations and suffers less from disease than other crops. The compulsory planting of food crops on a minimum of 12% of the land does not provide for all of Barbados' needs. Some 50,000 acres of cultivable land are devoted to sugar cane.

The tourist industry has grown in the last decade. Tourism and the developing industrial sector have replaced sugar as the main sources of revenue. About 15,000 Barbadians are employed in 130 factories, which is more than in tourism and sugar production. The largest source of employment, however, is in government services.

## DOMINICA

POPULATION. In 1980 the estimated population for the island of Dominica was 78,000. The largest cities are Roseau, the capital, with a population of 12,000 and Portsmouth with 3,000.

COMPOSITON. Most of the people of Dominica are descendants of the slaves. Dominica has the only remaining descendants of the native Carib people. Some 1,000 to 1,200 Caribs live on a government reservation.

LANGUAGE AND LITERACY. The official and commercial language is English. However, French Creole is spoken by the majority. Education is provided at 54 Government schools, three assisted denominational schools and 33 "temporary" schools.

RELIGION. Catholics constitute 87% of the population. The Church of England, Methodists and other Protestant denominations make up the remainder.

GEOGRAPHY AND CLIMATE. Dominica lies on the northern end of the Windward Island chain between the French islands of Martinique and Guadeloupe. It has a land area of 754 square kilometers (290 square miles). It is dominated by a high mountain range running the length of the island. The tropical climate is tempered by sea breezes. It lies within the hurricane belt and the island has been struck severely in the past. Temperatures vary little, between 25.5 and 32 degrees C. (78 to 90 degrees F.). Humidity ranges between 70 and 90 percent. Rainfall is great on the east side of the mountain but substantially less on the west.

HISTORY. Columbus discovered the island in 1493 but the warlike Carib Indians thwarted subsequent attempts to settle it. The French and British struggled for control of the island in the 18th century with ownership passing back and forth between them. The English gained lasting control in the early 19th century. Dominica became a member of the Federation of the West Indies in 1958 until the dissolution of the Federation in 1962. It became a State in Association with the United Kingdom in 1967. And on November 3, 1978 it became the independent Commonwealth of Dominica.

GOVERNMENT AND POLITICAL CONDITIONS. Mary Eugenia Charles became the first woman Prime Minister in the Caribbean in July, 1980 when her Dominican Freedom Party won national elections in an overwhelming victory. The Dominican Freedom Party is anti-communist and favors free-enterprise; this is a reversal of the previous government's leanings.

ECONOMY. The mainstay of the economy is the banana crop. However, a serious banana disease cut production by 50% in 1979. Limes and other citrus fruits are grown for export. Industries which support agriculture, such as canning, have been started. The only mineral mined is pumice, used in the production of cement and abrasives.

## GRENADA

POPULATION. Grenada had an estimated population of 108,000 in 1980. Its annual growth rate is 1.4%.

COMPOSITION. The majority of the people are of African descent (84%). Some 11% of the people are of mixed ancestry while 3% are East Indian. Less than 2% are of other races.

LANGUAGE AND LITERACY. English is the official, commercial and most generally used language. French Creole is used by a few. Education is compulsory but not enforced. There were 61 primary schools in 1973.

RELIGION. The Church of England, Church of Scotland, Methodist Church, Plymouth Brethren, Salvation Army, Seventh-day Adventist and Roman Catholic Church are all represented on Grenada. The Catholic Church is the largest, with 64% of the people, and the Anglican is next, with 21%.

GEOGRAPHY AND CLIMATE. The country of Grenada is made up of the islands of Grenada, Carricon and Petit Martinique. Together they have an area of 346 square kilometers (133 square miles). Grenada itself has a size of 312 square kilometers (120 square miles). It is the southernmost island in the Windward Chain. The island is of volcanic origin; the highest peak being Mt. St. Catherine (827 meters or 2,756 feet). Forests and streams cover much of the area.

Grenada has a tropical marine climate. Rainfall varies between 375 centimeters (150 inches) in the mountains and 100 centimeters (40 inches) in the southwest. Average annual temperature is 28 degrees C. (83 degrees F.).

HISTORY. Discovered by Columbus in 1498, the island was given the name Conception. Early settlement by the English in 1609 was so harrassed by the native Carib Indians that they abandoned it. Subsequent settlements by the French in 1657 and 1674 put the island into the possession of the French. The island was exchanged several times by the British and French until it wound up under British conrol in 1783.

On February 7, 1974 Grenada became independent. A coup d'etat in March, 1978 toppled the government of Eric M. Gairy and put the left-leaning government of Maurice Bishop and the New Jewel Party in power.

GOVERNMENT AND POLITICAL CONDITIONS. Grenada has been a member of the British Commonwealth with a Governor-General representing the Queen. There is a bicameral legislature, with a 12 member appointed Senate, and a 15 member elected House of Representatives. The constitution was suspended following the coup in 1979 which placed the left-wing New Jewel Movement in power with Maurice Bishop as Prime Minister.

ECONOMY. The main export crops are nutmeg, cocoa and bananas. Limes and lime products are also exported. There is a small industrial sector producing garments, animal feeds, concrete and handicrafts. There is a small tourist trade which partially offsets the chronic imbalance of trade.

### MARTINIQUE

POPULATION. The population of Martinique was estimated to be 315,000 in 1980. The average annual growth rate is minus .1%. Fort-de-France is the capital and largest city with a population of about 100,000.

COMPOSITION. Most of the people of Martinique are of African descent. There are some East Indians, Chinese and Europeans.

LANGUAGE AND LITERACY. French is the official language but a French Creole is spoken by most of the people. Education is compulsory between the ages six and sixteen.

RELIGION. Roman Catholicism is dominant but there are also Protestant and Hindu followers.

GEOGRAPHY AND CLIMATE. Lying between the islands of Dominica and St. Lucia of the Windward chain is the small island of Martinique. Its total land area is 1,100 square kilometers, (425 square miles). Generally hilly and mountainous, the island's highest point is Mt. Pelee (1,463 meters or 4,700 feet). The city of St. Pierre was totally destroyed in 1902 when the volcanic Mt. Pelee erupted.

Climate conditions are tropical. Rainfall is abundant. The average rainfall for Fort-de-France is 180 centimeters (70.8 inches). The temperature averages 25 degrees C. (77 degrees F.).

HISTORY. Columbus discovered Martinique in 1502 but the native Carib Indians were unfriendly. The Indians succeeded in discouraging European settlements until 1654 when a French colony was established. Soon, all the Caribs were subjugated. The island changed hands several times but eventually it was retained by France. It became an Overseas Department of France in 1946.

GOVERNMENT AND POLITICAL CONDITIONS. As an Overseas Department, Martinique is represented in the French Parliament by three members of the National Assembly and two members to the Senate. The French government is represented by a Prefect. The local legislative assembly is called the General Council, comprised of 36 members elected for six year terms.

ECONOMY. The economy of the island is primarily agricultural. Sugar, pineapples and bananas are the primary cash crops. The other major contributors to economic growth are tourism, sugar processing and its by products, and an oil refinery.

### ST. LUCIA

POPULATION. In 1980 the population of St. Lucia was 122,000 people. Castries, the capital, had a population of about

40,000. The annual growth rate is 1.7%.

COMPOSITION. Most islanders are black. Others include a mixture of European settlers (mainly French and British) and some descendants of Carib Indians.

LANGUAGE AND LITERACY. English is the official language but French Creole is also spoken. The literacy rate is about 80%.

RELIGION. Due to French influence, the island is predominantly Roman Catholic (90%). The capital, Castries, was elevated to an Archdiocese in 1975. The Anglican, Baptist, Seventh-day Adventist and the Methodist Churches are the other leading bodies.

GEOGRAPHY AND CLIMATE. St. Lucia lies between the French island of Martinique to the north, and St. Vincent to the south. The island has an area of 671 square kilometers (258 square miles). It is of volcanic formation, and is fairly hilly, the highest peak being Morne Gimie (944 meters, 3,145 feet). The average temperature is 26 degrees C. (79 degrees F.). The wet season is from May to August.

HISTORY. The date of St. Lucia's discovery by Europeans is unknown. The Carib Indians thwarted the first English attempts at settlement in 1624 and 1639. The French were more successful in 1651. However, the island subsequently changed hands 14 times until the British maintained control early in the 19th century. St. Lucia became an independent country within the British Commonwealth on February 22, 1979.

GOVERNMENT AND POLITICAL CONDITIONS. The Queen is represented by a Governor-General. There is a bicameral legislature: a 17 member Assembly and an 11 member Senate. The major political issue has been the question of independence. The ruling United Worker's Party supported independence while the opposition Labor Party fought against it.

ECONOMY. Two-thirds of St. Lucia's export earnings come from its major crop, bananas. However, total exports do not nearly match the import bill. Most of the budget comes from outside aid. Tourism is a growing industry, and it is hoped that a new free-trade zone and oil transhipment facilities will provide much need revenue.

POPULATION. St. Vincent had a total population of 114,000 in 1980. Of this, the small islands known as the Grenadines have a population of 8,000. Kingstown, the capital, has a population of 22,000.

COMPOSITION. Over 81% of the people are of African descent. Approximately 14% are mixed. East Indians account for over 2% while European whites account for about 1%.

LANGUAGE AND LITERACY. English is the only language spoken and used. Education is free but not compulsory, and is provided by 39 government, 11 Methodist, nine Anglican and two Roman Catholic schools. The literacy rate is about 80%.

RELIGION. Several Christian Churches are represented on St. Vincent including: Anglican, Methodist, Roman Catholic, Apostolic Faith Mission, Salvation Army, Seventh-day Adventist, Pilgrim Holiness, Plymouth Brethren, Pentecostal, Baptist and the Church of God. The Anglicans (47%) and Methodists (27%) are the largest Protestant bodies, while the Roman Catholics account for 13% of the people.

GEOGRAPHY AND CLIMATE. St. Vincent and its Grenadine Island dependencies lie at the lower end of the Caribbean chain. St. Vincent is a small island and the total land area for all the islands in the group is only 388 square kilometers (150 square miles). Running the length of the island is a mountain chain of volcanic origin. Mt. Soufriere (1,200 meters, 4,000 feet) is an active volcano which erupted in 1902, killing over 2,000 people, and again in 1979, destroying much of the island's crops.

St. Vincent's climate is tropical. About 70% of the rainfall occurs from May to November and the yearly total averages from 152 centimeters (60 inches) on the southeast coast to 375 centimeters (150 inches) in the central mountains. Although it is within the hurricane belt, St. Vincent seldom receives hurricane damage.

HISTORY. Inhabited by Carib Indians at the time of its discovery by Columbus in 1498, St. Vincent was left to the Caribs by subsequent British and French colonists. It remained a neutral island until it was ceded to the British in 1763. After several invasions and an insurrection by Caribs, the island was put firmly in British control.

In 1838 the imported slaves were freed. In 1846, Portuguese laborers were brought to the island, and East Indians arrived in 1861.

The island attained its independence in 1979. Just six monthes prior to independence, Mt. Soufriere erupted, forcing evacuation around the volcano and destroying half the island's crops.

GOVERNMENT AND POLITICAL CONDITIONS. As a member of the British Commonwealth, a Governor-General represents the Queen. A Prime Minister is responsible to the island's Parliament.

ECONOMY. St. Vincent is one of the poorest Caribbean countries. Its economy is based on agriculture, exporting bananas and arrowroot. Tourism and light industries are growing but inflation and unemployment are high.

## SELECTED BIBLIOGRAPHY AND INFORMATION SOURCES

The sources listed below are to help the reader find additional information on these islands and the Christian ministries there. This list does not try to be comprehensive or complete.

DOCUMENTS

Christian

Brathwaite, Joan, ed., Handbook of Churches in the Caribbean, Bridgetown, Barbados: CADEC, 1973.

Erskine, Noel Leo, Decolonizing Theology. Maryknoll, New York: Orbio Books, 1981.

Foy, Felican A., O.F.M., ed., 1980 Catholic Almanac, Huntington, Indiana: Our Sunday Visitor, 1980.

Pardee, Celeste, "Distribution of Religions in the West Indies," research paper delivered at Texas A and M University, 1975.

ORGANIZATIONS

Christian Action for Development in the Caribbean (CADEC), P.O. Box 616, Bridgetown, Barbados.

## ACKNOWLEDGMENTS

The information in this profile was taken from many sources which were the best available to the editors at the time of preparation. However, the accuracy of the information cannot be guaranteed. Views expressed or implied in this publication are not necessarily those of World Vision. The editors have tried to present the ministries of various organizations in an objective manner, without undue bias or emphasis. Where we have failed, we apologize for erroneous impressions that may result and request that comments and corrections be sent to MARC, 919 West Huntington Drive, Monrovia, California, 91016, USA. We appreciate and acknowledge the comments and contributions of various organizations and individuals in the preparation of this publication.

# III
# UNREACHED PEOPLES

This program is jointly carried out by the Strategy Working Group of the Lausanne Committee for World Evangelization and MARC, a ministry of World Vision International. For further information on the program, please write: MARC, 919 West Huntington Drive, Monrovia, CA 91016 U.S.A.

Within each country there are distinct groups of people. These groups must be viewed in the context of the country's history and way of life, for they are certainly part of a larger whole. But each group is unique too, and must be seen in a separate sense. We must look at countries and at people groups.

## WHAT IS A "PEOPLE GROUP"?

A people group is a part of a society that has some basic characteristics in common that cause it to feel a sense of oneness yet set it apart from other groups.

The unifying characteristic may be language, religion, economic status, occupation, ethnic origin, geographic location or social position.

For example, a distinct group based on ethnic, language and geographic characteristics might be the Quechua of Bolivia; while a sociological group might be the urban university students of France.

It is important to see that groups may share a common way of life and sense of oneness because of social, occupational, or economic characteristics, as well as language or ethnic origin.

## WHO ARE "UNREACHED AND UNEVANGELIZED PEOPLE?

Christians have different definitions of the terms "unreached" or "unevangelized". For our purposes we can describe an unreached or unevangelized people as a people who has not received or responded to the gospel. This unresponsiveness may be due to lack of opportunity, to lack of understanding, or because the people have not received enough information about the gospel message in its own language and through the eyes of its own culture so that it can truly respond to Christ.

We consider a people "unreached" when less than 20 percent of the members of the group are practicing Christians, that is are active members of the Christian community.

By "Christian" we mean adherents (church members, families and followers) of the historic Christian communions: Protestant, Anglican, Orthodox, Roman Catholic and such independent groups as may claim the Bible as the basis of faith and Jesus Christ as Lord and Savior.

## HOW CAN THESE UNREACHED PEOPLES BE EVANGELIZED?

To evangelize these unreached peoples we must first find out who they are. We must discover where they live and learn as much about their culture as possible. We should also know about the current Christian witness, the availability of scripture in the local language, and the receptivity of the group to the gospel.

With this information a culturally appropriate approach can be developed to reach a particular people group – an approach based on a realistic assessment of the group's culture and their needs. (See Planning Strategies for Evangelism, by Edward R. Dayton for more details on developing an approach.)

## WHAT NEEDS TO BE DONE?

To gather, store, and analyze this type of information is a tremendous job, but a necessary one if the Church today is going to fulfill the Great Commission.

To aid the Church in ths task, World Vision's Missions Advanced Research and Communications Center (MARC) maintains a computerized compilation of information on people groups from all over the world. This data is continually updated and expanded, and is published annually in a series entitled UNREACHED PEOPLES. Most of this information is supplied by individuals who send in MARC's survey questionnaires.

These questionnaire respondants provide the basic data that is needed to begin planning a way to reach peoples who have yet to know Jesus Christ. With this information, God's people can not only plan and act with greater efficiency, but they can also pray with greater insight.

The purpose of a world wide data gathering effort is to give Christians everywhere the information they need to think about their own situation and to seek to understand God's strategy for the people to whom God has called them.

As the Holy Spirit reveals new understandings of both the obstacles and the opportunities we face, we will be able to ask the right questions as to what God would have us do to reach the unreached.

## THE NEXT STEP...

On the following pages there is a brief
description of the peoples of Central
America and the Caribbean, followed by a
listing of the people groups from this
area for which there is some information
in the MARC data files. (See the most
recent volume of UNREACHED PEOPLES for a
complete list of MARC's unreached peoples
data). There is also a survey
questionnaire to provide more information
about these groups. Since people groups
are continually changing, it is important
to update and revise the material that has
been collected. The questionnaire can
also be used to provide new information on
other groups from around the world.

This information on specific peoples,
combined with country profiles, is an
excellent place to begin the planning
needed to reach the unreached. With this
foundation laid, God's strategy for
reaching a particular people can be
discovered.

## PEOPLE OF CENTRAL AMERICA
## AND THE CARIBBEAN

Whereas previous volumes of the World Christianity series have dealt with geographical regions in which the majority of the people groups are unreached, Central America and the Caribbean may present us with quite a different picture. With the exception of the East Indians on Trinidad, most groups are at least nominally Christian.

Analysis of the colonial legacy in the region provides information as to how this situation came about. Catholic priests accompanied the Spanish conquistadors on their missions of exploration and conquest. As the Indian populations were subjugated, they were forced to adopt Catholicism, at least in its outward forms. The same thing occurred when the French colonized the Caribbean islands. Although the Indian population of the islands was reduced by disease and warfare, the newly arrived slaves from Africa gradually adopted the Christian religious practices of their new culture. However, many of their existing beliefs and practices were allowed to continue alongside Christian doctrines and, thus, syncretism evolved rapidly.

The resulting religious form, known today as Christo-paganism, is widespread throughout the Central American and Caribbean region. Christo-paganism's beliefs vary widely, depending upon those elements brought to it by the various cultural groups in the region. The religious practices of Haitian Catholics who have been influenced by African religions are notably different from those practices of Guatemalan Indians who are "Catholics" yet retain their traditional Indian religious customs. There has been a marked resurgence of religious and cultural traditions within the past generation, particularly among blacks in the Caribbean. This resurgence is due in part to independence movements. Religions which incorporate elements of African traditional worship such as Vodun (Haiti), Rastafarianism (Jamaica), Santeria (Cuba), Pocomania, Shango and Rada (Trinidad and Tobago) are on the rise, displacing even the nominal influence of Christianity in many people's hearts.

There is evidence of widespread nominality even among Christians who are not influenced by any form of Christo-paganism. Religion is largely ignored by the masses. Among Roman Catholics in Central America, over 80% do not attend Mass regularly. In Cuba, the vast majority of people do not even claim to be Catholic anymore, whereas the island was once 85% Roman Catholic. Religion is seen as something only for women and children in Ladino culture. Nevertheless, Catholicism is firmly entrenched as a respectable cultural trait. But in terms of influencing the hearts and lives of the people, "popular Catholicism" is not particularly effective.

Although most Protestant churches are growing, several Protestant groups lack vitality. Adherents in many parts of Central America and the Caribbean are neither active nor committed to ongoing programs. For instance, among the blacks along the Mosquito Coast, Protestantism is often seen as a cultural trait rather than a life-changing influence.

Therefore, although most people groups consider themselves Christian, the nominal nature of their religious convictions leaves them, to all intents and purposes, unreached.

There are a few totally unreached people groups in this region. The largest is the East Indian population in Trinidad. These people were brought to the islands by the English as cheap labor around the turn of the century. Today they constitute about half the population of Trinidad and Tobago. Although many East Indians have become Christians through the ministry of the Presbyterians, they are still unreached. Smaller unreached people groups are found among the more remote tribes in Central America. Finally, small unreached communities of Chinese, Lebanese and Jews are scattered throughout the region.

The vast majority of Central American and Caribbean peoples have some knowledge of Christianity, albeit a distorted one in many cases. The major need of the Church among these nominal Christians is renewal and revitalization.

## INDEX BY GROUP NAME

The following is the basic listing of people groups for Central America and the Caribbean. Peoples are listed by their primary NAME, and effort has been made to standardize names and use the most commonly accepted English spelling. This listing includes the COUNTRY for which the information was provided, principal vernacular LANGUAGE used by the group, population estimate of the GROUP SIZE in the country listed and principal professed religion (PRIMARY RELIGION), which in some cases is less than 50 percent of the total group membership.

In addition, this index includes the estimated percentage of the group that practices Christianity in any recognized tradition (PRACTICING CHRISTIAN). Included in this percentage are Protestant, Roman Catholic, Orthodox, African Independent and other Christian groups. Excluded in this percentage were Christo-pagans and Christian cultic groups. It is important to note that this figure is the estimated percentage of practicing Christians within the group. If the group was listed in Unreached Peoples '79 or Unreached Peoples '80, the figure recorded here will most likely be different, because that volume recorded the percentage of professing Christians (or adherents), which most often will be a higher number. Thus these figures should not be compared or used as a time series, since the changes indicate a different kind of data. Differences might also be due to a new and better data source or revised data, as we are continually updating our files.

The index also lists a validity code (VALID) which estimates the accuracy and completeness of the data on a scale from 1 to 9. The code is:

1. The only information available at this point is the group name, country, language, population and primary religion The percentage listed under practicing Christians is at best a rough estimate.

2. There has been more data collected than the "baseline" information in 1, but it is scanty and/or of poor quality.

3. About one-half of the information on the unreached peoples questionnaire (Appendix B) has been collected, and information on Christian community, if any, is missing or probably inaccurate

4. Almost all the data on the unreached peoples questionnaire has been collected or the source document has supplied most of the necessary information.

5. Information has been supplied by a completed unreached peoples questionnaire and at least one other document.

6. In addition to 5, there is enough detailed information about the people group to write an accurate, up-to-date description.

7. There exists an extensive description of the people group in secular or Christian literature.

8. There has been a major research study (thesis or dissertation quality) done on the group which includes detailed information on Christian community.

9. In addition to 8, the study includes a thorough exploration of evangelism strategy for the particular group, based on first-hand experience.

The final column in this section indicates the year of the volume (YEAR) of Unreached Peoples in which a description of this group appeared.

| NAME | COUNTRY | LANGUAGE | GROUP SIZE | PRIMARY RELIGION | PRACTICING CHRISTIAN |
|---|---|---|---|---|---|
| Achi, Cubulco | Guatemala | Achi, Cubulco | 15,000 | Animism | <1% |
| Achi, Rabinal | Guatemala | Achi, Rabinal | 21,000 | Animism | <1% |
| Aguacateco | Guatemala | Aguateco | 8,000 | Animism | <1% |
| Black Caribs | Belize | Moreno | 10,000 | Cristo-Paganism | 1% |
| Black Caribs | Guatemala | Moreno | 1,5000 | Cristo-Paganism | 1% |
| Black Caribs | Honduras | Moreno | 20,000 | Cristo-Paganism | 1% |
| Cakchiquel, Central | Guatemala | Cakchiquel | 300,000 | Animism | <1% |
| Chinese | Costa Rica | Cantonese | 5,000 | Unknown | 1% |
| Chinese | Panama | Spanish | 25,000 | Trad. Chinese | 1% |
| Chorti | Guatemala | Chorti | 25,000 | Animism | <1% |
| Chuj | Guatemala | Chuj | 15,000 | Animism | <1% |
| Chuj of San Mateo | Guatemala | Chuj | 17,000 | Cristo-Paganism | 12% |
| East Indians | Trinidad & Tobago | English/Hindi | 400,000 | Hinduism | 5% |
| Ixil | Guatemala | Cuyolbal | 45,000 | Cristo-Paganism | 1% |
| Jacalteco | Guatemala | Jacalteco | 12,000 | Animsm | <1% |
| Jamaican Elite | Jamaica | Jamaican Patois | 800,000 | Secularism | ?% |
| K'anjobal of San Miguel | Guatemala | K'anjobal | 18,000 | Ancestor Worship | 10% |
| Kekchi | Guatemala | Kekchi | 270,000 | Cristo-Paganism | 3% |
| Mam | Guatemala | Mam | 470,000 | Cristo-Paganism | 7% |
| Miskito | Nicaragua | Miskito | 20,000 | Cristo-Paganism | <1% |
| Mopan Maya | Belize | Mopan Maya | 4,000 | Cristo-Paganism | 15% |
| Mopan Maya | Guatemala | Mopan Maya | 2,000 | Cristo-Paganism | 15% |
| Paya | Honduras | Spanish | 300 | Animism | <1% |
| Pocomchi, Eastern | Guatemala | Pocomchi, Eastern | 25,000 | Cristo-Paganism | <1% |
| Pocomchi, Western | Guatemala | Pocomchi, Western | 25,000 | Cristo-Paganism | <1% |
| Quiche | Guatemala | Quiche | 500,000 | Cristo-Paganism | 5% |
| Sumu | Nicaragua | Sumu | 2,000 | Cristo-Paganism | ?% |
| Teribe | Panama | Teribe | 1,000 | Cristo-Paganism | 15% |
| Tol | Honduras | Tol | 200 | Animism | <1% |
| Tzutujil | Guatemala | Tzutujil | 5,000 | Cristo-Paganism | 1% |
| Uspanteco | Guatemala | Uspanteco | 15,000 | Animism | <1% |
| Yucateco | Guatemala | Yucateco | 3,000 | Animism | <1% |

| INDEX BY COUNTRY | NAME | GROUP SIZE |
|---|---|---|
| CENTRAL AMERICA | | |
| Belize | Black Caribs (SEE: UP '79) | 10,000 |
| | Mopan Maya | 4,000 |
| Costa Rica | Chinese | 5,000 |
| El Salvador | Data not available at this time | |
| Guatemala | Achi, Cubulco | 15,000 |
| | Achi, Rabinal | 21,000 |
| | Aguacateco | 8,000 |
| | Black Caribs | 1,500 |
| | Cakchiquel, Central | 300,000 |
| | Chorti | 25,000 |
| | Chuj | 15,000 |
| | Chuj of San Mateo Ixtatan | 17,000 |
| | Ixil | 45,000 |
| | Jacalteco | 12,000 |
| | K´anjobal of San Miguel | 18,000 |
| | Kekchi | 270,000 |
| | Mam | 470,000 |
| | Mopan Maya | 2,000 |
| | Pocomchi, Eastern | 20,000 |
| | Pocomchi, Western | 25,000 |
| | Quiche (SEE: UP '79) | 500,000 |
| | Tzutujil | 5,000 |
| | Uspanteco | 15,000 |
| | Yucateco | 3,000 |
| Honduras | Black Caribs | 20,000 |
| | Paya | 300 |
| | Tol | 200 |
| Nicaragua | Miskito | 20,000 |
| | Sumu | 2,000 |
| Panama | Chinese | 25,000 |
| | Teribe | 1,000 |
| THE CARIBBEAN | | |
| Bahamas | Data not available at this time | |
| Cuba | Data not available at this time | |
| Dominican Republic | Data not available at this time | |
| Haiti | Data not available at this time | |
| Jamaica | Jamaican Elite | 800,000 |
| Trinidad & Tabago | East Indians (SEE: UP '79) | 400,000 |

235

# SURVEY QUESTIONNAIRE FOR UNEVANGELIZED AND UNREACHED PEOPLES

Do you see a group of people who are unreached or unevangelized? Identify them! As the Lord spoke to Ezekiel of old, so He speaks to us today. "Son of man, What do you see"?

Answers to the questions on these two pages will provide the minimum information needed to list this people group in the *Unreached Peoples* annual.

After you have read the directions, type or print your answers so they can be easily read. It is unlikely that you will have all the information requested. Do the best you can. What information you are lacking others may supply. If your information is a best guess or estimate, merely place an "E" after it. Send in what you have as soon as possible. Please ignore the small numbers next to the answers. They help others prepare your answers for the *Unreached Peoples* annual.

---

*"For this reason I bow my knees before the Father, from whom every family in heaven and on earth is named . . ."*
*Ephesians 3:14-15 (RSV)*

1. Name of the group or people: _____

2. Alternate name(s) or spelling: _____

3. Country where located: _____

4. Approximate size of the group in this country: _____

5. Vernacular or common language: _____

6. Lingua franca or trade language: _____

7. Name of religious groups found among this people:

| | % who are adherents of this religion | % who practice this religion |
|---|---|---|
| **CHRISTIAN GROUPS:** | | |
| Protestant | _____ % | _____ % |
| Roman Catholic | _____ % | _____ % |
| Eastern Orthodox | _____ % | _____ % |
| Other Christian: _____ (name) | _____ % | _____ % |
| **NON-CHRISTIAN GROUPS OR SECULARISM:** | | |
| _____ | _____ % | _____ % |
| _____ | _____ % | _____ % |
| _____ | _____ % | _____ % |
| _____ | _____ % | _____ % |
| TOTAL FOR ALL GROUPS: | 100 % | |

*"Brethren, My heart's desire and prayer to God for them is that they may be saved."*
*Romans 10:1 (RSV)*

8. In your opinion, what is the attitude of this people toward Christianity?

(01)☐ Strongly favorable    (02)☐ Somewhat favorable    (03)☐ Indifferent    (04)☐ Somewhat opposed    (05)☐ Strongly opposed

TURN THIS SHEET OVER FOR PAGE 2

52479B

9. Questionnaire completed by:

Name: _____ Date: _____

Organization: _____

Address: _____

_____

10. Who else might be able to provide information about this people?

Name                    Organization (if any)                Address

_____

_____

_____

11. If you are aware of any publications describing this people, please give title and author.

_____

12. What other information do you have that could help others to understand this people better? What do you feel would help in evangelizing them?    *(Use additional sheet if necessary.)*

*"And how are they to believe in him of whom they have never heard? And how are they to hear without a preacher?"*
*Romans 10:14 (RSV)*

13. Are you also sending in pages 3 and 4? ☐ Yes   ☐ No

Please send whatever information you have immediately. Do not wait until you have every answer.

Mail to:

Unreached Peoples Program Director
c/o MARC, 919 W. Huntington Drive, Monrovia, CA 91016 USA

Name of people group described_____ Your name ____

If you have any more information about this people group, please complete the following two
send in pages one and two now. If you can obtain more information later, send it in as soon as

## PEOPLE DISTINCTIVES—What makes them different? Why are they a pe

14. A number of different things contribute to create a distinctive people or group, one that in some
common way of life, *sees* itself as a particular group having an affinity toward one another, and differ
extent from other groups or peoples. What would you say makes the people you are describing distin
Check the appropriate box of as many of the following descriptions as *are important* in making this peop
distinctive. Use the following scale: "High" importance, "Medium" importance, "Low" importance. For example,
if you thought that the fact that they had a common political loyalty was of medium importance in unifying and
making a group distinctive, you would place an "X" in the middle box under "Medium".

Importance — High / Medium / Low

(01)☐ ☐ ☐ Same language
(02)☐ ☐ ☐ Common political loyalty
(03)☐ ☐ ☐ Similar occupation
(04)☐ ☐ ☐ Racial or ethnic similarity
(05)☐ ☐ ☐ Shared religious customs
(06)☐ ☐ ☐ Common kinship ties
(07)☐ ☐ ☐ Strong sense of unity
(08)☐ ☐ ☐ Similar education level
(09)☐ ☐ ☐ Other(s) _____
    *(please write in)*

Importance — High / Medium / Low

(10)☐ ☐ ☐ Common residential area
(11)☐ ☐ ☐ Similar social class or caste
(12)☐ ☐ ☐ Similar economic status
(13)☐ ☐ ☐ Shared hobby or special interest
(14)☐ ☐ ☐ Discrimination from other groups
(15)☐ ☐ ☐ Unique health situation
(16)☐ ☐ ☐ Distinctive legal status
(17)☐ ☐ ☐ Similar age
(18)☐ ☐ ☐ Common significant problems

15. How rapidly would you say the lifestyle of this people is changing? (check one)

(01)☐ Very Slow Change    (02)☐ Slow Change    (03)☐ Moderate Change    (04)☐ Rapid Change    (05)☐ Very Rapid Change

*"And to him was given dominion and glory and kingdom, that all peoples, nations, and languages should serve him." Daniel 7:14 (RSV)*

## PEOPLE LANGUAGES—What do they speak?

Please list the various languages used by the members of this people:

| LANGUAGE TYPE | Primary name(s) of their language(s) | Approximate % who *speak* this language | Approximate % of people over 15 years of age who *read* this language |
|---|---|---|---|
| 16. Vernacular or common language: | _____ | _____ % | _____ % |
| 17. Lingua franca or trade language: | _____ | _____ % | _____ % |
| 18. Language used for instruction in schools: | _____ | _____ % | _____ % |
| 19. Language suitable for presentation of the gospel: | _____ | _____ % | _____ % |

20. If there is Christian witness at present, what language(s) is being used? _____

21. Place an "x" in the boxes that indicate the status of Scripture translation *in the language you consider most suitable for communicating the gospel* (question 19):

| | CURRENT STATUS | | | AVAILABLE | | |
|---|---|---|---|---|---|---|
| | Not available | In process | Completed | In oral form | In print | On cassette or records |
| (POR)New Testament portions | ☐ | ☐ | ☐ | ☐ | ☐ | ☐ |
| (NT)Complete New Testament | ☐ | ☐ | ☐ | ☐ | ☐ | ☐ |
| (OT)Complete Old Testament | ☐ | ☐ | ☐ | ☐ | ☐ | ☐ |

22. Of the <u>Christians</u> present among this people, what percent *over 15 years of age can* and *do* read any language?

_____ %

52479C

...churches or missions (national or foreign) now active *within the area or region where this* ...ted, please give the following information:

...check here: ☐)

| ...N | YEAR<br>Year work<br>began in<br>this area | MEMBERS<br>Approximate<br>number of<br>full members<br>from this<br>people | ADHERENTS<br>Approximate<br>number of ad-<br>herents (com-<br>munity includ-<br>ing children) | WORKERS<br>Approximate<br>numbers of<br>trained pastors<br>and evangelists<br>from this<br>people |
|---|---|---|---|---|
| | _____ | _____ | _____ | _____ |
| | _____ | _____ | _____ | _____ |
| | _____ | _____ | _____ | _____ |

24. W... is the growth rate of the total Christian community among this people group?

(01)☐ Rapid growth  (02)☐ Slow growth  (03)☐ Stable  (04)☐ Slow decline  (05)☐ Rapid decline

25. In your opinion, what is the attitude of this people to religious change of any kind?

(01)☐ Very open  (02)☐ Somewhat open  (03)☐ Indifferent  (04)☐ Somewhat closed  (05)☐ Very closed

26. In your opinion, what is the attitude of this people toward Christianity?

(01)☐ Strongly favorable  (02)☐ Somewhat favorable  (03)☐ Indifferent  (04)☐ Somewhat opposed  (05)☐ Strongly opposed

27. Most people move through a series of more or less well-defined stages in their attitude toward Christianity. Parts of a people group will be further along than other parts. Here are ten categories that attempt to show this progression. However, locating people in some of these categories can be difficult, so to make things simpler some categories are combined in the questions that follow.

In your estimation, what percentage of this people can be described as those who: (These percentages are exclusive. Do not include people more than once. Your total should add up to 100%.)

Have no awareness of Christianity............................................................. _____ %

Have awareness of the existence of Christianity ............................................... _____ %

Have some knowledge of the gospel .......................................................... _____ %

Understand the message of the gospel ........................................................ _____ %

See the personal implications of the gospel ..................................

Recognize a personal need that the gospel can meet ......................................} _____ %

Are being challenged to receive Christ ........................................

Have decided for Christ, but are not incorporated into a fellowship
(may be evaluating their decision) ........................................................... _____ %

Are incorporated into a fellowship of Christians .............................................. _____ %

Are active propagators of the gospel .......................................................... _____ %

**TOTAL**  100 %

28. On the whole, how accurate is the information you have given us?

(V)☐ Very accurate  (F)☐ Fairly accurate  (E)☐ Good estimate  (G)☐ Mainly guesses

29. Are you willing to have your name publically associated with this information?

☐ No  ☐ Yes  ☐ Yes, with qualifications: _____

*"And you he made alive when you were dead, through the trespasses and sins in which you once walked . . ."*
*Ephesians 2:1-2 (RSV)*

*...earth... and tribe a... and peo... Revelation 14:6 (RSV)*